Looking Back at LBJ

Looking Back at LBJ

White House Politics in a New Light

Edited by Mitchell B. Lerner

 University Press of Kansas

© 2005 by the University Press of Kansas
All rights reserved

Published by the University Press of Kansas (Lawrence, Kansas 66049),
which was organized by the Kansas Board of Regents and is operated and
funded by Emporia State University, Fort Hays State University, Kansas
State University, Pittsburg State University, the University of Kansas, and
Wichita State University

Library of Congress Cataloging-in-Publication Data

Looking back at LBJ : White House politics in a new light / edited by
Mitchell B. Lerner.
    p. cm.
  Includes bibliographical references and index.
  ISBN 0-7006-1384-6 (cloth : alk. paper)
1. United States—Politics and government—1963–1969. 2. Johnson, Lyndon
B. (Lyndon Baines), 1908 1973.   I. Lerner, Mitchell B., 1968–   II. Title.

  E846.L66 2005
  973.923′092—dc22

                                                    2005000909

British Library Cataloguing-in-Publication Data is available.

Printed in the United States of America

10 9 8 7 6 5 4 3 2 1

The paper used in this publication meets the minimum requirements of the
American National Standard for Permanence of Paper for Printed Library
Materials Z39.48-1984.

Contents

Preface

AT A MEETING approximately three decades ago, a group of academics from the University of Texas and staff members at the Lyndon Baines Johnson Presidential Library agreed that in order to encourage scholarly research at the Library, someone should edit a diverse collection of essays written by experts in their fields, to demonstrate the type of work that could be done at the wonderful facility in Austin, Texas. Historian Robert Divine undertook the challenge, and in 1981 the first of three acclaimed volumes of *The Johnson Years* was published, with subsequent issues following in 1987 and 1994. The topics and authors varied throughout the three volumes, but two things remained constant: the high quality of the essays and the skill of Dr. Divine as editor. When he retired in the late 1990s, Bob left the series in the hands of someone who lacked many of his abilities: me. I can only hope that he does not come to regret that decision.

If Bob is to be proven perspicacious in his choice of successors, it will no doubt be due to the efforts of many people beyond myself. Nine authors have contributed their time, effort, and knowledge, and I owe my gratitude to each of them. I have also benefited from the expertise of a number of colleagues who generously agreed to read particular chapters or sections, or to discuss my thoughts and ideas about them. Among those who deserve special mention are Kevin Boyle, William Childs, Susan Hartmann, Michael Hogan, and Nicholas Evan Sarantakes. Mike Briggs at the University Press of Kansas encouraged me to undertake this project and has been patient and supportive throughout. He would have needed to be even more patient than he was had it not been for the support of the Ohio State University, which assisted my efforts in ways financial and otherwise. The same can be said for the wonderful people at the Johnson Library and the Johnson Foundation, especially Harry Middleton, Ted Gittinger, and Mike Parrish, all of whom provided irreplaceable assistance. And Bob Divine remains, as he has been throughout my entire career, a steady source of wisdom and support.

Readers will notice that this volume differs little from the three that preceded it. For various reasons the title has been changed, so this volume is perhaps best considered a stepchild, rather than a direct progeny, of the original series. Still, I have attempted above all else to remain true to the purpose articulated in the preface to the first volume: "to attempt to survey the materials in the Johnson Library and relate them to the existing body of scholarly literature on the Johnson Years." Accordingly, each author has been encouraged to produce an essay that contributes to the historiography not just through what it says but through the way it says it as well. In other words, each chapter should provide the reader with not only an expanded understanding of some aspect of the Johnson presidency, but also a glimpse into the newest historical materials and scholarship related to that topic. It is not my objective here—nor do I believe it to have been Bob's—to provide definitive answers about Lyndon Johnson's presidency. It is instead my aim to provoke questions, interest, and new avenues of scholarship about our thirty-sixth president. So, to quote Lyndon Johnson as he too inherited the mantle of a distinguished predecessor: "Let us continue."

M.B.L.
Granville, Ohio

1 | Introduction: Lyndon Johnson in History and Memory

Mitchell B. Lerner

IN HIS INTRODUCTION to the second volume of *The Johnson Years*, editor Robert Divine cited a "unifying element" in the collected essays about the Johnson presidency. "The common dilemma facing all the authors," he lamented, "is the absence of material in the [Lyndon B. Johnson Presidential] library by Johnson himself."[1] This obstacle should come as no surprise to anyone familiar with the president's work habits. LBJ was well aware that one of his greatest political assets was the dynamic force of his personality, and thus he was not one to put down on a memo that which he could speak directly. Since face-to-face conversations did not always fit his schedule, much of the "real" Lyndon Johnson came through over the phone lines. "He's a good man on that telephone," recalled Congressman Ed Hebert (D-La.). "He just likes the telephone."[2] Small wonder, then, that after the president spent eighteen minutes trying to reach Federal Bureau of Investigation liaison Deke DeLoach at home one Saturday night, only to fail because DeLoach's teenage daughter was on the phone, LBJ had technicians in DeLoach's bedroom the next morning to install a phone line to the White House.[3] And the second time that Johnson failed to reach aide Joseph Califano because he was in the bathroom, the president had a phone installed next to Califano's toilet within an hour.[4] For this reason, the Johnson Library, one of the nation's leading repositories of historical materials, has always faced the problem that its holdings revealed more about what Johnson's advisers were telling him than about what the president himself was thinking.

The situation began to change with the passage of the President John F. Kennedy Assassination Records Collection Act of 1992, which, in the wake of the controversial movie *JFK*, required that all records maintained by the federal government that were relevant to the assassination be opened to public and congressional scrutiny. In response, archivists at the Johnson Library released a previously sealed collection of taped phone conversations related to LBJ's ascension to the Oval Office.[5] These tapes, which had been born of Johnson's desire to have an accurate record of the deals that were being made in his political maneuverings, had been transferred to the control of the Library in 1973 with the stipulation that they remain sealed until fifty years after his death. Now, however, under congressional order, the library staff had opened Pandora's box. With the precedent established, and with the support of LBJ's family and closest advisers, the Library began in 1993 to process the rest of the collection of 643 hours of recorded White House phone conversations and 200 hours of meetings.[6] It was a fortuitous day for historians. "I felt for Johnson in a way that I couldn't have before," commented presidential historian Michael Beschloss after listening to some of the tapes, "because when you live through a man's life the way that you do when you're listening to tapes and essentially listening to his life hour by hour, you see the almost impossible situation that he was in."[7]

Problems with the tapes do exist. One cannot ascertain the extent to which LBJ's awareness of the taping system may have affected his behavior, nor can we know which comments may have been made in jest, in sarcasm, or even for the benefit of someone else in the Oval Office. The poor quality of some of the recordings presents its own challenges; in one incident, a White House secretary mistakenly transcribed Johnson's comment about "the Pakistani Ambassador" as "a pack of them bastards." Nevertheless, they have opened an unprecedented window into the American presidency. Scholars no longer need to be frustrated by Johnson's habit of responding to memos with a simple check next to "Approve," "Disapprove," or "See me." Now they could finally hear him voice his thoughts and concerns related to the issues articulated in those memos.

The result has been a wave of historical reexamination. Early scholarship, for example, generally lauded the president's accomplishments in the field of women's rights. In *The Presidency of Lyndon Johnson,* Vaughn Davis Bornet concluded, "The struggle of women to improve their position under the law and within the federal establishment achieved real gains under this president."[8] "He did believe that women were the stronger of the two sexes," recalled his secretary, Marie Chiarodo. "I know that he felt that women had a lot to contribute."[9] Certainly, Johnson deserves some accolades in this area, since by executive order he ended the practice of classifying civil service jobs by sex and banned gender-based discrimination by companies with government contracts. Still, one suspects that neither Bornet nor Chiarodo would have been as laudatory had they heard Johnson's phone conversation with aide Ralph Dungan in March 1964 about the possible appointment of Katherine May, dean of Wheaton College, to the Export-Import Bank:

President Johnson: And how old is she [May]?
Dungan: She's 47, as I recall.
President Johnson: That's a little old for me.
Dungan: [*Laughs.*] She's a spry 47.
President Johnson: Is she good-looking?
Dungan: No, she's—
President Johnson: Well, I'll be damned.
Dungan: [*Laughs again.*] Well, we're striking [out], we're going about three or four out of five.
President Johnson: What about Pat Harris?
Dungan: She's *very* attractive.
President Johnson: All right, now, what does she say, though?
Dungan: I haven't gotten to hear yet.[10]

Another conversation that same month, this one with National Security Adviser McGeorge Bundy, offers support for those historians who articulated the so-called stalemate thesis of the Vietnam War:

Bundy: What is your own internal thinking on this [Vietnam], Mr. President—that we've just got to stick on this middle course as long as there's any possible hope?
President Johnson: I just can't believe that we can't take 15,000 advisers and 200,000 people and maintain the status quo for six months. I just believe we can do that, if we do it right. Now, I don't know enough about it to know.
Bundy: God knows, I don't. The only thing that scares me is that the government would up and quit on us or that there would be a coup, and we'd get invited out.
President Johnson: There may be another coup, but I don't know what we can do. If there is, I guess that we just. . . . What alternatives do we have *then*? We're not going to send our troops in there—are we?[11]

This reemergence of the Johnson administration, and of Johnson himself, as a topic of interest for both historians and the general public should be unsurprising. It is not just that materials such as the tapes have provided new details but that the significance of the Johnson years has begun to emerge more clearly with the benefit of hindsight. In the wake of the turmoil of the late 1960s, it was hard for authors and the general public to focus on the details of LBJ's domestic record. People remembered that riots in Detroit left forty-three dead and seven thousand arrested; they remembered that half a million people marched in the 1967 Spring Mobilization; they remembered the street battles fought along Michigan Avenue between protesters and policemen outside the 1968 Democratic National Convention in Chicago. It was harder to pay much attention to a legislative agenda that forced lending institutions to disclose relevant information to consumers, that required the cleaning of junkyards, and that eliminated racially biased immigration quotas. More dramatic programs like Medicare (which paid almost $11 billion in medical bills for American seniors in its first full year of operation) were so complex and sweeping that they were easily reduced to caricatures of either all good or all bad for those with political agendas. And the great civil rights reforms of 1964 and 1965 became intertwined for many with the more immediate racial issues exploding across the nation. The same held true with regard to foreign policy, where Americans in the immediate post-Johnson period focused on Vietnam at the expense of an international record that also included a war in the Middle East and another in South Asia; a potential war between NATO allies Greece and Turkey over Cyprus; the capture of an American spy ship by an enemy (North Korea) and the attack against another by an ally (Israel); political crises in Brazil, Panama, the Dominican Republic, Indonesia, and elsewhere; and much more. Time, however, has brought a fresh perspective, and slowly Americans have begun to realize that there was more to the Johnson presidency than seemed apparent at first glance.

The emerging literature about the Johnson years thus began producing some new conclusions, particularly in the realm of foreign affairs. The earliest literature saw LBJ as simply uninterested in international relations, a domestic policy maven who focused almost exclusively on reforms at home. Johnson adviser (and historian) Eric Goldman described his boss as one who

> preferred to think about and deal with domestic relations than international affairs; . . . lacked extensive acquaintance with foreign leaders or significant knowledge of foreign civilizations . . . had no carefully thought out conception of the workings of the international system, few broad-gauged premises concerning diplomacy or war, even less feel or sense of things international. . . . Lyndon Johnson entered the White House not only little concerned with the outer world, but leery of it.[12]

Yet, as new evidence emerged, scholars began to challenge this depiction. The second generation of literature generally recognized LBJ as a president who was both active and interested in the shaping of American foreign policy. Their assessment of his conduct, however, was largely negative. Most of this scholarship focused on the Vietnam War, where Johnson's leadership was found wanting for many reasons. Some faulted him for too closely linking foreign policy with domestic politics, putting a primacy above all else on his own political standing.[13] Others found him to be concerned with personal credibility more than political credibility, depicting a president determined to resist any perception that he was weak and unmanly.[14] Some put an emphasis on economic motivations. Hence Patrick Hearden could place Vietnam within the literature of a world systems framework that found LBJ to be worried that a defeat in Vietnam would encourage a global resistance to the capitalist economic network directed by Washington, while Lloyd Gardner located the president's tragic flaw in his inability to recognize that his vision of bringing economic development to the world's poor was not enough to sate the forces of nationalism in Southeast Asia.[15] Many also saw Johnson as unwilling to break from traditional cold war assumptions that predisposed him to see the war not as an internal matter but as part of a larger struggle against world communist domination that risked both long-term American security and short-term American credibility.[16] Regardless of the specific critique, though, the consensus was clear: Lyndon Johnson had failed the country in Vietnam.

It was not just Vietnam, however, where his diplomacy was measured and found wanting. Critics extended their analyses into other regions to produce an image of a president whose diplomatic record was one generally marked by frustration and failure. Perhaps the defining voice for this sentiment was *Lyndon Johnson Confronts the World*, a collection of essays edited by Warren Cohen and Nancy Bernkopf Tucker. In ten chapters, the authors depicted a president whose foreign policy skills left much to be desired. "His appreciation of foreign nations," wrote one, "was shallow, circumstantial, and dominated by the personalities of heads of state that he had met. Lacking a detached critical perspective, he was culture-bound and vulnerable to clichés and stereotypes about world affairs."[17] Although the specific criticisms were wide-ranging, these authors charged LBJ with being obsessed with Vietnam at the expense of policymaking elsewhere; relying on racial and ethnic stereotypes in determining policy; taking positions on issues that he did not understand simply because of his need to feel that he was in command; and instinctively reducing complex world events to simplistic shades of good and bad within an unimaginative cold war framework. In the end, Tucker concluded, the administration's persistence "in pursuing an often unidimensional foreign policy severely limited its accomplishments elsewhere, strained friendships, aggravated animosities, and left a problematic legacy for subsequent occupants of decision-making posts in the White House, State Department, and Department of Defense."[18]

Recently, however, a new wave of scholarship has emerged, one that finds much more to praise in LBJ's diplomacy. The first such work, H. W. Brands's *Wages of Globalism*, was hardly bereft of criticism, especially on the topics of Vietnam and the Dominican intervention. Still, by recognizing the relative decline of American power since the end of World War II and the growing complexities of the world environment, the book provided the first generally positive scholarly assessment. "Considering the dimensions of the task," Brands concluded, "it is surprising he [Johnson] did as well as he did."[19] Subsequent authors followed his lead, usually stressing the daunting challenges and the declining American power that the president inherited. John Prados's study of arms limitations talks argued that, "although it fell to Richard Nixon . . . to sign the first SALT agreement, Johnson merits much more of the credit than he has been accorded."[20] Some went even further with their praise, including Thomas Schwartz, whose study of LBJ and Europe found the president to be "an astute and able practitioner of alliance politics, a leader who recognized how to assemble crossnational coalitions and work toward his overriding goals and objectives."[21]

Into this most contentious debate step four of the authors in this volume. Only one of the chapters, Mark Lawrence's study of the 1964 Panama crisis, echoes the positive view of Lyndon Johnson propagated in the most recent scholarship, and even then Lawrence attributes this success more to the unique circumstances surrounding the crisis than to Johnson's perspicacity. Nonetheless, he finds that the president's willingness to begin the process of revising the Panama Canal Treaty was "a remarkable gesture" that reflected "a flexible, creative, and even concessionary policy." At the opposite extreme, David Anderson examines the path to war in Vietnam and finds little to praise in Johnson's decisions or his motivation. LBJ is faulted on many grounds: for his unwillingness to be seen as lacking the courage and toughness of his predecessor; for his acceptance of basic cold war axioms that exaggerated the importance of Vietnam and rejected the possibility that it was an indigenous conflict; for his failure to understand the commitment and motivation of the enemy; and especially for his determination to preserve his political standing in order to obtain the domestic legislative agenda he so badly desired. In the end, Anderson concludes, Johnson lacked the political courage to either withdraw completely or escalate convincingly, instead adopting a gradualist approach that was "ad hoc, dilatory, dissembling, and not a picture of courage and purpose."

The other two foreign policy chapters fall somewhere in the middle. Peter Hahn's study of the Six Day War describes it as "a major setback for Lyndon Johnson." Yet Hahn recognizes that forces beyond the president's control were at work, and he notes the extent to which America's ability to shape the world was declining for reasons that had little to do with LBJ. Jeremi Suri offers a modified form of the criticism that Johnson subordinated foreign policy to domestic political imperatives, arguing that he was concerned not with passing legislation but with stabilizing the American political system itself in the face of massive popular unrest. By examining LBJ's policies toward the communist superpowers in 1968, Suri finds that a deeply rooted fear of the collapse of domestic order virtually paralyzed the president and drove him to "policy stagnation" in a situation that called for creative and bold initiatives. He recognizes, however, that Johnson was not alone in this predicament, as other global leaders met the same challenges with the same type of conservative responses, and he acknowledges that the roots of many of these problems lay in events, such as the Chinese Cultural Revolution, that were beyond the control of Lyndon Johnson. LBJ's diplomatic initiatives may have been unsuccessful during his last years in office, but it appears that, at least in Hahn and Suri's studies, events were in the saddle, and they rode mankind.

Although the four chapters have clear differences, they also have some points of agreement that may reflect at least a limited consensus emerging in the field of Johnson's diplomacy. Most obviously, the authors agree that LBJ was actively involved in the conduct of foreign policy during his administration. "He always will be judged personally by the measure of his administration's successes and failures," notes Anderson, "because they were his successes and failures." Clearly, this aspect of the early Johnson historiography is dead and buried. Interred next to it is the idea that the president acted in foreign policy only to advance his domestic agenda, as the authors also agree that while domestic politics played a role in his policy decisions, it was neither the sole factor nor even the predominant one. There also appears to be a consensus suggesting that Johnson was motivated less by a simplistic anticommunism than by a desire to defend the political status quo, both for himself at home and in regions deemed important elsewhere.

Hence the United States tried to placate both sides in the Middle East; sought rapprochement with China and the Soviet Union in 1968; and followed a policy of concession in Panama while doing the opposite in Vietnam because these approaches seemed most likely to preserve the existing order regardless of what form that order took. Although the three non-Vietnam chapters also recognize the extent to which LBJ and his advisers were concerned with the crisis in Southeast Asia, the authors also indicate that the Johnson White House was neither obsessed with it nor even greatly hindered by it in conducting American diplomacy. Perhaps most significantly, the same three authors note the importance of changing international conditions in shaping American policies in the Johnson era. For Suri and Hahn, writing about events in the chaotic environment of LBJ's final years, the president's intentions were clearly frustrated by the limits on American power; for Lawrence, the president was able to accomplish his aims in Panama specifically because the geopolitical conditions that limited his freedom to act elsewhere were missing.

Although there are clearly articulated schools of thought regarding Johnson's diplomatic record, the literature on his domestic policies is not as neatly defined. In some ways the evolution of scholarship about LBJ's domestic record has followed a path in almost direct opposition to the scholarship about his foreign policy. Rather than starting with a consensus and slowly evolving into competing schools of thought, this historiography began with two very different views that have slowly moved toward a common ground. In the earliest literature, Johnson emerged as either one of two extremes. His supporters depicted him as a genuine man of the people, a Texas populist determined to use the power of the presidency to help those in need, without thought of any personal gain.[22] His detractors offered a very different assessment, one that tended to emphasize an all-encompassing desire for power.[23] In 1967, Robert Sherrill's *Accidental President* described Johnson as lacking any moral values whatsoever. "The first thing we must do—and this is absolutely prerequisite to a better appreciation of Johnson—is admit that the man is not likeable," he wrote, "and that he is, in fact, treacherous, dishonest, manic-aggressive, petty, spoiled, and above all, accidental."[24]

Although these one-dimensional caricatures of LBJ and his presidency were soon replaced by more nuanced studies, a few works perpetuated their simplistic formulations. Jack Valenti's memoirs, *A Very Human President* (1976), which acknowledged that the president had flaws and made errors (particularly in Vietnam), nevertheless took every opportunity to credit him with both the finest results and the grandest motives; thus, for example, the reader learns that LBJ refused to appoint Robert Kennedy to the position of ambassador to South Vietnam in 1964 out of concern for his rival's physical safety in such a dangerous place.[25] On the opposite extreme is Robert Caro, who has authored three volumes that take the reader through Johnson's years in the Senate, all of which endorse the image of LBJ as being driven only by a personal lust for power.[26] Caro's works, despite being consistently interesting and well written, are marred by his failure to maintain objectivity. In the second volume, *Means of Ascent,* he overlooks the virulent racism of Coke Stevenson, Johnson's opponent in the famous 1948 Senate campaign, in presenting a simplistic story of evil (LBJ) cheating its way to triumph over good (Stevenson). The third volume, *Master of the Senate,* is more balanced than the first two but still never misses a chance to attribute the basest of motives to its subject. For example, having spent two and a half books attributing every Johnson action to a selfish quest for power, Caro now dismisses evidence suggesting that his motive in supporting the Civil Rights Act of 1957 might have been, at least in part, an earnest desire for social justice. Instead, he advances the imaginative claim that the Texas senator had simply convinced himself that a moral imperative existed in order to rationalize his involvement, rather than admit to himself that this was merely another self-serving step designed to advance his political career. In reality, for a southern politician to take a public role in shaping any civil rights legislation in the 1950s, even a law as weak as this, suggests that more than political motives may have been at work, but Caro seems as blinded by his need to attack as Valenti was to defend.

The majority of the literature over the past two decades, however, has moved toward a more moderate position. Among the early leaders in the field was Paul Conkin's *Big Daddy from the Pedernales.* While acknowledging that critics could fault specific Great Society reforms for doing either too much (and thus creating a large and intrusive federal bureaucracy) or too little (and thus leaving intact many of the problems that Johnson had pledged to address), Conkin argued that such attacks failed to recognize the larger legacy of the Great Society as a whole. His own analysis does not gloss over the shortcomings of specific reforms. The Community Action Program, for example, is depicted as both subversive of the existing order and ineffective in its attempts to lessen poverty in the United States. And he finds much to fault in the president's leadership, which he sees as marked by exaggerated rhetoric, a difficulty in communicating with the public as a whole, and an unwillingness to consider the possible future complications of his policies. However, by looking at the Great Society as the sum of many disparate parts, Conkin finds a moderate and largely successful program that reflected Johnson's own leanings toward consensus and flexibility and that were rooted in his personal background in the Texas Hill Country. "That, for a few brief years," he concludes, "Congress responded to these problems and concerns more promptly than ever before or since, at times more responsibly and in a few cases more daringly, was in part a product of the chaotic times, but also a product of the legislative magic of Lyndon Johnson."[27]

Current historical scholarship has begun to echo these conclusions. Two recent works in particular have begun the process of providing a detailed and detached analysis of the many aspects of the Great Society: Irving Bernstein's *Guns or Butter* (1996) and Robert Dallek's *Flawed Giant* (1998). Despite some specific interpretive differences, the two works agree that the Johnson presidency could not be reduced to simplistic notions of good and bad; that LBJ was a political moderate whose many personal flaws did not stand in the way of a generally positive legislative record; and that the Great Society merged elements of traditional New Deal liberalism, Texas populism, and Johnson's personal combination of ambition, political pragmatism, and genuine humanitarianism. In both books the shortcomings of the Great Society, and of LBJ himself, are on full display. Bernstein's examination of the Clean Water Act of 1965, for example, shows how the president largely jumped on the bandwagon established earlier by Maine senator Edwin Muskie, who had introduced such a bill almost three years earlier. And although he worked to ensure the passage of the not wholly ineffective 1965 version, Johnson quickly transferred its enforcement from the Department of Health, Education, and Welfare to the Department of the Interior, which had much closer ties to many leading polluters. Nor did he act to close the many loopholes that the law contained or to provide adequate funding for its enforcement. Bernstein is also quick to distribute credit to others, even offering the doubtful claim that almost all the Great Society legislation would have passed under Kennedy's administration, even the Civil Rights Act of 1964.[28] Dallek's study of the Model Cities initiative also shows how the president, caving in to political realities, scaled back his grand vision for a $2.4 billion program to address the needs of America's inner cities. Instead, as liberals attacked the initial plan as too little and conservatives as too much, he sought compromise and consensus, settling for a much more limited appropriation of $900 million over two years. Nor did he push for stringent application, instead watching as congressmen divided the funding among hundreds of cities, thus rendering it ineffective for all but political gain.[29]

However, both authors do find that LBJ's policies, like LBJ himself, left a positive legacy overall despite many specific shortcomings and a frequent failure to reach expectations. "Lyndon Johnson," Bernstein concludes, "has been short-changed. He has been charged with what went wrong and he has not been credited with what went right."[30] To prove that much did indeed go right, Bernstein provides a detailed look at seventeen pieces of legislation that he characterizes as "significant." The overall picture provided is one of a moderate and practical president who used his legislative mastery on behalf of many causes, including the advancement of his own political power, but especially on behalf of those Americans who could least help themselves. His legacy, Bernstein concludes, has been given short shrift because of a tragic flaw—his insistence that he could have both guns and butter at the same time—but it is a significant legacy nonetheless. Similarly, Dallek not only finds much that is laudatory in Johnson's legislative record but also credits him with playing an influential role in the development and preservation of modern liberalism. "Like FDR's New Deal," he concludes, "Johnson's poverty war and reach for a Great Society may seem somewhat outdated or inadequate to current challenges, but the humanizing force behind them abides and gives both men historical standing as visionaries who helped advance the national well-being and fulfill the promise of American life."[31] Dallek's evaluation of LBJ's educational reforms speaks for this interpretation as a whole: "The fact that the country's educational system works as well as it does has something to do with the federal support Johnson initiated in 1965. If his educational reforms did not lead to a great society, they have at least made for a better society."[32]

Most recent works have echoed these conclusions, finding in LBJ a pragmatic politician whose efforts to use the government to aid the American people were spread broadly across lines of income, race, and background. In *LBJ: A Life*, Irwin and Debbie Unger paint a portrait of a moderate liberal whose determination to help at all costs was matched by a politician's sense of what was possible and a conservative's commitment to preserve the basic foundations of the capitalist system. Medicare, they demonstrate, may have offered enormous benefits to many Americans, but they also note the extent to which LBJ's political horse trading to ensure its passage sparked massive medical inflation.[33] Bruce Schulman's *Lyndon B. Johnson and American Liberalism* explains that Johnson's vision of liberalism was determined to both emulate and surpass that of Franklin Roosevelt and, in doing so, ensured that his reforms offered something for all Americans while never losing sight of what was politically feasible. For LBJ, government was a necessity of life, one that could ensure an equality of opportunity, if not an equality of results, to individuals both at home and abroad. But his unwillingness to confront the "guns or butter" issue, and the backlash stemming from his civil rights reforms, eventually undermined his vision. LBJ, Schulman concludes, "left a record of achievement unmatched by any other president, and a legacy of failure, deceit, and bitterness."[34] John Andrew III, in *Lyndon Johnson and the Great Society*, finds in LBJ the ultimate symbol of "managerial liberalism," the idea that government could regulate the economy in such a way as to ensure prosperity while funding social reforms. But doing so required a serious challenge to the status quo, a massive commitment of energy and resources by the American people, and a rethinking of traditional American beliefs about federal assistance to individuals. Built on such an unstable base, and weakened by the controversies about civil rights and Vietnam, LBJ's consensus shattered.[35] In most of these recent accounts, the Great Society thus emerges as an opportunity lost, a missed chance for reform lost to the cultural divisions at home and the military conflict in Vietnam.

Although each of these books has much to praise, none of them provides a complete history of the Great Society.[36] There thus remains a striking gap in the historical literature of the Johnson period, one that no doubt reflects the daunting challenge that awaits anyone brave enough to attempt to synthesize such a massive collection of policies. Instead, historians have recently turned to providing a series of more narrowly focused studies, each examining in detail one aspect of Johnson's legislative record. The last decade has produced monographs about LBJ and Mexican-Americans; LBJ and Native Americans; LBJ and civil rights; LBJ and education policy; and LBJ and the judiciary. Collections of essays have also emerged to shed light on even more specific topics, addressing such issues as Johnson's administrative legacy and his use of the Council of Economic Advisers.[37] Most of these works conform to the emerging picture of the Great Society as a moderate collection that reflected LBJ's combination of idealism, New Deal liberalism, and political pragmatism. Yet much scholarly work remains to be done. In fact, it is revealing that so many of the authors whose work is collected here lament the dearth of attention paid to their particular subjects. David Shreve finds that ". . . Johnson's biographers have likely focused less attention on his administration's economic policies than any other major subject"; Robert Johnson notes that the

1964 farm bill is "not generally considered among the more significant of Johnson's tenure—or even of his first year in office"; and Thomas Clarkin explains that "most studies of Lyndon Johnson's presidency make no mention of his administration's efforts to assist American Indians."

Thus we come to the last five chapters of this collection, all of which use such narrowly focused studies to hint at larger conclusions about Johnson's domestic record. Two chapters—Thomas Clarkin on Native Americans and Julia Kirk Blackwelder on women—examine LBJ's policies and attitudes toward specific societal groups struggling to improve their positions within a largely closed social order. The authors reach similar conclusions, finding the president to be neither supportive of, nor even overly interested in, these efforts. Both also attribute his position to a combination of political factors and personal ideology; Lyndon Johnson, in these portrayals, was clearly never able to break free from the mental framework that dominated the political and social systems in which he had spent much of his life. Clarkin finds the president refusing to push for greater change in the government's policy toward Native Americans, specifically with regard to their desired shift from a "termination" program to one of "self-determination," because of the potential congressional opposition, the dearth of political pressure from Native Americans, and his own background and beliefs about the correct role of Native Americans in society. Similarly, Blackwelder finds a lack of commitment to women's issues in the Johnson White House, citing as the cause "the president's biases on gender, the political culture in which he functioned, and the scarcity and powerlessness of American feminists in the early 1960s." The authors do differ on LBJ's legacy in these areas. For Blackwelder, the president's unwillingness to push for serious structural reform meant that little was accomplished beyond the superficial gains embodied by his frenzied attempt to appoint 150 women to positions within his administration, an effort she shows to be neither as successful nor as meaningful as his supporters claimed. Clarkin, however, notes that while LBJ did not consciously help advance the position of Native Americans, the efforts of Great Society legislation (and in particular the controversial Community Action Program) to help the poor across the board had a number of beneficial consequences on the reservations.

If LBJ failed to have much influence in these areas, it was at least by his own choice. Michael Flamm shows that the same cannot be said for his attempts to calm the urban disorder that marked the latter years of his presidency. In his study of the "long hot summer" of

1967, Flamm reveals a president caught between a need to avoid appearing to be pandering to rioters and a desire to do whatever was necessary to bring stability to the inner city, all the while struggling to preserve a collapsing liberal coalition. In the face of such a severe domestic crisis, even the vaunted political acumen of Lyndon Johnson proved unable to find a solution, and in the end, here too he appears to have accomplished little. "The grand ambitions of the Great Society," Flamm concludes, "had given way to grim demands for 'law and order.'"

Yet the other two chapters find a president who was both active and successful in shaping a productive legislative agenda. For Robert Johnson, LBJ's handling of the 1964 farm bill represents both an example of the president's masterful political ability and a demonstration of the fact that political motivations of various types never strayed far from his mind. LBJ's skillful manipulation of this bill muted potential congressional opposition; reinforced his 1964 election campaign; strengthened his party's standing in the Farm Belt; and began the process of breaking down regional blocs in favor of a national coalition of moderates, a significant development on the road to civil rights and antipoverty legislation. David Shreve also embraces an activist picture of Lyndon Johnson, who believed that he could create a great society by moving beyond the generally accepted economic rules that dominated American fiscal policy. Rejecting as simplistic the standard story of "guns versus butter," Shreve instead credits LBJ with implementing a truly Keynesian policy that above all else saw no contradiction between full employment and price stability, and which would prove remarkably successful. "In the end," he concludes, "LBJ bequeathed to the nation unsurpassed prosperity and an auspicious beginning to both a war on poverty and a struggle for price stability at full employment." There are differences in the two portrayals, most notably in the question of motivation. Shreve finds LBJ's economic vision rooted in a genuine belief in its efficacy, but Robert Johnson notes that the president neither knew nor cared about the effectiveness of the farm bill. In the final analysis, however, both agree that Lyndon Johnson inherited situations fraught with obstacles and through his intelligence, his ability, and his energy, transformed them into victories for himself, his party, and the nation.

A number of unifying threads emerge from these chapters that may help future authors to better understand the nature of Lyndon Johnson and the Great Society as a whole. Most obvious is the portrayal of LBJ as never losing sight of the political ramifications of his actions. Johnson's response to riots in Detroit and Newark, Flamm demonstrates, was always influenced by an awareness of the political situation, and Robert Johnson's study shows the president to have supported four different versions of the farm bill at different times, not because of their contents but as part of a larger political strategy. There is also a general consensus that the president's vision of the Great Society was constrained by his deeply ingrained beliefs about the proper societal positions to be held by different segments of the population. LBJ wanted to help the poor out of poverty and *into* his perception of mainstream American society. He would not, however, help anyone to move *beyond* that perception of traditional society, as evidenced, for example, by his numerous refusals to embrace the cause of women's rights. In a related area, there emerges from these chapters a sense that paternalism lay at the heart of this domestic agenda, a paternalism that extended as far as his relationship with his predecessor's widow and the sense of obligation his administration felt to push Native Americans into the mainstream of American society. Even his fiscal policies seem to reflect paternalism, as David Shreve demonstrates that alongside all his sophisticated economic beliefs lay the fundamental idea that the economy was being manipulated to act against the best interests of those who could least defend themselves. "Some men want power simply to strut around the world and to hear the tune of 'Hail to the Chief,'" Johnson explained after leaving the White House. "Others want it simply to build prestige, to collect antiques, and to buy pretty things. Well, I wanted power to give things to people—all sorts of people, especially the poor and the blacks."[38]

These chapters also converge around a growing trend in the historical literature that suggests that LBJ's policies at home bear less responsibility for the collapse of American liberalism in the late 1960s than is sometimes assumed. In 1984, Allen Matusow's *Unraveling of America* pointed the finger of blame at liberals themselves, finding Kennedy and Johnson in particular to be unwilling to push for genuine structural change.[39] This failure, he suggested, divided the reform movement and opened the door to its repudiation. Eight years later, Thomas and Mary Edsall were even more specific, arguing that white reaction to the civil rights stance taken by the Johnson administration, and particularly the passage of the Civil Rights Act of 1964, lay at the heart of the decline of Democratic Party liberalism.[40] Recent historiography, however, has suggested that factors predating LBJ played critical roles.[41] Most of the chapters here offer support for the latter argument by suggesting that Lyndon Johnson inherited a collection of deeply rooted problems, and that the collapse of New Deal liberalism would likely have come regardless of who sat in the Oval

Office. Clarkin and Blackwelder in particular find that LBJ came to the presidency just as long-simmering tensions threatened to explode, and while Flamm rejects the idea that the coalition's collapse was attributable simply to pre-1960s racism, he does find that there was little Lyndon Johnson could have done to alleviate the security-related fears that proved to be its undoing. For many Americans, Flamm concludes, the issue of law and order became "not a conservative stratagem—it was a concrete issue based on real fear and actual circumstance that even a consummate politician like Johnson could not control."

If the conclusions reached by the nine authors here offer no definitive paradigm for better understanding Lyndon Johnson, it should not be surprising. One of his closest friends and political allies noted that there was "no adjective in the dictionary to describe him. He was cruel and kind, generous and greedy, sensitive and insensitive, crafty and naive, ruthless and thoughtful, simple in many ways yet extremely complex, caring and totally not caring . . . as a matter of fact, it would take every adjective in the dictionary to describe him."[42] In 1973, *New York Times* columnist Russell Baker wrote that LBJ was "a human puzzle so complicated nobody can ever understand it." Johnson, simply, was a complex man, a larger-than-life figure whose guiding principles likely cannot be—even should not be—reduced to one simple factor such as politics, personal power, or anticommunism. If historians and the general public are ever to understand these complexities, scholars will need to start by applying these newly available materials to studies of all aspects of his presidency, not just Vietnam and civil rights, and doing so in a broad, sweeping manner befitting the grand vision of the thirty-sixth president. This volume, while making no claims to providing definitive answers, hopes to offer at least a step in that direction.

Notes

1. Robert Divine, *The Johnson Years*, vol. 2, *Vietnam, the Environment, and Science* (Lawrence: University Press of Kansas, 1987), viii.

2. Lyndon Baines Johnson Presidential Library, Austin, Texas (hereafter LBJL) Oral History Collection, Edward Hebert Oral History, 15 July 1969, p. 29.

3. LBJL, Oral History Collection, Cartha D. Deloach Oral History, vol. 1, 11 January 1991, p. 30.

4. Joseph Califano, *The Triumph and Tragedy of Lyndon Johnson* (New York: Simon and Schuster, 1991), 26.

5. For a good history of the Johnson presidential tapes, see Michael

Beschloss, *Taking Charge* (New York: Simon and Schuster, 1997), 547–553, or the Johnson Presidential Library Web site at: http://www.lbjlib.utexas.edu/johnson/archives.hom/Dictabelt.hom/whsmain.htm (accessed 10 April 2004).

6. As of late 2003, the Library had released the phone conversations through March 1966, with the rest scheduled to follow over the next few years. The recordings of meetings have not yet been opened, and because of their poor quality and the higher level of security, their releases are likely to follow a slower trajectory.

7. Beschloss quoted in "HBO Films Artist Interviews," on the Web at http://www.hbo.com/films/pathtowar/artist_int_beschloss.shtml (accessed 15 December 2003).

8. Vaughn Davis Bornet, *The Presidency of Lyndon Johnson* (Lawrence: University Press of Kansas, 1983), 35.

9. LBJL, Oral History Collection, Marie Chiarodo Oral History, vol. 3, 16 August 1972, p. 18.

10. "Telephone conversation between Johnson and Ralph Dungan," 28 March 1964, 2:56 P.M., Citation no. 2696, tape WH 6403.18, program 1.

11. "Telephone conversation between Johnson and McGeorge Bundy," 2 March 1964, 12:35 P.M., Citation no. 2309, tape WH 6403.01, program 9.

12. Eric Goldman, *The Tragedy of Lyndon Johnson* (New York: Knopf, 1969), 379.

13. See, for example, Larry Berman, *Planning a Tragedy* (New York: Norton, 1983), in which the author concluded, "The President was involved in a delicate exercise of political juggling. . . . He chose to avoid a national debate on the war, to keep the reserves home, and to buy time for a domestic record meriting nothing less than Mount Rushmore" (146–148).

14. See, for example, Fredrik Logevall, *Choosing War* (Berkeley and Los Angeles: University of California Press, 1999).

15. Patrick Hearden, *The Tragedy of Vietnam* (New York: Addison-Wesley, 1991); Lloyd Gardner, *Pay Any Price* (New York: Ivan R. Dee, 1990).

16. See, for example, Brian VandeMark, *Into the Quagmire* (New York: Oxford University Press, 1995); Michael Hunt, *Lyndon Johnson's War* (New York: Hill and Wang, 1997); Robert Schulzinger, *A Time for War* (New York: Oxford University Press, 1991).

17. Waldo Heinrichs, "Lyndon B. Johnson," in *Lyndon Johnson Confronts the World*, ed. Warren Cohen and Nancy Bernkopf Tucker (New York: Cambridge University Press, 1994), 26.

18. Nancy Bernkopf Tucker, "Lyndon Johnson: A Final Reckoning," in Cohen and Tucker, *Lyndon Johnson Confronts the World*, 318. Many subsequent works echoed these conclusions. Michael Latham's study of the Panama crisis, for example, suggested that LBJ and his advisers "proved incapable of recognizing the relationship between the imperial past and the Cold War present," and Peter Felton's work on the Dominican intervention even suggested that the administration was most successful when the president was least involved. "Johnson's willingness to let others control the details of Dominican affairs," he concluded, "led to his ultimate success in Santo Domingo." Michael Latham, "Imperial Legacy and Cold War Credibility," *Peace and Change* 27 (October 2002): 499; Peter Felton, "Yankee, Go Home and Take Me with You," in *The Foreign Policies of Lyndon Johnson*, ed. H. W. Brands (College Station: Texas A&M University Press, 1999), 127.

19. H. W. Brands, *Wages of Globalism* (New York: Oxford University Press, 1995).

20. John Prados, "Prague Spring and SALT," in Brands, *Foreign Policies of Lyndon Johnson*, 20.

21. Thomas Schwartz, *Lyndon Johnson and Europe* (Cambridge, Mass.: Harvard University Press, 2003), 7.

22. See, for example, William White's book *The Politician*, which describes LBJ as "one of the most talented politicians in our history, alternatively confident and skeptical, outgoing and reserved, tough and compassionate, born to action but sometimes electing to pause in long thought." The book, White later admitted, had been written largely to present a favorable image of Johnson to the country and the world rather than to provide a dispassionate assessment. "I did very little research," he explained, "because it was not that kind of a book." LBJL, Oral History Collection, William White Oral History, 5 March 1969, p. 15.

23. The first such work was J. Evetts Haley's book *A Texan Looks at Lyndon*, which noted his "ambitious desires, his vanity and monumental egotism, his vindictive nature and his evil genius." J. Evetts Haley, *A Texan Looks at Lyndon* (New York: Buccaneer Books, 1964), 7.

24. Robert Sherrill, *The Accidental President* (New York: Grossman, 1967), 4.

25. Jack Valenti, *A Very Human President* (New York: Pocket Books, 1976), 140–141.

26. Robert Caro, *The Path to Power* (New York: Knopf, 1982); Caro, *Means of Ascent* (New York: Knopf, 1990); Caro, *Master of the Senate* (New York: Knopf, 2002).

27. Paul Conkin, *Big Daddy from the Pedernales* (New York: Twayne, 1987), 242.

28. Irving Bernstein, *Guns or Butter* (New York: Oxford University Press, 1996), 529–530.

29. Robert Dallek, *Flawed Giant* (New York: Oxford University Press, 1998), 317–322.

30. Bernstein, *Guns or Butter*, vii.

31. Dallek, *Flawed Giant*, 625.

32. Ibid., 203.

33. Irwin Unger and Debi Unger, *LBJ: A Life* (New York: Wiley, 2000), 366–367.

34. Bruce Schulman, *Lyndon B. Johnson and American Liberalism* (New York: Bedford, 1995), 164–165.

35. John Andrew III, *Lyndon Johnson and the Great Society* (New York: Ivan R. Dee, 1998).

36. Bernstein's book provides the best overview of the Great Society as a whole, but because it argues that LBJ's great failure was his insistence that he could make progress at home while fighting a war overseas, it loses focus on the Great Society as it shifts to Vietnam.

37. Julie Pycor, *LBJ and Mexican Americans* (Austin: University of Texas Press, 1997); Thomas Clarkin, *Federal Indian Policy in the Kennedy and Johnson Administrations* (Albuquerque: University of New Mexico Press, 2001); Robert Mann, *The Walls of Jericho* (New York: Harvest Books, 1997); Hugh Davis Graham, *The Uncertain Triumph* (Chapel Hill: University of

North Carolina Press, 1984); Bernard Firestone and Robert Vogt, eds., *Lyndon Baines Johnson and the Uses of Power* (New York: Greenwood Press, 1988).

38. Quoted in Doris Kearns Goodwin, *Lyndon Johnson and the American Dream* (Boston: St. Martin's Press, 1991), 54.

39. Allen Matusow, *The Unraveling of America* (New York: Harper Collins, 1984).

40. Thomas Edsall and Mary Edsall, *Chain Reaction* (New York: Norton, 1991).

41. See, for example, Mary Brennan, *Turning Right in the Sixties* (Chapel Hill: University of North Carolina Press, 1995); and Thomas Sugrue, *The Origins of the Urban Crisis* (Princeton, N.J.: Princeton University Press, 1996). Brennan demonstrates that the growing population in the Southwest was embracing conservative values in the late 1950s, and Sugrue reveals that the conservative backlash of the 1960s had its roots in a complex set of local conditions related to the economic decline of the industrial cities in the post–World War II era.

42. John Connally, quoted in Schulman, *Lyndon B. Johnson and American Liberalism*, 2.

2 | Exception to the Rule? The Johnson Administration and the Panama Canal

Mark Atwood Lawrence

HISTORY HAS GIVEN Lyndon Johnson low marks for his adminis-tration's performance in coping with the transformation of the third world during his years in office. The powerful assertion of nationalist grievances during the 1960s demanded creativity and flexibility, as U.S. national security increasingly depended on aligning the country with global forces of sociopolitical change. Instead, historians have argued, Johnson responded with rigidity in thought and action, embrac-ing a Manichaean understanding of the cold war and propping up the status quo wherever it was sagging. LBJ was "aware of change" in the international arena but was "slow to discard early Cold War assump-tions and unsure how to deal with new realities," writes one scholar with characteristic disdain.[1]

Johnson inspires particular criticism with respect to Latin America, where scholars have contrasted his administration's performance unfavorably with the more sophisticated policies of the Kennedy years. To be sure, many commentators argue that John F. Kennedy's Alliance for Progress has been overrated as a departure toward a more constructive U.S. relationship with Latin America.[2] But few dispute that LBJ squandered whatever promise the alliance possessed and left behind a heavy-handed policy based on militarism, narrow anticom-munism, and naked economic exploitation. During the 1960s, asserts one critic, "American leaders moved rapidly from the subtler ways of the alliance to the harsher means of social control, especially during the administration of Lyndon Johnson." Under Johnson, adds another, the focus of U.S. policy shifted from "development" to "stability," which became Washington's "holy grail" for a decade.[3] In that elusive quest, the administration ordered twenty-three thousand U.S. troops into the Dominican Republic in 1965, supported military coups in Brazil (1964), Bolivia (1964), and Argentina (1966), and generally hard-ened U.S. attitudes toward sociopolitical change throughout the region.

This pattern was not, however, without its exceptions. Above all, the Johnson administration's approach to Panama contrasts strikingly with its general performance in the Western Hemisphere. In the late 1950s and early 1960s, U.S. policymakers grew increasingly alarmed as Panama experienced the same kind of political and social turmoil that gripped much of Latin America. Protecting U.S. interests in the country, especially control over the Panama Canal, ranked as one of Washington's highest regional priorities throughout the Johnson years. At first, the administration responded to Panamanian unrest just as it answered similar challenges elsewhere—with diplomatic rigidity, manipulation of local politics, and force. Over time, however, Washington developed rare flexibility and imagination in its approach to Panama. On 18 December 1964, the president stunned the world by announcing that Washington would renegotiate the 1903 treaties under which the United States operated the canal and dominated the surrounding five-hundred-square-mile Canal Zone. Those treaties, lopsided arrangements rudely imposed on Panama during the era of Theodore Roosevelt's "big stick" diplomacy, had caused tension between Washington and Panamanian nationalists for half a century. Now, Johnson proclaimed, the United States was prepared for sweeping changes. The president declared U.S. willingness to "recognize the sovereignty of Panama" over the Canal Zone and, more generally, to seek an arrangement that was "just and fair and right" to both countries.[4]

Thus began the process that resulted fourteen years later in a new treaty and thirty-five years later in the official transfer of the canal to Panama, a process that lasted far longer than Johnson could have imagined but ultimately fulfilled his vision of a reconfigured U.S.-Panamanian relationship. At the handover ceremony on 14 December 1999, Jimmy Carter received the lion's share of credit for bringing the negotiations to fruition in 1978—a triumph of statesmanship in the face of fierce conservative resistance. Johnson's name was scarcely mentioned. Yet LBJ was the leader who had originally placed treaty revision on the U.S. agenda, a remarkable gesture at a time of mounting skepticism in Washington about the possibility of achieving U.S. objectives in Latin America through accommodating local demands for change.

Why did the administration take such an exceptional step in Panama? The question merits attention partly because Johnson's decision marked a watershed in U.S.-Panama relations and in the history of the canal. Even if the president failed to attain his objective during his term in office, his approach to the negotiations helped set the stage for dramas that played out in later years. The president's dealings with Panama also command scholarly inquiry because they illuminate the broader U.S. approach to the cold war during the 1960s. Johnson's response to Panamanian unrest in early 1964, his first foreign policy test after taking office, revealed patterns of behavior that would persist throughout his administration, above all LBJ's cultivation of a tough image and his careful management of political and bureaucratic adversaries. Even more revealing than the continuities, however, are the discontinuities between the administration's behavior in Panama and its performance with respect to other nationalist challenges. The Panama case sets in relief the rigidity and conservatism of Johnson's general approach by illuminating a peculiar set of circumstances in which he was open to a flexible, creative, and even concessionary policy.

This chapter argues that the administration followed such a course in Panama on the basis of three calculations it made over the course of 1964—a constellation of judgments that it was unable to make with respect to other third world trouble spots. First, Johnson concluded that he could manage the political risks associated with a policy of accommodation in Panama. Second, the administration calculated that ceding some rights in the Canal Zone, far from a sign of caving in to America's leftist enemies, would in fact help reduce the danger of radicalism in Panama by strengthening the rightist oligarchy that had served U.S. interests for decades. Third, the president determined that the bureaucracies most deeply invested in existing Canal Zone arrangements, especially the U.S. military, would not stand in the way of a new policy departure. Each calculation marked a necessary, but insufficient, condition for the transformation of U.S. policy in the months before Johnson's speech. Only after assuring himself in each and every way—political, geopolitical, and bureaucratic—did the president offer to renegotiate. That gesture, ostensibly one of the most forward-looking and generous U.S. foreign policy decisions of the cold war era, was, then, rooted in the same caution and conservatism that characterized Johnson era policymaking toward the third world more generally. Confident that generosity would cost him nothing at home and would strengthen the repressive forces of order in Panama, the president embraced an exceptional policy—an exception that proves the rule.

The Importance of Being Tough

On 7 January 1964, American students hoisted the U.S. flag up the flagpole outside Balboa High School near the Pacific end of the

Canal Zone, a deliberate violation of agreements specifying where the Stars and Stripes could be flown in the U.S.-dominated strip of territory. As school let out two days later, at least 150 Panamanian students marched to the school intent on responding by running their nation's colors up the flagpole. The ensuing confrontation led to a scuffle that injured several students and may have resulted in the tearing of the Panamanian flag. The marchers vacated the zone, but news of the clash spread quickly. Before the evening was out, rioting had erupted along a two-mile stretch of the Canal Zone border. Denouncing decades of U.S. domination, some two thousand Panamanians peppered the Canal Zone police with debris, smashed windows, and set fire to U.S. property. A twenty-year-old Panamanian student died as police shifted from tear gas to bullets to keep the mob out of the zone. Two hours into the fray, with canal police buckling, troops of the U.S. Southern Command went into action. Casualties mounted as U.S. snipers exchanged fire with armed rioters. By the time the Panamanian government called out its Guardia Nacional to restore order on 13 January, 4 U.S. soldiers and 21 Panamanians were dead, and more than 100 on each side lay injured.[5]

The damage reached far beyond the streets of Panama. After the first night of rioting, Panamanian president Roberto Chiari suspended his country's diplomatic relations with the United States. In a radio address, Chiari demanded an end to the rioting but declared that Panama would renew relations only if Washington agreed to renegotiate the canal treaties. Some U.S. officials suspected that the Panamanian leader, under mounting pressure before elections scheduled for May, was merely posturing to bolster his nationalist credentials and predicted that he would back down before seriously damaging relations with Washington. Chiari was, after all, hardly a radical. The president represented the deeply conservative oligarchy that had long cultivated close U.S. ties and run the country in the interests of the handful of families that dominated Panama. But Chiari showed no sign of giving in as the hours passed. On the contrary, he pledged that Panama's United Nations (UN) delegation would make a "vigorous denunciation" of U.S. "aggression" against his country. "I also want to promise the Panamanian people solemnly," he declared, "that my government will exhaust all recourses to carry out all measures to appeal to all possible organizations in order to obtain justice for the Republic of Panama once and for all and that national honor will suffer no loss whatsoever, and that the blood of the martyrs who perished today will not have been shed in vain."[6] He was equally categorical in a phone conversation with Johnson, demanding "complete revision" of the canal treaties to curtail U.S. privileges. Chiari reminded Johnson that President Kennedy had pledged in 1961 to review the treaties, but that the promise had gone unfulfilled. Panama, he declared, would wait no longer.[7]

Some powerful voices in the United States expressed a degree of sympathy for Panamanian complaints, blaming Americans in the Canal Zone for sparking the crisis and urging U.S. generosity. Among major newspapers, the *Washington Post* made the point most stridently. Balboa High students had done "their country about as much injury as it was in their capacity to accomplish," the *Post* asserted. To remedy U.S.-Panamanian relations, the paper urged the Johnson administration to offer concessions, including an increase in Panama's share of canal revenues and a reduction in disparities between salaries paid to American and Panamanian canal workers.[8] Similar ideas percolated through government agencies, where few officials had any fondness for the "Zonians." In one of its first analyses of the riots, the Central Intelligence Agency (CIA) complained that the Zonians had "fought every reasonable concession" to Panama over the years and were at it again, this time by flagrantly violating rules that had been painstakingly negotiated about the display of national flags.[9] At the State Department, the bureau for Panamanian affairs hurriedly drafted a list of concessions that Washington might offer to repair relations: redistribution of revenues, concession of some U.S. control over commercial activities in the zone, and return of unused sections of the zone to Panamanian authority. On these points, asserted Lansing Collins, chief of the Panamanian office, "there is some negotiating room."[10]

At the highest echelon of power, however, Johnson and his closest advisers had little interest in such proposals. To be sure, the president accepted that Americans had provoked the riots and blamed "our damn fool police" for starting the shooting.[11] But Johnson saw numerous reasons to reject Chiari's demands. For one, the president viewed the riots as a test of U.S. resolve to resist communist subversion. Despite widespread acknowledgment that Americans had initiated the crisis, intelligence reports suggested that Panamanian leftists had immediately seized on the flagpole incident to stir up trouble. The CIA named specific institutions—especially the "communist-infiltrated" Instituto Nacional, a high school near the border of the Canal Zone—as seedbeds of radicalism. Similarly, it pinpointed individuals—the "communist student leader" Victor Avila and the "pro-Castro" National Assembly delegate Thelma King, among others—as probable instigators of the riots.[12] Johnson readily embraced the theory of communist responsibility. "Kids started it and the communists got into it," the president asserted on the first day of the crisis. If the flag dispute had not come along, he said, "they would have kicked [the rioting] off in some other way, some other time."

U.S. fear of communist activity escalated in the following days. Intelligence reports suggested not only that "Castroites" and communists had penetrated the Panamanian government but also that Fidel Castro was preparing to send weapons into the country as part of a coordinated assault on U.S. interests. So seriously did Secretary of State Dean Rusk take these reports that he instructed U.S. diplomats remaining in Panama to begin planning joint U.S.-Panamanian military action to intercept Cuban arms. Meanwhile, the CIA reported that Panama's tiny communist party, the Partido del Pueblo, was growing bolder in its attempts to capitalize on the unrest. Communist leaders, including "persons who have visited behind the Iron and Bamboo curtains, have made trips to Cuba, and have been given training in guerrilla warfare by the Castro regime," were trying to maintain "strong prominent positions" during the crisis, "with the eventual objective of assuming an important role in the government," the CIA asserted. By the first week of February, that nightmare seemed to be coming true. "If Panama maintains its present position vis a vis the United States for one month more," claimed one wildly alarmist report, "it is probable that Panama will be the second socialist country in America." Already, the CIA alleged, the Partido del Pueblo had gained control over the government, dictating "practically every idea expressed by President Roberto Chiari" during the crisis.[13]

Johnson and his advisers concluded that the situation demanded toughness from Washington. To respond in any other way, they believed, would only embolden the radicals by creating the impression that the United States would back down under threat of violence. "I think the communists are going to cause trouble every place in this country they can," Johnson told Senate majority leader Mike Mansfield on the first day of the crisis. "I think we've got to get a little bit hard with them," the president added.[14] U.S. policymakers also manifested conventional cold war fears that softness in one country would encourage problems elsewhere. Trouble already seemed to be brewing. In Mexico City, U.S. diplomats reported on 11 January that the Communist Party and other leftist groups were taking to the streets in support of their Panamanian counterparts. In Argentina, leftists proposed sending arms to help Panamanians defend themselves against a U.S. crackdown. Meanwhile, U.S. diplomats watched as left-leaning newspapers in Venezuela, Colombia, Peru, and several other Latin American countries declared their sympathy for Panama's cause.[15] "The goddamn propaganda is all against us, and it's just everywhere," Johnson fretted.[16]

This standard cold war calculus intersected with a second reason for the administration's rejection of Chiari's renegotiation demand: Johnson's appraisal of his political needs. Many scholars of the 1960s have noted that Johnson, coming to power abruptly after the assassination of his predecessor, was uncertain in foreign affairs and feared, even more than other cold war presidents, that missteps would cost him politically.[17] The risks seemed especially grave in Latin America. U.S. politicians found advantage in the early 1960s in fingering Castro as the instigator of unrest throughout the hemisphere. Any move to appease Panamanian agitators therefore risked exposing the administration to damaging charges of playing into Cuban hands. Democratic congressman Daniel Flood of Pennsylvania, Washington's most outspoken defender of U.S. control over the canal, provided a taste of the rhetorical stakes when he accused the Kennedy administration of presiding over "another Munich" in 1962 by allowing the Panamanian flag to fly in the zone.[18] But even without Castro, Panama would have been a risky place for compromise. Since its construction in the first years of the century, the Panama Canal had held special symbolic power for many Americans. Johnson knew that the Zonians and their allies in Congress stood vigilant for any lack of U.S. determination to guard U.S. rights in the zone and would do their best to make any inattentive president pay a political price. Johnson also saw another reason for toughness. As the media repeatedly pointed out during the flag crisis, Panama represented his first foreign policy challenge as president. He knew that the nation and the world would judge him by how he handled it.[19]

Public opinion gave him good reason to believe that a hard line was the safest path. Approximately four hundred pieces of mail to the White House ran between ten and fifteen to one in favor of a "firm U.S. position," according to a memorandum prepared for the president on 11 January.[20] Gallup poll results a few days later showed similar tendencies. Of the 64 percent of Americans who were aware of the Panama issue, almost half urged a "firm policy," whereas only 9 percent favored concessions to Panamanian demands.[21] Such lopsided numbers impressed Johnson's political advisers, who had their eyes on the November presidential election. Richard Scammon, chief of the Commerce Department's census bureau and a Democratic political analyst, told Johnson he was "more than a little concerned with the potential trouble which Panama could cause us in November." The issue could cause "trouble, crises, problems, and difficulties ad infinitum ad nauseum [sic]," asserted Scammon, adding that concessions on the canal could give the Republicans their "first real solid muscled hit at the Administration." The adviser warned that Americans might turn against Johnson if he was seen "getting pushed around by a small country about an area which every grade school history book features with an American flag, a snapshot of Teddy Roosevelt, and an image of gallant engineers overcoming the mosquito."[22]

A chorus of conservative voices reinforced the administration's sense of political danger in Panama. A State Department survey found a "general consensus" in Congress for a "firm U.S. stand against Panamanian demands on the Canal," with some members even urging a "U.S. show of force."[23] A few liberals, sharing a sense that the United States was partly to blame for problems in Panama, struck a note of flexibility. Senate majority leader Mansfield, for instance, insisted that the "first thing we need is to keep our shirts on. . . . We are," he said, "a great and powerful nation, but we are not a nation of bullies."[24] But such comments paled beside bold rhetoric from Johnson's Republican adversaries, notably presidential aspirant Barry Goldwater. "That canal is ours, and we can't have other governments taking our property away," declared Goldwater, insisting that Johnson not "back down an inch."[25] Senate minority leader Everett Dirksen charged, "We are in the amazing position of having a country with one-third the population of Chicago kicking us around. If we crumble in Panama, the reverberations of our actions will be felt around the world."[26] Meanwhile, the *Wall Street Journal,* in contrast to liberal dailies, depicted concession as the path of softness and naïveté. "This disgraceful business ought to be a sharp reminder to all the sentimentalists who believe that we can uplift Latin America, and be loved for it, simply by handing out billions of [Alliance for Progress] dollars," the *Journal* insisted.[27]

Interwoven with Johnson's geostrategic and political calculations was a third reason for Johnson's belief that he must respond with firmness: his desire to cut the figure of a tough, manly leader. As historians Robert D. Dean and Fredrik Logevall have argued, Johnson worked hard to cultivate a reputation as a muscular president who would stand his ground no matter the cost.[28] During the Panama crisis, Johnson frequently boasted of his toughness, telling Democratic Senator Richard Russell on the first day, for example, that he had been "cold and hard and tough as hell" with Chiari. On one occasion, the president went further by casting himself in the role of the lone stalwart against State Department pressure to compromise. Following a meeting with department officials on 22 January, Johnson bragged to Russell that he "was the only man in the room who said no" to a gesture of compromise. He was "not one goddamn bit" prepared for such a move. "By God," Johnson insisted, "I ain't going to do it. I wasn't raised in that school."[29] Russell, LBJ's closest confidant in the early months of his administration, affirmed the president's sense of machismo. The Georgian praised Johnson for resisting the "weeping sob sisters" in the State Department and for giving the American people vigorous leadership. "The American people have been crying for someone that had some of the elements of Old Hickory Jackson in him," Russell told his friend. "Somebody . . . has just got to take the bull by the horns one of these days and just play the part of old Andrew Jackson."[30] Johnson soaked in the compliment without comment.

Motivated in all these ways, the Johnson administration laid down the policy that it would maintain over the following three months as the two countries struggled to repair their relationship. On the one hand, Johnson assured Chiari that once diplomatic ties had been renewed, Washington would talk with Panamanian leaders about the full range of problems that divided them. "In the appropriate circumstances and when peace has been restored, we will give sympathetic welcome to discussion of all troubles and problems with our Panamanian friends," LBJ specified in instructions for a delegation of U.S. officials dispatched to Panama in the first hours of the crisis. On the other hand, the president sternly rebuffed Chiari's key demand. Washington would never "negotiate under pressure of violence and breach in relations," he instructed his emissaries. The delegation was to inform Chiari that his demand for an immediate promise to revise the treaties was "unacceptable."[31] "If we go in there and start opening up [the] treaty under those conditions, we'd be the laughing stock of the world," Johnson declared.[32]

Panamanians were bound to see the U.S. position as yet another refusal to seek meaningful change, but Johnson considered it fair. Once Chiari backed down, Washington would be reasonable. But the Panamanian view was closer to the mark. Although the administration dangled the carrot of eventual cooperation throughout the three-month diplomatic standoff, Johnson was wary of giving any hint that the United States would make significant concessions and strongly emphasized the firmness of the U.S. rebuff to Chiari's principal demand. Fearing that the Panamanians might get the wrong idea from the softer side of his policy, Johnson took comfort in the fact that Tom Mann, the State Department's assistant secretary for inter-American affairs, led the U.S. delegation to meet with Chiari in Panama City. The president praised Mann as a "tough guy" who, in contrast to many State Department officials, could be counted on to state the U.S. position firmly.[33] Indeed, the president had appointed Mann to his post in 1963 with the expectation that the fellow Texan, a staunch anticommunist skeptical of the Alliance for Progress, would give U.S. policy in Latin America new vigor. Even with Mann in charge, though, the president worried that the vague assurance of future discussions conceded too much. "I'm afraid that we're going a bit further than we ought to go," Johnson complained to Russell. "It seems to me, that we're kind of giving in . . . and responding at the point of a pistol." The frustrating thing, Johnson said, was that the United States could not get away with a total rejection of Panamanian overtures. "I don't see how you can keep from listening," he reflected.[34]

Mastering the Political Risks

With Johnson and Chiari adamant about their positions, stalemate set in. The Mann delegation failed to generate any progress toward a solution and left Panama on 13 January. The focus of the dispute then shifted to a new forum, the Inter-American Peace Commission, a body of the Organization of American States (OAS) designed to mediate disputes between member nations. The results were the same. A five-member commission team produced a flurry of optimism on 15 January by issuing a communiqué inviting the two governments to reestablish relations and announcing that both had agreed "to discuss without limitation" all differences between their countries. The pitfall was that the Spanish-language text used the verb *negociar* where the English version used "to discuss" and *negociaciones formales* in place of "discussions."[35] Johnson immediately balked at language that appeared to commit the United States to renegotiation. A State Department spokesperson quickly pointed out the difference between "negotiation" and "discussion" and insisted that the United States was open only to "discussions." The deal unraveled. By the end of the month, the commission abandoned its efforts.

U.S. insistence on the communiqué's wording reflected Johnson's fears of exposing his administration to political attack for weakness in Panama. Some U.S. diplomats, more concerned with cold war geopolitics than electoral considerations, believed that Washington should accept the OAS formula in the interest of defusing a dangerous situation in Panama. Most significantly, Mann backed the commission's communiqué, apparently fearful that a prolonged confrontation would increase the chance of a leftist takeover in Panama. In a phone conversation with the president, Mann expressed hope that the OAS plan would alleviate an "explosive" situation. "We [need to] give time for tempers to cool and sit down and look at these things [the treaties]," said Mann, reflecting the State Department view that the United States could make concessions without sacrificing fundamental U.S. interests in the zone. "There are things we can credibly do," advised Mann. In any case, the assistant secretary suggested that history would judge the United States not by the words it used—"negotiate" or "discuss"—but by its deeds. To this assertion, the annoyed president replied that the administration's political fortunes, like it or not, rested on words. "You may not be around to judge [U.S. deeds] if they think we're sitting down to revise some treaties," Johnson warned Mann, implying that the administration might be voted out of office if it failed to take account of political realities that demanded toughness.[36] In the president's mind, electoral politics trumped geopolitics when the two diverged.

Johnson's approach served him well by the measure he considered most important. He received broad praise for his tough stand and, most important, felt little criticism from the Right after the first days of the crisis. The State Department detected a "wide consensus" among U.S. newspapers in favor of the president's approach.[37] Hawkish *Washington Post* columnist Joseph Alsop gave Johnson an especially strong endorsement, contending that the Panama crisis provided "a striking and pretty encouraging demonstration of President Johnson's approach to acute problems overseas."[38] In Congress, the president's achievement was evident not so much in forthright praise as in the thing that mattered more to him: the near-total absence of criticism. By showing unrelenting toughness, Johnson had succeeded in denying his critics an exploitable issue. The president probably also benefited from his efforts to involve Republican leaders in decision making. At a White House meeting on 19 January, for example, Johnson carefully solicited advice from prominent senators. Predictably, the president's Democratic allies embraced his position, asserting that any injustices in the U.S.-Panamanian relationship could be adjusted through discussions at a later date. On the other side, Dirksen found it impossible to outflank Johnson on the right. The minority leader merely urged the president to stick with the policy he had already staked out.[39]

Buoyed by broad support, the White House remained wary of any formula for resolving the crisis that could be interpreted as U.S. appeasement of Panama. At Panama's request, the OAS Council, the organization's committee of ambassadors, took up the controversy and developed a series of proposals during February and March. Repeatedly, the Johnson administration balked at language hinting at U.S. willingness to renegotiate. At one point, the president even disavowed a formula that the State Department had prepared and secretly handed to the OAS as a proposal that would surely win U.S. favor. That plan went beyond what Johnson was prepared to tolerate by specifying that the two sides would appoint special ambassadors "with sufficient powers to enter into agreements . . . including problems of existing treaties."[40] In a mid-March speech directed at his own bureaucracy as much as at Panama City, Johnson made his position clear. "Press reports indicate that the government of Panama feels that the language which has been under consideration for many days commits the United States to a rewriting and to a revision of the 1903 treaty," Johnson said. "We have made no such commitment and we would not think of doing so before diplomatic relations are resumed and unless a fair and satisfactory adjustment is agreed upon."[41] To drive home U.S. determination, the administration backed up its words with economic coercion. Secretary of State Rusk ordered U.S. diplomats to inform Panamanian officials that approval of new U.S. loans depended on security for officials who would monitor disbursement. Panamanians, increasingly aware of economic instability caused by the break in relations, could hardly have missed the threat.[42]

U.S. tactics paid off during the first days of April. Although Chiari apparently secured a $5 million loan from Francisco Franco's Spain, that sum was far too little to shore up Panama's crumbling economy, and the government came under mounting pressure from the Panamanian elite to end the crisis.[43] Well attuned to Chiari's bind, Johnson met with senior advisers on 1 April to edit the latest OAS proposal to suit U.S. tastes. Two days later, the Panamanian government accepted that plan. The carefully worded document called for reestablishment of diplomatic relations and the appointment of special ambassadors "with sufficient powers to seek the prompt elimination of the causes of conflict between the two countries, without limitations or preconditions of any kind." The deal specified that the ambassadors would aim for a "just and fair agreement which would be subject to the constitutional processes of each country."[44] Chiari hailed the agreement, but there was little doubt about which side had prevailed. The word "negotiate" was nowhere to be found. Nor did the agreement set a timetable or specifically mention the canal or the possibility of treaty renegotiation.

Johnson exulted over his triumph, boasting of his consistency during the crisis. "Our insistence on talking without precondition was our first and last position," Johnson bragged at the National Security Council (NSC) meeting that formally approved the deal.[45] Still, the president's actions in his moment of victory reflected a lingering concern with political hazards. The White House made sure to publicize the presence of Republican congressmen at the decisive NSC session. More important, the administration selected a prominent Republican, Robert B. Anderson, as the U.S. special ambassador who would take charge of talks with Panama. Given LBJ's sensitivities, Anderson was an ideal choice. A like-minded Texan with strong corporate connections, he promised to be a vigorous defender of U.S. interests. The U.S. Treasury secretary during the second Eisenhower administration, he would insulate Johnson from partisan attack.[46]

But the president probably had little cause for concern regardless of his choice. The resolution of the crisis won hearty approval across the political spectrum. William J. Jorden, a confidant of LBJ's and later U.S. ambassador to Panama, recalls in his memoir that observers gave Johnson "an A, some an A+," for his handling of the crisis.[47] Predictably, liberal newspapers applauded a deal that seemed to leave space for change.[48] Meanwhile, conservatives offered little criticism, and some found reason for praise. In an editorial contrasting sharply with the sneering tone it had taken in January, the *Wall Street Journal* praised the president's ability to hold firm while demonstrating a willingness to talk—a balancing act that the paper found more characteristic of tough-minded Republicans.[49] The implication was clear. Johnson had successfully co-opted his adversaries' agenda. Indeed, it was no coincidence that the strongest criticism of the president's Panama policy came from a fellow Democrat, Senate Foreign Relations Committee chairman J. William Fulbright. In a speech at the end of March, Fulbright berated Johnson for making the Panama crisis "a test of our bravery and will" and urged the administration to "go a little farther than half way in the search for a fair settlement."[50] There is no evidence that the president gave the intraparty attack much thought. That was not the kind of criticism that worried him.

Reappraising the Cold War in Panama

As the diplomatic crisis came to an end, then, the political dangers facing Johnson had lessened dramatically. The risk remained, of course, that the issue might reemerge to threaten his electoral chances in November. Unavoidably, the subject continued to attract media attention through the spring, as the two sides determined how they would proceed with the promised talks. Anderson traveled to Panama, and the chief Panamanian negotiator, prominent lawyer Jorge E. Illueca, flew to Washington for meetings with U.S. officials. But thereafter the administration succeeded in moving the matter exactly where it wanted it—safely onto the back burner. Bilateral talks during 1964 could have been held "in an igloo on the Arctic circle for all the attention they received from government or press," Jorden recalls.[51] In fact, the Johnson administration had little difficulty keeping the matter out of the spotlight, since the Panamanian government was in no position to force the pace of the talks. The hard-fought Panamanian presidential election in May distracted the government from its preparations and, after the election of Marco Aurelio Robles as Chiari's successor, produced so much turnover in Panamanian personnel that it would have been impossible to sustain momentum even if political leaders had tried. The Robles government, with a new cast of foreign affairs officials, was not inaugurated until October, by which time the imminence of the U.S. election ruled out any new initiatives.

If the calendar cooperated, so did the Republicans. Even as Goldwater attacked Johnson on Berlin, Vietnam, and other trouble spots in mid-1964, he had little to say about Panama. In a string of bland policy statements from April to July, Republicans revealed their inability to find political leverage. Just after the restoration of U.S.-Panamanian relations, a Republican study group issued an innocuous report that largely endorsed the president's policy. Relieved White House aide Gordon Chase applauded the paper's "constructive, bipartisan approach."[52] The administration found more reassurance a week later when a meeting of Republican officials issued a similarly benign statement demanding that if there was to be a new canal treaty, it must "not be negotiated under the club" of violence or threats.[53] Johnson could not have said it better himself. Nor did the Democrats have any reason to fear the canal issue as the November election drew closer. The Republican platform unveiled in July merely asserted the party's determination to "reaffirm this nation's treaty rights" while showing flexibility on some minor aspects of U.S. control.[54] Again, it was a virtual restatement of the Democrats' approach.

The declining political salience of the Panama issue created opportunities for Washington policymakers concerned with waging the cold war in Latin America, rather than protecting the president's political standing, to step to the fore—a critical moment in the evolution of U.S. policy. With the president's political interests secure, the foreign policy bureaucracy gained freedom to explore policy options that had been out of the question at the beginning of the year. The result was an increasingly sophisticated view, shared among a widening circle of policymakers, that the United States could best wage the cold war through precisely the opposite course from the one the president's personal interests had dictated. By showing flexibility and generosity, they calculated, the United States could bolster its long-term interests by undercutting Panama's Left and enabling the Chiari and Robles governments to claim credit as true champions of Panamanian nationalism. To be sure, this reappraisal of the cold war in Panama stood no chance of driving an immediate shift in U.S. policy. Through the November election, the president was determined to keep Panama out of the spotlight and to avoid any hint of weakness. But the geostrategic reappraisal provided a rationale for a dramatic change of policy that Johnson himself would find persuasive once he had achieved his sweeping electoral victory.

The shift rested on logic that a minority of U.S. officials, mainly within the State Department, had articulated as early as the first days of the diplomatic crisis. Assistant Secretary Mann, hardly a liberal, was among the most important exponents of the view that Washington should accommodate Chiari to some extent. Mann had little regard for Panamanian leaders, calling them "the most unreasonable people . . . you can imagine," but he dissented strongly from the prevailing view that communism was the root of the problem.[55] Communist activism was "not necessary to explain this outburst of anti-U.S. feeling which has spread to many leading Panamanians who have been friends of [the] U.S.," Mann wrote during his trip to Panama two days after the riots started.[56] In his view, unrest sprang not from an international conspiracy but from genuine nationalism that ran across the Panamanian political spectrum. A study by the State Department's Office of Intelligence and Research drew out the policy implications of this thinking, asserting that Chiari needed some sort of diplomatic victory if he was going to "keep a lid on the left." Though Americans might not like Chiari, the paper continued, he might be the best that Washington could hope for under the circumstances; so intense was Panamanian nationalism that no alternative leader could take a stance on the canal different from Chiari's and expect to remain in power.[57] The bottom line of such reasoning was clear. If Washington refused to budge on the canal, it risked destroying conservatives such as Chiari and opening the way for political instability and radicalization.

The clash between this view and Johnson's approach during the diplomatic crisis encapsulated the dilemma U.S. policymakers confronted in the 1960s as they crafted policy toward Latin America. Was turmoil principally the result of Soviet-sponsored conspiracy against U.S. interests, or did it stem mainly from socioeconomic grievances that extended far beyond the organized Left? Policy hung on the answer. In Panama, the dilemma weighed on U.S. policymakers as the diplomatic crisis dragged into spring 1964. If, as intelligence reports suggested, communists and Castroites had seized control over the Chiari government and driven it into confrontation with Washington, the best course lay in forcing Chiari to back down from his demand. If, as Mann urged, communist activity was more symptom than cause of Panama's problems, the best course lay in making concessions calculated to enhance moderate political forces that would, over time, diminish the radicals' appeal. Building up Chiari, in most respects an authoritarian figure of the type that had long served U.S. interests in Panama, might then prove a better solution than antagonizing him.

The latter view gradually became the dominant strand of U.S. thinking. The shift was possible mainly because of Johnson's success in neutralizing Panama as a political liability and his conviction that the United States had prevailed in a cold war test of wills. Having forced its opponent to back down, the administration could be satisfied that any future negotiations would be conducted from a position of strength. The stick had been successfully deployed; now the carrot—which had never entirely disappeared as part of Johnson's policy during the diplomatic crisis—could be offered with less fear that Washington's opponents would underestimate U.S. resolution. But these considerations by themselves do not suffice to explain the shift in policy during 1964. Three more specific calculations also helped to convince policymakers, including ultimately the president himself, that calculated generosity offered the best way to bolster U.S. interests in Panama.

First, U.S. officials, whatever their disagreements over communist strength back in January, found increasing evidence later in the year that radicals posed no serious threat in Panama. To gauge the Left's status, U.S. intelligence scrutinized a communist-organized National Youth Congress held in Panama just as the diplomatic crisis was coming to an end. The State Department's Office of Intelligence and Research was impressed not only by Chiari's efforts to obstruct the event but also by the low attendance and general lack of activism that it generated, failures that contrasted sharply with the Partido del Pueblo's enthusiasm for anti-American agitation just a few weeks earlier. "The contrast provides further proof that the trouble potential of Panama's Communists and Castroists is greatest when their objectives merge with those of other groups in society and focus on a genuinely popular cause," the report asserted. In January, it added, all segments of the Panamanian population had come together on the canal issue. By March, however, the climate had changed, and "responsible Panamanians in and out of government were not interested in aiding and abetting adventures of irresponsible youths."[58]

Washington gained further confidence as the 10 May national election approached. A detailed State Department report dated 20 April asserted that the Castro regime "still had some appeal among a few diehards" but concluded that committed communists, numbering only about three hundred, were in no position to seize power. The report went on to give one of the most elaborate expressions yet of a view that was rapidly becoming a consensus within the State Department: communist influence in Panama stemmed not from any significant base of support but from the Left's intermittent ability to tap into grievances that ran beneath the surface of Panamanian life. Most important, the Left appealed to Panama's disgruntled youth, a part of the population that the report described as "frustrated and discontented" due to the absence of opportunity for social advancement. Young Panamanians, the report continued, blamed Panama's elite and the United States, which they tended to associate with "the system." The study ridiculed ordinary Panamanians for expecting the United States to solve their problems for them. But it also indicated that Washington could help its cause by playing its hand carefully. "There is a large store of good will and admiration for the United States among the students and youth of Panama which, if diligently cultivated, can produce results favorable to the United States," the study insisted.[59] A White House memorandum picked up on this theme, asserting, "An unyielding U.S. position [on the canal treaty] would simply increase tensions in Panama, and make long-term arrangements more difficult."[60]

The second consideration that led the Johnson administration to reappraise its Panama policy was its satisfaction with the conduct and outcome of the Panamanian election. Reassurance sprang partly from the conspicuous lack of leftist agitation in the days around the vote. The CIA feared the worst, asserting on 7 May that "all the elements for a serious explosion very damaging to the U.S. security interests" were present in Panama.[61] Washington positioned a rapid-reaction force of thirteen hundred Marines off the Panamanian coast in case it was needed to reinforce the U.S. garrison in the Canal Zone. Two thousand more U.S.-based airborne troops prepared to intervene in the Canal Zone within ten hours of an emergency.[62] But no major disturbances occurred. U.S. officials were also pleased with the election's result. Panamanian law barred Roberto Chiari from running for a second term, setting up a race between his protégé, Marco Robles, and two rivals. One of those rivals, Juan de Arco Galindo, drew the bulk of his support from the same sector of the population that backed Chiari and Robles—elite Panamanians connected to the oligarchy. The other contender, Arnulfo Arias, was the twice-deposed president of Panama, an enigmatic populist with an authoritarian streak who had alternately repelled and intrigued Washington over the previous two decades. All three candidates campaigned on platforms emphasizing the need for new canal treaties and reform programs aimed at bringing advances to the mass of Panamanians. But in the end, the upper classes determined the outcome by closing ranks behind Robles, giving their candidate a narrow victory.

Washington policymakers hoped for a victory by one of the traditional conservatives and were relieved by Arias's failure. Yet few U.S. officials initially had much regard for Robles, whom they feared would fall prey to leftist influences just as they believed Chiari had. Robles was "just as crooked as any other [political leader] in living memory in Panama," the new U.S. ambassador, Jack Vaughn, reported following the election. Most alarming to Vaughn, Robles showed a "disconcerting readiness to cooperate with certain leftists."[63] As American officials learned more about Robles, however, their opinions shifted dramatically. Vaughn reported in June that the president-elect was working hard to combat the view among Americans that his desire to renegotiate the canal treaties amounted to "extremism and near-communism."[64] To the contrary, Robles cast that desire as part of a conservatively patriotic agenda that was not fundamentally anti-American. Vaughn was also impressed by Robles's choice for foreign minister, Fernando Eleta, scion of an elite Panamanian family noted for its strong conservatism. The U.S. ambassador praised Eleta for his "very lively sense of the realities of Communist inroads" in Panama, while Eleta's evident regard for the United States and for Franco's Spain also boded well.[65] As the new regime took office in October, opinion in Washington swung to outright enthusiasm. "Robles has pledged himself to [a] firm stand against communist agitation, in welcome contrast to his predecessor," Vaughn reported. "All this looks good and I believe there is much on the plus side of the ledger, much more perhaps than we had any right to expect."[66] With such a reliable regime in power, the Johnson administration gained confidence that it could bargain with Panama with little risk of playing into leftist hands.

The Robles government was not the only institution in Panama that reassured Washington. During the middle months of 1964, U.S. officials came to appreciate Panama's Guardia Nacional as another important source of anticommunist stability—the third consideration that led the Johnson administration to reevaluate its Panama policy. During the January riots, U.S. officials had been disappointed by the guard's timidity. Secretary of Defense Robert McNamara had regarded the force as a potentially significant ally for the United States and ordered the U.S. military commander in the Canal Zone to inform the Guardia that it could count on U.S. support in resisting a communist coup.[67] But the Guardia showed little interest in playing the role scripted for it at the Pentagon. Chiari refused to call out the force until the end of the third day of rioting, and the guard evidently accepted its limited role without dissent. Even after it went into action, it disappointed some U.S. officials by refusing to detain suspected leftist agitators—a function that U.S. officials had come to expect paramilitary organizations to perform in Latin America.[68]

By summer, however, U.S. opinion of the Guardia Nacional had changed dramatically. Around the time of the Panamanian election, U.S. diplomats repeatedly commented on the force's surprisingly strong role in preventing any disturbance by the Left while also positioning itself squarely behind Robles. The guard was "alert and capable," reported Vaughn, who predicted the guard would make sure there was no repetition of the January riots on election day.[69] When Panamanian leftists threatened to stage new anti-American demonstrations on the Fourth of July, U.S. embassy officials again took heart from the Guardia's firmness. Guardsmen positioned themselves along the Canal Zone border to prevent incidents, prepared, as one U.S. diplomat phrased it, "to nip in [the] bud any action [to] create trouble."[70] The embassy was not disappointed. The force not only suppressed anti-American unrest but also sent a band and color guard to participate in the Americans' holiday celebrations. Zonians showed their restored faith in the Guardia by giving the units a rousing ovation.[71] To be sure, the guard had not achieved the independent role it would seize four years later, when its commander, Omar Torrijos, executed a coup that ended civilian rule. But the force's actions over the course of 1964 pushed it back toward the center of national politics and restored Washington's confidence.

The Sea-Level Canal and the Forging of Consensus

Certain that Panamanian communism was in eclipse, pleased with Robles's conservatism, and reassured by the resurgent Guardia Nacional, the Johnson administration steadily, if quietly, leaned toward a new policy of accommodation. The new mood manifested itself first in Washington's efforts in the middle of the year to ease economic problems exacerbated by the diplomatic break. Shortly after the resumption of relations, the administration dispatched a team of experts to prepare for the restoration of existing aid programs and to assess possibilities for new projects. U.S. officials hoped that reopening the aid spigot would ease Panama's political tensions and win the population, especially young Panamanians, away from radicalism. Besides programs to improve Panamanian agriculture and transportation networks, aid agencies attached importance to educational initiatives, including scholarship programs and teacher-training projects designed, in the words of a U.S. embassy report, "to reach and influence Panamanian youth."[72]

But few had any illusions about the prospect of recasting U.S.-Panamanian relations through aid programs alone. Panama had, after all, remained a cauldron of anti-Americanism despite its status as one of the highest per capita recipients of Alliance for Progress aid.[73] A far more ambitious possibility—renegotiation of the treaties—gained appeal as a gesture that would curry favor with ordinary Panamanians and preserve conservative rule. The State Department remained the principal champion of the new approach, but others lent crucial support. Most important, Robert Anderson, Johnson's ambassador to the on-again, off-again U.S.-Panamanian talks, grew increasingly convinced that the United States should comply with unceasing Panamanian demands for new treaties and led the drive for the new approach in the weeks leading up to Johnson's momentous speech. Although there is no direct evidence of the president's changing attitude in October and November, the readiness with which he accepted Anderson's view in December suggests that he, too, was increasingly attuned to the logic of accommodation.[74]

It was by no means a simple matter, however, for Johnson to embrace the new policy, even after the November landslide further eased his political inhibitions. Two final obstacles stood in the way. First, there remained a risk that political sentiment might shift back in threatening directions if the White House seemed to engage in a bald giveaway of U.S. privileges. Second, the bureaucracies that benefited most heavily from existing canal arrangements, above all the Defense Department and the military, remained deeply skeptical of change and promised to resist any diminishment of U.S. rights. Only after satisfying himself on these matters did Johnson commit the United States to the new course. The key to overcoming these final roadblocks lay in the administration's shrewd manipulation of a peculiar futuristic fantasy that became a critical dimension of U.S. policy toward Panama in the second half of 1964—the prospect that the United States would dig a sea-level canal somewhere in Central America before the end of the century. That possibility equipped Johnson with a rhetorical tool that he used skillfully to generate bureaucratic consensus and to provide himself with an additional dose of confidence that he could offer concessions without significant opposition.

Americans had discussed the possibility of a sea-level passageway for more than a quarter century. Until the 1930s, the lock canal had accommodated all types of ships. With the advent of massive tankers, ore transports, and aircraft carriers, however, the canal's limitations started to show. Washington's first response was to begin excavating a new set of locks that could accommodate the latest generation of ships. But construction was discontinued in 1942, by which time U.S. resources were required elsewhere. Amid global war, Washington also began to doubt the wisdom of relying on a complicated lock system that lay vulnerable to attack. The idea of solving these problems by digging a sea-level canal, most likely using atomic explosions, gained momentum in 1947. In that year, Congress approved a plan to study the possibility of converting the existing lock canal and, at the same time, to investigate alternative routes elsewhere in Central America. But the idea languished until 1960, when rapidly increasing canal traffic, along with old worries about the locks' vulnerability, generated a flurry of new interest in the sea-level possibility. Over the following four years, the U.S.-controlled Panama Canal Company, the Atomic Energy Commission, and the Army Corps of Engineers undertook more intensive feasibility studies.[75]

New interest in the sea-level passageway also resulted from worries after 1958 that mounting political turmoil in Panama imperiled U.S. control over the existing canal. Anti-American riots in 1958 and 1959, U.S. fears of Castroite meddling in Central America following the 1959 Cuban revolution, and intensified Panamanian demands for renegotiation of the 1903 treaties persuaded the Kennedy administration that major changes in U.S. policy toward Panama were unavoidable. Construction of an alternative canal, until then seen as a solution to technical rather than political problems, gained appeal as a way to break free of the dilemma that increasingly confounded Washington: how to satisfy Panamanian nationalism while also preserving U.S. control. Digging a new canal promised to give the United States the freedom to relax its grip over the old canal while establishing a new, less controversial set of privileges in another location. It would be 1903 all over again, only this time Washington would be more careful about negotiating the terms.

If the new canal's appeal was obvious, the details—how and where to build it—were not. The Kennedy administration proved unable to resolve these questions and concluded in a 1962 National Security Action Memorandum that the United States had to await answers before it could move ahead with any reconfiguration of the U.S.-Panamanian relationship.[76] It took the flag riots to push the issue back onto the U.S. agenda. The Johnson administration devoted little thought to the idea during the diplomatic crisis. The president lacked familiarity with the complicated matter, and in any case he probably calculated that he stood to lose politically if he emphasized it. To stress U.S. hopes of excavating an alternative canal might, after all, have risked implying that Washington lacked the toughness to defend its existing rights. Once the president had proved his mettle and ended the crisis, however, Washington turned its attention to the sea-level idea as part of its wide-ranging consideration of long-term solutions to the Panama problem. The president successfully appealed to Congress for $17.5 million in new funds to accelerate engineering studies on five possible routes stretching between southern Nicaragua and northern Colombia.

The administration quickly encountered the same old uncertainties. Would any of the routes prove both financially and technically feasible? Could Washington negotiate terms to ensure control over a new canal? Would the nuclear explosions necessary to excavate the canal violate the Limited Test Ban Treaty? These questions had stymied the Kennedy administration, which refused to consider political matters before technical problems were solved. The Johnson administration chose a different approach. In contrast to his predecessor, Johnson valued the sea-level canal as much for the diplomatic and political purposes to which he could put it in the short term as for the theoretical benefits to U.S. trade and security over the long run. To be sure, the president supported further engineering surveys and appears to have sincerely believed that a new canal was realistic. But Johnson also viewed the prospect of a sea-level passageway as an important part of the solution to more immediate diplomatic, political, and bureaucratic problems. Increasingly, the administration exploited the sea-level canal idea as it sought to eliminate remaining pockets of real or potential resistance to the accommodationist policy that it preferred by fall 1964. In this effort, Johnson found advantage in the very uncertainties that had stymied the previous administration. With all the important decisions still to be made, Johnson discovered that the future canal could be a valuable rhetorical tool that could be shaped and reshaped to serve various purposes.

The administration first exploited the uncertainties surrounding the sea-level canal in mid-1964 as it sought to rein in Panamanian ambitions and to ensure that it would not be embarrassed by far-reaching demands. Shortly after the two countries resumed normal relations, Washington put the Panamanian government on notice by announcing that the United States and Colombia had reached an agreement on procedures for further cartographic studies of a possible canal running through northern Colombia. The Panamanian government could hardly miss the threat: If it drove too hard a bargain, the United States could simply choose to build a new canal in another country, thus negating the value of Panama's chief national asset. While *New York Times* columnist Marguerite Higgins called the ploy "a psychological stroke of genius," Panamanians saw it as psychological warfare. Shortly after the U.S.-Colombian understanding was announced, one Panama City radio station declared the agreement part of a U.S. "policy of blackmail, terror, and aggression" against Panama.[77] Undeterred, U.S. negotiators resorted to the tactic again in July when the two sides opened talks. At the first session, U.S. officials rejected an ambitious Panamanian agenda demanding immediate discussion of a declaration of Panamanian sovereignty in the Canal Zone and the fixing of a date for termination of all U.S. rights there.[78] The shocked U.S. delegation invited Secretary of the Army Stephen Ailes to brief the Panamanian delegation on U.S. planning for a sea-level canal that might be built outside Panama. The Panamanians relaxed their position.

In the fall, Johnson found that the sea-level canal could have as much political as diplomatic utility. Frequent assertions of the administration's interest in the new seaway helped Johnson assuage his political opponents, who could hardly object to concessions on the old canal if a new and improved one, invulnerable to attack, was part of the same agenda. It is surely no coincidence that the administration publicly emphasized the sea-level canal at precisely those moments when it felt most vulnerable to criticism. In April, after Washington agreed to U.S.-Panamanian talks, the administration announced its agreement with Colombia to explore routes in that country. In July, as the Anderson-Illueca talks got under way, the administration publicly pressed for legislation to fund new feasibility studies. And in December, when Johnson announced U.S. willingness to renegotiate the canal treaties, the president strongly emphasized his new intention. In his speech, Johnson began by declaring his intention to "press forward" with "plans and preparations" for the new canal.[79] Only after proclaiming that desire—an old idea about which, despite the fanfare, Johnson had little new to report—did Johnson announce the real news, U.S. willingness to renegotiate the 1903 treaties. In a background briefing for reporters on the same day, National Security Adviser McGeorge Bundy practiced the same strategy, obscuring U.S. concessions with strong emphasis on the new canal. Once the sea-level facility was operating, Bundy asserted, "the significance of the present lock operation will be reduced in effect to the negligible point."[80]

The administration's manipulation of the sea-level canal worked well. Although news media were quick to point out that a new canal remained far in the future, they readily accepted the administration's insistence that its decision to pursue the sea-level canal amounted to a major breakthrough and was the logical accompaniment of treaty revision. Newspapers emphasized the new canal in banner headlines on 19 December. The *Chicago Tribune,* for example, proclaimed, "U.S. Will Cut New Canal" across its front page, while a small, one-column subheading announced, "Panama Offered New Treaty."[81] Editorials, meanwhile, emphasized the new canal in praising the administration's announcement. The *Washington Post,* for instance, congratulated Johnson for taking "the sensible and equitable course" in pursuing the sea-level canal and renegotiating the old treaties in tandem. "The 1903 treaty is as politically archaic as the canal is technologically obsolete," the *Post* asserted.[82] Among prominent major publications, only the *Wall Street Journal* pointed to contradictions in Johnson's policy, noting that a U.S. decision to build a new canal outside Panama might damage U.S.-Panamanian relations and make any new provisions for joint operation of the old canal difficult to sustain.[83]

The sea-level canal was perhaps most important to the administration as a means of generating consensus within the national security bureaucracy. From as far back as the 1958 riots, the Panama issue had produced divisions between the State Department, on the one side, and the Defense Department and the Joint Chiefs of Staff, on the other. State Department officials naturally viewed the canal dispute principally as a problem of diplomacy and negotiation. Although they recognized the value of U.S. control, they consistently urged deference to Panamanian demands on small points of disagreement to preserve the most important U.S. rights and head off a devastating confrontation. The Defense Department and the military, by contrast, feared change of any kind in Panama. To these bureaucracies, the U.S. presence in Panama was critical not only to protecting and operating the canal but also to managing an elaborate regional defense establishment headquartered in the Canal Zone. At its Panamanian hub, the U.S. military maintained forces and supplies considered essential to countersubversion in the hemisphere, operated a research-and-development center for jungle warfare, managed elaborate communications and intelligence networks, and ran the School of the Americas to train military personnel from throughout Latin America. Any bid to scale back U.S. privileges threatened all these activities.

In order to go ahead with meaningful concessions to Panama, the administration had to overcome the military's reservations. The problem became especially acute only four days before Johnson's landmark speech, when army secretary Ailes refused to go along with drafts being prepared in the White House. The army particularly opposed proposals to cede unused Canal Zone land back to Panama and to limit the military's rights to operate commissaries. All Ailes would accept, reported one NSC aide, was "rearrangement" of provisions in the existing treaties "with minimal changes."[84] The Defense Department, it seemed, wanted "to offer as little as possible to keep control of the negotiations in its hands." Johnson responded to this resistance in two ways. First, he dispatched a CIA agent to Chicago to track down Dwight Eisenhower to obtain his approval for the concessions that Johnson planned to offer. To the administration's relief, Eisenhower, the avuncular former president with unimpeachable military credentials, agreed that Johnson could state publicly that he had approved of the plan—a gesture of support that the president invoked in the first minute of his speech.[85] While Johnson calculated that Eisenhower's backing would help ease any lingering problems with congressional and public opinion, his timing suggests that he was at least as concerned about reassuring the military.

Second, Johnson exploited the sea-level canal idea, whose vagueness once again proved useful. On 16 December, the Joint Chiefs of Staff accepted White House proposals related to the existing canal in return for modifications in language covering the sea-level project. The chiefs demanded especially that the United States avoid any quick commitments regarding the administration or operation of the new canal. The State Department had proposed a declaration that the new facility would come under either the multilateral control of an international commission or the bilateral control of the United States and the government of the country where it was built. The Joint Chiefs, wary of any plan to share authority, insisted that it was "premature" for the president to take any position on the matter and demanded that Johnson avoid committing the United States to any particular "method of control."[86] The White House could hardly object to such a modest request and removed all comment on the issue from the president's speech. With the last obstruction overcome, Johnson could go forward with his landmark speech without fear of bureaucratic dissent. Once again, the vagaries surrounding the new canal proved useful to Johnson, in this case as the linchpin of bureaucratic consensus. The fictitiousness of the sea-level canal enabled all sides to make of it what they wished.

Conclusion

The administration had good reason for satisfaction as 1964 came to an end. While the president's policy garnered praise from all but the fringes of the political spectrum, U.S. diplomats in Panama City reported that the new approach was yielding precisely the intended effect.[87] Ambassador Vaughn happily noted that Foreign Minister Eleta's first response to the news was to exclaim, "This will send the communists *al carajo* [to hell]."[88] Within a few days, events seemed to bear out that prediction. The "commies," Vaughn reported on New Year's Eve, had been "thrown badly off balance" by Johnson's speech, which the ambassador credited with creating "a sense of confusion among extremists here."[89] U.S. willingness to renegotiate had "pulled the rug from under the Panamanian left," embassy officials asserted in another report to Washington. Agitators intent on marking the anniversary of the 1964 riots with a new confrontation now had little hope of stirring anything up, reported the embassy, adding that Johnson's speech had helped channel Panamanian nationalism toward a "reasonable policy" that properly expressed the "true hope of the Panamanian people."[90]

Johnson failed, however, to realize his vision of a reconfigured relationship with a reliable, newly stabilized Panama. U.S.-Panamanian talks, which resumed in January 1965 with a new agenda and high hopes for quick success, dragged on for the next two and a half years as the two governments struggled to find an agreeable formula without agitating their political opponents at home. Finally, on 26 June 1967, they unveiled a forty-one-article accord that provided for joint administration of the canal, abolished the Canal Zone, and set an end date for all U.S. privileges in Panama in 2009 at the latest. Another treaty provided for joint defense of the canal, and a third gave Washington exclusive rights to build a sea-level canal in Panama provided it moved ahead within twenty years.[91] But the deals quickly unraveled amid political turbulence in Panama. Ultranationalists and leftists excoriated Robles for demanding too little in the negotiations. Wary of inflaming the situation, Robles refused to submit the treaties to the Panamanian assembly for ratification. His caution did neither him nor the agreements any good. Exploiting chronic economic woes and resurgent nationalist resentments, maverick populist Arnulfo Arias won Panama's 1968 presidential election. Arias showed little enthusiasm for his predecessor's handiwork. With the treaties obviously dead in Panama, Johnson saw no reason to send them to Congress, and his experiment in concession sputtered to a disappointing end. Only dramatic changes in U.S. and Panamanian politics would revive the treaties a decade later.[92]

The proximate cause of the treaties' failure during the 1960s lay in Panama. But Johnson's policy contributed to that outcome in its own way by propping up a political order that served U.S. interests but did little to address the socioeconomic problems at the heart of Panama's political turbulence. The administration's exceptional performance with respect to Panama must not, after all, be mistaken for genuine openness to change either in Panamanian society or in the conduct of U.S. foreign policy. On the contrary, Johnson's policy represented a shift in means rather than ends. The president, unwilling to run risks of any sort, embraced a policy of concession only after assuring himself that neither Congress nor the national security bureaucracy could criticize him effectively from the right. Equally important, the administration chose the exceptional course in Panama because of a growing certainty in 1964 that concessions would strengthen Panama's oligarchy—a regime that had become synonymous with cronyism, corruption, economic injustice, and partnership with the United States. Washington's willingness to reconfigure its relationship with Panama reflected acceptance that the Panamanian political landscape had changed in ways that the United States could no longer ignore. Beginning in the late 1950s, widespread social discontent placed the oligarchy on the defensive. To avoid being swept away, it had to either co-opt its critics by embracing some of their demands or resort to repressive force. Chiari and Robles embraced the first option, and in 1964 the Johnson administration concluded that its interest lay in helping them succeed.

U.S. policy toward Panama reflected the same objectives that dictated the more general U.S. approach to third world unrest during the Johnson years. While the administration opted for an uncompromising, even militaristic, policy to maintain the status quo in most areas, in Panama it settled on a policy of concession. The difference stemmed not from any fundamental divergence of purpose but from an exceptional set of circumstances that prevailed in connection with Panama —conditions generally absent as the administration crafted policy toward other areas that presented nationalist challenges to U.S. security. Most important, Johnson concluded in early 1964 that by staring down Chiari he had satisfied perceived geostrategic, political, and personal imperatives for toughness. Having established his credentials as an uncompromising leader, Johnson could consider concession without overwhelming fear that he would be accused of softness, a possibility that deterred him from compromise in other areas, including Vietnam. Johnson's judgment that he could embrace such an approach without provoking serious opposition from the military—largely the result of his ability to manipulate the sea-level canal idea, the single greatest oddity of the Panama situation—also contrasted with the administration's more general experience. In most U.S. foreign policy decisions related to third world areas, the military pushed the administration toward hard-line solutions. Finally, Johnson's confidence that accommodation would bolster rather than undercut U.S. interests stands apart from the administration's overall record. Robles's reliable anticommunism, the Guardia Nacional's resurgence, and the continued presence of massive U.S. force in the Canal Zone gave the administration confidence that it could offer concessions while containing demands for significant sociopolitical change. In no other area of the third world did Washington enjoy such comfort.

Notes

The author would like to thank Regina Greenwell, Mike Parrish, and especially Jocelyn Olcott and Susan Ferber for their help with this project.
1. Waldo Heinrichs, "Lyndon B. Johnson: Change and Continuity," in *Lyndon Johnson Confronts the World: American Foreign Policy, 1963–1968*, ed. Warren I. Cohen and Nancy Bernkop Tucker (New York: Cambridge University Press, 1994), 26. For other critical views, see Tucker, "Lyndon Johnson: A Final Reckoning," in Cohen and Tucker, *Lyndon Johnson Confronts the World*, 313, and H. W. Brands, *The Wages of Globalism: Lyndon Johnson and the Limits of American Power* (New York: Oxford University Press, 1995), 28–29.
2. See especially Stephen G. Rabe, *"The Most Dangerous Area in the*

48 | MARK ATWOOD LAWRENCE

World": John F. Kennedy Confronts Communist Revolution in Latin America (Chapel Hill: University of North Carolina Press, 1999), 180.

3. Thomas J. McCormick, *America's Half-Century: United States Foreign Policy in the Cold War and After,* 2d ed. (Baltimore: Johns Hopkins University Press, 1995), 146; Lars Schoultz, *Beneath the United States: A History of U.S. Policy toward Latin America* (Cambridge, Mass.: Harvard University Press, 1998), 358.

4. "Texts of Johnson Statement and Address by Robles," *New York Times,* 19 December 1964.

5. For accounts of the "flag riots" and their background, see William J. Jorden, *Panama Odyssey* (Austin: University of Texas Press, 1984), 38–53; Alan L. McPherson, *Yankee No! Anti-Americanism in U.S.-Latin American Relations* (Cambridge, Mass.: Harvard University Press, 2003), chap. 3; and Roberto N. Méndez, *Panama 9 de enero de 1964: Qué pasó y por qué* (Panama City: Imprenta de la Universidad de Panamá, 1999).

6. Panama City to State Department, 10 January 1964, box 64, National Security File (NSF), Country File (CF), Lyndon Baines Johnson Library (hereafter LBJL).

7. Transcript of phone conversation, Johnson with Chiari, 10 January 1964, box 64, NSF, CF, LBJL. For analysis of Panamanian decisions, see McPherson, *Yankee No!* chap. 3.

8. "The News from Panama," *Washington Post,* 11 January 1964.

9. CIA (Panama City) to various posts, 10 January 1964, box 64, NSF, CF, LBJL.

10. Gordon Chase to Bundy, 11 January 1964, box 64, NSF, CF, LBJL. The goal of redistributing canal revenues attracted the most support. In 1963, the canal yielded $5 million in net income, of which Panama received $1.9 million. See Walter LaFeber, *The Panama Canal: The Crisis in Historical Perspective* (New York: Oxford University Press, 1978), 133.

11. Telephone conversation (telcon), Johnson with Russell, 10 January 1964, WH6401.10, PNO 26, LBJL.

12. CIA cable 95543, Panama City to White House Situation Room, 10 January 1964, box 64, NSF, CF, LBJL; CIA cable SFI017, Panama City to White House Situation Room, 10 January 1964, box 64, NSF, CF, LBJL.

13. Mann to Martin, 14 January 1964, box 63, NSF, CF, LBJL; Rusk to Panama City, 15 January 1964, box 63, NSF, CF, LBJL; CIA cable, "Communist Direction of the 15 January Meeting at the University and the March to the Presidential Palace," 17 January 1964, box 63, NSF, CF, LBJL; State Department Bureau of Intelligence and Research report, "Castroist and Communist Involvement in the Panamanian Disorders," 31 January 1964, box 65, NSF, CF, LBJL; CIA cable, "Communist Exploitation of the Current Situation," 5 February 1964, NSF, CF, LBJL.

14. Telcon, Johnson with Mansfield, 10 January 1964, WH6401.11, PNO 12, LBJL.

15. Mexico City to State Department, 11 January 1964, box 2560, Central State Department File (CSDF), National Archives and Records Administration (NARA); U.S. Information Agency report, "Initial Foreign Reaction to the Panama Situation," 13 January 1964, box 64, NSF, CF, LBJL.

16. Telcon, Johnson with Russell, 22 January 1964, WH6401.19, PNO 2, LBJL.

17. For Johnson's attitude toward foreign policy, see especially Robert Dallek, *Flawed Giant: Lyndon Johnson and His Times, 1961–1973* (New York: Oxford University Press, 1998), 84–90.

18. Quoted in Michael L. Conniff, *Panama and the United States: The Forced Alliance* (Athens: University of Georgia Press, 1992), 119.

19. Lyndon B. Johnson, *The Vantage Point: Perspectives on the Presidency, 1963–1969* (New York: Holt, Rinehart, and Winston, 1971), 180. See also U.S. Information Agency report, "Initial Foreign Reaction to the Panama Situation," 13 January 1964, box 64, NSF, CF, LBJL.

20. White House memo, "Panama—Telegrams from the Public," 12 January 1964, box 64, NSF, CF, LBJL.

21. Figures cited in LaFeber, *Panama Canal*, 144.

22. Scammon's memo to White House aide Ralph Dungan, dated 17 January 1964, is cited in LaFeber, *Panama Canal*, 143–144.

23. State Department to Panama City, 11 January 1964, box 2560, CSDF, NARA. In a non-binding resolution in 1959, Congress had voted 380–12 against Eisenhower's proposals to permit the Panamanian flag to fly in the Canal Zone.

24. Quoted in Murrey Marder, "Johnson Bars Revision of Canal Treaties," *Washington Post*, 12 January 1964.

25. United Press International dispatch, "Goldwater Lays Crisis in Panama to Yielding," *Washington Post*, 16 January 1964.

26. Quoted in Jorden, *Panama Odyssey*, 74.

27. "Panamanian Campaigning," *Wall Street Journal*, 13 January 1964.

28. Robert D. Dean, *Imperial Brotherhood: Gender and the Making of Cold War Foreign Policy* (Amherst: University of Massachusetts Press, 2001), 210–228; and Fredrik Logevall, *Choosing War: The Lost Chance for Peace and the Escalation of War in Vietnam* (Berkeley and Los Angeles: University of California Press, 1999), 389–395.

29. Telcon, Johnson with Russell, 22 January 1964, WH6401.19, PNO 2, LBJL.

30. Telcon, Johnson with Russell, 10 January 1964, WF 6401.10, PNO 26, LBJL; Telcon, Johnson with Russell, 10 January 1964, WH6401.11, PNO 2, LBJL.

31. Johnson to USCINCSO, 11 January 1964, box 63, NSF, CF, LBJL.

32. Telcon, Johnson with Bundy, 11 January 1964, WH6401.12, PNO 2, LBJL.

33. Telcon, Johnson with Russell, 10 January 1964, WH6401.11, PNO 12, LBJL.

34. Telcon, Johnson with Russell, 11 January 1964, WH6401.12, PNO 1, LBJL.

35. State Department circular, 20 January 1964, box 64, NSF, CF, LBJL.

36. Telcon, Johnson with Mann, 14 January 1964, WH6401.14, PNO 1, LBJL.

37. State Department memo, "American Opinion Summary," 24 January 1964, box 63, NSF, CF, LBJL.

38. Joseph Alsop, "Johnsonian Diplomacy," *Washington Post*, 17 January 1964.

39. Jorden, *Panama Odyssey*, 73–74.

40. National Security Council study, "Panama Crisis—1964," box 1, National Security Council Histories, LBJL.

41. White House press release, "Remarks of the President," 16 March 1964, box 65, NSF, CF, LBJL.

42. Brands, *Wages of Globalism*, 39.

43. Jorden is the only author to write of the Spanish loan, but he provides no citations. See Jorden, *Panama Odyssey*, 70–71.

44. National Security Council study, "Panama Crisis—1964," box 1, National Security Council Histories, LBJL.

45. "Summary Record of National Security Council Meeting No. 526," 3 April 1964, box 1, NSF, NSC Meetings File, LBJL.

46. In the available documentation, neither Johnson nor his advisers explicitly acknowledged this logic. But historians have noted Johnson's pattern of appointing Republicans to difficult and politically risky diplomatic assignments. Most famously, he reappointed Henry Cabot Lodge as ambassador to Vietnam in 1965.

47. Jorden, *Panama Odyssey*, 91.

48. See, for example, "Truce with Panama," *New York Times*, 4 April 1964; "Fresh Chance on Panama," *Washington Post*, 5 April 1964; "Stern Lessons of the Canal Row," *Los Angeles Times*, 7 April 1964.

49. "The Politics of Foreign Policy," *Wall Street Journal*, 7 April 1964.

50. Tad Szulc, "Fulbright Says U.S. Must Shed 'Myths' and Think Daringly on Foreign Policy," *New York Times*, 26 March 1964.

51. Jorden, *Panama Odyssey*, 94.

52. Chase to Bundy, 8 April 1964, box 66, NSF, CF, LBJL.

53. United Press International dispatch, "Republicans Hear of Cuban Missiles," *New York Times*, 16 April 1964.

54. "Text of the Second Half of 1964 Republican Platform, as Approved by Committee," *New York Times*, 13 July 1964.

55. Telcon, Johnson with Mann, Moyers, 14 January 1964, WH6401.14, PNO 1, LBJL.

56. Mann delegation to State Department, 11 January 1964, box 64, NSF, CF, LBJL.

57. Director of Intelligence and Research to Rusk, 31 January 1964, box 65, NSF, CF, LBJL.

58. Director of Intelligence and Research to Rusk, 13 April 1964, box 66, NSF, CF, LBJL.

59. State Department report, "PANAMA—Plan for Action from Present to October 1964," 20 April 1964, box 66, NSF, CF, LBJL.

60. White House memo, "Panama," 28 April 1964, box 66, NSF, CF, LBJL.

61. CIA memo, "The Panamanian Situation," 7 May 1964, box 66, NSF, CF, LBJL.

62. Bundy to Johnson, 8 May 1964, box 66, NSF, CF, LBJL.

63. Vaughn to State Department, 1 June 1964, box 2559, CSDF, NARA.

64. Vaughn to State Department, 10 July 1964, box 66, NSF, CF, LBJL.

65. Vaughn to State Department, 20 July 1964, box 2559, CSDF, LBJL.

66. Vaughn to State Department, 8 October 1964, box 67, NSF, CF, LBJL.

67. Telcon transcript, McNamara with O'Meara, 14 January 1964, box 67, NSF, CF, LBJL.

68. See, for example, Mann to Martin, 30 January 1964, box 65, NSF, CF, LBJL; and Martin to Mann, 30 January 1964, box 65, NSF, CF, LBJL.

69. Vaugh to State Department, 1 June 1964, box 2559, CSDF, NARA.

70. Panama City to State Department, 2 July 1964, box 66, NSF, CF, LBJL.

71. Vaughn to State Department, 6 July 1964, box 2560, CSDF, NARA.

72. Panama City to State Department, 23 July 1964, box 2559, CSDF, NARA.

73. Between 1951 and 1961, the United States contributed about $7 million in economic aid to Panama. From 1961 to 1963, Washington spent $41 million. See LaFeber, *Panama Canal*, 132–133, 148–152.

74. Jorden's book, presumably based on interviews with participants, asserts that Johnson was "delighted" with Anderson's proposal during the 2 December White House meeting where Anderson formally proposed that the United States offer to renegotiate. Jorden, *Panama Odyssey*, 100.

75. "First Annual Report of the Atlantic-Pacific Interoceanic Canal Study Commission," 31 July 1965, box 71, NSF, CF, LBJL.

76. National Security Action Memorandum 152, 30 April 1962, box 64, NSF, CF, LBJL.

77. State Department report, "American Opinion Summary," 29 April 1964, box 66, NSF, CF, LBJL; Panama embassy to State Department, 17 April 1964, box 66, NSF, CF, LBJL.

78. Newbegin to Mann, 8 July 1964, box 66, NSF, CF, LBJL.

79. "Texts of Johnson Statement and Address by Robles," *New York Times*, 19 December 1964

80. Transcript of background briefing by Bundy, 18 December 1964, box 70, NSF, CF, LBJL.

81. Robert Young, "U.S. Will Cut New Canal," *Chicago Tribune*, 19 December 1964.

82. "A New Canal," *Washington Post*, 20 December 1964.

83. Philip Geyelin, "Offer to Revise Canal Pact Pleases Panama, but Choice of New Site Could Upset Accord," *Wall Street Journal*, 21 December 1964.

84. Robert M. Sayre to Bundy, 14 December 1964, NSF, CF, LBJL.

85. White House memo, "General Dwight D. Eisenhower's Comments on Draft Statement on Panama, Dated 14 December 1964," 17 December 1964, box 67, NSF, CF, LBJL; and McCone to Johnson, 17 December 1964, box 67, NSF, CF, LBJL.

86. Joint Chiefs of Staff to McNamara, 16 December 1964, box 67, NSF, CF, LBJL; and Sayre to Bundy, 17 December 1964, box 67, NSF, CF, LBJL.

87. The loudest fringe critic was Congressman Flood, who traced his lineage to Theodore Roosevelt and had long protested any U.S. compromise on the canal. Flood complained that Johnson's announcement marked the victory of the "Bolshevik Revolution of 1917 and the international communist conspiracy." See LaFeber, *Panama Canal*, 146. Although this author could find no opinion poll data related specifically to Panama, more general polls gave the administration good reason for confidence in early 1965. In polls over the first six months of 1965, between 50 and 60 percent of Americans expressed approval of the administration's handling of foreign affairs, whereas only 15 to 22 percent expressed disapproval. *Gallup Political Index*, Report No. 2, July 1965 (American Institute of Public Opinion, 1965).

88. Vaughn to State Department, 18 December 1964, box 67, NSF, CF, LBJL.

89. Vaughn to State Department, 31 December 1964, box 2560, NSDF, NARA.

90. Panama City to State Department, "Review of Political Developments, December 19–24," 24 December 1964, box 2558, CSDF, NARA.

91. For discussion of the 1965–1967 talks and the treaties, see Jorden, *Panama Odyssey*, 107–119.

92. For coverage of the 1970s, see Conniff, *Panama and the United States*, chap. 7.

3 | Lyndon Johnson and the Global Disruption of 1968

Jeremi Suri

RECENT SCHOLARSHIP HAS generally neglected the role of global social unrest in Lyndon Johnson's foreign policy calculations.[1] Close examination of the historical record, however, reveals that domestic attacks upon state authority within the United States and each of the other major international powers—what I have called the "global disruption of 1968"—undermined serious foreign policy initiatives during the last years of the 1960s.[2] Lyndon Johnson, like his counterparts in France, West Germany, the Soviet Union, and China, was unable to escape failed cold war endeavors and complete promising new overtures because he confronted deep dissent at home and stubborn resistance abroad. The president and other major leaders in the late 1960s became preoccupied with internal disorder. This new focus paralyzed foreign policy.

Social upheaval triggered efforts to build stability through great power cooperation.[3] This dynamic was particularly evident in U.S. relations with the People's Republic of China and the Soviet Union during Lyndon Johnson's last years in office. Domestic upheaval motivated the president and his foreign counterparts to seek new, but often ill-prepared, diplomatic overtures. Relations between the United States, China, and the Soviet Union failed to advance because the very internal forces that encouraged political change also limited the ability of leaders—particularly Johnson—to pursue new initiatives. The American president was too embattled at home to justify existing policies in Asia and Europe, but he was also too besieged to formulate creative new endeavors in these regions. During 1968, domestic discontent made Johnson a prisoner of the White House and the established cold war policies he wished to change.

The president recognized his predicament at the time. He recounts in his memoir:

> There was a restlessness in our land among many citizens, and in the Congress, regarding our role in the world. There was growing discontent over the burdens we had carried so long. Why, some people asked, was it necessary to keep U.S. troops in Europe

twenty-five years after World War II? Why were we fighting in Vietnam without the help of troops from any of the European countries we had helped to save? Why were we still spending money on aid to nations that seemed to be doing too little to help themselves?

Johnson lamented the manifest tendency for the American public to embrace an "isolationist reaction" against the reformist program he had pursued both at home and abroad.[4] Late 1968 was a period when the president and his close circle grasped for promising policy initiatives in a darkening environment of despair and disillusion. Lady Bird Johnson captured this atmosphere in a diary entry from August of that fateful year: "The world is in convulsions all around us—our party, our country—the whole world. Lyndon is plowing right on, working as hard as he can every day on those things he can control and assaulting those things vigorously that he has even a little hope of controlling. I know that it is a wracking year for Lyndon physically, and it must be mentally and spiritually as well."[5]

The Global Disruption of 1968

During the 1960s, one factor was preeminent in igniting the flames of revolution. Leaders promised their citizens more "progress" than ever before—through education, material consumption, and individual equality.[6] This was true for the United States, where President Johnson waged a "war on poverty" and promised citizens that he would build a truly "great society." Although he passed landmark legislation on issues related to civil rights and social welfare, Johnson failed to meet the rising popular expectations for reform that he had inspired.[7] A perception of "false promises" among young and ambitious citizens pervaded the language of dissent during this period. It contributed directly to protest activities throughout the United States and in many other nations.

The "global disruption of 1968" grew from the declining ability of leaders, like Johnson, to manufacture consent at home.[8] The president acknowledged this fact when he told his senior advisers in late 1967, following a summer of urban riots and battlefield setbacks in Vietnam, that "our people will not hold out four more years. . . . We are very divisive. We don't have the press, the newspapers or the polls with us."[9] Domestic and international events during 1968 made this problem far more intractable. Political elites displayed their determination to retain power through the use of force, but they did so at the cost of their domestic legitimacy. No longer could men like Johnson attempt to lead largely by persuasion. Order and unity now relied more heavily on police activities.[10]

Domestic turmoil confronted the president directly in April 1968, when rioting citizens set the nation's capital on fire. These upheavals began on the night of Thursday, 4 April, following the assassination of Martin Luther King Jr. in Memphis, Tennessee. The riots were not strategic undertakings, promising any durable accomplishment for the men and women who took to the streets. African Americans suffered the vast majority of all property damage and human injury. The violent reaction to King's assassination reflected a widespread desire to lash out against the circumstances of poverty and discrimination that the African American community seemed unable to overcome. "If we must die," Stokely Carmichael exclaimed, "we better die fighting back."[11]

Riots occurred in more than 120 cities following King's murder. The most devastating of disturbances took place in Washington, D.C., beginning only hours after James Earl Ray fired his fatal shot in Memphis. When news first reached the large African American community in the nation's capital, local figures forced city businesses to close early out of respect for their slain leader. "Martin Luther King is dead," crowds gathering at the busy intersection of Fourteenth Street and U Street shouted. "Close the store!"[12]

By 10:30 P.M. parading groups of African Americans began to smash windows and loot displayed merchandise. More than five hundred individuals marched into other, largely white neighborhoods. Some carried what they could—televisions, radios, clothing—from ransacked stores that they could not, under normal circumstances, afford to enter. Others stood in the middle of the street, throwing rocks and bottles at passing vehicles. After midnight, growing mobs began to light fires across town. When firefighters attempted to put out the blazes, they came under attack as well.

During the early morning hours of 5 April 1968, the city where Martin Luther King Jr. spoke of his "dream" for peaceful racial integration five years earlier became a war zone. Angry African Americans controlled many of the streets in the nation's capital. They badly outnumbered the local police officers, who had been hastily dispatched to maintain order. When the city's mayor—Walter E. Washington—attempted to survey the scene by car, he could only watch as the looting and burning continued around him. Instead of escorting the local leader through the damage, fearful police officers advised the mayor that "you better get out of here."[13] Despite their use of tear gas, nightsticks, and other implements, law enforcement personnel could not control or contain the rioting.

The mayor was not the only government official in danger. President Johnson, scheduled to attend a fund-raising dinner at the Washington Hilton Hotel, had to cancel his appearance for reasons of personal safety. Instead, Vice President Hubert Humphrey attended the affair. Substituting for the president in an environment filled with street violence, Humphrey must have felt a sense of déjà vu from his ill-fated trip to West Berlin almost exactly one year earlier, when protesters besieged his entourage.[14] As the riots spread through Washington, D.C., police officers had to surround the Hilton in large numbers to ensure the security of the vice president and other guests.[15]

Meeting with what he called "responsible Negro leaders" in the White House on 5 April, Johnson solicited advice for dealing with what had become a dire domestic crisis. Supreme Court justice Thurgood Marshall explained that "the important thing is to keep people out of the streets and change the mood in the country." The president agreed and explained, "I have taken every opportunity to get through to the young people." Recognizing his own failings at home and abroad, Johnson added: "How well I have gotten through remains to be seen."[16]

The president knew very well that, like most established political leaders at this time, he had lost the support of young citizens. As he spoke, public looting spread to within ten blocks of the White House. Members of Congress, cabinet officials, and other high-ranking figures became prisoners within their homes and offices. The rapid escalation of violence made the leaders of the "free world" fearful of walking or driving on their own streets.[17] Speaking on the telephone with Mayor Richard Daley of Chicago, the president described the "hell raising" around the nation's capital.[18] Late into the night of 5 April, rumors circulated around the White House of various assassination plots against American leaders, including both Johnson and Daley.[19] The U.S. government had contained adversaries abroad with relative success, but it was now physically imperiled by enemies within. Each additional sidewalk lost to the raging mobs represented another fallen domino, another further encroachment on the nation's security by its own citizens.[20]

On Saturday, 6 April 1968 more than eleven thousand troops from the U.S. Army entered Washington, D.C. They placed the nation's capital under military "occupation," applying virtual martial law. Soldiers patrolled each city block in the riot-torn areas. Personnel stationed at checkpoints on area highways stopped and searched all vehicles entering the city. Mounted machine guns appeared on the steps of the Capitol. A curfew from 6:00 P.M. to 6:00 A.M. required all residents to remain indoors during the hours of darkness. Citizens and soldiers alike compared the circumstances in Washington, D.C., to the "pacification" of villagers in Vietnam.[21]

The city returned to an eerie quiet by Sunday morning, 7 April. Army troops remained in Washington through the following weekend, gradually lifting the curfew and other restrictions on citizen activity. Twelve civilians died during the riots, a relatively small number compared with similar disorders in other cities. This should not, however, disguise the extreme violence of the events. During a four-day period local police fired more than eight thousand canisters of tear gas at unruly crowds, and 1,190 people suffered various injuries at the hands of rioters or those attempting to maintain order. Law enforcement personnel arrested more than 7,600 people. Property damage and government expenses during the riots exceeded $27 million.[22]

"Our nation is moving toward two societies," the National Advisory Commission on Civil Disorders warned before April 1968, "one black, one white—separate and unequal."[23] The upheavals that followed Martin Luther King Jr.'s assassination confirmed this pessimistic observation, but they also pointed to an even more discouraging phenomenon. America was divided not only by race but also by age. The rioting mobs on the streets of Washington and other cities were disproportionately composed of young men. Unlike their elder counterparts who had participated in the peaceful demonstrations of the civil rights movement, these urban youth saw little hope in gradual reform. They thought of themselves as "guerilla" fighters, not spiritual healers.

The African American crowds that ransacked the nation's capital and other cities shared more in language and behavior with their angry white counterparts in Berkeley and West Berlin than with the earlier civil rights marchers. Although the poor material conditions of the inner city differed markedly from the privileged circumstances of elite colleges, youth from different races harbored a common disaffection with the established channels of social reform. King's death appeared to provide the incontrovertible evidence that nonviolent change could not work. Revolutions required armed struggle. A growing cohort of young Americans—black and white—believed that they could redress inequalities and end the war in Vietnam only through increased violence. Members of the Black Power movement and student radicals forged loose alliances during the tumultuous months of 1968.[24]

Political leaders, including President Johnson, recognized this radical inclination among many youth. One could no longer dismiss them as an extremist fringe. With violence building in cities and universities, something clearly had to be done. Middle-aged leaders unaccustomed to dealing with angry young men and women were confounded and, quite frankly, scared. In September 1968 the Central Intelligence Agency (CIA) reported to the president that "there are, in fact, striking parallels between the situation today and the conditions of cynicism, despair, and disposition toward violence which existed after World War I and which later helped produce Fascism and National Socialism. . . . If this is so, there is a likelihood that dissidence will worsen and that its base will broaden."[25] Johnson had already announced his decision not to run for reelection as a reaction, in part, to violent domestic opposition.[26] He now had reason to fear that his efforts at securing a positive domestic and international legacy would be undermined by what the CIA identified as "restless youth" across the globe.[27]

U.S. Relations with China in the Shadow of Domestic Upheaval

President Johnson and his close advisers hoped to assuage public anguish in the late 1960s by forging a new diplomatic "opening" with North Vietnam's longtime patron—the People's Republic of China. Many American policymakers perceived Beijing as both a "belligerent" agitator in Southeast Asia and a necessary partner in building a "more peaceful" world community. An opening to China could help to reduce conflict in Vietnam and restore public faith in the actions of American leaders. Members of the Johnson administration began to plan for new contacts with China as early as 1966.[28]

Averell Harriman—one of Washington's most experienced diplomats—observed the contradiction between "giving full support to the war in Vietnam, while at the same time making a gesture towards Red China." Harriman affirmed a growing consensus among Johnson's advisers, however, when he argued that the president had to follow this course. He explained that Washington could rebuild international and domestic support for military activities in Southeast Asia only if it also initiated a "spectacular change in attitude towards Red China." The United States received widespread criticism for its stubborn refusal to acknowledge the authority of Mao's government on the mainland, even after almost every other major state established formal relations with the People's Republic. New forms of engagement with Beijing would, according to Harriman's logic, allow America to appear less intolerant in its foreign policy.[29]

A Johnson administration study of June 1966 noted that China had many advantages, despite Washington's opposition, in promoting "revolutionary change" throughout Asia. The United States could not wipe the area clean of Mao's influence, no matter how hard it tried to isolate and contain his regime. Instead, Washington had to deal with the "reality" of the People's Republic through a mix of pressures and enticements. Failure to offer Beijing cooperative signals, according to this study, only exacerbated difficulties and misunderstandings between the two states.[30]

Following lengthy deliberations among his advisers, on 12 July 1966 the president offered his clearest public call for Sino-American reconciliation.[31] After ritualistically affirming his determination to "make the Communists of North Vietnam stop shooting at their neighbors" and his opposition to "Communist China's policy of aggression by proxy," Johnson surprised many of his listeners. Toward the end of his speech he called for "reconciliation between nations that now call themselves enemies." "Lasting peace can never come to Asia," the president admitted, "as long as the 700 million people of mainland China are isolated by their rulers from the outside world." America, he explained, wanted to break the mainland's isolation by increasing informal contacts—including exchanges of news reporters, scholars, and health experts. China had "rejected" most of these contacts in the past, Johnson lamented, but he promised to "persist" in opening new doors to China out of a sincere desire for "cooperation" between Washington and Beijing. This was a public speech designed to broadcast a message of reconciliation to China and an image of presidential peacemaking to American citizens.[32]

Eight days later the president was even more unequivocal at a news conference. When asked about his recent "conciliatory attitude toward mainland China," he emphasized his wish for better relations between the United States and the People's Republic. This process, Johnson explained, had to begin with person-to-person contacts and clear signals about each state's peaceful intentions. "I feel," he said, "that we should do everything we can to increase our exchanges, to understand other people better, to have our scientists and our businessmen, our authors and our newspaper people exchange visits and exchange viewpoints." Abandoning common American criticisms of communist tyranny and aggression, the president expressed a sincere "hope that at a not too distant date mainland China will be willing to open some of the barriers to these exchanges."[33]

American overtures to Beijing in 1966 did not get very far. On 7 September Wang Guoquan, the Chinese ambassador to Poland, told John Gronouski, his American counterpart, that Mao's government would not allow itself to be "hoodwinked" by Johnson's rhetoric. Wang and Gronouski met as part of the ongoing Sino-American ambassadorial talks in Warsaw—initially begun on 15 September 1958 and continuing intermittently ever since. Contrary to Washington's hopes for a breakthrough after Johnson's dramatic speech, Gronouski reported that the Chinese representative reiterated the standard "attacks on U.S. aggression." Wang called Johnson's conciliatory rhetoric a "fraud" while Washington continued its war in Vietnam. Beijing would accept the "sincerity" of recent American overtures, the Chinese ambassador explained, only when the president removed all U.S. support from South Vietnam and Taiwan. This was, in Gronouski's words, "old ground" that no one expected would get very far.[34]

Convulsed by the early months of the Cultural Revolution, the Chinese largely ignored American overtures in 1966.[35] Mao's condemnations of Western "imperialism" and Soviet "revisionism" inspired a surge of activity in China, directed against any meaningful relations with the allegedly corrupt great powers. Between 1966 and 1967, groups of Red Guards besieged foreign diplomatic offices operated in Beijing by Great Britain, France, and even fellow communist states, like East Germany.[36] If anything, youthful revolutionaries on the mainland used Johnson's speech to confirm their injunctions against compromise with "counterrevolutionary" forces seeking to ingratiate themselves in Chinese society.[37] Chaos at home and American military escalation in Vietnam undercut the efforts of moderate figures—especially Prime Minister Zhou Enlai and Foreign Minister Chen Yi—who appeared favorably disposed to improving Beijing's relations with Washington. China's domestic extremism and self-imposed isolation in 1966 made a diplomatic breakthrough of any kind impossible. Instead of "surrendering" to corrupt external forces, radicals—like Kang Sheng—who gained influence over the Chinese Foreign Ministry demanded militant actions to prove that "the world had entered a new era of Mao Zedong thought."[38]

Watching the development of the Cultural Revolution from Washington, American policymakers were astounded by what Alfred Jenkins—a China expert on the National Security Council—called "the spectacle of the oldest civilization on earth methodically digging up its roots to the tune of raucous, uncivilized ballyhoo and bedlam." Jenkins counseled for caution to avoid antagonizing China with provocative threats. Washington also had to resist the temptation to address "moderates" on the mainland with its hopes for reconciliation. American overtures would sully the reputation, and imperil the safety, of the most receptive figures in China. "We can hope," Jenkins wrote, "that the chaos on the mainland may continue a while, and may prove to be in our interest in the denouement." "Meanwhile," he advised, "we should try not to provide a way out for a Mao in trouble, should he sooner or later require a particularly devilish devil."[39]

Adopting Jenkins's advice, the Johnson administration abandoned its inclination to seek a dramatic improvement in Sino-American relations. Policymakers continued to press discreetly for expanded contacts with Beijing, but the president put most overtures on hold. The United States would wait until a clear outcome emerged from what Walt Rostow called "China's vaulting chaos."[40]

Through the most disruptive months of the Cultural Revolution, the Chinese Foreign Ministry somehow managed to maintain limited contacts with the United States. The Sino-American talks in Warsaw, for example, continued. Even as Beijing rejected President Johnson's overtures in July 1966, Ambassador Gronouski observed that his meetings with Wang Guoquan remained "relaxed." Despite Chinese calls for isolation from the American "imperialists," Gronouski noted that Beijing's representatives continued to find the Warsaw meetings "useful."[41]

Zhou Enlai also employed contacts with Pakistan to send important messages to the United States. In March 1965 he had asked Pakistan's president, Mohammed Ayub, to tell Johnson that Mao's government intended to remain careful about its commitments in Vietnam. If American forces did not threaten Chinese sovereignty, Beijing's army would not engage U.S. soldiers directly. Neither government, Zhou explained, should trigger a replay of the Sino-American confrontation in the Korean War.[42]

Zhou used his connections with Pakistan to reaffirm Chinese caution and avoid American misperceptions during the most violent months of the Cultural Revolution. On 10 April 1966 he gave an interview to the Pakistani newspaper *Dawn* confirming that China wished to avoid any military confrontation with the United States.[43] Whether the Johnson administration received this particular message remains unclear. Zhou did manage, through Warsaw and Pakistan, to assure Washington that the chaos on the mainland would not create new sources of communist aggression in Asia.[44]

After the Chinese Foreign Ministry established its informal channel with West Germany in mid-1967, direct communications between Beijing and Washington began to improve as well.[45] On 8 January

1968, Ambassador Gronouski found his Chinese counterpart—the chargé d'affaires Chen Tung, substituting temporarily for Ambassador Wang Guoquan—incredibly forthcoming. The belligerent rhetoric and frequent references to American "imperialism" made during the Warsaw talks of the last two years did not find voice in this discussion. Chen focused his statements almost entirely on Taiwan, excluding the Vietnam War and other troubling issues from his presentation. Gronouski called the warmer Chinese attitude in Warsaw a "significant departure from the past performance." Walt Rostow forwarded this positive report directly to President Johnson.[46]

Signs of a more conciliatory Chinese attitude toward the United States proliferated in other forums as well. On 28 November 1968 Mao Zedong told E. F. Hill, the chairman of the Australian Communist Party, that the world had entered a period of "neither war nor revolution." Despite the belligerent rhetoric of the Cultural Revolution, the Chinese leader rejected the Marxist-Leninist argument that capitalism inevitably led to imperialism and war. "It seems," Mao explained, "that this rule no longer works now."[47] East German observers noted that comments like these from Mao, Zhou Enlai, and other Chinese figures in 1968 pointed to a new "nonconfrontational" stand toward Washington.[48]

British officials in Hong Kong also reported that after months of Red Guard threats to the island, Mao's government acted decisively in late 1967 and early 1968 to protect order along the shared boundary. In November 1967 the Chinese Foreign Ministry negotiated a series of very reasonable "understandings" with London's representatives. These arrangements included an exchange of Chinese and British prisoners, assured movement for workers from the mainland to the island, and, most important, guaranteed that citizens and leaders from the two sides would engage in "proper and normal" interactions. Both Chinese and British authorities pledged to prevent violent activities in or near Hong Kong.[49]

London's chief negotiator observed that the representatives from the mainland operated without any "attempt to browbeat or to shout political slogans or even adopt starchy attitudes," as was common during most of 1966 and 1967. The new professionalism of Chinese diplomats led the British to predict that after months of uncertainty "we can talk turkey with these people in the future." Like their Western counterparts, leaders in Beijing appeared intent on assuring domestic order and creating amicable relationships with the other great powers.[50]

In 1968 Mao confirmed his commitment to stability instead of continuous revolution when he purged many of the radicals who had recently assumed positions of authority in foreign affairs. As a consequence, the Foreign Ministry—like many other government departments—suffered from a shortage of staff. Only about 30 percent of its pre-1966 personnel remained in place. These circumstances reduced the breadth of the ministry's capabilities, but they also allowed moderates like Zhou Enlai and Chen Yi to exert more personal, and often secret, control over policy.[51]

Sino-American reconciliation grew from the work of these newly empowered moderates. The Cultural Revolution did not come to a close in 1968, but Chinese leaders now appeared determined to contain its disruptive effects on foreign policy. As Mao's government limited the activities of radicals during this period, it also turned to closer relations with traditional enemies—especially the United States.

Secret channels of communication and personal diplomacy allowed Chinese leaders to insulate their foreign activities from domestic criticism. Figures like Zhou Enlai used agreements with external powers to undermine Red Guard groups that had followed calls for cultural revolution in 1966, but now became too radical for the purposes of Beijing's leadership. Cooperation between Chinese and British authorities to protect order in Hong Kong reflected the conservative aims of Mao's government and its efforts to enlist external assistance for the sake of domestic stability. In his preparations for Sino-American reconciliation, Mao followed a similar tactic. He used relations with foreign barbarians to help restrain the internal rebels he had unleashed in earlier years. International détente would contribute to a needed domestic respite from continuous revolutionary upheaval.

By 1968 both Mao and Johnson sought improved relations between their states. The president was very receptive to the "China experts" in the United States who called for new overtures to Beijing in February of that year.[52] A Sino-American détente failed to reach fruition during this period, however, because the American government was so besieged at home that it could not concentrate on the new openings it sought overseas. Daily crises in Washington, D.C., and other American cities, as well as the battlefields of Vietnam, left officials with little freedom for long-range planning. In contrast to 1966 and 1967, thoughtful U.S. government deliberations about future relations with China are almost impossible to find in the records from 1968. Harry McPherson, one of Johnson's closest and longtime aides, recalls that during this period the White House became caught up in a perpetual crisis atmosphere that focused obsessively on domestic disorder. The president was isolated and unable to think beyond the daily course of troubles at home and in Vietnam. McPherson remembers that the president "could not go anywhere. . . . [T]hat was disastrous."[53] Johnson was a prisoner of domestic contention in the United States. The riots in Washington, D.C., during April 1968 indicated that the president had largely lost control of his own society. His administration lacked the authority, concentration, and internal coherence to formulate a new policy toward a longtime enemy. Domestic pressures motivated both Beijing and Washington to seek improved relations, but these conditions could only reach fruition when a new president, Richard Nixon, assembled the domestic mechanisms for the effective pursuit of this end.[54]

Lyndon Johnson's Overtures to Moscow in 1968

Despite his administration's failure to pursue promising opportunities for better relations with Beijing, in 1968 Lyndon Johnson made a series of important overtures to Moscow. This was not a significant change of policy, as was required for a prospective opening to China, but instead a new emphasis within an existing cold war framework. The president had desired improved relations with the Soviet Union from his first days in office. On nuclear issues, in particular, he sought to limit the horrific dangers of a confrontation between the superpowers. Having sat through the agonizing meetings of John F. Kennedy's "executive committee" during the Cuban missile crisis, Johnson wished to prevent a nuclear confrontation of this magnitude from recurring.[55] On 1 July 1968 the final signing of the Nuclear Non-Proliferation Treaty (NPT) by the United States, the Soviet Union, Great Britain, and fifty-nine other countries marked an important triumph for Johnson's long-standing efforts at arms control. The NPT also created a precedent for future disarmament negotiations between Washington and Moscow, scheduled to begin in 1968 as part of the Strategic Arms Limitation Talks (eventually known as SALT I).

During his first four and a half years in office, Johnson had displayed little enthusiasm for a major public meeting with his Soviet counterparts. Vivid memories of the personal acrimony and threatening behavior that followed from the last superpower summit—the meeting of John F. Kennedy and Nikita Khrushchev in Vienna on 3 and 4 June 1961—chastened the administration against the dangers of another face-to-face blowup over controversial issues, especially the Vietnam War.[56] In fact, the only superpower summit of the Johnson presidency was notable for its poor preparation, personal awkwardness, and public ambivalence.

On 19 June 1967, Aleksei Kosygin, chairman of the Soviet Council of Ministers, visited the United Nations to address an emergency special session of the General Assembly, following the Arab-Israeli Six Day War. As late as 21 June, when Kosygin was already in New York, members of the administration continued to debate the wisdom of a meeting with the president.[57] Fearful of the public fallout that would follow if the Soviet leader visited the UN but was not invited to see Johnson, on 22 June Secretary of State Dean Rusk proposed a meeting to Kosygin.[58]

On 23 and 25 June the two leaders met on the campus of Glassboro State College in Glassboro, New Jersey. They had no formal agenda, and their discussions ranged in an undisciplined manner from the Vietnam War to the Middle East, from arms control to the threats posed by the People's Republic of China. Both men showed a serious interest in bringing the Vietnam War to an end, but they failed to produce any substantive agreement. Due to the abbreviated and ad hoc nature of their discussions, they also failed to establish any serious personal rapport. As Johnson explained to former president Dwight Eisenhower after the final Glassboro meeting, "It was just largely conversation—pleasant, no vitriolic stuff, no antagonistic stuff, no bitter stuff, two or three little low blows below the belt every now and then."[59]

One year after Glassboro, Johnson's perspective on the value of "conversation" with the Soviet leader changed significantly. The global disruption of 1968 redoubled his desire to establish cooperative arrangements with Moscow, beyond arms control. As public order appeared to dissolve within the United States and abroad, an increasingly isolated president showed newfound interest in a major trip to the Soviet Union. Johnson now sought a display of superpower friendship to bolster his personal stature and quiet growing criticisms of his policy impotence.

In early June 1968 he asked his special assistant for national security affairs, Walt Rostow, to explore the issue with Secretary of State Rusk.[60] By the end of the month, rumors had already begun to circulate around Washington, indicating that Johnson hoped a new meeting with Kosygin would restore public confidence in the president. Sensitive to this charge, Rusk met with Soviet ambassador Anatoly Dobrynin on 1 July—immediately following the signing of the NPT—both to affirm Johnson's interest in a summit and to refute the gossip about his motivations. Rusk explained that "the president has in fact been thinking about the desirability of another meeting with Mr. Kosygin and felt that there was much to be gained from it." The secretary of state focused on arms control and a scheduled August conference of nonnuclear states to discuss the implications of the NPT. Rusk asserted that "there would be great advantage if the president and Mr. Kosygin could demonstrate before that meeting that the two of us are seriously engaged in the matter of offensive and defensive strategic missiles."[61]

Proposing a superpower summit on such short notice—"toward the latter part of July"—underscored Johnson's seriousness and his sense of urgency. The fact that the suggested topic was so narrow and offered almost no probability for a concrete breakthrough revealed that the president did, indeed, want to meet for purposes of public image rather than policy substance. In June 1967 Johnson hesitated to travel from Washington to New York for a discussion with Kosygin. Now, one year later, he offered to "make a non-stop flight to Leningrad" for "an official or state visit." As in 1967, both sides were ill prepared to achieve anything in their proposed meeting. In 1968, however, the White House saw important value in manufacturing an image of power and respect from foreign contacts. Johnson hated foreign travel, but he recognized that he could stage-manage a prestigious public event only on his adversary's territory, relatively free from the daily public protests in the United States and Western Europe.[62]

The president's attempt to use a summit meeting for domestic diversion is evidenced not only by the strange circumstances of the proposal but also by the overwhelming foreign policy objections to just such a meeting in the summer and fall of 1968. Clark Clifford, Johnson's longtime adviser and newly appointed secretary of defense, made a strong case against a summit on substantive grounds. Pointing to the crisis in Czechoslovakia and the possibility of Soviet military action against the Prague Spring in the near future,[63] Clifford warned: "You could get caught up in that and I'm just afraid it would be difficult for you to extricate yourself. You could have a talk with Kosygin and the day you talked with him Soviet troops could move on Czechoslovakia or the day after you left, troops could move in Czechoslovakia." Meeting with the Soviet leader in late July or early August 1968, Johnson risked getting "tied together" with an act of communist aggression. The president would appear to be condoning Moscow's repressive behavior. This, of course, would only further contribute to Johnson's image of weakness and desperation.[64]

Clifford observed that these risks of implicating the president in

Soviet aggression were not outweighed by the limited prospects, at best, of any substantive advance in relations between the two superpowers. The secretary of defense went through the possible topics of discussion between Johnson and Kosygin, indicating quite clearly that there was little chance of progress in a face-to-face meeting at this time:

> I think that we have to be careful about the reasons why the president was seeing Kosygin at this time. Is it because the president has a new plan that he is taking to Kosygin vis-à-vis Vietnam? Is there something new he wants to take him? Is it because the president's concerned about the Middle East—some development there? Is he concerned about NATO? You know, there's so much cooking right now. As far as starting off with Kosygin on a discussion of strategic limitation and ultimate reduction, I don't know. Right at this time, Mr. President, I wonder whether that's advisable. These are going to be long, difficult, exceedingly complex negotiations.[65]

Clifford added one more objection to the proposed summit. A meeting with Kosygin would complicate plans for Johnson to attend the Democratic National Convention in August. This would be a formative moment for the future of the Democratic Party, and Clifford assumed that the president would want to be closely involved with activities, even if he did not attend meetings in Chicago. Johnson's longtime adviser surely suspected that his chief hoped to maneuver at the convention for a return to the presidential race, probably as a candidate "drafted" by the party.[66]

Secretary of State Rusk recognized Clifford's objections and added the risk that Kosygin might use a meeting with Johnson at such a difficult moment to "turn up there with demands on Berlin or something." Referring again to the acrimonious Kennedy-Khrushchev encounter in Vienna, Rusk warned that "there's a little danger." He cautiously supported the idea of a summit so long as the crisis in Czechoslovakia was settled first.[67] This, of course, was a major condition. Events in Czechoslovakia continued to spiral through the summer of 1968, including more explicit attacks on Moscow's authority and a brutal Soviet-led invasion of the state on 20–21 August.

To the surprise of many, including Soviet ambassador Dobrynin, Johnson continued to push for a meeting with Kosygin after Moscow's tanks rolled into Prague. In fact, the president and prominent members of his administration appeared indifferent to, and at times even relieved by, Soviet military action. On the night of 20 August, when Dobrynin first alerted Johnson of the invasion, the ambassador received no rebuke, as he had expected, from the White House. Instead, the president reaffirmed his desire to visit the Soviet Union "in the nearest time."[68] Johnson surely regretted the suffering of the Czechoslovak people under repressive Soviet rule, but in the late summer of 1968 his clear priority was to arrange some kind of major public meeting with Moscow's leadership. As domestic disorder undermined the authority of elected officials across the globe, the president needed a public superpower event that would make him look presidential again. Johnson intentionally downplayed traditional American objections to Moscow's brutality in Eastern Europe.

On 5 September 1968 Llewellyn Thompson, the American ambassador to the Soviet Union, met at the White House with the president. National Security Adviser Walt Rostow gave Thompson a set of instructions indicating the following: "The President wishes to hold open the possibility of strategic weapons talks. His present idea is that he would open these talks at the highest level, not via the secretary of defense or the director, ACDA [Arms Control and Disarmament Agency]. Thompson should try to get any indication if there is any 'give on this subject' or any truly serious 'interest.'"[69] Rostow conveyed this message directly to Dobrynin on 7 September. He explained, "The President does not wish to launch the missile talks at a meeting lower than the Kosygin-Johnson level." Rostow suggested a summit date between 1 and 10 October, again barely one month's advance notice.[70]

The absence from these discussions of both the Czechoslovakia crisis and a clear indication of what Johnson and Kosygin could accomplish in their meeting is striking. Less than a month after Moscow crushed the most promising movement for communist reform in Eastern Europe, the president displayed an unseemly eagerness to embrace the Soviet leadership in public. Clifford's earlier objections to a summit of this kind were now stronger than ever. Johnson's presence in the Soviet Union could only legitimize and embolden Moscow's aggression. The president's only possible gains could come from an image of international importance.[71]

The Soviet leadership would not grant Johnson the public prestige that he craved.[72] The domestic disorder that made the president desperate for some overseas accomplishment also undermined his standing in the eyes of foreign leaders. As a lame duck finishing his last months in the White House, Johnson could not offer his Soviet counterparts any enduring agreements on strategic issues. A meeting with him would largely be about image, as the president recognized, and the leaders in Moscow saw no reason to lend Johnson any support in this area. After the election of Richard Nixon as president on 5 November 1968, the incoming administration alerted the Soviet Union of its explicit objections to a meeting with Johnson.[73]

Johnson's failure to procure a public boost in stature through a superpower summit late in his presidency does not mean his efforts were entirely ineffectual. Quite the contrary, they set an important precedent for Richard Nixon and the general framework of détente in the early 1970s. Internal challenges to leadership across the globe, and particularly within the United States, motivated the president to seek prestige and authority from cooperation, or at least the image of cooperation, with foreign figures. Johnson had discounted the value of superpower summits as late as the summer of 1967, but in 1968 he desperately turned to a meeting of this sort because of the unique image of power it could confer upon him. Visiting the Soviet Union, Johnson hoped, would produce a stage-managed display of cold war command, initiative, and beneficence—the very qualities his domestic detractors most diminished. As late as December 1968, he desired a public meeting of this kind to assure, at the very least, a positive gloss for his historical legacy.

Richard Nixon and his national security adviser, Henry Kissinger, worked against Johnson's summit hopes after the November 1968 election.[74] They waited almost four years to arrange their first meeting between the American and Soviet heads of state. Like Johnson, however, Nixon and Kissinger used their relationship with Moscow to bolster their public standing. As manifestations of dissent multiplied at home and among allies, foreign connections became a crucial justification for the exercise of White House power. Arms control discussions, particularly those leading up to SALT I, and the presidential visits to China and the Soviet Union in 1972 diverted attention from the continuing war in Vietnam and public discontent in nearly every major society. With greater skill and more propitious circumstances, Johnson's successors followed his lead in pursuing personal relationships with foreign adversaries as an antidote to diminishing domestic authority. Détente was a prolonged diplomatic reaction to the global disruption of 1968.[75]

Conclusions

Domestic turmoil during the late 1960s made American overtures to the largest communist states both necessary and impossible for Lyndon Johnson. The president needed new foreign contacts to recapture the political initiative he had lost in reaction to troubles at home. He found receptive counterparts in Beijing and Moscow, where leaders faced some similar internal problems. Johnson's efforts, however, constituted too little, too late. Preoccupied with violence on the streets of major Western cities and the battlefields of Southeast Asia, the White House could not formulate or implement a complex shift in America's long-standing cold war foreign policy. Johnson's search for better relations with China and the Soviet Union anticipated a period of détente among the great powers, but his administration was ill prepared to seize this new diplomatic ground. After Johnson declared on 31 March 1968 that he would not seek reelection, foreign leaders were hesitant to invest much of their own precarious political capital in relations with a lame-duck president.

In the case of the People's Republic of China, the Johnson administration recognized and pursued some promising avenues for rapprochement during 1966 and early 1967. Public violence in both the United States and China during late 1967 and 1968 put these nascent Sino-American maneuvers on hold. The White House was clearly distracted by domestic issues and the war in Vietnam. In response to the public attacks on his authority, Johnson became desperate for quick diplomatic accomplishments. The president and his close advisers recognized that while an opening between Washington and Beijing might lie on the horizon, it would involve a long and complex set of delicate negotiations. In 1968 Johnson had neither the time nor the patience for uncertain endeavors of this kind.

Improving relations with Moscow, or at least the appearance of these relations, seemed a simpler and quicker proposition for the White House. In marked contrast with his previous disinclination to meet Soviet leaders, Johnson devoted considerable energy during the second half of 1968 to arrangements for a public summit with Aleksei Kosygin. To the dismay of many close advisers and the surprise of Soviet representatives, the president was willing to accept Soviet aggression in Czechoslovakia as the cost of a superpower meeting. The administration had few concrete proposals for improved relations with Moscow, but Johnson continued to push for a summit in the hope that it would bolster his diminished political stature. He went so far as to approach president-elect Richard Nixon for endorsement of a Johnson-Kosygin meeting after the November 1968 election. Nixon rejected the outgoing president's proposal, as did the Soviet leadership, which now prepared to deal with a new American administration.[76] Johnson's overtures to Moscow in late 1968 reflect the pathetic low to which this monumental politician had fallen. The Vietnam War was only part of Johnson's problem. More fundamentally, internal upheaval diminished his ability to continue with the cold war status quo or pursue an alternative set of policies. This paradox points to the deep influence of social contention on foreign policymaking. The White House found itself paralyzed by the riots in Washington, D.C., and other cities, stuck in a failed Southeast Asian war, and cut off from crucial diplomatic openings. Johnson's attempts to manufacture a superpower summit without adequate preparations or appropriate international circumstances reveal how limited his options had become. The "imperial president" was now an imprisoned president in the White House. The man who promised, and sincerely pursued, a "great society" crumbled under the weight of what was a truly global disruption in 1968.

Domestic upheaval contributed to policy stagnation. During the early 1970s, détente would become a global framework for accepting this policy stagnation and stabilizing internal unrest. Lyndon Johnson's predicament pointed to an emerging era when the leaders of the United States, the People's Republic of China, and the Soviet Union would work closely together out of mutual concern for their domestic insecurity.

Notes

1. One notable exception is Mitchell B. Lerner, *The Pueblo Incident: A Spy Ship and the Failure of American Foreign Policy* (Lawrence: University Press of Kansas, 2002), 152–168. Lerner points to the public questioning of cold war assumptions about "liberal internationalism" during this period.
2. For an extended discussion of the "global disruption of 1968," see Jeremi Suri, *Power and Protest: Global Revolution and the Rise of Détente* (Cambridge, Mass.: Harvard University Press, 2003), 164–212.
3. For a more extended discussion of this point see ibid., 213–259.
4. Lyndon Baines Johnson, *The Vantage Point: Perspectives of the Presidency, 1963–1969* (New York: Holt, Rinehart and Winston, 1971), 491–492.
5. Diary entry, 27 August 1968, Lady Bird Johnson, *A White House Diary* (New York: Holt, Rinehart and Winston, 1970), 707.
6. This global phenomenon underlay Daniel Bell's analysis in *The End of Ideology: On the Exhaustion of Political Ideas in the Fifties* (Glencoe, Ill.: Free Press, 1960), 393–407.
7. For a classic account of how "rising expectations" can contribute to popular revolution during a period of reform, see Alexis de Tocqueville, *L'Ancien Régime et la Révolution* (1856; Paris: Gallimard, 1952), 226–231. See

also Arthur Marwick, *The Sixties: Cultural Revolution in Britain, France, Italy, and the United States, c. 1958–c. 1974* (Oxford: Oxford University Press, 1998), 247–287, 359–403.

8. Walter Lippmann was one of the first writers to use the phrase "manufacture of consent" for the manipulation of public opinion. See Walter Lippmann, *Public Opinion* (New York: Harcourt, Brace, 1922), 248. More recently, Edward Herman and Noam Chomsky have used the phrase to condemn the allegedly propagandist uses of the media by various government and business interests. See Edward S. Herman and Noam Chomsky, *Manufacturing Consent: The Political Economy of the Mass Media* (New York: Pantheon, 1988), especially 1–35.

9. Notes of the President's Meeting with Dean Rusk, Robert McNamara, Walt Rostow, Richard Helms, and George Christian, 3 October 1967, Folder: October 3, 1967—6:10 pm, Box 1, Tom Johnson's Notes of Meetings, Lyndon Baines Johnson Presidential Library, Austin, Texas (hereafter cited as LBJL).

10. Max Weber defined "legitimacy" as "voluntary compliance" with an authority deemed "valid." See Max Weber, *Economy and Society: An Outline of Interpretive Sociology*, ed. Guenther Roth and Claus Wittich (New York: Bedminster Press, 1968), 1: 212–301. The statistics on crime in the United States and other Western societies during this period point to both a precipitous increase in public violence and a more pervasive use of police power against threats to established authority. See Ted Robert Gurr and Erika Gurr, "Crime in Western Societies, 1945–1974," available through the Inter-university Consortium for Political and Social Research, ICPSR 7769, http://www.icpsr.umich.edu.

11. Quoted in Ben W. Gilbert and the staff of the *Washington Post, Ten Blocks from the White House: Anatomy of the Washington Riots of 1968* (New York: Praeger, 1968), 16.

12. Quoted in ibid., 16.

13. Quoted in ibid., 26.

14. See Suri, *Power and Protest,* 176.

15. See Gilbert, *Ten Blocks from the White House,* 36–37.

16. Notes of the President's Meeting with Negro Leaders, 5 April 1968, Folder: April 5, 1968—11:10 A.M., Box 3, Tom Johnson's Notes of Meetings, LBJL.

17. See Gilbert, *Ten Blocks from the White House,* 30, 36–37.

18. President's Daily Diary, 5 April 1968, p. 12, LBJL.

19. President's Daily Diary, 5 April 1968, p. 17, LBJL.

20. In April 1968 the Department of Defense created a permanent command center, under the immediate direction of the army, to coordinate military responses to domestic disorder across the country. This direct and intensive Pentagon preparation for internal violence revealed a high-level recognition that protests and riots—like those following the assassination of Martin Luther King Jr.—threatened the nation's security. See Clark Clifford Oral History, Interview VI, 24 April 1970, Internet Copy, p. 5, LBJL.

21. See Gilbert, *Ten Blocks from the White House,* 103–119; Maurice Isserman and Michael Kazin, *America Divided: The Civil War of the 1960s* (New York: Oxford University Press, 2000), 227–228.

22. Gilbert, *Ten Blocks from the White House,* 32, 105, 119.

23. *Report of the National Advisory Commission on Civil Disorders* (New York: Dutton, 1968), 1.

24. See Allen J. Matusow, *The Unravelling of America: A History of Liberalism in the 1960s* (New York: Harper and Row, 1984), 367–373.

25. CIA Report, "Restless Youth," September 1968, Folder: Youth and Student Movements, Box 13, Files of Walt W. Rostow, National Security Files, LBJL.

26. Robert Dallek, *Flawed Giant: Lyndon Johnson and His Times, 1961–1973* (New York: Oxford University Press, 1998), 519–530.

27. CIA Report, "Restless Youth," September 1968, Folder: Youth and Student Movements, Box 13, Files of Walt W. Rostow, National Security Files, LBJL.

28. See Memorandum from James C. Thomson Jr. of the National Security Council Staff to the President's Special Assistant (Bill Moyers), 15 March 1966, *Foreign Relations of the United States* (hereafter *FRUS*), 1964–1968, 30: 274–275.

29. Memorandum from the Ambassador at Large (Averell Harriman) to the President's Special Assistant (Bill Moyers), 3 June 1966, *FRUS*, 1964–1968, 30:318–319. For similar opinions from other close Johnson advisers, see Memorandum from the President's Special Assistant (Robert Komer) to President Johnson, 19 April 1966, ibid., 285–286; Memorandum from James C. Thomson Jr. to Walt Rostow, 4 August 1966, ibid., 364–366. Of all Johnson's close advisers, Secretary of State Dean Rusk was the most wary of establishing improved relations with Beijing. See Memorandum from Rusk to President Johnson and attachment, 22 February 1968, ibid., 645–650; Warren I. Cohen, *America's Response to China: A History of Sino-American Relations*, 3d ed. (New York: Columbia University Press, 1990), 192–194; Cohen, *Dean Rusk* (Totowa, N.J.: Cooper Square, 1980), 280–289.

30. "Communist China: A Long Range Study," prepared by the Special State-Defense Study Group, June 1966, *FRUS*, 1964–1968, 30:332–343.

31. On the deliberations behind Johnson's overtures to China in July 1966, see Memorandum from James C. Thomson Jr. of the National Security Council Staff to the President's Special Assistant (Jack Valenti), 1 March 1966, *FRUS*, 1964–1968, 30:262–264; Memorandum from the Consul General at Hong Kong (Edward E. Rice) to Walt Rostow, 15 April 1966, ibid., 282–284; "Communist China: A Long Range Study," prepared by the Special State-Defense Study Group, June 1966, ibid., 332–343. See also Cohen, *America's Response to China*, 193; Nancy Bernkopf Tucker, "Threats, Opportunities, and Frustrations in East Asia," in *Lyndon Johnson Confronts the World: American Foreign Policy, 1963–1968*, ed. Warren Cohen and Nancy Bernkopf Tucker (New York: Cambridge University Press, 1994), 105–107; Robert Garson, "Lyndon B. Johnson and the China Enigma," *Journal of Contemporary History* 32 (January 1997): 63–79.

32. Lyndon Johnson, "Remarks to the American Alumni Council: Asian Policy," 12 July 1966, PPP: LBJ, 1966: 718–722, quotations on 720–722.

33. President Johnson's News Conference, 20 July 1966, PPP: LBJ, 1966: 744–751, quotations on 747. See also Dean Rusk to All Diplomatic and Consular Posts, Guidance for Discussion of Communist China, 17 January 1967, Folder: POL 1 CHICOM-US, Box: 1974, State Department Central Files, RG 59, National Archives, College Park, Maryland.

34. Telegram from the Embassy in Poland to the Department of State, 7 September 1966, *FRUS*, 1964–1968, 30:383–386. On Sino-American talks in Warsaw, and their deadlock through 1967, see Kenneth T. Young, *Negotiating with the Chinese Communists: The United States Experience, 1953–67* (New York: McGraw-Hill, 1968), 161–298.

35. See Cohen, *America's Response to China*, 193.

36. On the night of 22 August 1967, a mob of Chinese Red Guards attacked and burned the British consulate in Beijing. For a firsthand account of this event, see D. C. Hopson, British Chargé d'Affaires in Beijing, to George Brown, 8 September 1967, PREM 13/1966, Public Records Office, Kew, London (hereafter cited as PRO). In late January 1967, a large group of Red Guards began a series of continuous demonstrations around the French embassy in Beijing. The Red Guards shouted through loudspeakers at all hours of the day and night, they restricted the movement of the ambassador, and they threatened to attack the embassy grounds. See Lucien Paye à Paris, 31 January 1967; Paye à Maurice Couve de Murville, 16 June 1967, Série: Asie, 1956–1967, Sous-série: Chine, Volume: 536, Les archives du ministère des affaires étrangères, Paris, France (hereafter cited as Quai d'Orsay); Note, 4 July 1967, Série: Asie, 1956–1967, Sous-série: Chine, Volume: 537, Quai d'Orsay. For an account of Red Guard attacks on East German diplomatic offices, see Hegen an Ulbricht et al., 1. February 1967, FBS 363/15322, Walter Ulbricht Nachlaß, Archiv für der DDR und Stiftung Archiv der Parteien und Massenorganisationen der DDR, Berlin-Lichterfelde (hereafter cited as SAPMO).

37. On the origins of the Cultural Revolution and its disruptive consequences for Chinese foreign policy, see Suri, *Power and Protest*, 114–121, 206–212. See also Tucker, "Threats, Opportunities, and Frustrations in East Asia," 107–110; Arthur Waldron, "From Nonexistent to Almost Normal: U.S.-China Relations in the 1960s," in *The Diplomacy of the Crucial Decade: American Foreign Relations During the 1960s*, ed. Diane B. Kunz (New York: Columbia University Press, 1994), 237–242; Yawei Liu, "The United States According to Mao Zedong: Chinese-American Relations, 1893–1976" (Ph.D. diss., Emory University, 1996), 435–443.

38. Barbara Barnouin and Yu Changgen, *Chinese Foreign Policy during the Cultural Revolution* (London: Kegan Paul, 1998), 57–62, quotation on 60; Kuo-kang Shao, *Zhou Enlai and the Foundations of Chinese Foreign Policy* (New York: St. Martin's Press, 1996), 196–197.

39. Alfred Jenkins to Walt Rostow 16 September 1966, *FRUS*, 1964–1968, 30:388–389.

40. Walt Rostow to President Johnson, 9 January 1967, ibid., 499–500. On America's discreet overtures for improved Sino-American contacts after July 1966, see Memorandum from James C. Thomson Jr. to Walt Rostow, 4 August 1966, ibid., 364–366; Action Memorandum from the Assistant Secretary of State for East Asian and Pacific Affairs (William Bundy) et al. to Secretary of State Dean Rusk, 1 December 1966, ibid., 471–475; William Bundy to Dean Rusk, 30 December 1966, ibid., 492–494.

41. Telegram from the Embassy in Poland to the Department of State, 7 September 1966, ibid., 383–386, quotations on 385–386. See also Telegram from Embassy in Poland to the Department of State, 25 January 1967, ibid., 509–512.

42. Shao, *Zhou Enlai and the Foundations of Chinese Foreign Policy*,

196–197. Zhou's statements do not contradict the evidence that Beijing contemplated a direct military confrontation with the United States in Vietnam. According to Qiang Zhai, in June 1965 Communist China pledged to deploy land forces *if* American soldiers invaded North Vietnam. If, however, the United States refrained from full-scale attack on the Hanoi government, Beijing advised the North Vietnamese and the National Liberation Front to fight on their own, with indirect support from the mainland. See Qiang Zhai, *China and the Vietnam Wars, 1950–1975* (Chapel Hill: University of North Carolina Press, 2000), 134.

43. Shao, *Zhou Enlai and the Foundations of Chinese Foreign Policy*, 197.

44. See Memorandum by the Board of National Estimates, Central Intelligence Agency, 23 September 1966, *FRUS, 1964–1968*, 30:401; Alfred Jenkins to Walt Rostow, 6 March 1967, ibid., 527–530.

45. On Chinese–West German contacts in 1967 and 1968, see Suri, *Power and Protest*, 226–228.

46. Telegram from the Embassy in Poland to the Department of State, 8 January 1968, *FRUS, 1964–1968*, 30:630–632; Letter from Ambassador Gronouski to Secretary of State Rusk, 11 January 1968, ibid., 632–634.

47. Conversation between Mao Zedong and E. F. Hill, 28 November 1968, *Cold War International History Project Bulletin* 11 (Winter 1998): 161.

48. Winzer an Ulbricht et al., December 1968, FBS 363/15322, Ulbricht Nachlaß, SAPMO.

49. Sir D. Trench, Hong Kong to Commonwealth Office, 26 November 1967, FCO 21/210, PRO; Trench to Commonwealth Office, 25 November 1967, FCO 21/210, PRO. One should note that the Chinese government did not show the same restraint in Macao. On this island—under a Portuguese colonial governor—Beijing helped to orchestrate continual demonstrations and riots. Faced with an ultimatum from the mainland in April 1968, Lisbon's representative ceded most authority over commerce and immigration in Macao to Chinese authorities. See "The Portuguese Capitulation in Macao," circa April 1968, FCO 21/233, PRO.

50. E. T. Davies, Hong Kong, to R. Whitney, Beijing, 15 December 1967, FCO 21/210, PRO. See also "The Cultural Revolution: Spring 1968," FCO 21/25, PRO; handwritten diary of British Foreign Minister Michael Stewart, 13 May 1968, Number: 8/1/5, Collection: STWT, Papers of Michael Stewart, Churchill Archives Center, Churchill College, Cambridge, England.

51. Barnouin and Changgen, *Chinese Foreign Policy during the Cultural Revolution*, 63–65; Shao, *Zhou Enlai and the Foundations of Chinese Foreign Policy*, 197–199.

52. The President's Meeting with China Experts, 2 February 1968, folder: February 2, 1968 Meeting with China Experts, box 2, Meeting Notes File, LBJL. Although Johnson expressed a desire for improved relations with Beijing, he also spoke of China as a common threat to the United States and the Soviet Union. In particular, the president described the Chinese as "cocky" and "chesty." See Record of Meeting between President Johnson, Anatoly Dobrynin, Averell Harriman, and Walt Rostow, 31 March 1968, 6:05 pm, folder: Rusk-Dobrynin, box 11, National Security File, Files of Walt W. Rostow, LBJL. This discussion took place just before Johnson went on television to announce that he would not seek reelection in 1968.

53. Harry McPherson, Oral History, Interview 5, Tape 2, p. 14, LBJL.

54. On this point, see Suri, *Power and Protest*, 232–245.

55. See Thomas Alan Schwartz, *Lyndon Johnson and Europe: In the Shadow of Vietnam* (Cambridge, Mass.: Harvard University Press, 2003), 16–26. On Johnson's role during the Cuban missile crisis, see Ernest R. May and Philip D. Zelikow, eds., *The Kennedy Tapes: Inside the White House during the Cuban Missile Crisis* (Cambridge, Mass.: Harvard University Press, 1997); Sheldon M. Stern, *Averting "The Final Failure": John F. Kennedy and the Secret Cuban Missile Crisis Meetings* (Stanford, Calif.: Stanford University Press, 2003).

56. As late as June 1967, members of the Johnson administration continued to refer to the acrimony that resulted from the Vienna Summit. See Memorandum by Zbigniew Brzezinski, Policy Planning Council 16 June 1967, *FRUS, 1964–1968*, 14:495; Walt Rostow to President Johnson, 21 June 1967, ibid., 500. In a clear reference to the Vienna Summit, McGeorge Bundy (now a special consultant to the president) warned Johnson that in meeting with the Soviet leader, "we don't want him to miss your strength." Bundy to Johnson, 22 June 1967, *FRUS, 1964–1968*, 14:507. Bundy and others in the White House recognized that Khrushchev had come away from the Vienna Summit thinking that President Kennedy was weak. This perception of Kennedy's weakness contributed to Khrushchev's subsequent belligerence around Berlin and Cuba. See Aleksandr Fursenko and Timothy Naftali, *"One Hell of a Gamble": Khrushchev, Castro, and Kennedy, 1958–1964* (New York: Norton, 1997), 129–134.

57. See Robert McNamara to President Johnson, 21 June 1967, *FRUS, 1964–1968*, 14:497–498; McGeorge Bundy to President Johnson, 21 June 1967, ibid., 498–499; Walt Rostow to President Johnson, 21 June 1967, ibid., 500–502.

58. Dean Rusk to the Department of State, 22 June 1967, *FRUS, 1964–1968*, 14:510–512. During his conversation with Rusk on 22 June, Kosygin suggested that the leaders of the two superpowers meet in a "farmer's house." "If they were in the Soviet Union," Kosygin explained, "this could be easily arranged for a meeting of a few hours."

59. Telephone Conversation between President Johnson and Former President Dwight Eisenhower, 25 June 1967, 9:44 P.M., *FRUS, 1964–1968*, 14:558. For detailed accounts of the Glassboro discussions, see ibid., 514–556.

60. Walt Rostow to President Johnson, 7 June 1968, *FRUS, 1964–1968*, 14: 649. A published footnote to this document explains that on 4 June 1968 Rostow wrote Johnson, asking, "Do you wish me to have an unofficial, exploratory word with Dobrynin on a Soviet trip, which you mentioned the other day?" Johnson responded: "Ask Rusk to give judgment & explore." Rostow's note indicates that this was originally the president's suggestion.

61. Memorandum of Conversation between Dean Rusk and Anatoly Dobrynin, 1 July 1968, *FRUS, 1964–68*, 14:655.

62. Ibid. During his 1 July 1968 conversation with Rusk, Dobrynin revealed that Richard Nixon, then a candidate for U.S. president, "has approached the Soviet government on three occasions about a visit to Moscow following the Republican Convention." Like Johnson, Nixon saw potential public relations value in a meeting with Soviet leaders. See also Memorandum of Conversation between Rusk and Dobrynin, 15 August 1968, ibid., 677.

63. On the Prague Spring and the crisis of Soviet authority in Czechoslovakia, see H. Gordon Skilling, *Czechoslovakia's Interrupted Revolution*

(Princeton, N.J.: Princeton University Press, 1976); Kieran Williams, *The Prague Spring and Its Aftermath: Czechoslovak Politics, 1968–1970* (New York: Cambridge University Press, 1997); Suri, *Power and Protest*, 194–206.

64. Record of meeting with President Johnson, Clark Clifford, Dean Rusk, and Tom Johnson, 29 July 1968, *FRUS, 1964–1968*, 14:666. This account is based on a tape recording of the meeting and a transcript prepared at the time by the president's secretary.

65. Ibid., 666–667.

66. Ibid., 667. On Johnson's maneuverings for a return to the presidential race in late 1968, see Dallek, *Flawed Giant*, 569–575.

67. Ibid., 669–670. In this meeting Clifford referred to the Vienna summit as a "calamity."

68. Summary of Meeting between President Johnson, Walt Rostow, and Soviet Ambassador Dobrynin, 20 August 1968, *FRUS, 1964–1968*, 17:236–241, quotation on 239. This account is based on a tape recording of the meeting. See also Notes of Cabinet Meeting, 22 August 1968, ibid., 248–249. On Dobrynin's surprise at Johnson's indifferent reaction to the Soviet invasion and the president's continued push for a Soviet-American summit, see Anatoly Dobrynin, *In Confidence: Moscow's Ambassador to America's Six Cold War Presidents, 1962–1986* (New York: Random House, 1995), 177–186. Johnson's under secretary of state for political affairs, Eugene Rostow, later explained that he and other policymakers in Washington worried most about the international anarchy that emerged as the authority of both superpowers, and especially the Soviet Union in Eastern Europe, began to "dissolve." "It's a nightmare situation," he warned. Eugene Rostow Oral History, 2 December 1968, p. 24, LBJL. See also Telegram from Walt Rostow to President Johnson, 31 August 1968, *FRUS, 1964–1968*, 17:263–264.

69. Instructions for the Ambassador to the Soviet Union, 5 September 1968, *FRUS, 1964–1968*, 14:691–692.

70. Walt Rostow to President Johnson, 9 September 1968, ibid., 695.

71. For a defense of Johnson's attempts to arrange a superpower summit after the Soviet invasion of Czechoslovakia, see Schwartz, *Lyndon Johnson and Europe*, 217–222.

72. Clifford predicted this in July 1968. See Record of meeting with President Johnson, Clark Clifford, Dean Rusk, and Tom Johnson, 29 July 1968, *FRUS, 1964–1968*, 14:674.

73. Henry Kissinger to President-elect Richard Nixon, 18 December 1968, ibid., 790. Johnson tried to convince Nixon to endorse a summit between Kosygin and the outgoing president. See Walt Rostow to President Johnson, 14 November 1968, ibid., 754–755; President Johnson to President-elect Nixon, 25 November 1968, ibid., 761–762. This is evidence of Johnson's desperation for a public meeting with Kosygin and his self-delusion about Nixon's likely reaction. As a seasoned politician, Johnson knew very well that no president-elect would want to see his predecessor undertake a superpower summit meeting just before the transition in American leadership.

74. Henry Kissinger to President-elect Richard Nixon, 18 December 1968, ibid., 790.

75. For a fuller elaboration of this argument, see Suri, *Power and Protest*, 213–259.

76. See note 73.

4 | An Ominous Moment: Lyndon Johnson and the Six Day War

Peter L. Hahn

AT 4:35 A.M. ON 5 JUNE 1967, National Security Adviser Walt W. Rostow awakened President Lyndon B. Johnson to report that an Arab-Israeli war had erupted. Johnson recalled in his memoirs that this news deeply disturbed him because he had worked hard to avert such hostilities, which seemed "potentially far more dangerous than the war in Southeast Asia." His concern peaked at 8:00 A.M., when Secretary of Defense Robert S. McNamara reported that Soviet premier Aleksei N. Kosygin had activated the "hotline," the Teletype link established after the Cuban missile crisis to enable Soviet and U.S. leaders to communicate instantly in a crisis. McNamara's words that "the hot line is up," Johnson recalled, "were ominous."[1]

After 1945, American policymakers devoted increasing attention to the Middle East. Because of the cold war, they deemed it crucial to deny the Soviets political or military influence in the region and to keep its vast oil resources and military bases in the Western camp. As British power waned, the United States accepted new responsibilities to protect the region's security and pro-Western alignment. The establishment of Israel in 1948 triggered an Arab-Israeli war in 1948–1949 and an enduring conflict that U.S. officials sought, in principle, to solve. Independence movements in the remnants of Britain's and France's Middle East empires spawned revolutionary nationalism and political instability that threatened to undermine Western interests across the Middle East.[2]

Having long recognized the Middle East as a potential source of regional and global conflict, the Johnson administration had pursued three broad objectives there prior to 1967. First, U.S. officials underscored the importance of practicing anti-Soviet containment. Johnson affirmed the doctrine of containment on a global scale and authorized military intervention in Vietnam to stop the spread of communism in Asia. His advisers cautioned that the Soviet Union also sought to gain influence in the Middle East by supporting revolutionary, anti-Western regimes and political movements. "The USSR is making a new push in the Middle East," Harold H. Saunders of the National Security Council (NSC) staff cautioned in June 1966, and is "gaining ground" in turning the United Arab Republic (UAR), Syria, and Iraq against the West. In view of the region's oil resources, military facilities, lines of communication, and human resources, U.S. officials resolved to stop such Soviet expansionism.[3]

Second, consistent with their containment objective, U.S. officials sought political stability in the Middle East. They aimed to preserve the territorial integrity of all states in the region against external attack, especially by the Soviet Union. They also sought to ensure the survival of Israel against Arab opposition. To safeguard Western oil interests, they worked to preserve the conservative monarchy in Saudi Arabia. To provide a buffer against the spread of anti-Western Arab influence or the renewal of conflict between Israel and radical Arab states, they bolstered Jordan with financial aid. State Department officials considered the $500 million dispensed to Jordan in 1957–1967, for instance, "a sort of insurance premium against an explosion." In addition, U.S. officials sought to reduce Arab-Israeli tensions over territory, fresh water, arms supply, and the status of Palestinian refugees, and to prevent the recurrence of Arab-Israeli war or the eruption of hostilities between Arab powers.[4]

Third, to promote Middle East regional stability, U.S. officials aimed to maintain a delicate balance between antagonistic factions in the region. To facilitate their quest for regional peace, they sought to remain on friendly terms with both Israel and its Arab neighbors. While outwardly supportive of Israel, the administration initially denied Israeli requests for arms supply on the reasoning that it would trigger Soviet arms supply to Arab states. The administration also sought to negotiate a resolution of a UAR-Saudi clash in Yemen. "Carrying water on both shoulders sometimes seems immoral and is always difficult," Saunders explained, in reference to the U.S. practice of maintaining friendly relations with all powers. But the only alternative was "being driven to choose half our interests, sacrifice half and let the USSR pick up our losses."[5]

Before 1967, the U.S. quest to promote containment, stability, and balance in the Middle East affected the quality of U.S. relations with the states of the region. U.S.-Israeli political relations appeared to rest on solid foundations of friendship and cooperation. President Johnson entered the White House reputed to be a longtime friend of Israel. In 1957, he had led Senate opposition to President Dwight D. Eisenhower's threat of sanctions against Israel, and in 1961 he had told Prime Minister David Ben-Gurion, "I am sure you know that you have many friends here." Days after becoming president, Johnson assured Foreign Minister Golda Meir and other Israeli officials that "the United States will continue its warm friendship with Israel." In June 1964, Johnson told Prime Minister Levi Eshkol that he personally was "foursquare behind Israel on all matters that affected their vital security interests."[6]

Under Johnson's leadership, the United States seemed to become closer to Israel. "No one who has an insider's view," Robert Komer of the NSC staff observed in 1965, "could contest the proposition that the US is 100% behind the security and wellbeing of Israel. We are Israel's chief supporters, bankers, direct and indirect arms purveyors, and ultimate guarantors." Komer and Golda Meir affirmed that "US/Israeli relations were on a solid footing." In words echoed in several policy statements, Saunders noted in 1966 that "Israel is a success and clearly here to stay—partly because of our help."[7]

Yet U.S.-Israeli relations were not without problems. Johnson vigorously promoted nuclear nonproliferation in the Middle East, for instance, and he deeply regretted Eshkol's refusal to renounce nuclear weapons. "The President has no give" on this issue, Komer noted in 1965. "For Israel to go nuclear would create the gravest crisis in US/Israeli relations." In addition, the Johnson administration affirmed the traditional U.S. opposition to Israel's policy of conducting major reprisals against neighboring states for terrorist attacks that apparently originated on their soil. When Israel launched a reprisal against Jordan in November 1966, U.S. officials strongly censured the action as a blow to the stability of the area.[8]

The tension in the U.S.-Israeli relationship stemmed in part from a conflict between domestic political pressure to favor Israel and State Department resolve to practice impartiality. State Department and NSC officials warned Johnson that favoritism toward Israel would imperil U.S. interests in the Arab states. The United States should establish a "reasonable balance" between Israel and the Arab states, they advised, "consistent with our special concern for Israel." The State Department argued that a "partisan policy in favor of Israel, cannot benefit Israel, because the West's ability to help Israel is in direct relation to the West's influence with the Arabs." Komer encouraged Johnson to insist that Israel "not . . . keep trying to force us to an all-out pro-Israeli policy" in light of "our Arab interests and our common aim of keeping the Soviets out of the Middle East."[9]

The Johnson administration also sought, with partial success, to nurture close relations with Arab states. Admitting that he was attracted to Jordan by "my deep interest in the Bible," Johnson assured King Hussein that he sought "close and cordial relations" with his country. Likewise, the president assured Saudi crown prince Faisal that "we are resolved as ever to stand solidly and steadfastly beside our valued friends in the area, including Saudi Arabia." U.S. relations with the UAR, by contrast, remained problematic. Johnson invited Premier Gamal Abdel Nasser to continue the "constructive cooperation" that developed between the two states in the early 1960s, and he applauded Nasser's willingness to accept U.S. initiatives on nuclear nonproliferation. But U.S.-UAR tensions mounted when Nasser refused U.S. initiatives to promote Arab-Israeli settlement, issued anti-U.S. propaganda, intervened in the civil war in Yemen, and accepted Soviet arms supply.[10]

U.S. decision making about arms supply to the Middle East revealed the complexity and difficulty of the U.S. quest to promote containment, stability, and balance in the Middle East. Citing Soviet arms supplies to the UAR, Israel requested permission to purchase U.S. tanks in 1964. Although he sensed that such a sale would have earned political rewards at home during an election year, Johnson initially declined the request on the hunch that it would undermine relations with Arab powers. Then, in 1965, U.S. officials deemed it essential to provide tanks to Jordan, both to enhance the stature of King Hussein and to deter him from accepting such weapons from the Soviet Union. To the modest disappointment of Israeli leaders, Johnson decided to offer tanks to both Israel and Jordan. Similarly, in 1966, Johnson sold advanced military aircraft to both Israel and Jordan to counter Soviet sales of such weapons to the UAR. Such arms deals, Saunders noted, were contrived to achieve "a deterrent balance" in the region.[11]

By early 1967, the Johnson administration's policy in the Middle East faced several obstacles. For one, Soviet political overtures to the UAR, Syria, and Iraq challenged the ability of the United States to remain friendly to those states, indirectly threatened the integrity of Saudi Arabia and Jordan, and portended a resurgence of Arab-Israeli conflict. Apparently with the endorsement of Soviet leaders, Syrian officials condoned terrorism against Israel as a means of demoralizing its population and discouraging immigration there. Palestinian refugees and other Arab nationalists directed some of their anti-Israeli passions against the traditional U.S. support of the Jewish state. Although relieved to have avoided crises in the region since 1963, administration officials recognized that conditions might worsen quickly.[12]

Political conditions in the Middle East indeed deteriorated rapidly in 1967. A series of incidents along Israel's borders with the UAR and Syria in late 1966 and early 1967 stoked tension. Infiltrators into Israel committed deadly acts of violence, Israel responded with forceful reprisals, United Nations (UN) authorities proved unable to settle tensions, and hostile rhetoric and passions escalated on all sides. Israeli fighters engaged and downed Syrian jets on 7 April, and in May a wave of violence in northern Israel prompted an Israeli threat to occupy Damascus and change the Syrian government. Amid reports that Israeli soldiers had mobilized for such an attack, the UAR and Syria consulted under their mutual defense pact. The Johnson administration counseled caution on all parties.[13]

The border tension escalated into a crisis on 16 May, when Nasser expelled the UN troops that had policed the Sinai since the end of the Suez-Sinai War in 1957. UAR forces occupied the evacuated UN observation posts on Israel's border and at Sharm al-Sheikh and advanced six hundred tanks and three infantry divisions into the Sinai. Rumors immediately surfaced that Israel would launch a preemptive strike against this provocation. Rostow advised Johnson that Nasser had acted in response to criticism from fellow Arab leaders that he had failed to defend Syria and Jordan against Israeli reprisals, and that the move would indeed deter Israeli reprisals against Syria. Because Israel remained militarily superior, however, Israeli preemption against the UAR posed the greatest immediate danger to regional peace. Johnson should urge Eshkol, Rostow advised, "not to put a match to the fuse."[14]

In this initial phase of the crisis, Johnson urged restraint on all powers. He asked Israel, Syria, and the UAR to cooperate with UN Secretary General U Thant, who visited Cairo in search of a peaceful resolution to the crisis. He advised Syria to curtail exfiltration of terrorists to Israel, the UAR to readmit UN soldiers to the Sinai, and Israel to refrain from a preemptive attack on the UAR. Secretary of State Dean Rusk warned Nasser that an unintended and punishing war might result from his maneuvers. Johnson wrote to Eshkol "to emphasize in the strongest terms the need to avoid any action on your side which would add further to the violence and tension in your area." Johnson also backpedaled from various U.S. commitments to Israeli security and instead reiterated the Tripartite Declaration of 1950, in which the United States had pledged to counter aggression from any quarter.[15]

Johnson maintained this position despite pleas from Israel for a security assurance. In view of Syrian terror, UAR provocation, and Soviet backing of the Arab states, Eshkol asked Johnson on 18 May to guarantee Israeli security publicly and to order a nearby U.S. destroyer to visit Eilat as a show of support. But U.S. officials rejected these requests on the grounds that they would confirm UAR allegations of U.S.-Israeli collusion and "provide a propaganda horse for the Arabs to ride." Israeli foreign minister Abba Eban ridiculed Johnson's suggestion that Israel allow UN soldiers to patrol its side of the border as part of a settlement of the crisis. The UN had no credibility in Israel, Eban asserted. "U.N. personnel would be welcome as tourists but not as Israel's protectors."[16]

Initially, U.S. officials were confident that the Soviet Union would not exert strong influence in the Middle East crisis. Soon after Nasser expelled UN forces from the Sinai, Soviet envoys, consulted by the State Department, agreed that Arab-Israeli war ought to be discouraged. State Department intelligence officers considered but rejected the thesis that the Soviets would encourage a Middle East war as means of hampering U.S. operations in Vietnam, on the rationale that such a war might escalate out of control and would likely lead to an embarrassing defeat of Moscow's Arab client states. But U.S. officials also expected the Soviet Union to offer little support of Western diplomacy to keep the peace because such support would alienate Arab leaders.[17]

The Middle East crisis deepened on 22 May, when Nasser closed the Straits of Tiran to Israeli shipping. UAR authorities declared that they would blockade the straits, stop and search ships, and seize strategic cargoes destined for Israel. Charging that such a blockade would imperil their military security and economic vitality, Israeli leaders threatened to fight to reopen the waterway. Other Arab leaders, including moderates such as King Hussein, warned that if the United States backed such action by Israel, then they would have to repudiate the United States in order to survive the public backlash. The Central Intelligence Agency (CIA) saw in Nasser's blockade a multipart gamble that the Soviets would back him, that the United States would refrain from intervention, that his army could defend itself in the Sinai, and that Israel would accept a UN-negotiated settlement rather than preempt. Such thinking convinced Lucius Battle that Nasser "had gone slightly insane," although Walt Rostow deemed Nasser's move "shrewd, but not mad."[18]

As tensions mounted, U.S. officials took four steps to head off war. First, Johnson promptly and publicly declared the UAR blockade "illegal" and "potentially disastrous to the cause of peace" and urged its reversal. Rostow told UAR ambassador Mustapha Kamel that under international law Israel had the right to send ships through the straits, that the UAR's closure constituted aggression, and that Nasser's action might cause "grave consequences." Within days, Johnson sent former secretary of the Treasury Robert Anderson to appeal to Nasser in person to resolve the crisis by lifting the blockade, but Nasser refused to desist.[19]

Second, U.S. officials encouraged the UAR and Israel to cooperate with UN diplomacy to end the crisis. "I want to play every card in the UN," Johnson told the NSC on 24 May. U.S. officials encouraged U Thant to visit Cairo, where he secured a pledge from Nasser not to attack Israel, and they endorsed Thant's special appeal, issued from New York on 27 May, for all powers to show restraint. Eban told Rusk, however, that Israeli officials "have absolutely no faith in the possibility of anything useful coming out of the U.N." On 2 June, Israeli ambassador Avraham Harman advised that the "farce in the United Nations be ended."[20]

Third, U.S. officials tried to restrain Israel from launching a military attack designed to reopen the Straits of Tiran. Johnson and his advisers realized that such a feat would require them to perform a delicate balancing act. If, at one extreme, they offered Israel no support, or if, at the other extreme, they firmly endorsed Israel's position on the straits, they might trigger the same outcome, namely, Israeli military action against the UAR. Such action would place the United States in a difficult situation, given that domestic political support of Israel would make it hard to fulfill U.S. pledges to counter intraregional aggression. Yet not stopping Israeli action, as ambassador to Cairo Richard Nolte warned, would incur "heavy cost to us in terms of political, economic, and other relationships in [the] Arab world." U.S. officials resolved to head off Israeli preemption both by warning firmly against the use of force and by offering alternative means to guarantee freedom of the seas.[21]

U.S. officials tried to implement this delicate policy in meetings with Eban, who visited Washington on 25–26 May. "We put the case against preemptive strikes to Eban very hard," Rusk wrote to Johnson after meeting the foreign minister, "both from the military and the political points of view. . . . Preemptive action by Israel would cause extreme difficulty for the United States." Johnson assured Eban on 26 May that "we will pursue vigorously any and all possible measures to keep the Strait open." The record of conversation reveals, however, that "with emphasis and solemnity, the President repeated twice, Israel will not be alone unless it decides to go alone." Johnson also refused to reissue a security guarantee on the grounds that he lacked congressional support and constitutional authority, without which a pledge "wouldn't be worth ten cents and Israel could get no help from the United States." Johnson also wrote to Eshkol that "it is essential that Israel not take any preemptive military action and thereby make itself responsible for the initiation of hostilities." On 30 May, Eshkol indicated that he would comply for "a further limited period."[22]

Fourth, U.S. officials decided to contest Nasser's blockade of the Straits of Tiran by organizing concerted action by Western maritime powers to break it. According to a plan conceived in the State and Defense departments, naval forces of various Western powers would assume positions in the Red Sea and pledge to protect merchant ships that plied the straits bound for Israel. Other Western naval vessels would concentrate in the eastern Mediterranean to deter Nasser from resisting the operation in the straits and to provide reinforcement if shooting erupted. "I want to see [British prime minister Harold] Wilson and [French president Charles] de Gaulle out there with their ships all lined up, too," Johnson told the NSC on 24 May. After discussing this plan with several allied powers, U.S. diplomats estimated that they would need three weeks to prepare an international agreement and put the plan in motion.[23]

The U.S. effort to head off war by appealing to the UAR to reverse course, endorsing UN diplomacy, restraining Israel, and organizing the maritime operation immediately encountered a series of problems. For starters, Israeli insecurity mounted quickly. Israeli intelligence predicted a sharp rise in infiltration raids under UAR protection and reported that UAR units in the Sinai were armed with chemical weapons. The Israeli people panicked over rumors that their country might be annihilated. "A surprise aerial attack on Israel could be expected at any moment," Israel Defense Forces (IDF) officials told U.S. Ambassador Walworth Barbour on 27 May, "knocking out their [Israeli] airfields and rendering a response ineffective." In this context, the historian Avi Shlaim notes, Eshkol's decision to wait for Western diplomacy to reopen the straits nearly provoked "an open rebellion" among military officers who favored immediate preemption. Such concerns rose after King Hussein flew to Cairo to sign a mutual defense treaty with the UAR on 30 May. In the absence of an ironclad U.S. security guarantee or promise to break the Gulf of Aqaba blockade, Eshkol wrote to Johnson, additional U.S. appeals for restraint "will lack any moral or logical basis."[24]

Second, administration officials realized that the task of organizing the maritime operation faced severe obstacles at home and among allied powers. Rusk and McNamara agreed that Johnson must secure congressional approval before placing troops in harm's way in the Middle East, but, because "the problem of 'Tonkin Gulfitis' remains serious," advised the president to delay asking for such approval until the UN exhaustively discussed the issue. Moreover, State Department negotiations with other maritime states on the logistics of implementing the Red Sea operation hit several bottlenecks. By 4 June, only seven states of fourteen approached pledged to adhere to the plan.[25]

Third, U.S. officials became painfully aware that the maritime plan faced political, economic, and military problems. Ambassador Nolte predicted with certainty that the UAR would resist blockade runners with "solid support [of] Soviet bloc and entire Afr[o]-Asian world as well as all Arabs, . . . unless faced by overwhelming military force." Retired ambassador Charles W. Yost, dispatched to Cairo to consult contacts in the UAR Foreign Ministry, advised that the maritime operation would not reopen the strait unless the United States assembled a "military force which would be out of proportion to real US interests at stake and would have most damaging repercussions on [the] US position throughout the Arab world." Tough words or financial sanctions designed to force UAR capitulation "will have precisely [the] contrary effect" of feeding Arab unity and provoking anti-U.S. demonstrations.[26]

The maritime operation also faced economic problems. Western powers had few financial levers to use against Arab states, a task force of officials from the State and Defense departments, White House staff, and CIA warned, but the Arab states "together would have powerful economic weapons to use against the Atlantic allies." If fighting erupted between the United States and the UAR, the task force concluded, the "oil-producing nations would take some action against the United States, ranging from scattered sabotage to sequestration of oil holdings and selective prohibition of exports." If those states seized Western oil firms, the United States would lose $1 billion per year in foreign trade and billions of dollars in capital investments, Britain would lose $1 billion, and international markets would be devastated. If they embargoed oil supplies to Europe or aviation fuels destined for the war in Vietnam, the United States would need to draw from its own reserves and impose rationing at home.[27]

The Pentagon also identified military reasons not to challenge Nasser's blockade. Although the Sixth Fleet projected a powerful presence in the Mediterranean, Chairman of the Joint Chiefs of Staff (JCS) General Earle G. Wheeler told the NSC on 24 May, available land forces included only fourteen hundred Marines stationed in Naples, a three-day sail from the likely zone of operations. U.S. antisubmarine warfare units in the Mediterranean, which would be needed against UAR submarines in the Red Sea, were unable to transit the Suez Canal, and the nearest alternative unit was based in Singapore, two weeks' travel time. Wheeler also anticipated that Turkey, Libya, and Spain might refuse to permit U.S. forces to use bases in their countries to support operations against the UAR. On 2 June, the JCS estimated that the navy needed thirty-one days to reposition ships from its Atlantic fleet to the Red Sea, and considered such a move "operationally unsound" because it would divide the Atlantic fleet, confine the task force to a small operating area, depend on an extended line of communication, and force a "reduction/degradation in other US commitments." Forces currently east of Suez could try to break the UAR blockade immediately, but "the capability of these forces to prevail, if attacked by major UAR forces, is doubtful." In addition, military action would not guarantee a free and open waterway.[28]

By early June, U.S. officials realized that they were boxed in by an impossible situation. Johnson and his top advisers remained convinced that Israel would escalate to war unless the UAR rescinded its blockade of the Straits of Tiran. Yet State Department officials warned that the maritime plan to reopen the straits appeared to Arab leaders as a U.S. capitulation to Israel, forced the pro-Western Arab states to endorse Nasser's position, eroded U.S. influence in the Arab world, and opened the door to Soviet influence. Ambassador to Syria Hugh H. Smythe considered the maritime plan "foredoomed" because it would lead quickly to U.S.-British military conflict with the UAR. He and other envoys to Arab states urged a "hands-off" policy. If the United States endorsed Israel's position in the conflict and then either Israel or the Western powers used force against the UAR, ambassador to Jordan Findley Burns Jr. added, "this will wreck every interest we have in North Africa and the Middle East and destroy our influence with the Arabs for years to come." Defense Department and CIA analysts warned that sending an unescorted tanker through the straits, let alone one escorted by the U.S. Navy, would trigger massive anti-U.S. propaganda by the UAR. "Nasser could severely damage the United States and West Europe, politically and economically," Deputy Assistant Secretary of Defense Townsend Hoopes noted, "without firing a shot."[29]

In such a situation, U.S. officials naturally considered the advantages of simply allowing Israel to escalate to hostilities. In contrast to the tactical difficulties of U.S. military operations in the Gulf of Aqaba, General Wheeler reported to the NSC as early as 24 May, "the Israelis can hold their own" in a war against the Arab states. Saunders suggested that if the United States had allowed Israel to preempt on 21 May, a better outcome might have resulted, namely, the defeat of

Nasser without U.S. involvement. "We ought to consider admitting that we have failed," Saunders suggested with some reservation, "and allow fighting to ensue." Rostow reported to Johnson that a Belgian official preferred letting Israel attack the UAR over accepting the burden of opening the straits with force. State Department officials considered the 1 June appointment of Moshe Dayan, who had commanded Israeli forces during the invasion of Egypt in 1956, to the position of minister of defense to be a sign that action would follow. In reference to Dayan and other Israeli hawks, Rostow told Johnson that "these boys are going to be hard to hold a week from now."[30]

Some scholars assert that in late May and early June, Johnson deliberately signaled to Israel that he would not object if it initiated military action against the UAR. William B. Quandt argues that despite Johnson's official protestations against war, the president subtly signaled Eshkol, in messages delivered through unofficial channels after 26 May, that he would not object if Israel preempted. In Quandt's view, Johnson abandoned his "red light" position of categorical opposition to Israeli action for a "yellow light" position of not opposing, while not specifically endorsing, an Israeli attack. "As for most motorists," Quandt concludes, to the Israelis "the yellow light was tantamount to a green one." Avi Shlaim observes that when Mossad director Meir Amit asked in early June how the United States would react to Israeli preemption, Secretary of Defense McNamara "gave Israel a green light to take military action against Egypt."[31]

As persuasive a case as Quandt and Shlaim make, three caveats limit the "yellow light" and "green light" theses. First, archival evidence demonstrates that Johnson remained skittish about Israeli preemption long after he might have flashed a yellow or green light to Eshkol. On 3 June, for instance, Johnson notified Eshkol of his diplomatic efforts to reopen the straits, confirmed his commitment to the survival of Israel and the territorial integrity of all Middle East states, and urged Eshkol to refrain from aggression. Rusk urged U.S. envoys in the Middle East to seek urgently some means to avert war. Even if Israel seemed determined to fight, he observed, "we cannot throw up our hands and say . . . let them fight while we try to remain neutral." "We are sorry this [war] has taken place," Johnson told the NSC on 7 June, two days after Israel attacked the UAR. "By the time we get through with all the festering problems we are going to wish the war had not happened." Johnson "has never believed that this war was anything else than a mistake by the Israelis," Rostow recalled months later. "A brilliant quick victory he never regarded as an occasion for elation or satisfaction. He so told the Israeli representatives on a number of occasions."[32]

Second, it seems plausible that Johnson expected Israel to initiate a test of Nasser's blockade of the Straits of Tiran rather than launch a full-scale attack on UAR forces in the Sinai. NSC officials apparently anticipated that Israel would send a ship into the straits on 11 June and would respond forcefully if the UAR stopped it. Thus they resolved to seek a compromise solution to the standoff by polishing the maritime plan or getting Nasser to rescind the blockade before that deadline. Apparently to deter Nasser from enforcing his blockade militarily, Rusk and State Department officials sent two messages to Nasser on 3 June reaffirming U.S. opposition to intraregional aggression. "The United States strongly opposes aggression by anyone in the area, in any form," Assistant Secretary of State for Near Eastern Affairs Lucius Battle assured Nasser. "Our future actions in the area will be firmly based on this policy which has benefited Egypt in the past." It seems doubtful that the State Department would have issued such assurances had it known that Israel would invade the Sinai on 5 June.[33]

Third, the legacy of U.S.-Israeli security relations and the evidence of U.S.-Israeli differences of judgment during the crisis of 1967 suggest that Israel would have launched a preemptive strike against the UAR regardless of the U.S. position. Israeli leaders were convinced by 5 June that UAR forces in the Sinai, armed with tanks and chemical weapons, posed a dire threat to their national survival, especially if the UAR launched a sudden air strike. It is reasonable to assume that they were prepared to address this threat by means of their own choosing regardless of the opinion of the United States, which was preoccupied in Vietnam and which occasionally pursued security objectives that clashed with Israel's. In several previous situations, most notably the Suez-Sinai War of 1956–1957, Israeli leaders took action to defend their national interests in defiance of U.S. advice. "You should not assume that the United States can order Israel not to fight for what it considers to be its most vital interests," Rusk cabled U.S. ambassadors on 3 June. "The 'holy war' psychology of the Arab world is matched by an apocalyptic psychology within Israel. Israel may make a decision that it must resort to force to protect its vital interests."[34]

The Israeli attack on the UAR on 5 June quickly escalated into a major war of territorial conquest. Eshkol justified the initial move as a defense against Nasser's "extraordinary catalogue of aggression." Rather than depend on the UN, he argued, Israel would "rely on the courage and determination of our soldiers and citizens." On the battlefields, Israeli forces demolished the UAR air force and rapidly occupied the Sinai. When Jordan and Syria entered the fray on the UAR's side, Israel delivered similar blows to their forces and occupied the West Bank and the Golan Heights. By the time the final cease-fire took effect on 10 June, Israel had soundly defeated three enemies and occupied enormous portions of their territory.[35]

U.S.-Arab relations deteriorated because of the war. Within hours of the outbreak of fighting, Rostow declared to Arab chiefs of mission in Washington that Johnson had tried to prevent hostilities and sought to restore peace. As their military fortunes collapsed, however, various Arab leaders charged that U.S. warplanes actually participated in the Israeli aerial attacks against them. U.S. officials rejected these charges as specious and privately attributed them to scapegoating by leaders anxious to fortify their political reputations in the face of embarrassing military setbacks. In any case, anti-U.S. passions soared among the peoples of Arab countries, mobs threatened the safety of U.S. nationals, and Arab governments severed diplomatic relations with the United States.[36]

U.S.-Israeli relations also suffered setbacks during the Six Day War. On 8 June, Israeli warplanes attacked the *Liberty*, a U.S. Navy intelligence-gathering ship sailing off the coast of the UAR, killing thirty-four U.S. sailors. For reasons that remain mysterious, Johnson called off a counterstrike by nearby naval units. Israel later explained the incident as a result of errors in reconnaissance and communications and apologized for it, and Johnson accepted the apology and refrained from publicly investigating the episode.[37] Yet the attack angered many U.S. officials. Rusk reported to Eban "very strong feeling" in Congress over the matter. "There is no excuse for repeated attacks on a plainly marked U.S. naval vessel," an NSC official wrote. Israeli apologies "do not change the fact that this most unfortunate attack occurred."[38]

As the June War unfolded, the United States adopted a three-track policy. First, it sought to end the war as soon as possible. To accomplish this aim, U.S. officials pushed a simple cease-fire resolution through the UN Security Council on 6 June. They resisted a Soviet amendment ordering Israel to evacuate the territory it occupied, and the Soviets relented in light of Israel's mounting battlefield gains. U.S. officials argued to Israel that continued fighting would undermine King Hussein's authority and deliver Jordan to radical leaders. Israel "must look to its own interest in the Arab world," Rusk warned, and not allow the king to "go down the drain." Having occupied the West Bank and under pressure from the Soviet Union as well, Israel accepted a truce with Jordan on 7 June. U.S. officials also brokered a UAR-Israeli cease-fire on 8 June, after the IDF reached the Suez Canal and encircled UAR units in the Sinai. U.S. officials elicited Syrian acceptance of the cease-fire on 9 June, but the fighting continued at Israeli initiative. Ordered by Johnson to "put pressure on Israel to accept a cease fire," Under Secretary of State Nicholas deB. Katzenbach warned Ambassador Harman that Israel must comply because the Soviets were "busy saber rattling." Israel accepted the final cease-fire on 10 June.[39]

The Johnson administration's second major objective was to prevent Soviet political or military involvement in the war, which would seriously imperil Western interests in the Middle East and perhaps lead to a global conflict. In a series of "hotline" messages, Johnson appealed to Soviet premier Kosygin to repudiate Arab charges of U.S. military involvement in Israel's attack and to collaborate to achieve UN cease-fire resolutions. Kosygin indicated that he supported UN diplomacy to end the fighting in principle, but tensions arose over the terms of the cease-fire resolutions when the Soviets promoted the proviso forcing Israel to relinquish the territory it occupied. Tensions peaked on 10 June, when Kosygin severed relations with Israel and warned Johnson that "necessary actions will be taken, including military," unless Israel accepted the cease-fire with Syria. Fearing the worst, Johnson ordered the Sixth Fleet to move from a holding pattern toward the battle zone of the eastern Mediterranean, cognizant that Soviet submarines would detect this maneuver. The mood around the White House reportedly became somber and heavy until news arrived that Israel approved the cease-fire. Only then did U.S. officials celebrate the fact that the war spelled a major defeat for the Soviet Union because its client states had performed miserably. "The Russians," Johnson noted 14 June, "had lost their shirts in the Middle East war."[40]

The role of the Soviet Union has become an issue in the literature on U.S. diplomacy in the Six Day War. Judith Klinghoffer suggests that the Soviet Union caused the war by goading Arab powers to provoke Israel as a means of distracting the United States from its war in Vietnam, and that U.S. officials tacitly approved Israel's preemption on 5 June after detecting the Soviet move.[41] During the war, however, State Department officials repudiated rumors that the Soviets sought a settlement involving simultaneous U.S. de-escalation in Vietnam and Soviet restraint in the Middle East. In fact, they noted Soviet allegations that the United States had instigated the Middle East crisis to divert international attention from Southeast Asia.[42]

Third, the United States sought to build a permanent peace settlement over the ashes of the Six Day War. As early as 5 June, Rusk and Rostow advised Johnson that in addition to seeking cease-fires, the United States should promote a permanent peace settlement that reopened the Straits of Tiran, redeployed UN soldiers on both sides of the UAR-Israel border, ended the arms race in the Middle East, settled the refugee crisis, and promoted economic development of the entire region. Success in such an endeavor, the State Department advised, would depend on the ability of the United States to restore its traditional policy of acting amicably toward all Middle East powers. Zbigniew Brzezinski of the State Department's Policy Planning Council and Special Assistant McGeorge Bundy recommended that Johnson publicly propose a comprehensive peace plan at once, before the Soviet Union drove a wedge between the West and the Arab states by proposing a pro-Arab peace plan.[43]

Johnson administration officials realized that the success of any U.S. peace plan would depend on the willingness of Israel to compromise. King Faisal and other Arab statesmen, for example, made clear to the United States that Israel must relinquish its wartime territorial gains as part of any settlement. "Only Israeli concessions of some kind, at the right time," NSC staff member W. Howard Wriggins noted, "will make it politically possible for Arab leaders to overcome their humiliation, accept Israel as a legitimate Middle Eastern country and acknowledge its transit and security requirements."[44]

Yet U.S. officials soon realized that extracting concessions from Israel would prove difficult. Flushed with their dramatic and unanticipated victory over three Arab states, Israeli leaders gradually resolved to use the occupied territories to secure their own terms in any peace settlement. To dislodge Israel from the occupied territories against its will, Harry McPherson advised Johnson after touring Israel, would require actual U.S. military force, not merely a threat of economic sanctions as Eisenhower had issued in 1957. "We are clearly for both territorial integrity in the Middle East and for peace," Rostow advised Johnson. "Our powers to make peace, however, are extremely limited."[45]

In addition, political factors within the United States mitigated against pressuring Israel to concede against its will. Johnson should issue public "assurances of a real, guaranteed, and meaningful peace" consistent with Israeli wishes, political advisers Larry Levinson and Ben Wattenberg recommended. "From a domestic political point of view, . . . this would be a highly desirable action." On 8 June, leaders of twenty-one Jewish organizations told Vice President Hubert H. Humphrey that they endorsed a permanent peace settlement on Israel's terms. An aide who monitored Gallup polls reported to Johnson that most Americans "strongly sympathize with the Israelis."[46]

In such a context, U.S. peacemaking diplomacy achieved little. On 19 June, Johnson announced a plan for settlement, including mutual recognition, arms limitations, resolution of the Palestinian refugee crisis, freedom of transit, and independence of all area states. The UN General Assembly, however, considered but failed to vote on a draft resolution acknowledging these principles. At the Glassboro summit in late June, Johnson elicited Kosygin's approval of his principles, although Kosygin insisted that Israel withdraw unconditionally from the occupied territories before the Arabs made concessions, a position that Johnson rejected. In July, Johnson expressed his frustration that the Soviets would gain politically if the Arab-Israeli situation remained unsettled. He directed his advisers to recruit some other power to mediate peace treaties because "we can't put it together again."[47]

By fall 1967, U.S. efforts to make peace bore little fruit. Israel's position seemed to harden, the NSC noted in September, even as the Arab positions moderated. "The outlook for the moment is for deadlock," Rusk told the cabinet, because of disagreement over enforcement of Johnson's five principles for peace. The UN finally adopted Resolution 242 incorporating the essence of Johnson's principles for settlement, but deep disagreements over implementation blocked progress toward an actual resolution. In fact, violent incidents between the military forces of the UAR and Israel occurred in September–October 1967 and erupted into the War of Attrition by mid-1968. Embittered by their massive military defeats and territorial losses in 1967, Arab states became increasingly dependent on the Soviet Union for military and political backing as they waged limited war against Israel. Because of the perception that such Arab aggression enjoyed Soviet backing, the United States bolstered Israel. Despite his best efforts, Johnson proved unable to avoid the emergence of a close parallel between the Arab-Israeli conflict and the U.S.-Soviet cold war.[48]

The Arab-Israeli conflict confronted Lyndon Johnson with a difficult and dangerous situation. From 1963 to 1967, the president proved able to maintain a policy of containment, stability, and evenhandedness in the Middle East and to avert an escalation in the Arab-Israeli conflict. Maintaining amicable relations with Israel and various Arab states seemed to protect U.S. vital interests in the region. In 1967, however, this policy collapsed under the strain of a UAR-Israeli crisis. Johnson administration officials tried to defuse the crisis by persuading the UAR to reverse its provocative actions, restraining Israel from preempting against the UAR, promoting UN peacekeeping diplomacy, and promoting a multilateral operation to reopen the Straits of Tiran.

Such U.S. diplomacy failed, however, to avert the outbreak of full-scale warfare on 5 June 1967.

Johnson and his advisers succeeded only modestly in achieving their objectives once the war erupted. They were able to end the fighting by negotiating a series of cease-fire accords by 10 June, but only after passions had been inflamed and territorial boundaries had been substantially redrawn. They were able to deter Soviet intervention in the war, but only after Kosygin threatened to use force against Israel. The administration also proved unable to achieve a permanent peace accord in the aftermath of the war. The territorial and security issues stemming from the 1967 episode would fester and haunt U.S. policy-makers for years to come.

U.S. relations with the Arab states and Israel remained problematic through the Johnson presidency. Prior to 1967, U.S. diplomats aimed to preserve friendly ties with the conservative regimes in Jordan and Saudi Arabia and tried to repair strained relations with the more radical governments in the UAR and Syria. By defending Israeli transit rights during the crisis of 1967, however, U.S. officials earned the wrath of Arab peoples and leaders who experienced the humiliating military defeats of June. U.S. relations with Israel appeared to rest on more solid footing, given the strong sympathy that Israel enjoyed in U.S. domestic politics. At the official level, however, pre-1967 tensions over U.S. arms supply policy and Israel's reprisal policy were exacerbated by Johnson's reservations about Israel's preemption, Israel's attack on the *Liberty*, and Israel's uncompromising postwar position on peacemaking.

Events in the Middle East also strained the U.S.-Soviet relationship already frayed by Vietnam and other issues. While it remains unproved that Soviet leaders deliberately provoked the 1967 war, it appears that they showed little enthusiasm for Western efforts to avert hostilities. To a degree, U.S. and Soviet leaders collaborated to achieve the cease-fires during the Six Day War, but tensions between them rose when the Soviets threatened to intervene against Israel and Johnson ordered the U.S. Navy to sail toward the battle zone. The two superpowers also failed to agree on the optimal terms for a permanent peace after the war.

U.S. power in the Middle East declined during the Johnson administration. The president found it impossible to implement an initiative among maritime powers to lift the Aqaba blockade, to achieve a UN settlement of the Israeli-UAR standoff, to convince Nasser to relent from an act of brinkmanship, or to restrain Israel from provoking general hostilities. After 10 June, Israel enjoyed sufficient military power and political confidence to resist U.S. pressures, modest though they were, to make concessions needed for settlement, while the Arab states remained sufficiently bitter to reject U.S. calls for compromise. In the Suez-Sinai War of 1956–1957, U.S. officials had proved adept at terminating the hostilities and forcing the attacking powers to relinquish their gains. In 1967, by contrast, the United States retained no such power.

Not coincidentally, limitations on U.S. power and influence in other areas of the world became obvious at roughly the same time. Despite massive commitments of firepower, manpower, and financial resources, the U.S. military effort in Vietnam sputtered and stalled short of victory in 1967–1968. Throughout the third world, anti-U.S. nationalism gained prominence and influence. In the international financial realm, balance of payments problems triggered a crisis for the dollar in the late 1960s. Perhaps these simultaneous problems resulted from overcommitment in Vietnam and elsewhere; perhaps they resulted from the dynamics of international competition in the multipolar world order that emerged in the 1960s and replaced the bipolar world of the late 1940s and 1950s. Whatever the cause, the decline of U.S. power became apparent in the Middle East, as events spun out of the control of officials in Washington.

The Arab-Israeli War of 1967 represented a major setback for Lyndon Johnson. It undermined his broad policy objectives in the Middle East, complicated his diplomatic endeavors in other parts of the world, threatened to escalate into a superpower showdown, and revealed the limits of his power to control international developments. Perhaps that is why Johnson considered the news of war on 5 June so ominous.

Notes

1. Lyndon Johnson, *The Vantage Point: Perspectives on the Presidency, 1963–1969* (New York: Popular Library, 1971), 287.

2. Peter L. Hahn, *Caught in the Middle East: U.S. Policy toward the Arab-Israeli Conflict, 1945–1961* (Chapel Hill: University of North Carolina Press, 2004); Warren Bass, *Support Any Friend: Kennedy's Middle East and the Making of the U.S.-Israeli Alliance* (New York: Oxford University Press, 2003).

3. Saunders to Rostow, 24 June 1966, U.S. Department of State, *Foreign Relations of the United States (FRUS), 1964–1968,* 21: *Near East Region; Arabian Peninsula* (Washington, D.C.: Government Printing Office, 2000), 29–31.

4. State Department paper, 8 February 1967, *FRUS, 1964–1968,* 21: 39–

41. See also Rusk to Johnson, 16 January 1964, *FRUS, 1964–1968,* 18:*Arab-Israeli Dispute, 1964–1967,* 17–23 (Washington, D.C.: Government Printing Office, 2000); State Department paper, 8 February 1967, *FRUS, 1964–1968,* 21: 39–41.

5. Saunders to Rostow, 24 June 1966, *FRUS, 1964–1968,* 21: 29–31. See also Douglas Little, "Choosing Sides: Lyndon Johnson and the Middle East," in *The Johnson Years,* vol. 3, *LBJ at Home and Abroad,* ed. Robert A. Divine (Lawrence: University Press of Kansas, 1994), 150–197.

6. Minutes of meeting, 30 May 1961, Records of the Foreign Ministry, Political Files, RG 130.23, 3294/8, Israel State Archive, Jerusalem, Israel (hereafter cited as RG 130.23 with appropriate filing designations); Komer to Johnson, 2 June 1964, White House memorandum of conversation, 1 June 1964, National Security File (NSF), Country File (CO), box 142, Lyndon Baines Johnson Presidential Library, Austin, Texas (hereafter LBJL). See also Johnson to Eshkol, 2 January 1964, *FRUS, 1964–1968,* 18: 1–2.

7. Komer to Bundy, n.d. [12 August 1965], White House Central File (WHCF) (Confidential), box 9, LBJL (hereafter cited as WHCF with appropriate file designations); Komer memorandum for the record, 8 October 1965, NSF, Name File, box 7, LBJL; Saunders to Rostow, 24 June 1966, NSF, Memos to President: Rostow, box 8, LBJL. See also Komer to Johnson, 18 January 1966, unsigned memoranda, 19 May and 2 November 1966, NSF, CO, boxes 139–140, LBJL.

8. Komer to Bundy, n.d. [12 August 1965], WHCF (Confidential), box 9, LBJL. See also Bundy to Johnson, 8 March 1964, NSF, Memos to President: Bundy, box 1, LBJL; memorandum for the record by Komer, 16 May 1964, NSF, Bundy File, box 18, LBJL; Komer to Johnson, 28 May 1964, White House memorandum of conversation, 1 June 1964, Komer to Johnson, 3 June 1964, NSF, CO, box 142, LBJL; paper by Brewer, 12 January 1966, Averell Harriman Papers, Subject File, box 433, Library of Congress (LOC); Wriggins and Saunders to Rostow, 16 November 1966, Wriggins to Rostow, 23 November 1966, *FRUS, 1964–1968,* 18: 664–666, 683–685.

9. Head to Bundy, 7 April 1964, NSF, CO, box 138, LBJL; State Department background paper, 22 May 1964, Komer to Johnson, 28 May and 2 June 1964, NSF, CO, box 142, LBJL. See also unsigned memorandum of conversation, 25 November 1963, Ball to Johnson, n.d. [May 1964], NSF, CO, boxes 138, 142; memorandum by Harriman, 30 December 1963, Harriman Papers, Subject File, box 433.

10. Johnson to Hussein, 2 January 1964, Johnson to Faisal, 15 June 1964, *FRUS, 1964–1968,* 18: 2–3; 21: 444–445. See also Johnson to Nasser, 27 February 1964, memorandum of conversation by Davies, 25 May 1964, Rusk to Johnson, 8 August 1964, Johnson to Nasser, 13 August 1964, Johnson to Nasser, 18 March 1965, *FRUS, 1964–1968,* 18: 45–46, 138–142, 193–195, 205–206, 408–409. For a fuller discussion of Johnson's early relations with Arab states, see Little, "Choosing Sides," 151–161.

11. Saunders to Rostow, 24 June 1966, *FRUS, 1964–1968,* 21: 29–31. See also Feldman to Johnson, 4, 14 March 1964, Bundy to Johnson, 8 March 1964, NSF, Memos to President: Bundy, box 1, LBJL; Feldman to Johnson, 11 May 1964, memorandum of conversation by Palmer, 25 February 1965, State Department background paper, 26 July 1966, NSF, CO, boxes 138–139,

144–145, LBJL; Komer to Johnson, 8 February 1966, NSF, Name File, box 6, LBJL; Komer to Johnson, 22 February 1966, *FRUS, 1964–1968*, 18: 556–557.

12. Saunders to Rostow, 16 May 1967, *FRUS, 1964–1968*, 21: 41–48.

13. NSC, *History of Middle East Crisis*, vol. 9, appendix P, box 20, NSF, LBJL, pp. 1, 5–13 (hereafter *NSCH*).

14. Rostow to Johnson, 17 May 1967, NSF, NSC History, vol. 1, box 17, LBJL. See also *NSCH*, 13–20.

15. Johnson to Eshkol, 17 May 1967, NSF, NSC History, box 17, LBJL. See also Rostow to Johnson, 19 May 1967, Country File: Israel, box 144, NSF, LBJL; Smythe to Rusk, 20 May 1967, Rusk to Nolte, 22 May 1967, NSF, NSC History, vol. 13, box 22, LBJL; Johnson to Nasser, 22 May 1967, NSF, CO, box 144, LBJL; circular telegram by Rusk, 18 May 1967, Johnson to Eshkol, 21 May 1967, NSF, CO, box 144, LBJL.

16. Rusk to Barbour, 20 May 1967, Barbour to Rusk, 21 May 1967, quoted in *NSCH*, 20–34. See also Eshkol to Johnson, 18 May 1967, Barbour to Rusk, 18 May 1967, NSF, NSC History, vol. 13, box 22, LBJL; Johnson to Eshkol, 21 May 1967, in *NSCH*, 26–27; memorandum of conversation by Saunders, 21 May 1967, NSF, NSC History, vol. 1, box 17, LBJL.

17. Rusk to embassy in Moscow, 18 May 1967, Denney to Rusk, 19 May 1967, NSF, NSC History, vol. 13, box 22, LBJL; Hughes to Rusk, 23 May 1967, NSF, NSC History, vol. 6, box 19, LBJL.

18. Minutes of NSC meeting, 24 May 1967, NSF, NSC Meetings file, box 2, LBJL; Rostow to Johnson with attachment, 25 May 1967, NSF, NSC History, vol. 2, box 17, LBJL. See also Barbour to Rusk, 21 May 1967, quoted in *NSCH*, 24; Nolte to Rusk, 23 May 1967, NSF, NSC History, vol. 13, box 22, LBJL; CIA to White House Situation Room, 25 May 1967, CIA Records, On-line Retrieval Information System (ORIS); Burns to Rusk, 26 May 1967, NSF, NSC History, vol. 2, box 17, LBJL.

19. Johnson quoted in *NSCH*, 37; Rostow to Nolte, 22 May 1967, NSF, NSC History, vol. 13, box 22, LBJL. See also Rusk to Embassy at Cairo, 22 May 1967, NSF, NSC History, box 17, LBJL; Anderson to Johnson and Rusk, 2 June 1967, NSC History, vol. 3, box 18, NSF.

20. Minutes of NSC meeting, 24 May 1967, NSC Meetings file, box 2, NSF, LBJL; Rusk to Johnson, 26 May 1967, Country File: Israel, box 142, NSF, LBJL; Rusk to Barbour, 3 June 1967, quoted in *NSCH*, 97. See also *NSCH*, 60–61.

21. Nolte to Rusk, 26 May 1967, Office File of White House Aides: George Christian, box 4, LBJL. See also cable from Amman, 1 June 1967, NSC History, vol. 3, box 18, NSF, LBJL; circular cable by Rusk, 26 May 1967, *NSCH*, 59–60; Rusk to Johnson, 26 May 1967, memorandum by Saunders, 27 May 1967, NSF, NSC History, vol. 2, box 17, LBJL.

22. Rusk to Johnson, 26 May 1967, Country File: Israel, box 142, NSF, LBJL; unsigned memorandum of conversation, 26 May 1967, Johnson to Eshkol, 27 May 1967, Eshkol to Johnson, 30 May 1967, NSF, NSC History, box 17, LBJL. See also memorandum for the record by Saunders, 19 May 1967, Rostow to Harman, 20 May 1967, Rostow to Johnson, 27 May 1967, NSF, NSC History, box 17, LBJL; minutes of NSC meeting, 24 May 1967, NSF, NSC Meetings, box 2, LBJL; Rusk to Johnson, 26 May 1967, NSF, CO, box 142, LBJL.

23. Minutes of NSC meeting, 24 May 1967, NSC Meetings file, box 2, NSF, LBJL. See also *NSCH*, 64–66; Eshkol to Johnson, 2 June 1967, NSF, NSC History, vol. 3, box 18, LBJL.

24. Barbour to Rusk, 27 May 1967, quoted in *NSCH*, 64; Avi Shlaim, *The Iron Wall: Israel and the Arab World* (New York: Norton, 2000), 236–240, quotation on 240; Eshkol to Johnson, 30 May 1967, NSF, NSC History, vol. 2, box 17, LBJL. See also circular cable by Rusk, 30 May 1967, NSF, NSC History, vol. 14, box 22, LBJL.

25. Rusk and McNamara to Johnson, 30 May 1967, NSC History, vol. 3, box 18, NSF, LBJL. See also *NSCH*, 84–86, 93–96, 103–105.

26. Nolte to Rusk, 26 May 1967, Office File of White House Aides: George Christian, box 4, LBJL; Yost to Rusk, 2 June 1967, Country File: Egypt, box 107, NSF. See also Rusk to Nolte, 30 May 1967, NSF, NSC History, vol. 14, box 22, LBJL.

27. Battle to Control Group, 31 May 1967, quoted in *NSCH*, 76.

28. Wheeler to McNamara, 2 June 1967, NSC History, vol. 3, box 18, NSF, LBJL. See also minutes of NSC meeting, 24 May 1967, NSC Meetings file, box 2, NSF, LBJL.

29. Rostow to Johnson, 28 and 29 May 1967, Rusk and McNamara to Johnson, 30 May 1967, Hoopes to McNamara, 2 June 1967, NSC History, vol. 3, box 18, NSF, LBJL; Smythe to Rusk, 1 June 1967, Burns to Rusk, 2 June 1967, NSF, NSC History, vol. 14, box 22, LBJL.

30. Minutes of NSC meeting, 24 May 1967, NSF, NSC Meetings file, box 2, LBJL; Saunders to Rostow, 31 May 1967, LBJL; Rostow to Johnson, 2 June 1967, NSF, NSC History, vol. 3, box 18. See also Rostow to Johnson with attachments, 1 June 1967, NSF, NSC History, vol. 3, box 18, LBJL; Saunders to Rostow, 1 June 1967, NSF, NSC Meetings, box 58, LBJL; situation report, 1 June 1967, NSF, NSC History, vol. 10, box 21, LBJL.

31. William B. Quandt, *Peace Process: American Diplomacy and the Arab-Israeli Conflict Since 1967* (Washington, D.C.: Brookings Institution, 1993): 25–48, quotation on 48; Shlaim, *Iron Wall*, 241.

32. Circular cable from Rusk, 3 June 1967, NSF, NSC History, vol. 15, box 23, LBJL; memorandum for the record by Saunders, 7 January 1969 [7 June 1967], NSF, NSC Meetings, box 2, LBJL; memorandum for the record by Saunders, 17 November 1967, NSF, NSC History, box 18, LBJL. See also Johnson to Eshkol, 3 June 1967, NSC History, ME Crisis, vol. 3, box 18, NSF, LBJL; Richard B. Parker, *The Politics of Miscalculation in the Middle East* (Bloomington: Indiana University Press, 1993), 114–122.

33. Battle to Nolte, 3 June 1967, NSF, NSC History, vol. 15, box 23, LBJL. See also unsigned memorandum, 3 June 1967, NSF, NSC History, vol. 3, box 18; circular cable from Rusk, 3 June 1967, NSF, NSC History, vol. 15, box 23, LBJL.

34. Circular cable from Rusk, 3 June 1967, NSF, NSC History, vol. 15, box 23, LBJL.

35. Eshkol to Johnson, 5 June 1967, NSC History, vol. 3, box 18, NSF, LBJL. See also Davis to Rostow, 7 June 1967, NSC History, vol. 3, box 18, NSF, LBJL; Rostow to Johnson, 7 June 1967, NSF, NSC History, vol. 4, box 18, LBJL; *NSCH*, 106–123.

36. Circular cables from Rusk, 5, 7 June 1967, NSF, NSC History, vol. 15, box 23, LBJL; CIA situation reports, 6–10 June 1967, CIA Records, ORIS.

37. On the basis of the testimony of surviving crew members, writers such as James Ennes, Donald Neff, and Andrew Cockburn and Leslie Cockburn speculate that Israel attacked the ship to prevent the United States from detecting Israeli mobilization against Syrian forces in the Golan Heights and reporting such intelligence to the regime in Damascus, while James Bamford suggests that Israel acted to prevent detection of its mass killings of Egyptian prisoners of war in nearby Sinai. In contrast, scholars such as David Schoenbaum accept the Israelis' "honest error" argument. James M. Ennes, *Assault on the Liberty: The True Story of an Israeli Attack on an American Intelligence Ship* (New York: Random House, 1979); Donald Neff, *Warriors for Jerusalem: Six Days That Changed the Middle East* (New York: Linden, 1984), 246–275; Andrew Cockburn and Leslie Cockburn, *Dangerous Liaison: The Inside Story of the U.S.-Israeli Covert Relationship* (New York: HarperCollins, 1991, 152–53; James Bamford, *Body of Secrets: Anatomy of the Ultra-secret National Security Agency from the Cold War through the Dawn of a New Century* (New York: Doubleday, 2001), 185–239; David Schoenbaum, *The United States and the State of Israel* (New York: Oxford University Press, 1993), 157–159.

38. Rusk to embassy Tel Aviv, 9 June 1967, NSF, NSC History, vol. 15, box 23, LBJL; unsigned memorandum, 9 June 1967, NSC History, vol. 4, box 18, NSF, LBJL. See also CIA situation report, 8 June 1967, CIA memorandum, "The Attack on the Liberty," 13 June 1967, CIA Records, ORIS. During a conference on the 1967 war, held in 1992, former Israeli officials continued to argue that the attack was an honest mistake, while former U.S. officials continued to reject that argument. See Richard Parker, ed., *The Six-Day War: A Retrospective* (Gainesville: University Press of Florida, 1996), especially the exchange between former U.S. ambassador Talcott W. Seelye and former Israeli ambassador Ephraim Evron (266–270).

39. Rusk to Barbour, 6 June 1967, quoted in *NSCH*, 129; memorandum for the record by Saunders, 22 October 1968 [10 June 1967], NSC History, vol. 4, box 19, NSF, LBJL; Katzenbach quoted in *NSCH*, 148. See also Nathaniel Davis to Rostow, 6 June 1967, NSC History, vol. 3, box 18, NSF, LBJL; CIA situation report, 8 June 1967, CIA Records, ORIS; Nolte to Rusk, 8–10 June 1967, NSF, Country File, box 107, LBJL; *NSCH*, 106–117, 123–124, 145–150.

40. Johnson to Kosygin, 10 June 1967, Kosygin to Johnson, 10 June 1967, NSF, NSC History, vol. 7, box 19, LBJL; unsigned memorandum of conversation, 14 June 1967, Diary Back-Up file, box 68, LBJL. See also Eshkol to Johnson, 5 June 1967, NSC History, vol. 3, box 18, NSF, LBJL; memorandum for the record by Saunders, 7 January 1969 [7 June 1967], NSC Meetings, box 2, NSF, LBJL; unsigned memorandum, 9 June 1967, NSC History, vol. 4, box 18, NSF, LBJL; memorandum for the record by Saunders, 22 October 1968 [10 June 1967], NSC History, vol. 4, box 19, NSF, LBJL; CLC to Harriman, 14 June 1967, Harriman Papers, box 432, LOC.

41. Judith Klinghoffer, *Vietnam, Jews, and the Middle East: Unintended Consequences* (New York: St. Martin's Press, 1999).

42. Circular cable by Rusk, 9 June 1967, NSF, NSC History, vol. 15, box 23, LBJL.

43. Rostow to Johnson, 5 June 1967, NSF, NSC History, vol. 3, box 18, LBJL; Rostow to Embassy in London, 7 June 1967, NSF, NSC History, vol. 4, box 18, LBJL; State Department paper, 8 June 1967, paper by Brzezinski, 14

June 1967, NSF, NSC History, vol. 7, box 19, LBJL; Bundy to Johnson, 9 June 1967, Diary Back-Up File, box 68, LBJL.

44. Wriggins to Rostow, 8 June 1967, NSF, Country File, box 107, LBJL. See also Wriggins to Rostow, 6 June 1967, NSF, Country File, box 107, LBJL; Rostow to Johnson, 7 June 1967, Hughes to Rusk, 7 June 1967, Faisal to Johnson, 12 June 1967, Rostow to Johnson, 13 June 1967, NSF, NSC History, vol. 4, box 18, LBJL.

45. Rostow to Johnson, 13 June 1967, NSC History, vol. 5, box 18, NSF. See also McPherson to Johnson, 11 June 1967, NSC History, vol. 4, box 18, NSF, LBJL; Smith to Johnson, 11 June 1967, Rusk to Embassy in Jidda, 15 June 1967, Rusk to Embassy in Amman, 16 June 1967, Rostow to Johnson, 27 June 1967, Diary Back-Up file, boxes 68, 70, LBJL; Barbour to Rusk, 13 June 1967, NSF, NSC History, vol. 16, box 23, LBJL; Parker, *Politics of Miscalculation*, 126–127.

46. Levinson and Wattenberg to Johnson, 7 June 1967, NSC History, vol. 3, box 18, NSF, LBJL; Panzer to Johnson, 10 June 1967, WHCF, NS-D, box 193, LBJL. See also Barbour to Rusk, 7 June 1967, NSF, NSC History, vol. 4, box 18, LBJL; Humphrey to Johnson, 8 June 1967, WHCF, NS-D, box 193, LBJL.

47. Notes on meeting by Tom Johnson, 18 July 1967, Tom Johnson Notes File, box 1, LBJL. See also circular cable by Katzenbach, 27 June 1967, NSF, NSC History, vol. 16, box 23, LBJL; notes on meeting by Tom Johnson, 12 July 1967, Tom Johnson Notes File, box 1, LBJL; circular cable by Rusk, 12 August 1967, Harriman Papers, box 432.

48. Minutes of Cabinet meeting, 1 November 1967, Cabinet Papers, box 11, LBJL. See also summary notes of NSC meeting, 13 September 1967, NSF, NSC Meetings, box 2; David A. Korn, *Stalemate: The War of Attrition and Great Power Diplomacy in the Middle East, 1967–1970* (Boulder, Colo.: Westview Press, 1992); Yaacov Bar-Siman-Tov, *The Israeli-Egyptian War of Attrition, 1969–1970: A Case Study of Limited Local War* (New York: Columbia University Press, 1980); Parker, *Politics of Miscalculation*, 127–129.

5 | A Question of Political Courage: Lyndon Johnson as War Leader

David L. Anderson

"IF THE AMERICAN PEOPLE don't love me," Lyndon Johnson remarked to White House fellow Doris Kearns in 1968, "their descendants will."[1] At that time and for good reasons, the president was convinced that the public perceived his leadership as a failure because the American war in Vietnam seemed to be mired in a bloody stalemate. He was equally convinced, however, that the verdict of history would be more approving. There is now a large body of historical scholarship that assesses Johnson's performance as war leader. A vigorous debate has persisted from the time of the war to the present regarding the extent of the president's personal responsibility for what Johnson biographer Robert Dallek terms "the worst foreign policy disaster in the country's history."[2] A focus on Johnson during the 1965 escalation of the American war in Vietnam and on his decisions in early 1968 to end that escalation provides a measure of his leadership. In both cases he deluded himself that he was acting with political courage. In truth, his behavior reveals an inherent desire to follow the path of least resistance.

Historians have developed a number of criticisms and some defenses of Johnson's performance as war leader, including some speculative scenarios about the course of American involvement in Vietnam if John Kennedy had lived. In view of Johnson's well-known sensitivity to comparisons with the Kennedys, he would likely have been deeply offended to read these estimations, which generally contend that Kennedy would not have allowed the U.S. military intervention to be as large or go as long as did his successor. Kennedy did not live to face the imminent collapse of an independent South Vietnamese government as LBJ did in 1964, but the invocation of the Kennedy record as a means for analyzing Johnson does help historians ask important questions. Studies that compare what Kennedy might have done with what Johnson actually did rely heavily on estimations of the ability of the two men to exercise independent judgment in foreign policy and to demonstrate the high level of credibility and trust that would have been required to reverse a decade of U.S. policy commitment in Southeast Asia. One of the more recent presentations of this alternate scenario is by historian Howard Jones. He carefully avoids a categorical statement that Kennedy would not have escalated U.S. military intervention as Johnson did, but Jones argues that Kennedy had a secret plan (unknown to Johnson) that was, in fact, "a pattern of withdrawal in the making."[3]

It would have taken an enormous act of political courage for either president to defy the prevailing cold war consensus in America about the global danger of expansive communism and to resist the overconfidence, which had emerged from the glorious victories of World War II, in the moral and military force of a seemingly invincible United States. As he aspired to be president, Kennedy had made courage a touchstone of his political persona in various ways, including publication of his 1956 book, *Profiles in Courage,* and what Robert Dean terms "the narrative of warrior heroism" from his military service in the Pacific.[4] Whether or not President Kennedy was politically courageous or dangerously reckless regarding international issues such as Cuba or Berlin remains a point of contention. Whether he would have had the political courage to allow Hanoi to triumph in Vietnam without first waging a major fight can never be known.

On the other hand, Johnson's decision to escalate the American military intervention in Vietnam and to persist in that intervention for three years at great cost to the United States and Vietnam can be and has been examined in detail. Historians and biographers have developed a mass of knowledge about Johnson's personality and experience, his relationship with his advisers, his historical and ideological frame of reference, and his political calculations. All this research confirms that it is not a simple question of how this president could have gone so wrong. As historian Allan Nevins writes in the foreword of *Profiles in Courage,* "the right course is not always clear" in the pulling and tugging of political life.[5] Even with hindsight, military and diplomatic historians disagree about whether the United States was wrong not to cut its losses and seek a negotiated settlement earlier or to increase more quickly and decisively its military, political, and economic intervention in Vietnam.[6] Did Johnson not know the right course? The majority of expert opinion today holds that the United States, to avoid the Vietnam disaster, should have withdrawn earlier or never have intervened at all. Most of the speculation on Kennedy's hypothetical course supports this interpretation. The nonhypothetical question, however, focuses on his successor. Did Johnson know or at least sense that withdrawal was the right course and yet lack the political courage to make the right decision? Present evidence suggests that he did.

After becoming president in November 1963, Johnson believed that he was following the courageous course in Vietnam. Two days after Kennedy's death, the new president told his aides that the United States had to do something and not let South Vietnam "go under." Otherwise, he explained, the Chinese and the "fellas in the Kremlin" will "think we're yellow and we don't mean what we say."[7] Such a Soviet and Chinese perception of American weakness would, he feared, invite World War III. Equally frightening to Johnson was domestic reaction. He later told Kearns about actual nightmares in which he saw Robert Kennedy declaring that "I had betrayed John Kennedy's commitment to South Vietnam. That I had let a democracy fall into the hands of the Communists. That I was a coward. An unmanly man. . . . I could hear the voices of thousands of people. They were all shouting at me and running toward me: 'Coward! Traitor! Weakling!'"[8] As political scientist and practicing psychologist Blema Steinberg has concluded, "Psychologically, Johnson could not tolerate the prospect of being found lacking in courage in comparison with his predecessors."[9]

Successful statesmanship requires courage, but courage alone is not a guarantee of successful policy. Few would disagree that Abraham Lincoln exhibited great political courage and statesmanship, but Lincoln also understood the challenge of making correct decisions: "There are few things wholly evil or wholly good. Almost everything, especially of Government policy, is an inseparable compound of the two, so that our best judgment of the preponderance between them is continually demanded."[10] Johnson and the men who advised him perceived "militant imperial anticommunism" to be both good and heroic.[11] To affirm the use of U.S. armed forces to fight armed communist insurgents in Vietnam was, for them, akin to the physical courage of the soldiers, sailors, marines, and airmen whom they sent to do the fighting. Physical courage is not, however, the same as moral courage. The physical act of courage is often instinctive, spontaneous, and unreflective, but the moral act of courage is often deliberate, considered, and highly reflective. What constitutes moral or political courage, as Lincoln implied, is ambiguous; it can be rationalized out of existence and is more difficult to exercise than the more direct act of placing one's body in harm's way. Johnson often wore on his lapel the Silver Star ribbon awarded him after he rode as a passenger on a single harrowing combat flight during World War II. The commendation is one of the nation's highest recognitions of military valor, and the merits of its presentation to Johnson, then a member of Congress and a naval reserve officer, were questionable.[12] The United States does not award ribbons for political heroism. If it did, would Johnson have been so bold as to have claimed his service as commander in chief during the Vietnam War was courageous?

On a number of occasions, Johnson confided to his closest aides that he did not want war. "I want war like I want polio," he claimed privately, but "what you want and what your image is are two different things."[13] He did not relish bombing Vietnamese civilians. He anguished over sending young Americans to war. "I am the fellow that wakes up in the morning with a report that fifty of our boys died last night," he exclaimed to Martin Luther King as an illustration of his desire for peace.[14] On another occasion, after giving a short speech to troops preparing to leave for Vietnam, he confided to his top aides, "I told myself—I am at heart a sentimental guy at times like those—that I sure regret having to send those men."[15] Yet, from March 1965 to March 1968, he persisted in waging war, bombing civilians, and sending men to battle. He could not bring himself to say no to war. He did not seem to have the courage to do so. What drove him to pursue a military course through these months and years cannot be reduced to one factor. Many influences were at work both on Johnson and on the U.S. policy process. For the president himself, however, was there a false sense of courage that compelled him initially to choose war? On 31 March 1968, did he discover a true moral courage that enabled him to announce that he would not seek reelection and would begin limiting the war effort?

Johnson told a gathering of congressional leaders on 2 April 1968 that he had never wanted to be president. He was not being strictly honest with himself and the group at that moment, however, because he certainly had always sought power. To abdicate that power ran against the grain of this strong, tough man whose "style," according to journalist William S. White, was based on the "belief that life is not made for the sluggard or the timid."[16] The assassination of John Kennedy had suddenly thrust the responsibilities of the presidency upon him, including the decade-old policy of U.S. support for the Republic of Vietnam. After several weeks in the White House, Johnson shared his personal doubts about Vietnam with National Security Adviser McGeorge Bundy: "I just don't think it's worth fighting for, and I don't think we can get out. It's just the biggest damn mess."[17] The office was unanticipated, and the commitment in South Vietnam may have been unwanted, but consistent with his style he plunged into both full of vigor.

Johnson was an energetic and demanding executive, a confessed workaholic. After taking office, he achieved tremendous legislative successes in obtaining passage of Kennedy's New Frontier domestic initiatives and later his own even more ambitious Great Society reforms. Through the force of his personality, a dynamic combination of charm and intimidation, he could effectively manage powerful congressional leaders and cabinet officers to gain dramatic results. The Civil Rights Act of 1964 and the Medicare system of old-age health insurance approved in July 1965 stand as just two of the monuments to his domestic leadership. It has been natural for students of Johnson's presidency to ask how his prodigious talents in the domestic sphere translated into foreign policy in general and Vietnam policy in particular.

Most observers agree that on domestic and foreign issues the policies of the Johnson administration were the policies of the president himself. He was a dominant personality. He was six foot three, full of energy and emotion, a skilled actor, and a shrewd judge of people. He was also intelligent and worked hard at mastering details. Whether one met him in person or talked with him on the telephone (his favorite form of communication), Johnson was a physical and intellectual presence who made it clear to everyone that he was in charge. Thus, he always will be judged personally by the measure of his administration's successes and failures because they were his successes and failures.[18]

During and immediately following the war, historians and journalists in general criticized the American military intervention in Vietnam so consistently that historian Robert Divine labeled these negative assessments the orthodox scholarly interpretation.[19] Since Johnson was the president who made the fateful decisions to begin regular bombing in Indochina and to deploy not just U.S. military advisers but combat troops to South Vietnam, and because his leadership style was so notoriously overbearing, much of the early literature about the war placed the weight of accountability for bad decisions squarely on him. As journalist David Halberstam wrote in one of the classic larger-than-life portraits of Johnson, "That energy, when properly harnessed by him was marvelous, but given his powers, his drives, his instinct to go forward, it was disastrous if he was harnessed to the wrong policies."[20]

Despite consensus among observers that the president played a central role in Vietnam policy, there is an extensive variety of opinions about why he so seriously mishandled the issue. Johnson has his defenders, such as his aides Walt Rostow and Dean Rusk or so-called revisionist historians such as Michael Lind, who argue that the decision to Americanize the war in Vietnam was a correct response to international threats against U.S. interests.[21] Overwhelmingly, though, the historical verdict is harsh. John Burke and Fred Greenstein support David Halberstam's view that Johnson's demands for personal loyalty from his advisers stifled open and constructive policy discussion in the White House. Frederick Logevall, Doris Kearns, and H. R. McMaster see a deeply insecure man behind Johnson's bullying manner. Couple this insecurity with a lack of interest and experience in foreign policy, as noted by Eric Goldman and David Kaiser, and Johnson appears incapable of independent and creative foreign policymaking. Other analysts, such as Waldo Heinrichs and Sandra Taylor, seize upon Johnson's presumed provincialism (his rural southern origins and teachers college education) and lack of cultural understanding as the problem. Although George Herring cautions against the temptation to place too much emphasis on Johnson's personal traits, he also acknowledges that the impatient president was not well suited to appreciate the subtleties and complexity of counterinsurgency warfare. In sum, this catalog of shortcomings portrays a president fundamentally incapable of making sound policy in Vietnam.[22]

In recent years, interpretations of Johnson's leadership have begun to appear that are more complimentary of his foreign policy abilities, while still acknowledging the blot of Vietnam on his record. Dallek, for example, terms Johnson a "tough-minded realist" who was not confused about policy goals and who employed his considerable political skill at home and abroad in a "double game" of constantly reaffirming U.S. commitment to a long war while keeping the door open for a negotiated settlement.[23] Other scholars have mined the archives to find that, in the words of H. W. Brands, Johnson did a "fair job" in dealing with questions involving France, West Germany, Turkey-Greece, the Arab-Israeli conflict, India-Pakistan, Indonesia, and the Caribbean. "Though Johnson handled the war in Vietnam disastrously, with the fault lying partly in the stars and partly in himself," Brands observes, "he did better managing other aspects of the transition to a world no longer dominated by the United States."[24]

Thomas Schwartz argues forcefully that "the Vietnam War should not be allowed to block a more dispassionate assessment of Johnson's foreign and domestic policies."[25] Schwartz carefully examines policies toward Britain, France, West Germany, and the Soviet Union and finds that Johnson, despite his "ugly American" persona, had real achievements in sustaining the U.S. alliance with Western Europe, encouraging détente with the USSR, and expanding trade and monetary cooperation. These overlooked successes suggest to Schwartz that "Johnson gambled that fighting a limited war would allow him to move ahead with 'thawing' the Cold War in Europe."[26] The gamble in Vietnam paid off, Schwartz explains, because it shielded the president from being labeled an appeaser and enabled him to improve relations with the USSR while also avoiding armed conflict with China. On the other hand, Johnson lost his gamble when the fall of the American-backed Saigon government in 1975 tarnished the U.S. reputation for invincibility. On balance, however, Schwartz implies that, in the end, Johnson's ability to keep the United States at the center of Western alliance politics paid an ultimate dividend in the peaceful end of the cold war that mitigated the defeat in Vietnam.[27]

This gambler image and the possibility of a link to the big jackpot in ending the cold war in Europe suggest elements of courage and purpose in Johnson's Vietnam policy that are not so apparent in the record. The cold war undeniably shaped Johnson's worldview and that of his senior advisers. They accepted the political axiom that an effective president could not dare to appear soft on communism. "Had all American leaders not thought that all international events were connected to the Cold War," Robert Schulzinger writes, "there would have been no American war in Vietnam."[28] Johnson's decision to make Vietnam a cold war battleground does not reveal any meaningful global strategy leading to the ultimate demise of the Soviet Union and the end of the cold war. Early in his presidency he accepted uncritically the prevailing strategy of containment. He left implementation of that strategy in Southeast Asia to Secretary of Defense Robert McNamara, Secretary of State Dean Rusk, McGeorge Bundy, and other holdovers from the Kennedy team, while he devoted his own attention to the domestic agenda. Beginning with the escalation decisions in 1965 and continuing through 1968, Johnson became increasingly preoccupied, even obsessed, with the war and its details. He poured much of his great reservoir of energy and emotion into driving his aides for solutions to the Vietnam morass. His declassified telephone conversations, now available through 1965, reveal an executive who was informed and who could ask tough questions of powerful assistants and members of Congress. Throughout this process, however, LBJ's Vietnam decisions were often ad hoc, dilatory, dissembling, and not a picture of courage and purpose.

Johnson was definitely not a timid leader or one devoid of goals. His objectives throughout his presidency were clear: first to build what he called the Great Society at home and second to contain global communism. Although he characterized the Great Society as "the woman I really loved," he did not compartmentalize U.S. policy between foreign and domestic.[29] He understood that he would have to be effective abroad to accomplish his domestic agenda. He also believed that, just as government initiatives could improve the lives of people at home, American initiatives abroad could improve the lives of people throughout the world. He explained to Bundy:

> What I really think our role in the world is is . . . to have enough power to prevent weak people from being gobbled up and then sharing what we have to prevent people from dying at forty with disease and starving to death and growing up in ignorance. . . . I am trying to do it at home. I would like to do it abroad. If they'd let me, I'd like to take my fifty billion that we are spending on defense, and I'd like to spend ten to fifteen billion of it in these countries where they die at thirty-five, in the Africas and Asias of the world, and I would like to do something about health and education and all these things that are desirable.[30]

It was a grand vision to attempt to bring the benefits of democracy and economic betterment to everyone in the United States and the world. The conflict in Vietnam, however, posed a threat to the achievement of that goal that Johnson was unable to master. He tried to treat the war through crisis management rather than long-term strategy. The Vietnamese revolutionaries were stronger and their own vision for Vietnam was more unshakable than he and his aides anticipated. Despite Johnson's good intentions, he and his advisers flailed about in Southeast Asia in much the same way as did the U.S. ground and air forces they sent on armed reconnaissance missions in the combat area. Costs mounted for Americans and Vietnamese in a process that became increasingly difficult to rationalize, and one that Johnson could not bring himself to acknowledge was a mistake.

Johnson was a narcissist, but it was not his personality as much as it was his political pedigree that shaped his responses. He had little understanding of the Vietnamese experience in the first half of the twentieth century, but he was deeply imbued with the presumed lessons of his own country's experience. He had entered public life during the Great Depression, became an administrator in one of Franklin Roosevelt's social welfare programs, and remained an ardent New Dealer in political philosophy throughout his congressional and presidential career. When World War II came, he embraced the liberal internationalism that Roosevelt espoused in the struggle to defeat Nazi tyranny. Along with many of his contemporaries in the American leadership, he easily transferred the World War II crusade to combat dictatorship to the postwar commitment to contain communism. Equal to his enduring faith in the power of government to be a positive influence at home was his acceptance of America's ongoing obligation and ability to improve the condition of all people.[31]

Although historians must be wary of memoirs and public speeches as authoritative sources, Johnson's own writings and pronouncements summarize well his perception of the challenges that Vietnam presented to the United States as he contemplated escalating the U.S. involvement. On 7 April 1965, he made an important speech at Johns Hopkins University that was broadcast live to the nation. In his memoirs he wrote that the purposes of the address were to provide a clear explanation of why the United States had begun regular bombing of North Vietnam in March, to encourage Hanoi to work with Washington for a peaceful settlement, and "to describe what peace and cooperative effort could do for the economic development of all of Southeast Asia." In a key passage he envisioned a massive project for the Mekong River comparable to the highly successful Tennessee Valley Authority (TVA) of the New Deal. "For our part," he pledged, "I will ask the Congress to join in a billion dollar American investment in this effort as soon as it is under way."[32] Johnson was inviting Vietnam to participate in the Great Society. If North Vietnam rejected the offer, the president could always say to himself and others that he had presented a peaceful alternative. There is little reason to doubt, however, that the Mekong proposal was genuine. Ever since his first visit to South Vietnam as vice president in 1961, he had maintained that the answer to the communist challenge was to provide economic development for the people of Asia, who were less fortunate than Americans. A Vietnamese TVA fit Johnson's deal-making methods that had brought him so much success in domestic politics. It seemed to him to be an irresistible offer of immediate and long-term benefits that President Ho Chi Minh and the Politburo in Hanoi could not refuse. "Old Ho can't turn me down," he assured his press secretary Bill Moyers.[33] North Vietnam's leaders rejected the proposal, however, and dismissed the billion dollars as "bait" or a "bribe." "They had no interest in cooperating with their neighbors in a peaceful way," LBJ recorded in his memoirs; "they preferred to take them over by force."[34]

That Johnson thought he could, in effect, buy off a hardened revolutionary like Ho Chi Minh in the way he could offer an incentive to a labor union leader—he told Moyers that AFL-CIO chief George Meany would have "snapped" at an offer of $100 million—seemed naive. The president never gave up the thought, however, that somehow American beneficence could woo the Vietnamese away from communism. "I want them to say when Americans come, this is what they leave—schools, not long cigars," he announced in 1966 as the war grew more violent; "we're going to turn the Mekong into a Tennessee Valley."[35] In March 1968, in the wake of the Tet offensive, he still urged his advisers, "Let's do what we said we would do at Johns Hopkins."[36]

Hanoi spurned and impugned Johnson's generous offer of aid in 1965, and the president declared subsequently that he was not surprised. His memoirs include a dramatic map of Southeast Asia in 1965, with dark black lines converging from north and south on South Vietnam, Cambodia, and Thailand. The caption reads: "The Communist pincers—Djakarta-Hanoi-Peking-Pyongyang axis on the move."[37] Although obviously oversimplified, Johnson's point was that "Ho Chi Minh's military campaign against South Vietnam was part of a larger, much more ambitious strategy being conducted by the Communists." He maintained that President Sukarno of Indonesia had conspired in late 1964 with Chinese foreign minister Chen Yi to pressure South Vietnam from two directions, force a political collapse in Saigon, and precipitate "an ignominious American withdrawal. . . . The entire region would then be ripe for plucking. That was the prospect we faced as we debated what to do in Vietnam and Southeast Asia in the critical months of 1965."[38]

Hyperbole aside, it is evident that because of his compulsive personality and his perception of a geopolitical crisis in the making, Johnson was going to do something rather than nothing. He did not want to be a war president, but neither was he a reluctant warrior. He dismissed the notion that the conflict in Vietnam was a civil war. In his view, North Vietnam was engaged in overt aggression against South Vietnam that required a military defense, which only the United States could provide. In his brief announcement on 28 July that he was ordering an increase in U.S. troops in Vietnam from 75,000 to 125,000, he avowed that the United States would "convince the Communists that we cannot be defeated by force of arms or by superior power." He added: "We did not choose to be the guardians at the gate, but there is no one else."[39]

In July 1965, Johnson chose the stick over the carrot in Vietnam. He was preparing to do battle, and he turned to the military to wage it. This momentous decision to send U.S. combat divisions to Vietnam to wage a ground war in Asia was difficult for him. Thousands of pages have been written analyzing this choice. The volume of this analysis confirms the significance of the move to Americanize the ground war, but, despite all the intellectual energy expended on explaining his decision, the reasons remain fairly clear. Johnson and most of his senior advisers believed that they had no choice. They judged that negotiations were impossible unless the United States was prepared to concede to a neutralization of Vietnam, which was tantamount to a political victory for Hanoi. Notably, within Johnson's inner circle, Under Secretary of State George Ball proposed negotiation as an option, but he could not answer the concern that compromise equaled defeat or give Johnson what the president considered an "action" alternative to the deployment of American forces. The president could see no good choice and shared his frustration with his wife, Lady Bird: "I can't get out. I can't finish with what I've got. So what the hell do I do?"[40] Since considerations of geopolitics, ideology, and domestic American politics (the Great Society legislation was going through final voting in Congress) made unthinkable any appearance of outright surrender to an ally of the USSR and the People's Republic of China, the Johnson administration chose to make a military defense of South Vietnam.[41]

What defined Johnson's war leadership was not that he chose war, but that he tried to proceed by measured steps that disguised the magnitude of the decision in order to avoid public debate. A notorious example of his manipulation of open discussion was the near-unanimous passage of the Gulf of Tonkin Resolution in August 1964 authorizing the use of U.S. armed forces against North Vietnam. Johnson allowed congressional leaders to believe that North Vietnamese attacks (some of which were unconfirmed) on U.S. ships were unprovoked, when in fact American naval patrols in the Gulf of Tonkin were actually in support of secret South Vietnamese raids against the North. The July 1965 decision to escalate dramatically the American troop strength in Vietnam came after lengthy, top secret discussions with aides that invited no public or congressional input. The president revealed the escalation to the press almost matter-of-factly in the midst of a routine press conference in a purposeful attempt to minimize publicity of this major move. Moreover, units were deployed in stages with little fanfare. These incremental increases, which often meant giving military commanders some but not all of what they had requested, and the secrecy surrounding them revealed a pattern of attempting to conduct war on the sly.

Was Johnson's gradual and deceptive escalation an indication of political and strategic prudence or of a lack of political and strategic courage? The initial decision to choose war did not require particular courage because it was generally supported by the public and Congress. There was a high degree of cold war inevitability and inertia in that action that made it an American decision rather than a Johnson decision. What was Johnsonian was the political calculation in this and subsequent White House actions. It is enormously significant that the passage of the Great Society legislation and the resulting expectations of domestic change occurred over the same months that the U.S. military role in Vietnam leaped upward. For example, on 6 August 1965, Johnson signed the Voting Rights Act, a cornerstone of the Great Society's efforts on behalf of millions of disadvantaged and often disenfranchised African American citizens. On 11 August a white policeman in the Watts section of Los Angeles made a traffic arrest of a black motorist, and within hours this economically depressed black ghetto erupted in five days of violence that produced thirty-four deaths, hundreds of injuries and arrests, and millions of dollars in property damage. The causes of this terrible outburst were complex, but the president was immediately on the political defensive. In a call to Attorney General Nicholas Katzenbach, Johnson demanded prompt action on voter registration and on the investigation of the origins of the Watts riot because "people are trying to say the Great Society caused all of this."[42]

In other conversations it was evident that Watts and Vietnam were on the president's mind at the same time. He could list in detail the challenges that confronted young African American men. He explained:

Fifty-three out of one hundred rejected last month for the Army, many of them Negroes. So, the white boys are doing the fighting. . . . They won't let them [young African Americans] go in because their IQ is too low or health is too low or they don't know how to brush their teeth or shave. Bob McNamara thinks we ought to be pulling a bunch of them in and letting them do some of the fighting. . . . We have just got to find some way to wipe out the ghetto, find housing, put them to work.[43]

This idea eventually became Project 100,000, a special enlistment program that critics characterized as a devious way to shift the human costs of the war to the black underclass. From Johnson's perspective, however, the Vietnam War and the Great Society were both about making the world better and thus were interconnected. If he could propose a TVA for the Mekong River, he could envision military service, even in wartime, as an escape from the ghetto for black males.

Johnson's distinctive approach to Vietnam decision making is especially visible in several confidential consultations he initiated with former president Dwight Eisenhower. Although he carefully avoided a public critique of Johnson, General Eisenhower privately advised the president that "you have to go all out" in Vietnam.[44] Eisenhower had given President Harry Truman almost identical advice in June 1950 at the outset of the Korean War: "Our nation has appealed to the use of force. We must make sure of success. We should move quickly . . . to concentrate and use whatever forces may be required, including American ground troops."[45] After Johnson initiated Rolling Thunder—a continuing air campaign against North Vietnam—in March 1965 and sent two battalions of U.S. Marines to guard the Danang air base, Eisenhower complained that the number of troops was inadequate for the needs of General William Westmoreland, the U.S. commander in South Vietnam. He advised Johnson to "untie Westmoreland's hands."[46] He also objected to the restricted pattern of the Rolling Thunder bombardment and urged that U.S. air and naval forces hit North Vietnam with "everything that flies."[47] Johnson worried that the huge price tag for such an air and land assault would drain resources from his ambitious domestic plans and that conservative members of Congress would use the military necessity argument to derail the Great Society. It would be an understatement to say that the fiscally conservative Eisenhower did not share Johnson's enthusiasm for the Great Society and downplayed Johnson's concerns. In a key July 1965 phone conversation, Eisenhower's confidence contrasted sharply with Johnson's hesitations. The president asked the commander of the Allied victory over Nazi Germany outright, "Do you really think we can beat the Vietcong?" Eisenhower candidly acknowledged that it was hard to say, but he still believed that "we should go ahead."[48]

This particular conversation alone did not decide Johnson's policy course that on 28 July led him to approve orders that would bring the total of American forces in South Vietnam to 175,000 by the end of the year. Eisenhower agreed with the move, however. After a news story appeared noting that Eisenhower had not sent combat troops to Vietnam in the 1950s, the former president immediately called Johnson on 18 August. He declared that "the conditions of today are vastly different from those of '55." Eisenhower recalled that there were only about six hundred U.S. military advisers in Vietnam when he left office, but he also noted that he "did say constantly we are going to support Vietnam, but at that time it had not come to a military stand." He went on: "By reasons beyond your control and mine, the damn thing did become military—simply during the two or three years before you came in [a reference to the Kennedy administration period]. Now I have constantly said that in the condition that it is today I support the President consistently and fully." He reassured Johnson that there was no division between them and that "nothing else could have been done" other than the course the administration had taken in Vietnam.[49]

Despite these reassurances, Eisenhower grew increasingly frustrated with Johnson's seeming inability to go for the jugular with Hanoi. He thought that the timid pace of escalation was far from sufficient. Through his former presidential aide General Andrew Goodpaster, Eisenhower sent a reminder to the commander in chief of the dictum of classic military strategist Baron von Clausewitz to avoid acting by "driblets." To win, he explained, you "should sweep the enemy with overwhelming force. . . . This is no time for 'piddling steps.'"[50] Johnson saw great political danger, however, in expanding the U.S. role in Vietnam too quickly. He had estimates from economists that the war could require a federal defense budget for the next fiscal year of $110 to $112 billion, which would necessitate a tax increase. He told McNamara that he could not go to Capitol Hill with such a request because "George Mahon [chair of the House Appropriations Committee] would eliminate the whole poverty program." McNamara agreed that "if you go to 110 to 112 your Great Society is going to be gutted." "You're the only guy I talk to who sees it," the president responded. Johnson then instructed McNamara to submit a budget of $57 billion with an explanation to Congress that expenditures for Vietnam could not be predicted. Johnson reasoned that the administration could "put off a decision on extra troops until February–March," that is, until after the budget debate, and then a supplemental appropriation could be sought.[51]

As 1965 ended, Johnson was maneuvering to protect funding for the Great Society while waging a limited war. He was trying not to "stir the right wingers," who wanted more bombing, but he also did not want to provide political capital to media and congressional critics who wanted a bombing halt. The administration announced a Christmas Day pause in the Rolling Thunder campaign. On Christmas morning, Bundy raised with Johnson the question of informally extending the aerial cease-fire. He thought it would make a good public impression if the president himself made a Christmas Day statement that the United States would not be the one to end the holiday truce. Since Bobby Kennedy had given a reporter a similar suggestion earlier in the morning from the Idaho ski slopes, Johnson declined to issue a comment because he thought it would look like Kennedy "is kind of running things."[52] Although publicly quiet, Johnson kept the pause in effect past Christmas. He instructed Rusk and others to check with the British, the Poles, and other sources to see if there were any new signals of diplomatic opportunities because of the current suspension of bombing. The chance of starting negotiations was the argument that Kennedy had used for a pause. Johnson labeled the *New York Times* "the fat daddy of the pause." If the "pause boys . . . can tell who the hell is interested in it, we might announce it." As far as he could see, the Russians, Chinese, and North Vietnamese had no current interest in talks. Referring to James Reston, editor of the *Times*, Johnson declared, "If Scottie's got a better source than we have, we've got to have it."[53]

By 27 December, Westmoreland and Admiral Ulysses S. Grant Sharp, the commander in chief of U.S. Pacific forces, were pressing for resumption of the air attacks on the North. When reporters in Vietnam asked air force officers why the bombing had not resumed, the answer was that Washington would not allow it. "I just wish that damn bunch of military people would keep their mouths shut," Johnson fumed.[54] He knew that he would soon resume bombing, but he also knew that a recent Gallup poll reported that 43 percent of the public thought the administration's diplomatic efforts had been inadequate. "I feel the ice cracking under me and slipping on the domestic scene," he confided to General Maxwell Taylor, former U.S. ambassador to Saigon, who continued to serve as a special consultant to the president. Johnson figured "the odds are 95 to 5 that nothing would happen" diplomatically with a pause, "but we would be able to say to the doubting Thomases, and a good many of them are in the Senate, and a good many of the 43 percent of the American people that we paused for five days last year and nothing happened. We paused eleven to twelve days this year. We have gone the last mile. We need it now to get the support and the unity we need." Johnson quoted to Taylor a cable from Sharp to the Joint Chiefs of Staff (JCS): "The armed forces of the United States should not be required to fight the war with one arm tied behind their backs. I urgently recommend that Rolling Thunder commence immediately." Taylor advised Johnson that it would be all right to "try out the pause for political purposes and then go back and hit them as Sharp suggests." Johnson responded, "Well, I'd hit them harder after I go back."[55] In 1966 Johnson began working to contain pressures on him from both sides. The stand-down of Rolling Thunder remained in place until 31 January, when bombing of the North resumed. By June U.S. troop levels in the South had increased by eighty thousand over December.

Despite Eisenhower's earnest efforts to be discreet in his advice to the president, on one occasion he made a public slip that brought

Johnson's conduct of the war into sharp focus. On 30 September 1966, during a press conference to promote the candidacy of his brother Earl for a local office, the former president responded to a question about the war with the remark that winning it quickly should take precedence over "the war on poverty, on getting to the moon, or anything else."[56] Senator Mike Mansfield, who opposed further escalation, challenged the general "to make his views known" to the president, if he had "specific ideas as to what he would do if he were in Johnson's shoes."[57] Immediately after reading Mansfield's statement, Eisenhower telephoned the White House. He assured Johnson, "They want me to say publicly how to win the war. I won't do it. I won't divide the United States when it needs unity."[58] It was evident, however, that Eisenhower would have chosen a major war in Vietnam over implementing the Great Society, which was a choice that Johnson would not make. Even after Johnson's gradual approach pushed troop levels to four hundred thousand in 1967, Eisenhower still thought he was "holding back" and advised him to err on the side of too much rather than too little.[59] Johnson remained determined, however, to protect his Great Society and not let Congress convert the domestic reform mobilization to a foreign military mobilization. He continued to believe that the United States had the material resources and political will to do both, to provide what journalists termed both guns and butter.

As the war grew in size, cost, and controversy in 1966 and 1967, the question of political courage became increasingly relevant. Johnson needed to make some tough choices, but he exhibited an inability to make strategic decisions and provide firm guidance to the military. This pattern could be accounted for, in part, as a continuation of the premium he placed on compromise and consensus in reaching political decisions, something that he had mastered in his days as Senate majority leader and that had helped him push the Great Society through Congress. What worked for a legislative leader, however, did not work well for a commander in chief. McNamara and the JCS argued repeatedly over bombing strategy. Marine commanders differed with Westmoreland on the merits of large unit campaigns versus village security and pacification. Senior officers in the army also questioned the cost-effectiveness of Westmoreland's search-and-destroy tactics. Johnson liked to boast of the good personal relationship he had with the generals, but often the top brass did not know what he was really thinking. Not until the communists' Tet offensive in early 1968 forced a reassessment did Johnson invite a genuine review of the debates over strategy and tactics.[60]

Johnson's indecision was indicative of a failure of political nerve.

As the increased level of the American war effort extended to a year and then two years, it became more apparent that military escalation, if not a complete mistake, was at least based on a serious underestimation of the costs and benefits to the United States. As some journalists, members of Congress, and antiwar street protesters made this point, Johnson became increasingly defensive. He avoided facing facts. He devoted much of his own time to the war but would not discuss it candidly with the public and was obsessively secretive. He personalized the domestic debate. He complained to an aide: "I can't trust anybody. . . . Everybody is trying to cut me down, destroy me."[61] He characterized his critics as traitors, disloyal to him and to the country. To invoke the notion of treason was to portray his own actions as a heroic defense of American interests. Close observers of the president, such as Bill Moyers, worried that his defensiveness reflected a growing paranoia.[62]

In February 1967, Johnson told his aides that the policy in Vietnam "was operating on borrowed time." The communists were waging an "all-out psychological war" that was eroding his administration's political base, but, he calculated, "In the country the support for more vigorous military action is at least 3–1, even if the war should get rougher and we face serious consequences. . . . We have probed for talks and found nothing substantial. Now we must act strongly."[63] Westmoreland launched the largest ground operations of the war but was unable to deliver a knockout blow to the enemy's forces, which largely avoided direct engagement with the more heavily armed Americans. On Washington's orders, Westmoreland increased the pacification or civic-action efforts of his forces, but they made little progress in eroding communist political influence in rural areas. The JCS requested an increase of two hundred thousand ground troops. By May, McNamara had seen enough and sent Johnson a blunt memorandum. "The war in Vietnam is acquiring a momentum of its own that must be stopped," he wrote, predicting that sending ever larger numbers of troops "could lead to a major national disaster" and "would not win the Vietnam war." His recommendation was a combination of military operations at present levels, pacification, and diplomacy as a lever not for victory but "toward negotiations and toward ending the war on satisfactory terms."[64]

Johnson was not done, however. Through 1967 he continued to take a middle course among the options, as he had done since 1965. He approved only fifty-five thousand of Westmoreland's requested two hundred thousand additional troops but did not request a review of the search-and-destroy tactics of the ground war or a limit on the air war. He was refusing to face the inconsistencies in U.S. strategy that were tantamount to no strategy at all. On 1 November 1967, McNamara sent Johnson a new memo that "addressed fundamental questions that had to be answered." In his memoirs, McNamara describes how he tried to convey that "I understood just how hard it would be for the president to consider abandoning the conventional wisdom on Vietnam and changing course. But that was what I was recommending."[65] The memo specifically outlined a policy of "stabilization," which included (1) "no increase . . . in US forces above the current approved level," (2) "a bombing halt [that] is likely to lead to talks with Hanoi," and (3) "programs which involve (a) reduced US casualties, (b) procedures for the progressive turn-over to the GVN [South Vietnamese government] of greater responsibility for security in the South, and (c) lesser destruction of the people and wealth of South Vietnam."[66]

Johnson demanded evidence and reassurance that, in fact, more than two years of American military effort was producing results in Vietnam. Was he simply making political calculations in preparation for the 1968 election year or was he trying to buck up his courage? Either way, National Security Adviser Walt Rostow gave him what he wanted. Rather than engaging McNamara in direct discussion (much as he had avoided candor with congressional leaders), Johnson shared the memo with Rusk for comment and instructed Rostow to solicit reactions to the paper from a select group without identifying its author. Rostow began quietly contacting Taylor, ambassador to Vietnam Ellsworth Bunker, presidential confidants Clark Clifford and Abe Fortas, and a few others. He also convened the Wise Men to meet with Johnson on 2 November. This unofficial advisory group, mostly former high-level officials of the caliber of former secretary of state Dean Acheson, had served the president as a generally supportive sounding board in the past. McNamara was present at the meeting, as were most of the men Rostow would be polling, but no mention was made of the memo. The minutes of the meeting indicate that the president set the agenda: "He wanted to know if our course in Vietnam was right. If not, how should it be modified? He said he is deeply concerned about the deterioration of public support and the lack of editorial support for our policies." Based on JCS and CIA briefings of the previous day, the group was very positive in its assessments. Clifford, for example, termed the war "an enormous success" and recommended that "if we keep up the pressure on them, the will of the Viet Cong and the North Vietnamese will wear down." The president declared that there was a consensus that "generally everyone agrees with our present course in the South." Rostow added, "The progress taking place will help win support. He said that there are ways of guiding the press to show light at the end of the tunnel."[67]

Rostow had, in fact, also guided this internal policy review to show progress. George Allen, the CIA's senior Vietnam analyst who helped to prepare the regular briefings that his bosses gave the White House, observed that the administration's policy process was "ad hoc." Without a systematic approach, Allen noted, "policies tend to be excessively dominated by aggressive individuals . . . rather than by rational deliberation." Rostow considered it to be one of his responsibilities to build support for the president's policies. In mid-1967 he had informed Allen that "the president needed a [CIA] summary that would help him convince a number of congressmen and other White House visitors in coming weeks that the pacification effort was on track." Allen protested that such a report would not be objective and, after some heated discussion with the national security adviser, declined to "be a party to 'cooking the books' in the manner he was suggesting."[68] Rostow subsequently got a statement of progress to his liking from another CIA office. His efforts paid off in the briefings to the Wise Men. In reflecting later on the meeting, McNamara wrote that "the Wise Men had no clue that all this was going on."[69] His reference was to his own negative memo, but it was a comment on the entire process.

Westmoreland, a political general, came back to Washington in late November to offer the public reassurances of progress that the White House desired. Such maneuvering may have been blatant presidential politics. Privately, however, Johnson embraced the claims of success. In December, he placed an internal memorandum in the record in which he referenced the collected results of Rostow's inquiries about McNamara's recommendation of 1 November, the meeting of 2 November (which he characterized as "a full discussion"), and personal consultations with General Westmoreland and Ambassador Bunker. He recorded his rejection of McNamara's "policy of stabilization" and of "a unilateral and unrequited bombing standdown." He agreed with the third point to "review the conduct of military operations in South Vietnam."[70] Publicly and privately, the president refused to confront the possibility that the war was a mistake. It was a sign of a failure of political courage.

In January 1968, the communists' surprise Tet offensive, followed by a request from Westmoreland for 206,000 more troops, prompted a real reevaluation of the progress of the war, not a staged review as had occurred in November. Clark Clifford, one of the most confident of the Wise Men, had replaced the disillusioned McNamara in January, and Johnson turned to the new defense secretary to conduct the review. Initially the president continued to express confidence to his aides: "I do not share the view that many people have that we took a great defeat."[71] One of his principal concerns was the $5 to $7 billion cost of Westmoreland's request. "Let's hope for the best but expect the worst," he told aides. "I guess that will be that Westmoreland will need more troops."[72] By early March, Clifford's meetings with civilian and military officials in the Pentagon had raised enough doubt about a military solution to the war to lead the administration to reject the huge request for troops. What to do next, however, remained unclear. Press and public opposition to the war intensified, and many influential businessmen began to note the damaging economic impact the war was having on the United States. On 26 March, internal discussions within the White House finally brought Johnson to a decision.

It was an emotional day for the president. He met in the morning with General Earle Wheeler, chairman of the JCS, and General Creighton Abrams, who would soon replace Westmoreland in Vietnam. Although they could report that Westmoreland had the tactical situation in hand, Johnson's personal stress was evident. "Our financial situation is abominable," he anguished, because the federal deficit was so high that it threatened the value of U.S., British, and Canadian currency. Congress would never approve a tax increase without reduced appropriations. "What happens when you cut poverty, housing and education?" he worried and launched into a brief monologue:

> This is complicated by the fact it is an election year. I don't give a damn about the election. I will be happy to keep doing what is right and lose the election. . . . The country is demoralized. . . . I will have overwhelming disapproval in the polls and elections. I will go down the drain. I don't want the whole alliance and military pulled in with it. I wouldn't be surprised if they repealed the Tonkin Gulf Resolution. Senator Russell wants us to go in and take out Haiphong [North Vietnam's primary port city]. . . . The Times and the Post are all against us. Most of the press is against us. . . . We have no support for the war. This is caused by the 206,000 troop request, leaks, Ted Kennedy and Bobby Kennedy.[73]

Johnson was still agonizing, as he had from the beginning of the escalation in 1965, over the threat of the war to appropriations for the Great Society, over political pressures from both conservatives and liberals, and over the Kennedys.

In the afternoon Johnson and his top aides met with the Wise Men. Dean Acheson spoke for the majority of the external advisers: "We can no longer do the job we set out to do in the time we have left and we must begin to take steps to disengage." Although there was a minority view that "we should not act to weaken our position," McGeorge Bundy was accurate in his observation about the Wise Men that "there is a very significant shift in our position."[74] Arthur Dean explained, "Mr. President, all of us got the impression last night listening to General DePuy, Mr. Carter [Carver] and Mr. Habib that there are no military conclusions in this war—or any military end in the near future." Maxwell Taylor added that the picture he received from the briefings "is not the one I have developed over a period of time." Johnson responded that "the first thing I do when you all leave is to get those briefers last night."[75] A transcript of the tape recording of the meeting indicates that Johnson added, "I want to so I can evaluate it and may come to the very same conclusion that everybody else here has. I haven't heard some of these theories. Maybe I haven't gotten the whole story. I gather that it is different from what I have been getting top-side."[76]

Johnson's ruminations with the generals and the session with the Wise Men revealed to him that the war was not working. The president's intimidating manner and Rostow's flawed sense of loyalty had led to a lack of candor in previous White House briefings. The national security adviser's selective policy review of November had not served Johnson well. The meetings on 26 March forced him to see through the illusion of progress and positive scenarios. The following day General William DePuy from the Pentagon and George Carver from the CIA gave Johnson the same briefing that the Wise Men had received, and the president insisted they must have changed it because "what you are telling me couldn't account for the inferences they drew."[77] Johnson's incredulity was the product of his former unwillingness to face what were widely held and publicly expressed doubts about the war. His self-delusion had been undermining his ability to be objective. The assessment now before him was not that the war was lost. Wheeler, Abrams, and the briefers indicated that there were a host of military and diplomatic options that still could be exercised. The message was that the strategic value of Vietnam and the costs to the United States of further escalation had to be recalculated realistically.

On 31 March, Johnson informed a national television audience that he was ordering limits on the bombing of the North and offering negotiations. At the end of the speech he added his own bombshell that he would not seek reelection as president. He told congressional leaders a few days later that he had called together fifteen men from inside and outside the government, heard their views, "and as a result made this speech proposal Sunday night."[78] What had prompted his dramatic response to that session? Had he finally mustered the political courage that he had been lacking?

As he had done when he inherited the Vietnam policy process in 1963, Johnson rationalized as courage a course of action that he felt he had little choice but to take. The meetings and briefings of 26–27 March led him to sense that the Vietnamese enemy was too strong and the popular approval in the United States too weak to continue the course he had been following. Johnson may have wanted it to be otherwise, but, as political scientist Richard Neustadt notes, he "knew how to count and, having looked about him, evidently felt he had no other option."[79] From her talks with Johnson after he left the White House, Kearns believed that "he ingeniously reasoned that he could withdraw from politics without being seen as a coward." History would record, he thought, that "he acted nobly at this critical moment."[80] Adding to Kearns's assessment, psychologist Steinberg has argued that "Johnson had a sufficiently strong ego to accept the realities" as revealed by the Wise Men's reversal and the public outcry over the war.[81] She reasoned that he chose de-escalation and withdrew as a candidate in 1968 just as he had chosen escalation in 1965 to protect his ego from the humiliation of political defeat.

Johnson's 31 March announcement of his political retirement—his abandonment of "personal partisan causes"—at the end of a speech on "our search for peace in Vietnam" was, in effect, clear evidence of the high correlation between his personal political leadership and the conduct of the American war.[82] He may have chosen to believe that he was sacrificing himself—falling on his own political sword—in an act of political courage. People around him in the days between the briefings and the speech noted, however, how "frazzled" and exhausted he appeared.[83] He had run a high-stakes political race to launch the Great Society and contain communism in Vietnam before facing the voters in the November 1968 elections. He had lost that race, and he knew it. He told the congressional leadership on 2 April that he was "tired of begging anyone for anything."[84] He was throwing in the towel.

In the final analysis, Johnson had persisted too long in seeking an American solution to Vietnam's internal political conflict. Would John Kennedy have made the same political calculation? Would he have had the same "courage" to stop escalation sooner? Johnson kept waiting for Westmoreland to bail him out of what was increasingly discernible as a military stalemate. Johnson never wanted a big war because he wanted no war at all. Some military historians and others have complained that he could have done more, but, as it was, the United States was already doing more damage to itself and to Vietnam than the level of American interest in the region could tolerate. Johnson would rather have been building dams in Vietnam, not firebases.

Johnson did not lack political courage in domestic politics. He showed tremendous personal growth and commitment in championing civil rights legislation, for example. He translated his sensitivity for the economic and social plight of African Americans trapped in poverty and disadvantage into action that moved an often reluctant Congress to approve dramatic reforms. He demonstrated a confidence and daring in fashioning progressive legislation that he had cultivated from his earliest days as a New Dealer. In Vietnam, however, political courage failed him. He could profess the same sensitivity for Vietnamese farmers and for young American soldiers at war as he had for economic and social stresses on Americans at home, but the wherewithal to say no to the agony of Vietnam was missing. He used fears—real and imagined—of communist aggression, conservative political backlash, and personal humiliation to talk himself out of giving in to his doubts about the human costs of war. It was difficult to say no to the pressures for escalation and easy to say yes to incremental increases of force. Lyndon Johnson's war leadership was not a profile in courage.

Notes

1. Doris Kearns, *Lyndon Johnson and the American Dream* (New York: New American Library, 1976), 361.

2. Robert Dallek, *Flawed Giant: Lyndon Johnson and His Times, 1961–1973* (New York: Oxford University Press, 1998), 626.

3. Howard Jones, *Death of a Generation: How the Assassinations of Diem and JFK Prolonged the Vietnam War* (New York: Oxford University Press, 2003), 11. See also Fredrik Logevall, *Choosing War: The Lost Chance for Peace and the Escalation of War in Vietnam* (Berkeley and Los Angeles: University of California Press, 1999), 395–400.

4. Robert D. Dean, *Imperial Brotherhood: Gender and the Making of Cold War Foreign Policy* (Amherst: University of Massachusetts Press, 2001), 48. See also David M. Barrett, *Uncertain Warriors: Lyndon Johnson and His Vietnam Advisers* (Lawrence: University Press of Kansas, 1993), 16, on the enormous political obstacles facing any president who would have considered announcing a withdrawal from Vietnam in 1964 or 1965.

5. John F. Kennedy, *Profiles in Courage*, foreword by Allan Nevins (New York: Pocket Books, 1957), ix.

6. For a discussion of Vietnam War historiography, see David L. Anderson, "The Vietnam War," in *A Companion to American Foreign Relations*, ed. Robert Schulzinger (Oxford: Blackwell, 2003).

7. A. J. Langguth, *Our Vietnam: The War, 1954–1975* (New York: Simon and Schuster, 2000), 269.

8. Kearns, *Lyndon Johnson and the American Dream*, 264–265.

9. Blema S. Steinberg, *Shame and Humiliation: Presidential Decision Making on Vietnam* (Pittsburgh: University of Pittsburgh Press, 1996), 123.

10. Quoted in Kennedy, *Profiles in Courage*, 207.

11. Dean, *Imperial Brotherhood*, 239.

12. Robert Dallek, *Lone Star Rising: Lyndon Johnson and His Times, 1908–1960* (New York: Oxford University Press, 1991), 238–241.

13. Notes of meeting, 20 March 1968, Tom Johnson's Meeting Notes, box 2, Lyndon Baines Johnson Presidential Library, Austin, Texas (hereafter LBJL).

14. Telephone Conversation between Lyndon B. Johnson and Martin Luther King, 20 August 1965, 5:10 P.M., Citation no. 8578, Recordings and Transcripts of Telephone Conversations, LBJL.

15. Notes of meeting, 20 March 1968, Tom Johnson's Notes of Meetings, box 2, LBJL.

16. William S. White, *The Professional: Lyndon B. Johnson* (Boston: Houghton Mifflin, 1964), 251. See also notes of meeting by Jim Jones, "April 2, 1968, 8:42 AM Congressional Leadership Breakfast," Meeting Notes File, box 2, LBJL.

17. Telephone Conversation between Johnson and McGeorge Bundy, 27 May 1964, 11:24 A.M., Citation no. 3522, Recordings and Transcripts of Telephone Conversations, LBJL.

18. H. W. Brands, "Introduction," in *The Foreign Policies of Lyndon Johnson: Beyond Vietnam*, ed. H. W. Brands (College Station: Texas A&M University Press, 1999), 4; Logevall, *Choosing War*, 390.

19. Robert A. Divine, "Vietnam Reconsidered," *Diplomatic History* 12 (Winter 1988): 79–93.

20. David Halberstam, *The Best and the Brightest* (Greenwich, Conn.: Fawcett, 1972), 522.

21. Interview with Walt Rostow, 7 June 1996, National Security Archive on-line, www.gwu.edu/~nsarchiv/coldwar/interviews/episode-9/rostow1.html (accessed 7 August 2003); Dean Rusk with Richard Rusk, *As I Saw It*, ed. Daniel S. Papp (New York: Norton, 1990); Michael Lind, *Vietnam: The Necessary War* (New York: Free Press, 1999).

22. John P. Burke and Fred I. Greenstein with Larry Berman and Richard Immerman, *How Presidents Test Reality: Decisions on Vietnam, 1954 and 1965* (New York: Russell Sage Foundation, 1989); Logevall, *Choosing War*; Kearns, *Lyndon Johnson and the American Dream*; H. R. McMaster, *Dereliction of Duty: Johnson, McNamara, the Joint Chiefs of Staff, and the Lies That Led to Vietnam* (New York: HarperCollins, 1997); Eric F. Goldman, *The Tragedy of Lyndon Johnson* (New York: Knopf, 1968); David Kaiser, *American Tragedy: Kennedy, Johnson, and the Origins of the Vietnam War* (Cambridge, Mass.: Harvard University Press, 2000); Waldo Heinrichs, "Lyndon B. Johnson: Change and Continuity," in *Lyndon Johnson Confronts the World*, ed. Warren I. Cohen and Nancy Bernkopf Tucker (New York: Cambridge University Press, 1994);

Sandra C. Taylor, "Lyndon Johnson and the Vietnamese," in *Shadow on the White House: Presidents and the Vietnam War, 1945–1975*, ed. David L. Anderson (Lawrence: University Press of Kansas, 1993), 113–129; George C. Herring, "The Reluctant Warrior: Lyndon Johnson as Commander in Chief," ibid., 87–112.

23. Robert Dallek, "Lyndon Johnson as a World Leader," in Brands, *Foreign Policies of Lyndon Johnson*, 12, 14.

24. H. W. Brands, *The Wages of Globalism: Lyndon Johnson and the Limits of American Power* (New York: Oxford University Press, 1995), vii. See also Robert A. Divine, "The Johnson Revival: A Bibliographical Appraisal," in *The Johnson Years*, vol. 2, *Vietnam, the Environment, and Science*, ed. Robert A. Divine (Lawrence: University Press of Kansas, 1987), 17–18.

25. Thomas Alan Schwartz, *Lyndon Johnson and Europe: In the Shadow of Vietnam* (Cambridge, Mass.: Harvard University Press, 2003), 225.

26. Ibid., 235.

27. Ibid., 234–237. Mitchell B. Lerner, *The Pueblo Incident: A Spy Ship and the Failure of American Foreign Policy* (Lawrence: University Press of Kansas, 2002), argues similarly that, despite some problems, Johnson handled well the difficult crisis in Korea in 1968 and maintained key alliances and regional stability to achieve the best possible outcome available.

28. Robert D. Schulzinger, *A Time for War: The United States and Vietnam, 1941–1975* (New York: Oxford University Press, 1997), 329.

29. Kearns, *Lyndon Johnson and the American Dream*, 263. See also Jeffrey W. Helsing, *Johnson's War/Johnson's Great Society: The Guns and Butter Trap* (Westport, Conn.: Praeger, 2000), 255–256.

30. Telephone Conversation between Johnson and McGeorge Bundy, 31 May 1965, 12:45 P.M., Citation no. 7852, Recordings and Transcripts of Telephone Conversations, LBJL.

31. Lloyd C. Gardner, *Pay Any Price: Lyndon Johnson and the Wars for Vietnam* (Chicago: Ivan R. Dee, 1995), xi–xii.

32. Lyndon Baines Johnson, *The Vantage Point: Perspectives of the Presidency, 1963–1969* (New York: Popular Library, 1971), 133–134.

33. Quoted in Stanley Karnow, *Vietnam: A History* (New York: Penguin, 1984), 419. See also Gardner, *Pay Any Price*, 55.

34. Johnson, *Vantage Point*, 134.

35. Kearns, *Lyndon Johnson and the American Dream*, 279. See also Gardner, *Pay Any Price*, 197.

36. Notes of meeting, 20 March 1968, Tom Johnson's Notes of Meetings, box 2, LBJL.

37. Johnson, *Vantage Point*, 606.

38. Ibid., 134–136.

39. *Public Papers of the Presidents of the United States: Lyndon B. Johnson, Containing the Public Messages, Speeches, and Statements of the President, 1965* (Washington, D.C.: Government Printing Office, 1968), 794–796. See also Herring, "Reluctant Warrior," 87; Gary R. Hess, *Presidential Decisions for War: Korea, Vietnam, and the Persian Gulf* (Baltimore: Johns Hopkins University Press, 2001), 94; and Kearns, *Lyndon Johnson and the American Dream*, 344.

40. Lady Bird Johnson, *A White House Diary* (New York: Holt, Rinehart and Winston, 1970), 248.

41. For especially useful analyses of the July 1965 decision, see Larry Berman, *Planning a Tragedy: The Americanization of the War in Vietnam* (New York: Norton, 1982); David M. Barrett, *Uncertain Warriors: Lyndon Johnson and His Vietnam Advisers* (Lawrence: University Press of Kansas, 1993); and Logevall, *Choosing War.*

42. Telephone Conversation between Johnson and Nicholas Katzenbach, 17 August 1965, 11:55 A.M., Citation no. 8544, Recordings and Transcripts of Telephone Conversations, LBJL.

43. Telephone Conversation between Johnson and John McCone, 18 August 1965, 12:10 P.M., Citation no. 8550, ibid. See also Office of Assistant Secretary of Defense (Manpower and Reserve Affairs), *Description of Project One Hundred Thousand,* April 1968, Office of the Secretary of Defense Historical Office, Washington, D.C.

44. Memorandum of telephone conversation, 2 July 1965, Palm Desert-Indio series, box 10, Dwight D. Eisenhower Post-Presidential Papers, Dwight D. Eisenhower Library, Abilene, Kansas (hereafter DDEL).

45. Dwight D. Eisenhower, *Mandate for Change, 1953–1956* (New York: New American Library, 1963), 118.

46. Andrew J. Goodpaster memorandum, 9 April 1965, Palm Desert-Indio series, box 9, DDEL.

47. Goodpaster memorandum, 13 May 1965, ibid.

48. Memorandum of telephone conversation, 2 July 1965, box 10, ibid.

49. Telephone Conversation between Johnson and Dwight Eisenhower, 18 August 1965, 6:15 P.M., Citation no. 8555, Recordings and Transcripts of Telephone Conversations, LBJL.

50. Goodpaster memorandum, 3 August 1965, Palm Desert-Indio series, box 9, DDEL.

51. Telephone Conversation between Johnson and Robert McNamara, 22 December 1965, 10:10 a.m., Citation no. 9327, Recordings and Transcripts of Telephone Conversations, LBJL.

52. Telephone Conversation between Johnson and McGeorge Bundy, 25 December 1965, 12:50 P.M., Citation no. 9337, ibid.

53. Telephone Conversation between Johnson and Bundy, 27 December 1965, 9:35 A.M., Citation no. 9338, ibid.

54. Ibid.

55. Telephone Conversation between Johnson and Maxwell Taylor, 27 December 1965, 8:56 P.M., Citation no. 9339, ibid.

56. *New York Times,* 1 October 1966.

57. *New York Times,* 2 October 1966.

58. Memorandum of telephone conversation, 3 October 1966, Palm Desert-Indio series, box 10, DDEL.

59. Goodpaster memorandum, 7 April 1967, box 10, ibid.

60. George C. Herring, *LBJ and Vietnam: A Different Kind of War* (Austin: University of Texas Press, 1994), 182; Herring, "Reluctant Warrior," 97–98.

61. Quoted in Hess, *Presidential Decisions for War,* 122. See also Herring, *LBJ and Vietnam,* 183.

62. Langguth, *Our Vietnam,* 367–368; Dallek, *Flawed Giant,* 281.

63. Walt W. Rostow, Notes of Meeting with President Johnson, 17 February 1967, *Foreign Relations of the United States, 1964–1968,* vol. 5, *Vietnam, 1967* (Washington, D.C.: Government Printing Office, 2002), 185 (hereafter *FRUS*).

64. Memorandum from McNamara to Johnson, 19 May 1967, ibid., 437.
65. Robert S. McNamara, *In Retrospect: The Tragedy and Lessons of Vietnam* (New York: Random House, 1995), 307. See also George C. Herring, *America's Longest War: The United States and Vietnam, 1950–1975*, 4th ed. (New York: McGraw Hill, 2002), 217.
66. Memorandum from McNamara to Johnson, 1 November 1967, *FRUS, 1964–1968*, 5: 949–950.
67. Memorandum from Jim Jones (presidential assistant) to Johnson, 2 November 1967, ibid., 954–970.
68. George W. Allen, *None So Blind: A Personal Account of the Intelligence Failure in Vietnam* (Chicago: Ivan R. Dee, 2001), 237–242.
69. McNamara, *In Retrospect*, 309.
70. Memorandum for the file by Johnson, 18 December 1967, *FRUS, 1964–1968*, 5: 1118–1120. Comments on McNamara's memo by Taylor, Bundy, Fortas, Clifford, Rusk, and Bunker are found in ibid., 978–1061. For Rostow's summary for the president of the comments on McNamara's memo, see chart in "Vietnam, conduct of War in (sensitive), President's Memo, McNamara's Memo," Files of Walt W. Rostow, National Security File (NSF), box 3, LBJL.
71. Notes of meeting by Tom Johnson, 6 February 1968, *FRUS, 1964–1968*, 6: 139.
72. Notes of the president's meeting with senior advisers, 9 February 1968, "Mar. 31 Speech, Vol. 7, Meeting Notes," National Security Council (NSC) Histories, NSF, Box 49, LBJL.
73. Notes of meeting, "March 26, 1968, 10:30 AM, Meeting with Gen. Wheeler, JCS, and Gen. Creighton Abrams," Tom Johnson's Notes of Meetings, box 2, LBJL.
74. Notes of meeting, 26 March 1968, *FRUS, 1964–1968*, 6: 471.
75. Memorandum from Tom Johnson to the president, 27 March 1968, "March 26, 1968," President's Appointment File (Diary Backup), box 93, LBJL.
76. Transcript of Meeting in the Cabinet Room, 26 March 1968, *FRUS, 1964–1968*, 474n6.
77. Quoted in Townsend Hoopes, *The Limits of Intervention: An Inside Account of How the Johnson Policy of Escalation in Vietnam Was Reversed* (New York: David McKay, 1969), 218. See also Notes of Meeting by Tom Johnson, 27 March 1968, *FRUS, 1964–1968*, 6: 481–483; and Clark Clifford with Richard Holbrook, *Counsel to the President: A Memoir* (New York: Doubleday, 1992), 517–519.
78. Notes of meeting by Jim Jones, "April 2, 1968, 8:42 AM Congressional Leadership Breakfast," Meeting Notes File, box 2, LBJL.
79. Richard E. Neustadt, *Presidential Power and the Modern Presidents: The Politics of Leadership from Roosevelt to Reagan* (New York: Free Press, 1990), 189.
80. Kearns, *Lyndon Johnson and the American Dream*, 360.
81. Steinberg, *Shame and Humiliation*, 304.
82. *Public Papers of the Presidents of the United States: Lyndon B. Johnson, Containing the Public Messages, Speeches, and Statements of the President, 1968–1969* (Washington, D.C.: Government Printing Office, 1970), 468–476.
83. Langguth, *Our Vietnam*, 490.
84. Notes of meeting by Jim Jones, "April 2, 1968, 8:42 AM Congressional Leadership Breakfast," Meeting Notes File, box 2, LBJL.

6 | The "Long Hot Summer" and the Politics of Law and Order

Michael Flamm

IN NOVEMBER 1967, President Lyndon Johnson received some bleak news from speechwriter Ben Wattenberg, who reported that "whites will vote readily for a Negro for Congress or Senate, but not for City Hall—not when the Police Department and/or the Board of Education may be at stake. That is where the backlash is; that is where the fear is."[1] After three years of mounting street crime, political demonstrations, and civil disorders, the fear was pervasive despite the desperate—and, in the end, doomed—efforts of Lyndon Johnson to contain it. In the wake of major riots in Newark and Detroit that summer, millions of white Americans, suburban and urban, demanded an immediate restoration of "law and order." The issue had first moved from the margins to the mainstream of national politics in 1964, when Arizona senator Barry Goldwater made "crime in the streets" a central theme of his presidential bid. But it had failed to resonate with most voters because Johnson was too popular, Goldwater was too conservative, and, above all, conditions were too tranquil.[2] By 1967, however, "law and order" had taken center stage. By 1968, it was the most important political issue in the United States—and the most potent political weapon in the conservative arsenal.

Conservatives maintained that the breakdown in public order was the result of three developments aided and abetted by liberals. First, the civil rights movement had popularized the doctrine of civil disobedience, which promoted disrespect for law and authority. Second, the Supreme Court, in a series of decisions such as *Escobedo* and *Miranda*, had enhanced the rights of criminal defendants at the expense of law enforcement.[3] Finally, the Great Society trumpeted by the White House had directly or indirectly rewarded undeserving minorities for their criminal behavior during urban riots. It was a cogent narrative with visceral appeal.

Liberals, by contrast, could not craft a compelling message. They first denied the problem and then insisted with some merit that the only truly effective way to fight disorder was through an assault on root causes like poverty and unemployment. They also tried to define crime control as a local matter, which, constitutionally and logistically, it was.[4] But the definition seemed rather convenient when liberals had already classified virtually every other social ill, most notably public education, as a national imperative. By 1967, many white voters believed that the Johnson administration neither shared their pain nor understood their frustration.

When precisely and why exactly urban white voters began to desert the Democratic Party and embrace the Republican Party—or abandon electoral politics altogether—is a subject of considerable interest for scholars and commentators. Thomas and Mary Edsall, authors of *Chain Reaction,* identify the critical moment as the 1960s and the main cause as the white reaction to the civil rights movement and Johnson administration programs. The Democratic Party, they and others contend, then compounded the crisis by responding to the grievances and demands of a black militant minority while ignoring the fears and desires of a white "silent majority."[5]

But historian Thomas Sugrue argues that urban antiliberalism predated the Johnson administration and determined the "politics of race and neighborhood" in the North in the 1940s and 1950s. In *The Origins of the Urban Crisis,* he details how opposition to racial integration dominated local elections even in Detroit, where liberal organizations like the United Auto Workers presumably held sway. Therefore, the conservative backlash of the 1960s was not, according to Sugrue, "the unique product of the white rejection of the Great Society. Instead it was the culmination of more than two decades of simmering white discontent and extensive antiliberal political organization."[6]

Neither interpretation is wholly persuasive. Sugrue has convincingly documented the existence and virulence of northern racism at the municipal level. But the disintegration of the New Deal coalition at the national level was not inevitable. Prior to the early 1960s, many urban whites in effect split their ballots. They balanced support for conservative local candidates opposed to residential integration with support for liberal national candidates committed to civil rights.[7] More important, both the Edsalls and Sugrue place too much emphasis on the role of racism and too little on the role of security. After 1964 the distance between voters and issues narrowed as anxiety over the loss of public safety widened.[8] The unraveling of the liberal political coalition therefore was not simply the result of a racial backlash against civil rights. Nor was it solely a result of specific actions taken—or not taken—by Johnson. It was, rather, due largely to the growing sense that the administration could not ensure personal security or contain social disorder, which increasingly seemed like the inevitable by-product of modern liberalism.

During the "Long Hot Summer" of 1967, more than one hundred cities erupted in violence. But it was the riots in Newark and Detroit that eroded what confidence remained among most officials in the White House. The critical distinction that they had tried to draw between race and crime was shattered, perhaps permanently. The careful emphasis on federalism—the notion that "law and order" was a local responsibility—lay in ruins. And the abiding faith that the Great Society would calm social unrest was replaced by the gnawing fear that it had somehow contributed to the civil disorders. For Johnson, under siege from every direction, including his own party, no relief appeared in sight. "I do not know what they think we can do," he complained bitterly to his former attorney general.[9]

I

Although Newark had remained quiet during the Harlem riot of 1964 and the Watts riot of 1965, it was as promising a place for an eruption as any other in America. The poverty, unemployment, and crime rates were high. It had a police department that was, proportionately, the largest in the country—yet was, by most accounts, riddled with corruption and rife with brutality. It also had an overcrowded and dilapidated school system. And with the arrival of summer, tens of thousands of teens were on the streets, unemployed and unoccupied because of budget cutbacks in the recreation program.[10]

On the evening of Wednesday, 12 July, a black cab driver named John Smith sustained serious injuries after he was arrested by Newark police. As rumors of police brutality spread, a confrontation between officers and bystanders erupted outside the Fourth Precinct police station, near the massive Hayes Housing Project. A barrage of rocks and a few Molotov cocktails smashed against the station. Scattered looting was later reported. The next day, the mayor called the Smith affair an "isolated incident" but promised an investigation by a panel of citizens and the appointment of the city's first black police captain. That evening, a protest march disintegrated into widespread looting. At midnight the overwhelmed police were told to use "all necessary means—including firearms—to defend themselves." Early Friday morning, the mayor requested that Governor Richard Hughes dispatch the state police and National Guard. "The line between the jungle and the law might as well be drawn here as any place in America," declared Hughes, who sent in more than three thousand Guardsmen.

Late Monday evening they withdrew. Left behind were twenty-three dead, twenty-one of whom were black residents of Newark.[11]

The deaths left even temperate observers angry. During his appearance on *Meet the Press* that Sunday, Roy Wilkins of the National Association for the Advancement of Colored People (NAACP) bristled at assertions that he should have done more to halt the riot. "Nobody ever asked the Chamber of Commerce to stop a white riot; nobody ever asked the Ministerial Alliance to stop the riot," he retorted. "They realize rioters are not part of the church or part of the business community, but the minute something happens in a Negro community they say, 'Why don't you Negroes get together, you law-abiding Negroes, and stop all the rest of these Negroes?'" When columnist Robert Novak asked whether he favored a "massive effort to disarm the Negroes in the ghettos," Wilkins replied, "I would be in favor of disarming everybody, not just the Negroes." Brushing aside Novak's objection, he then added, "I wouldn't disarm the Negroes and leave them helpless prey to the people who wanted to go in and shoot them up." But why, interjected Novak, should blacks in Newark have rifles? What do they have to fear? "Why does anyone have rifles?" responded Wilkins. "The NRA is carrying on a tremendous lobbying campaign for Americans to own rifles. Every American wants to own a rifle. Why shouldn't the Negroes own rifles?"[12] Even in air-conditioned studios far from the ghettos, tempers were rising.

In Washington, the president anxiously watched the situation unfold. Ready to help an old friend and fellow Democrat, Johnson on Friday had offered Hughes whatever he needed—support the governor declined. But the president remained sensitive to conservative claims that his administration rewarded rioters and that poverty workers had helped to incite the riot. He also was determined to maintain the division of responsibility mandated by federalism. When Hubert Humphrey on Saturday confirmed that the White House had offered assistance, Johnson was furious. Inform the vice president, he told Califano, that "he has no authority, spell it out, N-O-N-E, to provide any federal aid to Newark or any other city, town or country in America." Four days later, the president met with Roy Wilkins and Whitney Young. "I was struck by their despair," recalled Califano. "The nation was at a flash point with pent-up frustration and anger, and these leaders seemed bewildered by the rush of events . . . [and] numbed by their lack of influence."[13] They were not alone.[14]

At the cabinet meeting on Wednesday, Johnson urged his officials to do more for the cities, to challenge critics about what they would do, and to redouble efforts to get the administration's story told. At his press conference the day before, the president had followed his own advice. "No one condones or approves—and everyone regrets—the difficulties that have come in the Wattses, the Newarks, and the other places in the country," he said. Then, after defending the Office of Economic Opportunity (OEO), Model Cities, and the entire poverty program, he acknowledged the depth of the crisis in the ghetto. "We can't correct it in a day or a year or a decade," he declared. "But we are trying at this end of the line as best as we can."[15] By the end of the weekend, it was clear that was not good enough.

Unlike Newark, Detroit was not a textbook case of a riot waiting to happen. Led by respected white liberals like Mayor Jerry Cavanagh and Commissioner Ray Girardin, it was seen by many as a "model city."[16] Black incomes were significantly above the national average—and the gap between blacks and whites had narrowed dramatically since 1960. The unemployment rate was also low in comparison to that in other urban areas.[17] But the Motor City was not truly a "model city." Although many of the unions had finally begun to accept African Americans, discrimination remained rampant, with blacks concentrated in unskilled or low-skill jobs. The city schools were overcrowded. Black housing was segregated and in poor quality, if not in national terms, then in comparison to white housing.[18] Above all, the police had a local reputation for brutality that poisoned community relations, particularly among blacks in the troubled Twelfth Street section.[19] Once again, the stage was set.

Early Sunday morning, 23 July, four days after Johnson spoke to the cabinet about Newark, officers raided five "blind pigs," or private social clubs. By midmorning, allegations of police mistreatment had spread, and the riot was under way.[20] The arrival of the state police and National Guard, however, merely added fuel to the fire. The latter in particular were poorly prepared, with little training for riot control. They were also ill equipped, with obsolete weapons, inadequate maps, and a severe shortage of radio equipment (so severe that at times they had to depend on pay telephones). And they were overwhelmingly nonurban whites (only forty-two of the eight thousand Guardsmen in Detroit were black), with little knowledge of the city or respect for African Americans. "I'm gonna shoot at anything that moves and that is black," declared one Guardsman upon arrival.[21] His sentiments were typical.

On Monday, the riot reached a crescendo of violence as the temperature climbed to ninety degrees. In a desperate effort to restore order, the Detroit police, National Guard, and state police began to shoot looters. As in Newark, "official violence" mounted as fatigue, fear, rage, and resentment fueled a loss of restraint on the part of law enforcement. The situation now clearly demanded the U.S. Army. Yet throughout the day Republican George Romney and the White House shadowboxed. Legally, the governor had to issue a formal request affirming that a state of insurrection existed and that all available resources were exhausted. Politically, he was a presidential candidate and loath to admit (like New Jersey Governor Richard Hughes) that he could not handle the situation himself.[22]

For his part, Johnson mistrusted the Republican (unlike the Democrat Hughes) and was not eager to assume responsibility for the racial crisis.[23] "I knew what I had to do," recalled Johnson in his memoirs, "but I could not erase from my mind the awful prospect of American soldiers possibly having to shoot American citizens. The thought of blood being spilled in the streets of Detroit was like a nightmare. I could imagine the inflammatory photographs appearing within hours on television and on the front pages of newspapers around the world."[24] The president had little choice, however. While Romney and Attorney General Ramsey Clark negotiated the timing, language, and details of the deployment, Johnson agreed that the paratroopers should assemble at Selfridge Field, thirty miles outside Detroit. He also sent former Deputy Secretary of Defense Cyrus Vance to survey the situation. At first Vance reported that the disorder was under control—an assessment that received a mixed reaction from community leaders as well as state and local officials. Then night fell, and the violence intensified. "The situation is continuing to deteriorate," Vance reported to the president shortly after 11:00 P.M. He advised that Johnson sign the executive order. "Well," said the president glumly, "I guess it's just a matter of minutes before federal troops start shooting women and children." Twenty minutes later, Hoover informed him that "Harlem will break loose within thirty minutes. They plan to tear it to pieces." With no apparent alternative, Johnson committed the army paratroopers and federalized the National Guard.[25]

The president's worst nightmare was not realized. The paratroopers from the 101st and 82nd Airborne, many of whom had protected black children at Central High School in Little Rock, Arkansas, in 1957, soon restored relative peace with minimal force.[26] By late Tuesday most of the looting and firebombing had ended, although scattered reports of sniper fire continued. By Thursday the worst civil disorder of the century to date—until the Los Angeles riot of 1992—was over.

On Saturday the paratroopers departed, followed by the National Guard three days later. Left behind were forty-three dead, thirty-three of whom were black, fifteen of whom were looters.[27]

II

The intervention of the U.S. Army had saved lives and property. It might have saved even more if it had happened sooner—a "haunting question," according to Johnson.[28] Yet the deployment had also significantly weakened the facade of federalism so carefully maintained by the administration. No longer could the White House assert with plausibility that "law and order" was exclusively a local matter. Moreover, the deliberate manner in which the president ultimately agreed to intervene—combined with the defensive way he presented his actions—contributed to the perception that the administration had played politics while Detroit burned.[29] The result was a further loss of credibility for Johnson, who could ill afford it. Afterward, the White House faced the additional challenge of aiding the victims without appearing to reward the rioters—a delicate task that was complicated by a bitter internal debate over whether black radicals had conspired to produce the riots.[30]

At around midnight on Monday, 24 July, the "spin control" began with an appearance by Johnson on national television. With Hoover, Clark, and McNamara at his side, the president demonstrated his continued sensitivity to the potential intersection between racial violence and civil rights by emphasizing that the movement was in no way connected to the events in Detroit, which the "vast majority of Negroes and whites" condemned. In legalistic language, the brief speech also managed to mention six times in seven minutes how Romney's inability to maintain order had forced Johnson's hand.[31] White House Counsel Harry McPherson thought the wording politically maladroit, a clear case of shifting the blame, but the president was swayed by the advice of an old friend, Justice Abe Fortas. When Califano likewise expressed dismay at the speech's partisan tone, Johnson retorted, "I had the best damn constitutional lawyer in the country write that statement."[32] Perhaps he had, but the message nonetheless backfired and instead generated sympathy for Romney.[33]

A week later, the governor fired back at a press conference, charging that the administration's hesitation had cost lives and property. "I think the President of the United States played politics in a period of tragedy and riot," he said strongly. At his press conference that same day, Johnson brushed aside the charge. But clearly it stung. First, the president had Clark respond immediately. Then, in a request that Hoover saw as "fraught with political dynamite," Johnson asked the director of the Federal Bureau of Investigation to get a tape of Romney's TV and radio statement of 24 July in which he vacillated on the need for federal troops. Finally, the president had the attorney general issue another statement after Romney repeated his allegation before the Kerner Commission on 12 September. In the statement, Clark went through the chronology of 24 July hour by hour. "Any delays in dispatch of federal troops resulted from Governor Romney's indecision," he concluded, noting that the governor had not even fully deployed the National Guard when he finally made his request. "This is excellent," commented Johnson, who had also arranged to have the Vance report on the riot released that day. "Pity it didn't get out properly and get better play."[34]

A similar level of defensiveness was evident in the administration's handling of the poverty programs, which came under fire precisely because of Detroit's reputation as a city of racial progress and harmony. Even as paratroopers patrolled the streets in Detroit, officials in the White House were tabulating telegrams to see whether the public blamed the War on Poverty.[35] On 27 July, Califano's office put out the word: "No new programs for Detroit without clearance from us." In response, Shriver asked "how to get out of the dog house," noting that of the twenty-three thousand OEO workers in riot cities, only five were booked by police, and none were convicted. Two days later, the OEO director informed Califano that forty volunteers from the Volunteers in Service to America (VISTA) program would arrive in Detroit that day and that he was trying to find others to keep the schools in Newark open. Shriver's efforts met with scant approval. To his aide Califano was blunt: "Call OEO and make sure they don't send anything into Detroit" without prior authorization.[36]

The difference in outlook between Califano and Shriver mirrored the divisions and uncertainties within the White House about how to proceed, especially given the difficulty of distinguishing between extraordinary riot-induced needs and ordinary inner-city needs. "Should applications from these cities for ordinary HEW, HUD, Labor, OEO projects be given special treatment?" asked an aide. Most officials, he reported to Califano, felt the answer was no, for "political (we don't want to reward rioters), economic (we should not use our limited resources inefficiently by subsidizing a poor project just because it is from Detroit), and administrative (we don't want to bother altering our routine) reasons." The debate posed a larger dilemma for the

White House, which McPherson summarized succinctly: "We talk about the multitude of good programs going into the cities, and yet there are riots, which suggests that the programs are no good, or the Negroes past saving." Neither explanation held much appeal. The loss of liberal confidence was evident—and growing.[37]

The 2 August meeting of the cabinet exposed other deep divisions within the White House. Johnson, Shriver, and Secretary of Labor Willard Wirtz sparred over the political and policy merits of work programs versus poverty programs.[38] The issue that generated the most heated exchanges, however, was whether black radicals like Stokely Carmichael and Rap Brown had incited the riots. In his presentation, Clark said that relatively few blacks were involved, making it imperative that the administration seek to support the responsible blacks and isolate the radical agitators. A stubborn man who consistently placed principle ahead of politics, he contended that the best response to the riots was to pass the Safe Streets Act, impose effective gun control, and upgrade National Guard training.[39] Citing incidents of police and National Guard overreaction, which could trigger "guerrilla war in the streets," the attorney general said that "a racial war can only be avoided by [the] disciplining of ourselves." Talk of a conspiracy, he added, merely drew attention away from the deeper social roots of the riots. In any event, he maintained, at present the Justice Department could not make a case against either Brown or Carmichael.[40]

The reaction was fast and furious. "It is incredible to think you can't make a case," declared Secretary of the Treasury Joe Fowler. Clark replied that there was little evidence of a conspiracy based on arrest figures. "But there are fifty-two cities potentially about to explode," stated Humphrey. Both Secretary of Health, Education, and Welfare John Gardner and Secretary of State Dean Rusk also expressed disbelief at Clark's statement. Rusk said that Carmichael had personally threatened his life—as well as the lives of McNamara and the president. And Gardner warned that "those who organize or incite riots are generally the last to be picked up and arrested." The final word came, naturally, from the president. "I don't want to foreclose the conspiracy theory now," he said. "Keep that door open. . . . Even though some of you will not agree with me, I have a very deep feeling that there is more to that than we see at the moment."[41] Privately, he would later express to Califano his deep disappointment with Clark.[42]

Whether Johnson seriously entertained the idea that the riots were the product of a conspiracy is unclear, although he was willing to ponder the possibility at times. According to one scholar, the president became convinced a conspiracy existed, perhaps fostered by communists, an idea Hoover encouraged. "The FBI always knew when and where the next riot was going to take place and it had always taken place when and where they predicted," Johnson told Katherine Graham, the *Washington Post* publisher. For his part, Califano disagreed: "I don't think he thought for five minutes that there was a conspiracy. The only thing we ever worried about was whether Chinese communist money was going to the Black Panther groups."[43]

The debates inside the cabinet were reflective of the debates that were taking place outside the government, where racial differences had hardened into divisions. Twice as many whites as blacks saw the riots as organized. Twice as many blacks as whites, by contrast, blamed the disorders on discrimination, poor housing, and unemployment. "The Black Muslims are finally putting through the plan they threatened years ago," said a white college student from Rhode Island. But a black farmer from Mississippi disagreed: "The Negro has been down and mistreated all his life, and the Federal government has opened doors for him and he is determined to keep them open." The races also differed predictably in their assessment of police brutality. Blacks typically (by a 2–1 margin) cited it as a major factor. Whites overwhelmingly (by an 8–1 margin) rejected it. And more than 60 percent of whites thought the police should use deadly force against looters, compared with less than 30 percent of blacks, although a substantial majority of both groups agreed that looters were criminals.[44]

Other points of consensus existed. Americans of all races agreed that the riots had hurt the civil rights cause, harmed ghetto residents the most, and attracted only limited support. They also shared the belief that new federal programs would reduce the chance of further unrest. But behind the apparent consensus lurked racial ambiguities. African Americans saw their demands as a principled response to white discrimination. White Americans saw their concessions as a practical response to black disorder. "They need food, work, and education," said an elderly Californian, "but . . . they just use these as excuses to riot." A Michigan housewife complained, "They have everything I have and some have even more."[45]

Underlying these sentiments was more evidence that race relations remained confused and contradictory. In the aftermath of the riots, a substantial and increasing number of whites said that they had no problem with the presence of blacks in public spaces like restaurants, bathrooms, and theaters. Yet a disturbing and increasing number also continued to express prejudiced attitudes. In July 1966, 65 percent of whites thought blacks had less ambition, and 50 percent thought they had "looser morals." In August 1967, the respective figures rose to 70 percent and 58 percent. Survey questions about whether blacks had "less native intelligence" or desired "to live off the handout" generated similar though lower numbers.[46]

One sentiment, however, united all Americans: fear. Both races now felt more uneasy on the streets than they had a year earlier. The number of whites fearful for their personal safety rose from 43 to 51 percent by August 1967. "You just never know what's going to happen," declared a white mother from suburban Michigan. "I'm afraid to go downtown any more." The comparable figure among African Americans was 65 percent. "On Friday and Saturdays I don't walk the streets," said a young black man from Philadelphia, who added that the police, not the rioters, were his main concern. But a black laborer from Dayton, Ohio, refused to draw distinctions. "Rocks and bullets have no names on them," he said simply.[47] By the end of the "Long Hot Summer," the combustible combination of race, radicalism, and riots had exploded the liberal faith that the War on Poverty would constitute a war on disorder.

III

The riots in Newark and Detroit dashed the administration's flagging hopes that the Great Society would generate both social justice and social peace. From the left and the right came devastating rhetorical assaults. Conservatives charged that the riots were criminal acts incited or exploited by radical conspirators armed with revolutionary intent. The radicals were in turn aided or abetted by liberals whose social programs had first instilled a sense of entitlement among the rioters and then rewarded them for their lawlessness. Radicals charged that the riots were political rebellions triggered by acts of police repression and suppressed by white elites determined to preserve a racist and exploitative political and economic system. According to this view, the War on Poverty was a cruel hoax, an insidious effort to prop up rather than tear down a fundamentally flawed system. Thus by 1968 both conservatives and radicals were united and vocal in their condemnation of the Great Society and the "false expectations" it had supposedly bred. The criticism rang loud and clear.

By contrast, liberals were divided and hushed, unable to offer a unified or amplified defense of the antipoverty program. Outside the administration, the belief grew that the Great Society was too modest in scope and had failed to bridge the considerable and corrosive gap in economic achievement between blacks and whites (the "relative deprivation" thesis). Inside the administration, the sense was that the War on Poverty was a victim of its own success, however limited (the "rising expectations" thesis). Neither explanation would prove persuasive in the aftermath of the disorders in Newark and Detroit.

Perhaps the clearest statement of how ideological foes viewed the civil disorders came from a somewhat unlikely source: Tom Hayden.

> To the conservative mind the riot is essentially revolution against civilization. To the liberal mind it is an expression of helpless frustration. While the conservative is hostile and the liberal generous toward those who riot, both assume that the riot is a form of lawless, mob behavior. The liberal will turn conservative if polite methods fail to stem disorder. Against these two fundamentally similar concepts, a third one must be asserted, the concept that a riot represents a people making history.[48]

A radical activist, Hayden had a vested interest in depicting liberalism and conservatism as two sides of the same coin. Yet he had outlined accurately how each camp generally defined—or wished to define—what the riots represented.

For the Right, the riots represented the logical culmination of liberalism's failure as well as a political opportunity to drive home the point. "Rioting has become part of the American way of life, like football, strikes, conventions and picnics," wrote one conservative. Although he and others differed on whether communists had incited or exploited the riots, they agreed that radicals like Carmichael and Brown had helped to spark the riots not only through traditional means but through the news media, which constantly transmitted images of police brutality uncontrasted with depictions of antipolice harassment. "The big scene always features a savage cop beating a fallen victim, preferably female," complained the *National Review,* conveniently forgetting that conservatives rarely neglected to depict crime victims as innocent white women. At the same time, the "electronic global village" created by television had turned rioting, like youth fashions and rock music, into a global phenomenon.[49]

Nevertheless, the main targets of conservative outrage were domestic liberalism and the Johnson administration. Whereas liberals once accused conservatives of falsely conflating race and disorder, conservatives now accused liberals of falsely conflating poverty and disorder. "There is indeed a problem of the slums," conceded the *National Review.* "And there is the problem of rioting and civil disobedience. But the two are not the same problem, and it is distinctively Liberal fatuity to suppose that they are." If the riots had a root cause, conservatives charged, it was not poverty, since the American economy was in robust health. Rather, the collapse of "law and order" was in part due to a lack of moral leadership from the White House, which included a vice president who had declared that if he lived in a slum he would "lead a mighty good revolt." But, above all, it was the unintended but inevitable consequence of the administration's War on Poverty, which had perversely fostered a dangerous degree of dependency and irresponsibility among urban blacks, many of whom were now angry and frustrated, without the individual initiative and moral integrity to make progress on their own. Sending more aid to riot-torn cities under the guise of humanitarian assistance would only exacerbate the crisis by rewarding criminality and feeding the frustration.[50]

The revolutionary potential of the urban disorders constituted for radicals one of several points of intersection with the conservative construction. Like the Right, the Left perceived the riots as spontaneous eruptions at the moment but with the potential for coordinated action in the future. As an editorial in the Nation predicted, with a measure of despair and excitement, "Sooner or later, sporadic local uprisings are pretty sure to escalate into action organized on a national scale with some degree of liaison and discipline instead of extemporaneous looting. And then what?"[51] Like many conservatives, radicals also sought to assign political agency and revolutionary consciousness (at least inchoate) to the rioters, whom they asserted were by no means marginal or isolated members of their community. On the contrary, as the Kerner Commission would confirm, the participants had relatively high levels of education, were active in the civil rights movement, and enjoyed substantial support from fellow African Americans.[52] And although some rioters were motivated by a combination of greed, boredom, or rage, most were careful to channel their emotions into actions aimed deliberately at those they saw as the agents of their oppression—white businessmen and policemen.[53]

Thus in Newark the first target of the rioters was the Fourth Police Precinct, a symbolic site of social control (it was located adjacent to the Hayes Housing Project) and the actual location of police brutality (it was where cabdriver John Smith was beaten while in custody). Firemen were harassed, according to a local white teacher and civil rights activist, so that "the two symbols of [ghetto] degradation—white businesses and rat-infested tenements"—would burn. But careful calculation also motivated the rioters, according to another white radical. "Economic gain was the basis of mass involvement," contended Hayden, who observed that the looters were careful to avoid black establishments. "The [white] stores presented the most immediate way for people to take what they felt was theirs," he added, noting that the looting took place because organized protests against gouging merchants had previously proved futile.[54]

A third piece of common ground between radicals and conservatives was their antipathy toward Johnson and the Great Society. While the Right attributed great influence to the antipoverty program—if only as a negative force—the Left gave it little credit and attacked it as a political sham, a token gesture motivated by white guilt and intended to deflect black demands for structural change.[55] With dispassionate statistics, socialist Michael Harrington calculated that the United States spent relatively less on welfare than any other advanced country. In passionate prose, Eldridge Cleaver argued that the "War on Poverty, that monstrous insult to the rippling muscles in a black man's arms, is an index of how men actually sit down and plot each other's deaths, actually sit down with slide rules and calculate how to hide bread from the hungry."[56] Although an obvious exaggeration, Cleaver's vivid and gendered description exemplified the depth of animosity between liberals and the Left by late 1967.

With criticism mounting from all directions, the White House scrambled to mount a defense. In typical fashion, the administration attempted to craft a balanced and inclusive message that would satisfy reasonable critics on both sides. In a typical statement, Congressman Emanuel Celler of Brooklyn, a staunch liberal and Johnson ally, echoed the administration's position when he told the American Jewish Committee that white flight, white racism, and the white backlash were partly responsible for the riots because they had contributed to urban frustration and violence. But, he was quick to add, "law and order" was as necessary for blacks as for whites. "Riots are a form of self-indulgence and ultimately boomerang," he maintained. "That we understand the reasons for the riots is important. That we do not use the reasons for excuses is equally important."[57] The speech was moderate and reasoned. Whether it or the countless others like it had any larger impact is doubtful.

A major problem for liberals was the seeming coherence and internal logic of the arguments advanced by their opposition. Also important, however, were divisions within their own ranks, which were caused in part by a growing lack of confidence in the correctness of their policies. Outside the White House, many liberals contended that the War on Poverty had done too little too slowly. Despite some progress, blacks remained victims of "relative deprivation," with high unemployment rates and low income levels in comparison to whites.[58]

In the words of Joseph Rauh of the Americans for Democratic Action, they were "the have-nots of a society who have waited too long for the full rights, privileges, and advantages available to other citizens in this democratic society." To secure those privileges and advantages, it was time for the federal government to commit itself to all-out war, with massive jobs programs and large-scale income redistribution policies. Where the money would come from (barring an immediate withdrawal from Vietnam) and how the administration would push these measures past a hostile Congress were questions left largely unanswered. "I wish [Congress] had let us experiment with different programs, admitting that some were working better than others," Johnson remarked later. "But I knew that the moment we said out loud that this or that program was a failure, then the wolves who never wanted us to be successful in the first place would be down upon us at once."[59]

Inside the White House, both the prescription and the remedy advanced by more extreme liberals met with little favor. Instead, the preferred explanation was that the Great Society had engendered hopes that were beyond immediate realization. Ironically and tragically, the opportunities provided had only increased the frustrations felt by many ghetto residents. At bottom, then, the riots were a product not of conspiracy but of "the revolution of rising expectations," a phrase that became popular within the administration after the summer of 1967. To be sure, the progress toward economic and political equality for blacks was slow and limited, especially in the inner city. As Johnson himself conceded, "God knows how little we've really moved on this issue despite all the fanfare. As I see it, I've moved the Negro from D+ to C−. He's still nowhere. He knows it. And that's why he's out in the streets. Hell, I'd be there too."[60] But there was progress, which the president regularly trumpeted. Between 1963 and 1966, federal spending on the poor through the Community Action Program and Aid to Families with Dependent Children rose by more than 50 percent. By 1967, the proportion of blacks in the middle class had doubled since 1960, and the unemployment rate among blacks on the whole had dropped by more than 50 percent since 1958. Even Detroit reported considerable improvement.[61]

Then the Motor City went up in flames. How could the White House now sell the War on Poverty as a cure for disorder? With the "model city" in smoldering ruins, the administration was forced on the defensive, uncertain how to demonstrate that the Great Society was not in fact fueling unrest in the cities. "People say the anti-poverty program helped riots," explained an aide to Califano, "and we gather statistics to show they didn't."[62] It was a losing game, and Johnson knew it. The riots in Newark and Detroit had raised the rhetorical and political stakes, leaving the administration in an increasingly desperate plight. The support for the War on Poverty had faded. The effort to contain the demands for "law and order" within the parameters of federalism had failed. The attempt to compartmentalize civil rights and civil disorders had collapsed. The future of liberalism appeared in serious doubt.

To ordinary Americans the future appeared equally uncertain. A poll taken in August indicated that the public now perceived the riots as the nation's most serious problem—more serious even than the Vietnam War.[63] The disorders also strengthened the white backlash and reduced white support for civil rights and the Great Society.[64] A North Carolina mother of two wrote that although she had supported the movement when it began, she now felt it had gone too far. She opposed sending federal aid to Newark in the wake of the riot because she worried that it would act as "an incentive to others to loot, destroy and kill."[65]

For conservatives, the riots were an essential plank in the tripartite "law-and-order" platform—as important as street crime and political demonstrations. In 1964 Johnson had promised that his War on Poverty would constitute a war on crime. Now, in the aftermath of Detroit and Newark, conservatives charged that civil disorder represented the ultimate breakdown of civil society and the ultimate bankruptcy of modern liberalism, whose social programs had apparently backfired. First, the War on Poverty had encouraged irresponsibility among the disadvantaged. Then, administered by distant bureaucrats with little regard for local traditions or values, it had rewarded lawlessness, pandered to criminals, and squandered the hard-earned tax dollars of hardworking Americans. To add injury to insult, liberals in the end had failed even to protect law-abiding citizens, black and white, from the violence that threatened to engulf them. The Great Society had reaped what it had supposedly sowed—urban destruction rather than renewal.[66] By claiming that the disorders were at least in part the product of the welfare state, conservatives thus mounted a frontal assault on contemporary liberalism even as they tapped into the racial roots of white fear.

For liberals, that fear proved impossible to dispel. It affected the white residents of urban neighborhoods, who had some cause to fear black muggers and burglars, as well as the homeowners in homogeneous suburbs and small towns, who had less cause even though many of them had only recently fled crime-ridden cities where friends and family still resided. But regardless of actual circumstance, white fear of racial violence and social chaos was real and cut across class and geographic borders. It was reinforced by conservatives who successfully blended the urban disorders with street crime and antiwar demonstrations under the rubric of "law and order." Contributing to the atmosphere of anarchy perceived by many middle-class whites were the rallies and rhetoric of radicals, who claimed that the riots were not criminal acts per se but political protests.[67] Ironically, the Left thus strengthened the connections the Right had drawn between race and crime, civil disorder and civil disobedience, violent demonstrations and peaceful rallies.

Caught in the crossfire and trapped in no-man's-land were moderate liberals, who tried in vain to separate the distinct phenomena (although all were often technical violations of the law). In a typical response, the attorney general declared, "I think we would have to be very careful in considering demonstrations and lawlessness and rioting as the same thing."[68] On the one hand, liberals denied that the riots, in contrast to the antiwar protests, were "political" in any meaningful sense, in part because that would undercut what support remained for the Great Society. On the other hand, they strained at considerable political cost to emphasize how important yet overlooked elements of "law and order," such as suburban juvenile delinquency and white-collar crime, were not driven by race.[69] Though logical, the arguments of liberals often fell on ears deafened by thunderous rhetoric from conservatives and radicals, whose opinions served to blur distinctions, exclude complications, and heighten anxieties. Above all, the conservative construction amplified the sense that the nation was coming apart at the seams, that it faced a crisis of authority unprecedented since the 1860s.

To allay that anxiety, the president in December 1967 gave a joint interview to the major television networks. "Our big problem is to get at the causes of these riots," he said. "The answer is jobs. The answer is education. The answer is health care. Now, if we refuse to give them those answers, people are going to lose hope, and when they do, it is pretty difficult to get them to be as reasonable as we think they should be."[70] It was the mainstream liberal line, spoken with apparent conviction. But within the White House the confidence, energy, and will to pursue those solutions was almost exhausted.

Other officials also maintained that the country remained fundamentally healthy despite the summer's physical devastation and psychological scars. "I can't think of another country that would have this sort of civil disorder," noted Wattenberg, "and still talk about the 'socio-economic roots' of the disorder and the 'culture of poverty' and not go out and crack a few heads."[71] Shortly after Christmas, the president's pollster reported with satisfaction that the public seemed to have accepted the administration's Vietnam policy. Therefore, it was time "to shift gears to the domestic side. The big issue here is crime, civil rights, disorders, etc. Here too the Administration should seize the middle ground between the domestic hawks and doves."[72] His confidence was misplaced, as the search for that middle ground, at home and abroad, would prove futile. But his contention was correct—the politics of "law and order" would prove decisive in 1968.

In that critical election, the impact of the other great issue, Vietnam, was ambiguous for two reasons. First, although voters generally ranked the war as the most critical issue facing the nation, they also indicated—with the exception of liberals and the young—that Vietnam was a distant, impersonal concern. By contrast, private polls commissioned by the Democratic Party indicated that "law and order" was an immediate, personal priority with virtually all Americans. The vast majority, reported Humphrey's pollster, wanted order restored without reservation or hesitation. "[It] is not a covert demand for anti-Negro action," he added. "The demand is spread through all segments of the population."[73] Second, most voters could not distinguish between the candidates, both of whom pledged to bring the war to an end. Even in late October, survey data led the president's pollster to conclude that Vietnam was "cutting for neither Humphrey nor Nixon."[74] Nor was inflation—an important political issue and economic problem by 1968—providing a significant edge to either party. By contrast, when it came to "law and order," most Americans had a clear idea where the two men stood—and by a considerable margin preferred the conservative Republican to the liberal Democrat.[75]

The Nixon campaign skillfully used television to tap directly into the fear and anxiety felt by many Americans. In one powerful commercial, a middle-aged, middle-class, white woman walked nervously down a deserted city street as darkness fell and an announcer recited crime statistics.[76] Ultimately, Nixon won the election by a narrow margin.[77] But the victory for conservatism was of epic proportions. In 1964, Johnson received 43.1 million votes, 61 percent of the total. In 1968, Humphrey received 31.2 million votes, 43 percent of the total. Almost 12 million voters, including 5 million from urban areas, had either abstained or defected to Wallace or Nixon, who together claimed almost 57 percent of the popular vote.[78] The Republican nominee had reversed the results of 1964 in large part because a significant majority of white Americans believed that, unlike his Democratic opponent, he could and would restore authority, stability, and security, that under his leadership the disorder of the past four years would at last come to an end.

The grand ambitions of the Great Society had given way to grim demands for "law and order." The outcome left Johnson perplexed. "Somehow," he wrote in his memoirs, "in the minds of most Americans the breakdown of local authority became the fault of the federal government."[79] But for most white Americans, "law and order" was not a conservative stratagem—it was a concrete issue based on real fear and actual circumstances that even a consummate politician like Johnson could not control. Constrained by the limits of federalism and the logic of liberalism, he could do little to halt the violence and disorder or prevent his presidency from becoming the most prominent political victim of "crime in the streets."

Notes

1. Wattenberg to LBJ, 21 November 1967, Ex PL/Kennedy, Robert F., Box 26, White House Subject Files (WHSF), Lyndon Baines Johnson Presidential Library, Austin, Texas (hereafter LBJL).

2. For an expanded discussion of the 1964 election, see Michael W. Flamm, *Law and Order: Street Crime, Civil Unrest, and the Crisis of Liberalism in the 1960s* (New York: Columbia University Press, 2005), chap. 2.

3. Although police departments expanded at twice the rate of population growth during the 1960s, both clearance and conviction rates fell—the direct result of court rulings, according to conservatives. Lucas A. Powe Jr., *The Warren Court and American Politics* (Cambridge, Mass.: Harvard University Press, 2000), 399–400, 408.

4. In 1968 state and municipal governments still employed more than ten times as many full-time law enforcement officers as the federal government. Special Message to the Congress on Crime and Law Enforcement, 7 February 1968, *Public Papers of the Presidents of the United States: Lyndon B. Johnson, Containing the Public Messages, Speeches, and Statements of the President, 1968–1969* (Washington, D.C.: Government Printing Office, 1969), 2: 185.

5. Thomas Byrne Edsall and Mary D. Edsall, *Chain Reaction: The Impact of Race, Rights, and Taxes on American Politics* (New York: W. W. Norton, 1991), 9. For a similar national perspective, see Allen J. Matusow, *The Unraveling of America: A History of Liberalism in the 1960s* (New York: Harper and Row, 1984). For a similar local perspective, see Jonathan Rieder, *Canarsie: The Jews and Italians of Brooklyn against Liberalism* (Cambridge, Mass.: Harvard University Press, 1985).

6. He also argues that miscegenation was the main fear of whites in the 1950s. I would contend that by the 1960s street crime represented the main fear. Thomas J. Sugrue, "Crabgrass-Roots Politics: Race, Rights, and the Reaction against Liberalism in the Urban North, 1940–1964," *Journal of American History* 82 (September 1995): 578. See also Thomas J. Sugrue, *The Origins of*

the Urban Crisis: Race and Inequality in Postwar Detroit (Princeton, N.J.: Princeton University Press, 1996).

7. Thus a Charlestown, Massachusetts, housewife, Alice McGoff, could support the Civil Rights Act of 1964 but later oppose forced busing. See J. Anthony Lukas, *Common Ground: A Turbulent Decade in the Lives of Three American Families* (New York: Knopf, 1985), 26.

8. "As issues became more salient and politics intruded on more individuals, there was a heightened awareness of discrepancies between what the parties stood for as opposed to what they were believed to stand for." Norman H. Vie, Sidney Verba, and John R. Petrocik, *The Changing American Voter* (New York: Cambridge University Press, 1979), 269.

9. Telephone conversation, LBJ with Katzenbach, 25 January 1967, 7:45 P.M., Tape K67.02, PNO 3, LBJL.

10. *Report of the National Advisory Commission on Civil Disorders*, 56–60. An application for Model Cities aid in 1967 noted that Newark had the nation's highest percentage of poor housing; the most crime per one hundred thousand residents; the heaviest per capita tax burden; and the highest rates of venereal disease, maternal mortality, and new cases of tuberculosis. The city was also second in infant mortality, second in birth rate, and seventh in absolute number of drug addicts despite its relatively small size. Tom Hayden, *Rebellion in Newark: Official Violence and Ghetto Response* (New York: Random House, 1967), 3, 5–6; and "The Real Tragedy of Newark," *U.S. News & World Report*, 31 July 1967, 30. Conditions have hardly improved in Newark since. See Ronald Smothers, "In Riots' Shadow, a City Stumbles On," *New York Times*, 14 July 1997, B1, B4.

11. Only 1.2 percent of the New Jersey National Guard were black and less than 1 percent of the New Jersey state troopers were black. *Report of the National Advisory Commission on Civil Disorders*, 60–69; Hayden, *Rebellion in Newark*, 9, 14–16, 34, 38, 45.

12. Meet the Press, 16 July 1967, Box 78, Administrative File (IV), NAACP Papers, Library of Congress (LOC).

13. Johnson diplomatically rejected their suggestion that communists had supplied the snipers with rifles by stating that Hoover was checking into it. Joseph A. Califano Jr., *The Triumph and the Tragedy of Lyndon Johnson: The White House Years* (New York: Simon and Schuster, 1991), 210–211.

14. Newark officials were "in a state of shock" on Sunday, according to Warren Christopher, who had joined the Justice Department that weekend. Warren Christopher Oral History (OH), interview by T. H. Baker, 18 November 1969, LBJL.

15. President's News Conference, 18 July 1967, *Public Papers of the Presidents of the United States: Lyndon B. Johnson, Containing the Public Messages, Speeches, and Statements of the President, 1967* (Washington, D.C.: Government Printing Office, 1968), 2: 701–702.

16. "Detroit's Mayor," *U.S. News & World Report*, 7 August 1967, 16.

17. *Report of the National Advisory Commission on Civil Disorders*, 85–86, 89–91; Sidney Fine, *Violence in the Model City: The Cavanagh Administration, Race Relations, and the Detroit Riot of 1967* (Ann Arbor: University of Michigan Press, 1989), 1–93. See also "The Fire This Time," *Time*, 4 August 1967, 13–14.

18. *Report of the National Advisory Commission on Civil Disorders,* 85–86, 89–91; Fine, *Violence in the Model City,* 1–93.

19. Fine, *Violence in the Model City,* 95–125. See also Jerome Cavanagh OH, interview by Joe B. Frantz, 22 March 1971, LBJL.

20. Police Commissioner Ray Girardin later explained that police feared it was a diversion. Garry Wills, *The Second Civil War* (New York: New American Library, 1968), 84. Another factor was that the police had put down a riot in 1966 using similar tactics—in addition to a show of overwhelming force, a point forgotten in 1967. Jerome Cavanagh OH, interview by Joe B. Frantz, 22 March 1971, LBJL.

21. Many of the soldiers held racist beliefs, and few had any personal familiarity with Detroit. A reporter described an encounter with the crew of an armored personnel carrier. "We're lost!" said the officer. "Can you tell us where we are? We're from Grand Rapids." Fine, *Violence in the Model City,* 196–199.

22. The mayor, safety director, and governor would exchange accusations in the aftermath. The governor could not make up his mind, charged Girardin, a Cavanagh loyalist, claiming that he and the mayor had always wanted federal troops. Wills, *Second Civil War,* 51. In Romney's defense, he was concerned that use of the term "insurrection" might void insurance coverage. Fine, *Violence in the Model City,* 193–196, 199–203.

23. Johnson lacked trust or confidence in Romney, who he felt was running for president. Joseph Califano, interview with author, 8 August 1995.

24. Lyndon Baines Johnson, *The Vantage Point: Perspectives of the Presidency, 1963–1969* (New York: Holt, Rinehart and Winston, 1971), 170.

25. Tom Johnson's Notes of the President's Activities During the Detroit Crisis (TJN), 24 July 1967, Box 1, LBJL.

26. The twenty-seven hundred paratroopers fired only 201 rounds, most of them in the first few hours. They were permitted to load their weapons only if an officer gave the order. Throckmorton attempted to have the National Guard unload their weapons as well but had less success. *Report of the National Advisory Commission on Civil Disorders,* 100. See also "An American Tragedy, 1967," *Newsweek,* 7 August 1967, 20.

27. The death toll in Detroit and other cities may have been higher than reported. As one guardsman recalled, "We were supposed to fill out all those goddam reports after every exchange of fire. You can't fight a battle and be filling out forms. We just shot and forgot. When we killed a sniper or looter, he either died in a burning building or we threw him into one." Wills, *Second Civil War,* 56. For the official figures, see *Report of the National Advisory Commission on Civil Disorders,* 106–108. For a recent analysis of the lingering impact that the riot has had, see Robyn Meredith, "5 Days in 1967 Still Shake Detroit," *New York Times,* 23 July 1997, A10.

28. Johnson, *Vantage Point,* 173.

29. "The Romney-LBJ Feud: Who Played Politics in the Rioting?" *U.S. News & World Report,* 14 August 1967, 14.

30. We knew, recalled Califano, "that we had to find a way to get them aid without appearing to bow to the rioters." Joseph Califano, interview with author. "In this picture," concurred Christopher, "we were always walking a difficult line of wanting to assist the cities in their relief and rehabilitation, but at the same time not wishing to have the occasion of a riot made the rea-

son for a city to get preferential treatment on its normal programs." Warren Christopher OH, interview by T. H. Baker, 18 November 1969, LBJL. McPherson felt that the issue of rewarding rioters was "hollow" because the administration had a moral obligation to assist all in need and lacked the funds "to 'reward' anybody, if 'reward' means the massive rebuilding of slum areas. We didn't have it before and we don't now." Harry McPherson, *A Political Education: A Washington Memoir* (1972; Austin: University of Texas Press, 1995), 360–361.

31. Remarks to the Nation after Authorizing the Use of Federal Troops in Detroit, 24 July 1967, *Public Papers of the Presidents: Lyndon B. Johnson, 1967*, 2: 716.

32. Johnson later claimed that the language was for constitutional purposes only. "But my doubts were as deep as those of the reporters I tried to persuade," recalled a dubious McPherson. McPherson, *Political Education*, 360; Califano, *Triumph and the Tragedy of Lyndon Johnson*, 218.

33. Even Cavanagh, a Romney foe, believed that Johnson's speech had engendered sympathy for the governor. Jerome Cavanagh OH, interview by Joe B. Frantz, 22 March 1971, LBJL.

34. President's News Conference, 31 July 1967, *Public Papers of the Presidents: Lyndon B. Johnson, 1967*, 2: 727; Ramsey Clark statement, 12 September 1967, Box 15, Warren Christopher Papers (Christopher MSS), LBJL. See also Califano to LBJ, 12 September 1967, Box 24, Handwriting File, LBJL; Fine, *Violence in the Model City*, 216.

35. Califano to LBJ, 26 July 1967, Box 22, White House Office Files (WHOF) of John Robson and Stanford Ross, LBJL.

36. Gaither to Califano, 27 July 1967, Box 43, WHOF of James Gaither, LBJL; Muriel Hartley to Jim Gaither, 1 August 1967, Box 43, WHOF of James Gaither, LBJL; Notes of the President's Meeting with the Cabinet, 2 August 1967, Box 9, Cabinet Papers, LBJL.

37. Nimetz to Califano, 9 August 1967, Box 58, WHOF of Joseph Califano, LBJL.

38. Notes of the President's Meeting with the Cabinet, 2 August 1967, Box 9, Cabinet Papers, LBJL. See also Minutes of the Meeting, 2 August 1967, Box 9, Cabinet Papers, LBJL.

39. "Ramsey ultimately did, in every instance that I saw, just what Ramsey thought the right result was," recalled an aide. Bruce Allen Murphy, *Fortas: The Rise and Ruin of a Justice* (New York: William Morrow, 1988), 295–296.

40. Notes of the President's Meeting with the Cabinet, 2 August 1967, Box 9, Cabinet Papers, LBJL. See also Minutes of the Meeting, 2 August 1967, Box 9, Cabinet Papers, LBJL.

41. Ibid.

42. Of Clark, Johnson said: "If I had ever known that he didn't measure up to his daddy [former attorney general and justice Tom Clark], I'd never have made him Attorney General." Yet Johnson remained loyal to Clark and apparently never sought to replace him. Califano, *Triumph and the Tragedy of Lyndon Johnson*, 221–222.

43. Nicholas Lemann, *The Promised Land: The Great Black Migration and How It Changed America* (New York: Knopf, 1991), 190. Joseph Califano, interview with author.

44. "After the Riots: A Survey," *Newsweek*, 21 August 1967, 18–19;

Panzer to LBJ, 11 August 1967, Box 398, WHOF of Fred Panzer, LBJL; Hazel Erskine, *Public Opinion Quarterly* 31 (Winter 1967–1968): 655–677; *Report of the National Advisory Commission on Civil Disorder* (New York: Bantam Books, 1968), 302; Panzer to LBJ, 29 August 1967, Box 39, Ex JL 6, White House Subject Files (WHSF), LBJL.

45. Ibid.

46. Ibid.

47. Ibid.

48. Hayden, *Rebellion in Newark,* 69.

49. Phillip A. McCombs, "Who Is behind the Race Riots?" *National Review,* 20 September 1966, 334–335; James Burnham, "Care and Feeding of Riots," *National Review,* 24 September 1968, 951; James Burnham, "The Collective Organizer," *National Review,* 22 August 1967, 895.

50. "Bulletin," *National Review,* 2 August 1966, 1; "Watts to Detroit," *National Review,* 22 August 1967, 885–887; "The Permanent Insurrection," *National Review,* 8 August 1967, 835–838. See also Ervin to Mrs. John Burchard, 16 March 1968, Box 200, Senator Sam J. Ervin Jr. Papers (Ervin MSS), Southern History Collection (SHC).

51. Editorial, "The Three Revolutions," *Nation,* 14 August 1967, 98–99.

52. Surveys in Detroit and Newark confirmed that a significant number of the residents in selected neighborhoods had participated to some degree in the riots and that participants on average had more education than nonparticipants, although less than those who had actively opposed the riots. The surveys also showed, however, that a significant majority of blacks were either passive bystanders or active counterrioters (that is, they attempted to stop the riots). *Report of the National Advisory Commission on Civil Disorders,* 7: 132–133. See also Richard A. Cloward and Frances Fox Piven, *Regulating the Poor: The Functions of Public Welfare* (New York: Random House, 1971), 228–229, 233, 238–239. Newark, according to Hayden, was one of those moments when the "people take leadership in their own hands." Hayden, *Rebellion in Newark,* 14.

53. Almost all the major riots of the 1960s were precipitated by police actions. Police harassment and brutality remained major causes of black resentment. Robert M. Fogelson, "From Resentment to Confrontation: The Police, the Negroes, and the Outbreak of the Nineteen-Sixties Riots," *Political Science Quarterly* 83 (June 1968): 217–247.

54. Lewis M. Moroze, "Lethal Indifference," *Nation,* 14 August 1967, 105–107; Hayden, *Rebellion in Newark,* 30, 32.

55. In 1965, Saul Alinsky called the War on Poverty "history's greatest relief program for the benefit of the welfare industry." Social workers were, he added, "pimps of the poor." The antipoverty program was, he concluded, "a macabre masquerade and the mask is growing to fit the face, and the face is one of political pornography." Saul Alinsky, "The War on Poverty: Political Pornography," *Journal of Social Issues* 21 (January 1965): 41–47. In March 1968, the black caucus at the Lake Villa Conference called for an end to the War on Poverty because it was a paternalistic reform. David Farber, *Chicago '68* (Chicago: University of Chicago Press, 1988), 87.

56. *Report of the National Advisory Commission on Civil Disorders,* 143. The Harrington statement was cited in "Crime and Insurrection,"

Nation, 31 July 1967, 68–69. See also Eldridge Cleaver, *Soul on Ice* (New York: Dell, 1968), 136.

57. Celler was chairman of the House Judiciary Committee and chief sponsor of the Safe Streets Act, the administration's main anticrime measure. Celler to the American Jewish Committee Appeal for Human Relations, 2 November 1967, Box 540, Celler MSS, LOC.

58. Almost four times as many nonwhites as whites still lived in poverty (defined by the Social Security Administration as an annual household income of less than $3,335 for a family of four). The median black family income was less than 60 percent that of whites. Only 28 percent of black families were in the middle class, compared with 55 percent of white families. And although the overall unemployment rate for blacks had fallen to 8.2 percent by 1967 (3.2 percent for married black men), it remained twice as high as for whites. In the central cities it was between 16 and 20 percent. *Report of the National Advisory Commission on Civil Disorders*, 14, 251–253.

59. Joseph Rauh to Congress, 12 July 1967, Box 11, Joseph L. Rauh Papers (Rauh MSS), LOC; A. Philip Randolph to LBJ, 19 July 1967, Box 64, Administrative Files (IV), NAACP Papers, LOC; Doris Kearns, Lyndon Johnson and the American Dream (New York: Harper and Row, 1976), 291.

60. Kearns, *Lyndon Johnson and the American Dream*, 305.

61. James Gaither OH, interview by Michael L. Gillette, 12 May 1980, LBJL; Douglass Cater, interview with author, 13 July 1995; Robert Dallek, *Flawed Giant: Lyndon Johnson and His Times, 1961–1973* (New York: Oxford University Press, 1998), 330; Ben Wattenberg OH, interview by T. H. Baker, 23 November 1968, LBJL; *Report of the National Advisory Commission on Civil Disorders*, 14, 251–253. The White House deliberately tabulated the unemployment figures in the most favorable light, but they accurately reflected the administration's outlook. For an alternative assessment, see William Hamilton Harris, *The Harder We Run: Black Workers since the Civil War* (New York: Oxford University Press, 1982), 153.

62. Douglass Cater, interview with author; James Gaither, interview with author, 25 September 1995; James Gaither OH, interview by Michael L. Gillette, 12 May 1980, LBJL; Matthew Nimetz OH, interview by Steve Goodell, 7 January 1969, Tape no. 1, LBJL.

63. In September 1966, 24 percent viewed racial unrest as the nation's most important problem. By August 1967, that figure had jumped to 79 percent—higher even than the 76 percent who believed the war in Vietnam to be the nation's most pressing overseas concern. Fred Panzer to Marvin Watson, 3 August 1967, Box 20, FG 11–8–1/Panzer, Fred, WHSF, LBJL.

64. In Cleveland 80 percent of whites voted Republican, and in Boston it was 50 percent. In Gary, the figure was 90 percent. A Croatian precinct that was 68 percent Democratic in 1964 was now 93 percent Republican. Wattenberg to LBJ, 21 November 1967, Box 26, Ex PL/Kennedy, Robert F., WHSF, LBJL.

65. Mrs. Charles W. Ratchford to Ervin, 18 July 1967, Box 180, Ervin MSS.

66. For a concise and typical statement, see "Senator Sam Ervin Says," 3 August 1967, Box 451, Ervin MSS.

67. This view found considerable favor in the scholarly world. See Cloward and Piven, *Regulating the Poor*, 228–229, 233, 238–239.

68. Law Day USA Special, 30 April 1967, Box 20, Ramsey Clark MSS, LBJL.

69. Daniel Patrick Moynihan, "The Politics of Stability," 23 September 1967, Box 57, WHOF of Harry McPherson, LBJL.

70. A Conversation with the President, 19 December 1967, *Public Papers of the Presidents: Lyndon B. Johnson, 1967*, 2: 1164–1165.

71. Wattenberg to McPherson and Cater, 22 December 1967, Box 260, Statements File, LBJL.

72. Fred Panzer to Jim Jones, 28 December 1967, Box 20, FG 11–8–1/ Panzer, Fred, WHSF, LBJL.

73. Minutes, 27 September 1968, "Pers Pol: Campaign Policy Committee Minutes," Box 1, Personal Political Files, 1968 Campaign Files, Humphrey MSS, Minnesota Historical Society (MHS); memo, Evron Kirkpatrick to Freeman, 4 October 1968, "Pers Pol: Freeman, Orville L.," Box 1, Personal Political Files, 1968 Campaign Files, HHH Papers, MHS.

74. Charles Roche to LBJ, 22 October 1968, Box 3, WHOF of Charles Roche, LBJL; Voter Opinion on Campaign Issues, Box 9, Research Files, 1968 Campaign Papers, Humphrey MSS, MHS; Panzer to LBJ, 28 October 1968, Box 26, Ex PL/Nixon, Richard, WHSF, LBJL.

75. "Narrow Victory, Wide Problems," *Time*, 15 November 1968, 19; "Nixon's Hard-Won Chance to Lead," *Time*, 15 November 1968, 24–25. George Reedy to LBJ, 5 October 1968, Box 26, Ex PL/Nixon, Richard, WHSF, LBJL; Theodore H. White, *The Making of the President 1968* (New York: Atheneum, 1969), 467; Gerald Hursh to Orville Freeman, 27 September 1968, Box 16, Citizens for Humphrey Files, 1968 Campaign Papers, Humphrey MSS. For an expanded discussion of the 1968 election, see Flamm, *Law and Order,* chap. 9.

76. "Woman," Nixon campaign commercial, 1968, Political Advertisement, 1954–1984 (1984), compiled by Marshall Reese, available from Electronic Arts Intermix, Inc., New York.

77. "Narrow Victory, Wide Problems," 20; "The Way the Voting Went—And Why," *U.S. News & World Report*, 18 November 1968, 40, 42; "Nixon's Hard-Won Chance to Lead," 22.

78. Ibid. See also Timothy Thurber, *Hubert H. Humphrey and the African American Freedom Struggle* (New York: Columbia University Press, 1999), 219.

79. Johnson, *Vantage Point*, p. 549.

7 | Politics, Policy, and Presidential Power: Lyndon Johnson and the 1964 Farm Bill

Robert David Johnson

IN EARLY MARCH 1964, President Lyndon Johnson privately described a pending piece of legislation as "almost as important—not quite—as civil rights."[1] These words referred to the 1964 farm bill, a measure not generally considered among the more significant of Johnson's tenure—or even of his first year in office.

The 1964 farm bill, however, is more significant than might appear at first glance. Beyond providing a textbook example of how congressional logrolling and effective presidential leadership can transform a bill into a law, the measure's path to passage reveals much about the legislative and political realities of the six months following John Kennedy's assassination, as Lyndon Johnson settled into the White House and the 1964 presidential campaign took shape. In the initial weeks of his tenure, Johnson challenged long-established tradition by making an ability to shepherd legislation through Congress a tangible asset in presidential politics. By doing so, he shifted the playing field to an area where he possessed an overwhelming advantage over any possible foe. In 1999, C-Span asked sixty historians, journalists, and presidential scholars to rate the presidents in ten categories. In nine of the ten, George Washington, Abraham Lincoln, or Franklin Delano Roosevelt received the highest ranking. But in one category—relations with Congress—first place went to Johnson.[2] The intensity and productivity of his dealings with the institution the *Washington Star* considered his "first and lasting love" represented one of Johnson's sharpest breaks from his predecessor.[3] Among twentieth-century chief executives, Franklin Delano Roosevelt might have pioneered the strategy of benefiting politically from performing presidential duties, but no previous president had positioned legislative success in and of itself as a political test—because no previous president had shared Johnson's confidence that he could perform the task.

More than any piece of legislation considered in 1964, the farm bill offers insight into Johnson's political thoughts and strategy. Between December 1963 and April 1964, the president backed four separate versions of farm legislation, shifting gears in each case for political reasons: he admitted on several occasions that he did not even know the specific provisions of each bill. The development of the bill thus went beyond logrolling to show how political concerns—of varied types—influenced Johnson's early domestic policy decisions. In the process, Johnson gradually abandoned an attempt to replicate the approach of his political hero, FDR, who had tried to placate the South by showering the region with federal largesse. As the intensity of southern opposition to the administration's social agenda became clear, the president used the farm bill to improve his political standing in other ways: by appeasing potential congressional enemies; by fortifying his reputation for political leadership; and, most innovatively, by wooing Republicans uncomfortable with the party's hardline stance on foreign policy and civil rights. In the end, then, the 1964 farm bill became a vessel for understanding Lyndon Johnson's political vision for mid-1960s America.[4]

In 1964, the prominent political scientist Theodore Lowi observed, "Agriculture is the field where the distinction between public and private has been almost completely eliminated."[5] Indeed, for the two decades that preceded Lowi's statement, farm policy had swung wildly back and forth between ideological extremes, with partisanship or belief systems generally explaining the shifts. The defining event of the postwar years, the Brannan Plan of 1949, sought to enhance federal regulatory power over farm production in exchange for providing a guaranteed income—rather than the traditional approach of guaranteed prices—for farmers.[6] The Farm Bureau, a free-market agricultural organization, led the opposition to the measure, which congressional Republicans denounced for its expense and the sweep of its federal authority. In July 1949, the plan lost in the House by almost seventy votes; Democratic setbacks throughout the Midwest in the 1950 midterm elections provided a further cautionary tale for those, as the Farm Bureau gloated, "who would place the national farm program on a partisan political basis."[7]

Even Brannan's most committed opponents, though, could hardly have guessed how dramatically his successor would shift policy. Following the 1952 election, Dwight Eisenhower appointed Ezra Taft Benson to lead the U.S. Department of Agriculture (USDA). A prominent figure in the Mormon Church and a hard-line conservative, Benson considered price supports not only economically but also morally pernicious.[8] Accordingly, he championed flexible price supports, in which the subsidy level varied according to the crop's market value. He inspired intense opposition: Louisiana senator Allen Ellender, for instance, called the secretary "the God-damndest hypocrite that ever lived" and announced that if Benson, whatever his church position, went to heaven, Ellender himself would decline the opportunity.[9] More to the point, Benson's dogmatism coincided with an economic downturn that made him a polarizing and unpopular figure in the Midwest. (In 1960, Quentin Burdick became the first North Dakota Democrat elected to the Senate in nearly fifty years on the strength of his slogan, "Beat Benson with Burdick.") By the end of Eisenhower's term, farm policy had become an issue that both parties used to score political points.[10]

Though Democrats as a whole benefited politically from their opposition to Benson, John Kennedy did not. In the 1960 campaign, the Massachusetts senator fared poorly in the Farm Belt, carrying only Minnesota and Missouri—and these states only barely, with 50.6 percent and 50.3 percent, respectively. He had no particular interest or expertise in agricultural matters: as late as 1963, Kennedy asked the Department of Agriculture to explain the difference between fixed and flexible price supports, a distinction that formed the central ideological debate regarding agricultural policy for the preceding generation.[11] Since the president's key advisers were similarly uninterested in farm issues, an unusual amount of power devolved to Secretary of Agriculture Orville Freeman, a three-term former governor of Minnesota who had failed to win reelection in 1960. (Freeman joked that he was appointed largely "because Harvard doesn't have a College of Agriculture.") Like Brannan before him, Freeman championed more government controls, dubbing his agenda "ABCD"—shorthand for abundance, balance, conservation, and development.[12]

Doubts about the government's ability to solve the agricultural problem, however, characterized the approach of what the USDA itself considered "this urban oriented administration."[13] (In a conversation with John Kenneth Galbraith, Kennedy was said to have remarked: "I don't want to hear about agriculture from anybody but you, and I don't want to hear about it from you."[14]) With Kennedy loath to offer a comprehensive farm package, the early 1960s featured piecemeal measures, usually initiated by Congress, delaying consideration of more controversial issues, such as cotton, wheat, and beef. Filling the resulting vacuum, in January 1963, Harold Cooley (D-N.C.), chairman of the House Agriculture Committee, introduced a bill to establish what he called a "one-price cotton" system.

Over the preceding decade, Congress had extended subsidies to cotton farmers and exporters, with the unintended consequence of forcing U.S. textile mills to purchase their cotton at a rate 8.5 cents per pound higher than their foreign competitors. Rather than terminating the system, however, Cooley's bill envisioned a "triple subsidy," with the federal government extending payments to domestic mills as well. The bill thus promised a more costly cotton policy and an even more complex subsidy system. Kennedy offered lukewarm support, largely because the Agriculture Committee chair, who was already "making unpleasant noises" about lack of support from the administration, had made perfectly clear his commitment to aid the textile industry. Cooley's intensity caused both Freeman and Under Secretary of State George Ball to speculate that the congressman "must actually take money personally" from southern textile lobbyists.[15]

Using his considerable power as chair, Cooley pushed his bill through the House Agriculture Committee in March 1963, but the measure then became caught in a bind common to agriculture legislation: it could not obtain sufficient votes from nonfarm representatives without reducing subsidy levels, but the very act of cutting subsidies would render it useless to its advocates.[16] As Congress deadlocked on cotton legislation, wheat matters took center stage. In 1962, Congress returned to earlier principles by passing legislation to establish a mandatory acreage control program for wheat, coupling the limitations with higher subsidy rates. But, as Orville Freeman noted, "agriculture, perhaps more than any other subject, lives in a 'jungle of historical has-beens' full of 'semantic booby traps.'"[17] To neutralize charges of reviving the Brannan Plan, the wheat measure included a provision for a referendum of wheat farmers to ratify the scheme.[18] The Farm Bureau mobilized against the administration's proposal, cleverly presenting farmers with a choice of "Freeman or Free Men" while assuring farmers that rejecting the certificate plan would lead to an even more generous government program."[19]

Throughout the spring, Freeman remained confident about receiving the two-thirds total necessary in the referendum.[20] Instead, on 21 May 1963, some 597,776 farmers, representing 52.2 percent of the total vote, cast ballots against the certificate plan. Of the twenty-eight states that participated in the referendum, the administration surpassed the two-thirds level in only two (Kentucky and North Carolina). In Ohio, where Freeman had predicted victory, the yes vote totaled 22.6 percent. Only Kansan farmers cast more votes than their Ohio counterparts; in the Sunflower State, 41.8 percent voted yes.[21] After the vote, *Fortune* predicted that if Republicans used "the wheat vote as the start of a campaign for the gradual reversal of federal intervention in farm economics," they could end any chance that Democrats would penetrate the Farm Belt in the 1964 election.[22]

Four days after the vote, Freeman admitted that he had "not yet been able to get a clear reading on this matter."[23] To administration critics in Congress, the lesson was simple. According to an up-and-coming young congressman, Bob Dole (R-Kans.), who represented the largest wheat-producing district in the country, farmers voted no to "protest the almost overwhelming regulations."[24] Kennedy, meanwhile, immediately phoned Freeman to express his concern. A week later, he spent forty minutes with the secretary discussing the political fallout.[25]

With the wheat program in disarray, attention returned to cotton legislation, whose condition likewise offered little cause for optimism. Cooley, bolstered by an aggressive lobbying effort from textile mills and the Cotton Council, kept his bill alive throughout the summer. But he was nowhere near a majority. In desperation, majority leader Carl Albert (D-Okla.) and majority whip Hale Boggs (D-La.) penned a letter to all Democrats claiming that the measure would gradually lower cotton price supports, increase protection for small cotton farmers, and decrease consumer prices.[26] The plea failed to move the bill forward, though, partly because its claims were so transparently false. But the president's ambivalent attitude also weakened the measure's chances. As late as November 1963, one Kennedy staffer conceded, "The Administration has never yet really said what it wanted in a Cotton bill"—or even "whether it wanted one."[27]

"Let us continue," urged Lyndon Johnson in his first address to Congress as chief executive. Promising to implement his predecessor's program with renewed vigor, Johnson also retained nearly every prominent Kennedy staffer, deeming a perception of continuity critical to establishing his legitimacy as chief executive. Still, despite the rhetoric, the new president moved in directions quite different than those of his predecessor. Six areas of policy (agriculture, the budget, poverty, civil rights, Vietnam, and Latin America) dominated the national agenda for the first six months of 1964. Of these, Johnson wholly maintained Kennedy's approach only concerning civil rights—and even here, powerful political reasons reinforced Johnson's personal commitment to the issue. This southern chief executive needed to prove himself a national leader, and, given Robert Kennedy's close identification with the question, any significant alteration in policy ensured strong resistance from the attorney general. In the other areas, Johnson initiated subtle but substantive changes, usually in ways that simultaneously improved his political standing.

On agricultural matters, Johnson had little choice but to embark in a new direction, since Kennedy's defeats in 1963 bequeathed a farm policy in total disarray. Moreover, Johnson had a greater interest in and knowledge of farm policy than had his predecessor. Intellectually, he had a clear bias in favor of generous price supports: the New Deal, to which he traced his ideological roots, had operated under this principle. The scope of the change from Kennedy to Johnson was sharp and immediate. As *U.S. News & World Report* observed, "Unlike Mr. Kennedy, who left farm matters largely to Agriculture Secretary Orville Freeman, Mr. Johnson has taken personal charge of administration farm policy." More than personalities, or even Johnson's more adroit legislative skills, explained the shift from Kennedy to Johnson. Johnson entertained a differing vision of how agricultural issues related to his broader political strategies and interests. In particular, he believed that generous farm subsidies could help him maintain southern support despite the region's conservative attitude on social questions, especially civil rights. The Cooley bill offered the first sign of how he would use agricultural questions to cushion the Democrats against the fallout from the party's support for civil rights.[28]

The fight at hand seemed futile. Shortly before the assassination, one House leader privately admitted that he chiefly desired a vote as quickly as possible not because he thought the bill would pass but because he wanted to "get it over with" and stop complaints from the cotton lobby.[29] Similarly, within the administration, Freeman "merely went through enough motions to live up to commitments."[30] This pessimism seemed well founded. Mayor Richard Daley, who controlled a key bloc of Chicago House Democrats, described the Cooley offering as a "bill for one section of the country only": since "Southerners don't vote for civil rights," he promised that midwesterners would not endorse a cotton subsidy.[31] Meanwhile, a group of House liberals led by Robert Kastenmeier (D-Wis.), Richard Bolling (D-Mo.), and Frank Thompson (D-N.J.) opposed the measure from what congressional liaison Larry O'Brien termed "long suppressed desires to wreak vengeance on certain supporters of the bill because of their positions on civil rights."[32]

To Johnson, though, placing the administration's prestige behind the textile mill subsidy made good political sense. First, the Cooley measure offered a ready-made opportunity to reach out to southerners alienated by Democratic activism on civil rights. The New Dealer in Johnson believed, as had Franklin Roosevelt a generation before him, that federal programs addressing the region's economic backwardness would keep the South loyal to the Democrats. In addition, the Cooley bill enjoyed strong support from House Speaker John McCormack, who had ties to textile interests once powerful in Massachusetts. (In a bizarre argument, McCormack privately termed passing the Cooley bill a fitting tribute to John Kennedy's memory.) With an opportunity to pacify both southerners and McCormack, Johnson gambled that "the nature and geography of the doubtful Democrats" would ultimately ensure their votes.[33] House Republicans were another story. From the right, Clifford Hoeven (R-Iowa), the ranking member on the House Agriculture Committee, denounced the "dangerous precedent" of the government bailing out a prosperous industry.[34] From the left, Silvio Conte (R-Mass.) pointedly commented, "At a time when we should be national, we are being sectional."[35] Conte's remark offered the first sign of the fierce resistance that moderate Republicans would mount against the measure. With no reason to appease the South, they saw the bill as an opportunity to distinguish themselves from the Democrats on civil rights.

As late as the day before the vote, the *Washington Star* termed the bill's prospects "cool"; Cooley, a self-described "un-hyphenated, un-splintered, worker-in-the-vineyard Democrat," complained that his "very, very partisan" opponents had "frightened or intimidated" many in the House.[36] In reality, a major impediment to the bill was Cooley's personal unpopularity, which forced Johnson to put his prestige on the line. The president told McCormack to "use my name in any way you need"; privately, the Speaker asked colleagues whether they wanted "to start out President Johnson's administration with a defeat."[37] Undecided congressmen were heavily courted: on the day before the vote, Thomas Morris (D-N.M.) received sixteen calls from the White House and the congressional leadership urging him to support the bill.[38] (He did.) In what the *Wall Street Journal* termed Johnson's "farm bill wizardry," the House passed the bill by a surprisingly comfortable 216-to-182 margin.[39]

Johnson doubted that the bill would "do a hell of a lot of harm or good one way or the other."[40] Focused on the political benefits of consolidating his southern base, the president devoted little attention to the specifics of the Cooley measure or Freeman's legislative strategy on cotton issues. Freeman and his deputies, who had never been enthusiastic about the Cooley bill, considered its final form "much less desirable" than even the original cotton measure.[41] And so, with President Kennedy's consent, Freeman had rested his hopes on a bill sponsored by Senators Herman Talmadge (D-Ga.) and Hubert Humphrey (D-Minn.), which would allow farmers to base subsidy payments on a sliding scale to benefit farmers who grew fewer than fifteen bales of cotton. The senators wanted to create a single price for U.S. cotton while eliminating the subsidies to exporters and the need for payments to textile mills. This, Talmadge claimed, would "put the cotton business back on a free enterprise basis"—but it also would protect the interests of small farmers.[42] In the fall of 1963, at Freeman's recommendation, Kennedy supported the Cooley bill in the House and the Talmadge/Humphrey bill in the Senate. Freeman then expected to use the administration's political muscle to produce a conference committee measure resembling the Senate bill.[43]

Jettisoning the Cooley bill, however, would directly harm one interested party—the textile mills. Cooley, the industry's chief spokesman in the House, dismissed the Talmadge bill as "not acceptable" and promised to fight it in conference.[44] In the upper chamber, Cooley's Tarheel State colleague, B. Everett Jordan, took up the effort. On the cotton question, Jordan's mantra was straightforward: "Get relief for the textile mills."[45] (He had spent his entire adult life as a textile manufacturer until being appointed to a Senate vacancy in 1958.) Before 1963, Jordan had done little to distinguish himself in the Senate. Nor was he an intellectual powerhouse: indeed, Richard Russell (D-Ga.) once commented on how his colleague "labors very earnestly to understand that two and two equals four."[46]

Jordan confirmed Russell's observation when he called the White House the day after Cooley's bill passed. Like Cooley, he dismissed the Talmadge measure as unsound and considered it "absolutely imperative that this [Cooley] bill get through the Senate and get it through here quick." To reinforce his argument, he claimed that his state's largest underwear supplier had reported that large buyers of textiles, such as J. C. Penney, had stopped making long-term purchases and instead were working on a ten-day basis. At a time when major tax reform and civil rights measures were before Congress, Jordan described the cotton bill as "the most imperative thing facing this country right now."[47]

Ordinarily, such a bizarre plea from a junior senator would have met with a disinterested response. But Jordan was not a typical junior senator: as chair of the Rules and Administration Committee, he would oversee the recently authorized investigation into Bobby Baker, secretary of the Senate from 1955 through 1963 and Johnson's protégé in the late 1950s. Under pressure, Baker had resigned his post in the fall of 1963, though not before reports surfaced that he had amassed a fortune of more than $2 million on an annual salary of under $20,000. John Williams (R-Del.), hailed by supporters as the "conscience of the Senate," helped push through a resolution authorizing the Rules Committee—the committee of jurisdiction, since the upper chamber had no Ethics Committee—to investigate the finances of any current or former Senate employee. (In addition, unbeknownst to the Democrats or the White House, the Delaware senator was also soliciting information regarding rumors of "sex orgies" and "unnatural sex acts" in the vice presidential office during Johnson's tenure.)[48] On the same day that the House passed the farm bill, the Rules Committee convened in executive session to begin its hearings on Baker.[49]

At a time when Johnson was attempting to define himself to the nation, the Baker affair recalled less flattering aspects of the president's past. Although Johnson boasted of his humble upbringing, he entered the presidency with a net worth estimated at $14 million, including ownership of a large ranch in Texas and an Austin television station, KTBC.[50] No direct evidence existed that he had abused his public position to advance his private interests, but, as Johnson biographer Robert Dallek has suggested, the Federal Communications Commission did issue a number of rulings favorable to KTBC. Furthermore, Johnson had arrived in the Senate under an ethical cloud: vote fraud almost certainly accounted for the eighty-seven votes that provided the margin of victory for "Landslide Lyndon" in the 1948 Texas Democratic primary. Finally, his reputation as a "wheeler and dealer," though valuable during his stint as Senate leader, now conflicted with his appearing statesmanlike.[51]

In short, the president had every reason to fear a high-profile set of hearings on Baker. Given Jordan's power to shape the course of the inquiry, Johnson entertained his pleas on the cotton bill. In return, the North Carolina senator promised "to keep the Bobby thing from spreading" and to resist media pressure to leak information: "They keep boring in, and they ain't going to get anything out of Everett." But Jordan also—none too subtly—implied that his willingness to do the president's bidding would depend on how hard Johnson fought for the Cooley bill.[52]

Jordan's plea had an immediate and decisive effect. As he had promised the North Carolina senator, Johnson telephoned Orville Freeman to discuss strategy the next day. Less than three weeks into the new administration, the two men had struggled to develop a comfortable working relationship. Freeman considered Johnson personally uncouth, conservative, and excessively influenced by special interests; at several points, the secretary contemplated resignation. In Freeman's opinion, the outcome of the "wheat referendum and the reports of the unpopularity of production control programs" made the "acutely politically sensitive" president hostile to bold initiatives.[53] Johnson, meanwhile, complained about the secretary's habit of submitting lengthy memorandums and disparaged—with good reason—Freeman's political abilities.[54]

Johnson had already decided to jettison the secretary's approach to the cotton bill. Despite having assured Freeman that he would support the Talmadge bill in the Senate, the president now reversed course.[55] "I'm in a hell of a shape," he complained, "if we're against the Cooley bill." He disingenuously claimed that after assuming "you and Kennedy knew what you were doing," he had not understood Freeman's plan to bypass the Cooley bill once it arrived in the upper chamber. A stunned Freeman reminded the president of the Talmadge bill's superiority, but Johnson no longer agreed: "They tell me," repeating Jordan's J. C. Penney story, "that every damn fellow in the country has quit buying right now." Abandoned by the administration, the Talmadge bill was dead.[56]

Dubious about Freeman's commitment to the new course, the president transferred farm bill strategizing to the White House and decided to gain a sense of the Senate situation by approaching Allen Ellender, chair of the Senate Agriculture Committee.[57] One of the most unusual members of the Senate, Ellender entered politics as a protégé of Huey Long, whom he succeeded in the upper chamber in 1936. Although no friend of liberals, the Louisianan never fully shed his populist heritage, combining an obsession with restraining federal expenditures with a desire to ensure that government programs did not exclusively benefit the wealthy and corporate interests. These two beliefs reinforced his disdain for the Cooley bill, which he feared would cost far more than its proponents had promised and whose benefits, he recognized, would accrue primarily to the textile industry. Under these circumstances, Ellender concluded that he would prefer no bill at all.[58]

Ellender conceded that the administration "might be able to logroll the bill through." But, he supposed, nobody "wants to do that."[59] That, of course, was exactly what Johnson intended to do, since the Cooley bill otherwise had no chance. And so, for the second time in scarcely two weeks, the administration dramatically altered its approach to farm legislation. Fortunately for the president, an appropriate logrolling measure existed. The day after the 1963 wheat referendum, Ellender privately remarked that the wheat farmers could "stew in their own juice" before he would support another subsidy measure.[60] Wheat-state Democrats, facing a disastrous 1964 summer wheat crop, had no such luxury. With prices predicted to dip as low as $1.25 per bushel, farmers' income could fall by around $700 million.[61]

Two freshmen, Quentin Burdick and George McGovern (D-S.D.), took the lead. McGovern, who in 1962 had captured his seat by fewer than one thousand votes, introduced a measure to establish a voluntary marketing certificate plan for wheat. Under the bill's provisions, farmers who voluntarily agreed to acreage limitations would receive a certificate, worth $.75 per bushel, which then would be passed on to millers before processing. The idea all but replicated the terms rejected in the wheat referendum, except that it did not technically mandate participation. The difference was semantic: as George Aiken, the ranking Republican on the Agriculture Committee, observed, "I would question whether it is really voluntary in that it would create a situation where a producer would have to participate 'or else.'"[62]

In the aftermath of the wheat referendum, the wheat legislation's chances seemed even more remote than the cotton bill.[63] In the Senate, Ellender rejected a request from McGovern to open hearings on the bill.[64] In the House, Graham Purcell (D-Tex.), chairman of the Wheat Subcommittee, also declined to act. Once again, however, Johnson's accession to the presidency made an impact. Immediately after speaking with Ellender, Johnson urged Purcell to convene hearings.[65] Purcell did as ordered. The president then brought leaders of eighteen farm organizations to the White House to develop a common agenda. Although he delivered what Freeman termed an "incoherent rambling kind of statement about the nature of our economy" and how it treated farmers unfairly, Johnson's message was clear: the Cooley and McGovern measures were no longer separate. The pairing was an awkward one, since the two initiatives offered radically different approaches to the farm problem. Cooley called for subsidizing the middlemen on cotton matters, while McGovern structured a program in which the wheat middlemen would bear most of the cost.[66] Regardless, the measure was now the "cotton-wheat" bill.[67]

The president delivered his State of the Union address on 8 January, after which he focused on a major crisis with Panama abroad and passing Kennedy's tax reform bill at home. He took a high profile on agricultural matters only once in the ensuing month, on 31 January, when he sent a bland farm message to Congress. Johnson's legislative strategy, however, demonstrated signs of success. While the Cooley bill had passed the House with almost no Republican support, the new cotton-wheat measure attracted two prominent GOP backers, North Dakota senator Milton Young and Kansas senator Frank Carlson. Young even took on the thankless chore of confronting the Farm Bureau, which denounced the McGovern bill as a "bread tax" based on an overly "complicated" certificate scheme.[68]

Within the Senate Agriculture Committee, only Ellender strongly opposed the bill, and he contented himself with peppering administration witnesses with difficult questions.[69] But the agriculture chair possessed a weapon more potent than his wit. Although he could not block the measure entirely, he could delay it. And given the legislative realities of early 1964, delay might work as well as outright defeat.

In February 1963, John Kennedy had submitted a civil rights bill calling for a four-year extension of the Civil Rights Commission, strengthening voting rights statutes, requiring courts to give "expedited treatment" to voting rights cases, prohibiting the application of different tests for different voters in federal elections, and establishing a sixth-grade education as proof of literacy for the purpose of voter registration. Even this relatively modest offering stalled in Congress until events in Birmingham, Alabama—where police chief Bull Connor turned fire hoses and police dogs on peaceful civil rights protesters, including children—shifted the national ground on the issue. Kennedy responded by supplementing the February bill with provisions allowing the attorney general to file desegregation suits aimed at public schools and colleges and calling for "equal access" to all public accommodations.[70]

Overcoming the determined opposition of the autocratic chair of the Rules Committee, Howard Smith (D-Va.), and benefiting from the political atmosphere following the assassination, the measure cleared the House in late January 1964. That left the enormous obstacle of obtaining Senate approval. Largely due to the efforts of Johnson, then majority leader, the upper chamber had approved civil rights measures in 1957 and 1960, but only in watered-down form. The ability of southern Democrats to filibuster had blocked bolder reforms, and a similar threat existed in 1964.[71]

In early 1964, the administration lacked the votes needed to impose cloture. And so falling behind the civil rights measure in the Senate calendar could delay consideration of the cotton-wheat bill until the summer, rendering the measure politically useless for the election. With cotton-wheat thus threatened, Johnson personally pleaded with Ellender to "give us some kind of a farm bill." Harboring no illusions that he could persuade the senator of the merits of the measure, he appealed to partisanship: "This is an election year. Democrats are up. If we don't have that farm bill, they're going to catch hell." Ellender relented, and four days later the Agriculture Committee reported the bill.[72]

Once the bill reached the Senate floor, critics targeted the peculiar alliance between an administration backing civil rights and southern senators such as James Eastland (D-Miss.), who served as the measure's floor manager. That it reached the Senate calendar through a roll call vote that placed it ahead of the civil rights measure further exposed the administration to attacks from the bill's most consistent critics: moderate Republicans. Kenneth Keating (R-N.Y.), for instance, joined Johnson in sporting a strong civil rights record—and in having an eye on the November election. The New York senator teamed with other northeastern Republicans, such as Vermont's George Aiken and Maine's Margaret Chase Smith, in questioning the bill's merits. But Keating also criticized the administration's "supplanting the civil rights bill with the farm bill." He saw no reason for speedy consideration—on either ideological or tactical grounds. Ideologically, the administration seemed to have pushed the "grave problems of human rights . . . into the background." Tactically, meanwhile, it amazed Keating that the administration would allow a lever against a southern filibuster to "be completely surrendered now by first taking up the farm bill."[73]

Johnson cared little about charges regarding the program's specifics. But Keating's attacks—echoed by a *New York Times* editorial on the same subject—threatened to nullify the bill's political benefits.[74] In the short term, these concerns melted away. The multiregional, bipartisan coalition that Johnson had helped assemble pushed the measure through the Senate by a vote of 55 to 35. Freeman termed the result a classic "example of how the special power groups can exercise pressure and how we get Government by special interest groups."[75] But Richard Russell was closer to the mark, pointing to Johnson's legislative acumen to explain passage of a measure that a month before he believed needed a "miracle" to clear the Senate.[76]

What Russell, from cotton-growing Georgia, considered divine others viewed more critically. Of the nation's major newspapers, only the *St. Louis Post-Dispatch* endorsed the bill; the *New York Times* chastised Johnson for "playing politics with the farm bloc at the expense of the consumer."[77] Doris Fleeson of the *Washington Star* denounced cotton-wheat as "an unusually crass and costly election-year measure."[78] The *Christian Science Monitor* termed the measure "a misguided political effort to buy the farm vote in an election year."[79] In the most scathing appraisal of the bill, the editors of the *New Republic* mockingly declared, "Happiness in LBJ's Washington is something for everyone. Seldom have so many people been offered such a variety of things as in the Administration's wheat-cotton legislation." Indeed, the whole scheme "perfectly fit the requirements of an election year" in which "President Johnson must keep a firm footing in the South, the Midwest, and the West—much of it Goldwater country not long ago."[80]

Lyndon Johnson, perhaps with some justification, does not enjoy a reputation as a political visionary. But throughout the early months of his presidency, he recognized, to a much greater extent than did his advisers, how significantly the civil rights bill would realign southern politics. He also recognized, to a much greater extent than did his advisers, that the Democratic Party would need traditionally Republican votes to retain its majority status. He developed this theme in more detail later in 1964, when he began speaking of the "frontlash"—the prospect of Republicans fleeing to the Democratic column because of nominee Barry Goldwater's positions on social issues. In many ways, the cotton-wheat bill represented the first step in Johnson's frontlash campaign. Johnson initially had backed the cotton measure as an early payoff to southern supporters and with the hope that the Senate would produce a more just bill. Everett Jordan's intervention ended that possibility: letting Freeman twist in the wind, the president abruptly shifted course, and the bill's function became almost exclusively to improve his political standing.

But the continuing resistance to civil rights among southern senators made it increasingly unlikely that using federal generosity to appeal to the South would succeed. Indeed, in the wake of its support of the civil rights bill, the administration had grown so unpopular in the South that any association with the president threatened the political well-being of southern moderates. The likes of Gillis Long (D-La.) and Pat Jennings (D-Va.) worried that voting for the bill, despite the economic benefits it would bring to the region, would expose them to attacks from conservative primary challengers.[81] Meanwhile, southern conservatives required intense lobbying even to consider backing the measure. James Eastland, for instance, suggested that "the least thing" Johnson could do for southerners "is give them a pat on the back" in exchange for their votes—advice a chief executive fearful of being perceived as too pro-Southern would hardly welcome.[82] In fact, as the debate proceeded, Johnson's association with the cotton bill threatened to cause him political harm, by providing an opening for northern Republicans to demonstrate their greater commitment to civil rights. Attacks from figures such as Keating and Conte suggested that GOP liberals recognized the opportunity.

As the South grew less certain about the president, the significance of wheat-growing areas increased. The Farm Belt, including Wisconsin, Minnesota, the Dakotas, and parts of Montana, Wyoming,

Missouri, Illinois, and Nebraska, had been (except for Minnesota and, usually, Missouri) Republican territory since the election of 1938. But during Eisenhower's last three years in office, Democrats captured Senate seats in Wisconsin, Wyoming, Minnesota, and North Dakota. In 1960, despite the presence of a Catholic heading the ticket, Democratic challengers only narrowly lost in Iowa and South Dakota, while the party reelected incumbents in Montana, Illinois, and Missouri.[83] And in 1962, Democrats George McGovern and Gaylord Nelson claimed seats in South Dakota and Wisconsin.

Tantalizing signs existed that Johnson could duplicate the success of figures like McGovern or Nelson. In early March, polls showed the president running ahead of all potential GOP opponents in Iowa, which only one Democrat had carried in the previous six presidential elections, and in North Dakota, which had last gone Democratic in 1936.[84] Johnson exulted, "We've got a chance—not much—but a little chance to hold a few farm states," provided he could prevent a collapse in wheat prices.[85] The bill itself, the president still believed, "won't make a damn" difference in terms of public policy. But the political benefits could be enormous: in addition to denying the GOP nominee traditionally Republican electoral votes, ending the "all-Republican delegations from the Midwest" would "let us control this Congress."[86] Failure, meanwhile, had its own risks: the *Wall Street Journal* wondered if the wheat question "could become the Johnson administration's first economic headache."[87]

"Freeman doesn't handle his business very well up there," Johnson once commented privately.[88] While the president was preoccupied with the confluence of the civil rights, tax, and cotton-wheat measures in the Senate, he suffered his first serious legislative setback in the House. On 4 February, the House Agriculture Committee tabled (and thus killed) an administration bill to expand the federal food stamp program. The food stamp plan, one of John Kennedy's first initiatives, had been launched in 1961 through an executive order. It allowed needy families to purchase at a price below face value government food stamps, which then could be used to buy groceries. Initially available in eight communities, food stamps were offered in forty communities in twenty-two states within two years, after which Kennedy introduced legislation to provide $700 million to nationalize the program.[89]

Johnson strongly supported the food stamp plan, which he viewed as a building block for his antipoverty program. But with the measure apparently certain to pass and more pressing matters to distract him, the president left Freeman to manage the bill. This decision backfired.

The secretary, who admitted that the "very difficult stage of trying to pass legislation . . . is the part of this job I like the least," relied on assurances from the bill's chief House sponsor, Leonor Sullivan (D-Mo.), that the committee would comfortably report the measure.[90] Instead, all fourteen committee Republicans, representatives of the party's conservative wing, denounced food stamps as a welfare initiative for which farmers disproportionately bore the costs. As an alternative, they advocated the direct-distribution food program, under which the Agriculture Department donated surplus government-owned agricultural goods to the states for direct, free distribution to the needy. (Critics portrayed this idea as a humiliating dole that offered a diet limited to food in surplus.) Meanwhile, turning on its head Johnson's logic that economic questions would trump civil rights concerns and keep southerners in the Democratic Party, several southern Democrats worried that nationalizing the food stamp program would benefit blacks in their home communities. As a result, five Democrats—Thomas Abernethy (Mississippi), E. C. Gathings (Arkansas), George Grant (Alabama), Paul Jones (Missouri), and Watkins Abbott (Virginia)—voted with the committee's Republicans to table the bill.[91]

The vote polarized the House Democratic caucus. Northern Democrats, seeking retribution for their southern colleagues' blocking initiatives important to the party's liberal wing, began targeting measures on which they could exact revenge, such as a tobacco research bill. Unfortunately for the president, since the Senate had significantly amended the Cooley bill—indeed, the upper chamber had added a whole new component with the wheat certificate plan—the measure had to return to the House for reconsideration. As congressional liaison Larry O'Brien noted, Democrats from the North and East "have just had it with farm bills" and were eager to rebel against the "one-way street" blazed by "arrogant" southern colleagues.[92] Carl Albert, not one prone to overstatement, considered the situation "the worst thing I've seen in a long time" and recognized that food stamps had become "the key" to ensuring the cotton-wheat bill's passage.[93] The administration needed to find a way to reverse the Agriculture Committee's action and bring the food stamp bill to the floor, where it had the votes to pass.

Promising no "more flops like that food stamp [vote] in the committee," Johnson began lobbying individual House members, and with unusual intensity—even for him.[94] The president announced that he would do "anything and everything that I need to do, day and night, commit anything to anybody to get that thing passed."[95] With Johnson personally calling several wavering members of the Agriculture Committee and Cooley "desperately" trolling for votes among southerners, on 9 March the five-vote committee majority against the food stamp program evaporated, replaced by a narrow 18-to-16 tally to report the bill.[96] The House leadership quickly announced that it would bring the food stamp initiative to a vote before the cotton-wheat measure, all as part of a newly dubbed farm bill.[97]

As had occurred frequently throughout the bill's tortured legislative history, reasons beyond the specific merits of the program explained the president's actions. The sudden opposition of northerners to administration initiatives—even if seemingly tailored to aid the South only—frustrated Johnson. These were the very Democrats who "ought to want us to go into the election and carry something besides the big cities."[98] He envisioned a Democratic Party in which northern Democrats would recognize that the only way liberals could enact their agenda was "by getting some votes in the South and West."[99]

Internal regional warfare in the Democratic caucus threatened to doom not only the cotton-wheat bill but also the more ambitious initiative Johnson was about to propose: on 16 March, the president sent to Congress a long-delayed plan to combat poverty. Without a relatively unified Democratic caucus, the poverty bill had no chance of passage: the administration expected minimal Republican support. And so the farm bill's rationale changed yet again. It began as a textile subsidy desired by a relatively small but powerful band of congressmen and endorsed by Johnson, somewhat hurriedly, in the hopes of reassuring his southern base. It then became a measure for the president to appease a senator whose actions in coordinating the Baker inquiry would directly affect his political fortunes. It then evolved into the cotton-wheat bill, a classic logrolling measure—but one with the political purpose of stimulating what the *Wall Street Journal* termed "big political inroads" for the Democrats in the Midwest.[100] And now it emerged as a model for a powerful triregional coalition that could come together on all domestic economic issues.[101]

By increasing the stakes, however, Johnson also galvanized the administration's opponents. As White House counsel Myer Feldman noted, "This is a critical battle for the Farm Bureau as well, because they've put everything on the line in this fight."[102] The organization launched a massive lobbying effort that included busing hundreds of farmers to Washington to urge their representatives to oppose the administration's proposal. (The bureau's star attraction, the "Singing Farmer," regaled congressmen with tunes detailing the dangers of government regulation.) Meanwhile, the House Republican leadership had detected an opening to inflict a rare defeat upon the administration. On 10 February, minority leader Charles Halleck (R-Ind.) convened the House Republican caucus, which voted to oppose the farm bill formally. As a result, the number of expected GOP supporters for the bill dropped from twenty-five to ten.[103]

Johnson urged Democrats to respond in kind. Denouncing the "mean, vicious Republicans," the president wondered whether the GOP action provided an excuse for publicly "making a political issue out of it."[104] He even toyed with the idea of appearing before a joint session of Congress to champion the bill, but Carl Albert vetoed the idea.[105] The GOP Policy Committee's action made the legislative arithmetic look troublesome. With only 181 firm Democratic votes, the loss of the anticipated Republican support meant Johnson needed to pick up around 25 more Democrats, a hard task after the contentious House battles over civil rights and the tax bill.[106] By late March, Carl Albert had all but conceded defeat. "We just can't handle them," the majority leader lamented. "We have nothing particularly to offer them, and we've got a bunch of recalcitrants."[107] Perhaps, Albert mused, Johnson's personal involvement could turn the tide, but time conspired against the administration: the Easter recess was scheduled for the second week of April, and both Albert and Johnson believed that the return home to their districts would increase pressure on undecided congressmen to oppose the bill.

In mid-March, the House took up the farm bill; one week later, it received a remarkably favorable rule (over the opposition of Rules Committee chairman Howard Smith) that permitted only one hour of debate and prohibited amendments—despite the fact that the whole body had never even considered the wheat bill. As the matter reached its climax, controversy flared anew between Johnson and his agriculture secretary. On the surface, Freeman admitted, the battle was taxing: he confessed that he could not escape thoughts "about our current legislative contest" even when he was in church. But, he argued, the publicity generated by "a fierce contest like the current one" provided an opportunity to educate the electorate about agricultural affairs. Freeman worried that "our farm program, even by generally knowledgeable people, is considered patchwork, a series of sometimes contradictory improvisations." With the spotlight on farm policy, the secretary urged the president to use his bully pulpit to "draw some attention to the fact that we do have a long term, consistent, logical program."[108]

Johnson rejected Freeman's idea out of hand: selling the bill as a patchwork measure was its only chance for passage. By this stage, in fact, the president had made so many promises to so many different congressmen that even his chief lobbyists wondered about the bill's exact provisions. To get a better handle on affairs, Henry Wilson, Larry O'Brien's deputy in the Congressional Liaison Office, spent a Sunday afternoon with Ken Birkhead, his counterpart in the Agriculture Department. Wilson found the subject "so widely complicated that I can't read a departmental paper on it without requiring a special definition for every fourth word." The normally cooperative Birkhead, meanwhile, provided "so many qualifications that by the time you've absorbed them all you've forgotten the question." Wilson wondered how, "if it's so politically important that these farmers be prevented from losing this income," GOP congressmen could be "so unanimously stupid about it."[109] He prepared a special question-and-answer document for the liaison office to use with individual congressmen, but for O'Brien the matter was simpler: passage would benefit the party, and therefore Democrats should vote aye.

What the *Wall Street Journal* described as the "Johnsonian tactics in ramming the farm bill through the House" dominated debate when the bill came up for final consideration on 7 and 8 April.[110] Clarence Brown (R-Ohio) opened debate with a tirade condemning the president's "reprehensible, dictatorial, and un-American" behavior.[111] Brown, the ranking minority member of the House Rules Committee, compared limiting debate to a situation in which "like the members of the German Reichstag under Hitler, we will be called upon to say 'Ja' or 'Nein,' and that will be our only response."[112] The whole affair provided "a pure and straightforward demonstration of what 'raw and bloody power politics' can mean."[113]

The debate lasted until well after midnight. Behind the scenes, Johnson monitored events: as one wavering Democrat noted, "The phone lines from the White House to my office have been pretty busy."[114] The climax of what the *New York Times* termed a "long, boisterous, and bitterly partisan session" came when Republicans vented their frustration by loudly booing John McCormack and jeering Wayne Hays (D-Ohio).[115] From the other side, Chet Holifield (D-Calif.) more than matched Clarence Brown's hyperbole by comparing the GOP performance to "the story told in the Bible where our savior condemned those who sat in public places and offered audible prayers and professed to be men of great piety."[116] When the roll call concluded, the administration had triumphed, by a narrow margin of 211 to 203. Northern Democrats favored the measure 113 to 25, southern Democrats 88 to 11. House Republicans voted 167 to 10 against.

Johnson's lobbying effort had clearly paid dividends. Three weeks before the vote, Carl Albert had forwarded to the president a list of the sixty-four House Democrats who had not committed to supporting the bill.[117] On the early morning of 8 April, thirty-eight of these members sided with the administration, and another five did not vote. That success allowed the administration to overcome the thirty House Republicans who had voted for the Cooley bill in December but voted no in April. (Twelve of the switchers came from New Jersey, New York, and Massachusetts alone, showing the effectiveness of the Conte-Keating attack against the bill.) In the aftermath, *National Review* discovered congressional Republicans "shaken from another exposure to the Johnson Treatment."[118]

While widespread (and, in hindsight, incorrect) speculation existed about the long-term policy effects of the bill's passage, the *Wall Street Journal* came closest to the mark when it interpreted the measure as an example of the "growing presidential intervention in legislative strategy."[119] Indeed, on three separate occasions—in early December, before the initial passage of the Cooley bill; a few weeks later, when the bill looked stalled in the Senate Agriculture Committee; and in the weeks before the measure finally cleared the House—only direct action by Johnson kept the bill alive. In the process, of course, the president did everything he could to close off discussion of broader agricultural principles, and, to the extent he succeeded, he helped keep in place a subsidy system that would persist until the mid-1990s. The political payoff, however, was considerable. Though the farm bill did not, as he had desired, pay substantial dividends in the South, it did accomplish its goal of aiding his (and his party's) standing in the Midwest.[120] Moreover, it helped appease a senator critical to his overall standing and provided a tactical model of legislative strategy to which he would return later in the year, on a matter—the poverty bill—closer to his heart. The president's observation of the cotton-wheat bill as "almost as important—not quite—as civil rights" was obviously made, in part, for effect. But the statement also provided a sense of the measure's surprising significance in his political calculations as the 1964 election got under way.

Notes

1. President Johnson and Larry O'Brien, 7 March 1964, 4:15 P.M., Recordings of Telephone Conversations—White House Series, Recordings and Transcripts of Conversations and Meetings, Lyndon B. Johnson Presidential Library, Austin, Texas (hereafter LBJL). All transcriptions done by author.

2. http://www.americanpresidents.org/survey/historians/35.asp (accessed 10 January 2003).

3. *Washington Star*, 3 December 1963.

4. James Sundquist, *Politics and Policy: The Eisenhower, Kennedy, and Johnson Years* (Washington, D.C.: Brookings Institution Press, 1969). For other manifestations of this viewpoint, see Allen Matusow, *The Unraveling of America: A History of Liberalism in the 1960s* (New York: Harper and Row, 1984); John Morton Blum, *Years of Discord: American Politics and Society, 1961–1974* (New York: Norton, 1991), 135–162; Robert Collins, "Growth Liberalism in the Sixties," in *The Sixties: From Memory to History,* ed. David Farber (Chapel Hill: University of North Carolina Press, 1994), 11–47; Mark White, "Introduction: A New Synthesis for the New Frontier," in *Kennedy: The New Frontier Revisited,* ed. Mark White (New York: New York University Press, 1998), 10–12.

5. Theodore Lowi, "How the Farmers Get What They Want," *Reporter,* 21 May 1964.

6. John Mark Hansen, *Gaining Access: Congress and the Farm Lobby, 1919–1981* (Chicago: University of Chicago Press, 1991), 112–120; *New Republic,* 2 May 1949.

7. Allen Matusow, *Farm Policies and Politics in the Truman Years* (Cambridge, Mass.: Harvard University Press, 1967), 192–221; J. Roland Pennock, "Party and Constituency in Postwar Agricultural Legislation," *Journal of Politics* 18 (1956): 171–181.

8. Willard Cochrane, *Toward an Understanding of Farm Policy* (Minneapolis: University of Minnesota Press, 1979), 30–31.

9. Ellender quoted in Orville Freeman, "Memorandum for the Files," 14 January 1964, Orville Freeman Papers, Box 11, Minnesota State Historical Society, St. Paul. *Wayne Darrow's Washington Farmletter* noted that in Congress, "there's a growing suspicion that a Pharaoh is in power that knows not Joseph." *Wayne Darrow's Washington Farmletter,* 17 January 1953.

10. Cochrane, *Toward an Understanding of Farm Policy,* 28–33; Hansen, *Gaining Access,* 143–152.

11. Orville Freeman to Myer Feldman, 4 June 1963, WHCF, Box 468, John F. Kennedy Presidential Library.

12. Orville Freeman to President Kennedy, 30 August 1963, Orville Freeman Papers, Box 10, Minnesota State Historical Society. Careful to avoid "the semantic pitfall of controls," Freeman boasted in 1963 that he had "managed to substitute the term 'supply management' for the traditional 'control' label." Orville Freeman to John Kennedy, 5 February 1963, Orville Freeman Papers, Box 9, John F. Kennedy Presidential Library.

13. Willard Cochrane to Orville Freeman, 5 November 1963, Freeman Papers, Box 10, Minnesota State Historical Society.

14. D. E. Hathaway to Council of Economic Advisers, "Current Limits Affecting Farm Policy," 16 November 1961, Kermit Gordon Papers, Box 23, John F. Kennedy Presidential Library.

15. Orville Freeman diary, 14 January 1963, Orville Freeman Papers, Box 14, Minnesota State Historical Society; Claude Desautels to Larry O'Brien, 28 March 1962, Office of Congressional Liaison Papers, Box 4, John F. Kennedy Presidential Library. When the House began considering cotton legislation in late 1962, Cooley publicly informed textile representatives, "We want to help you." He asked only that they propose a specific program. U.S. House of Representatives, Committee on Agriculture, *Hearings, Preliminary Hearings on Cotton Legislation,* 88th Cong., 1st sess., p. 41 (13 December 1962).

16. Willard Cochrane to Orville Freeman, 5 November 1963, Freeman Papers, Box 10, LBJL; *Congressional Quarterly Weekly Report*, 21 June 1963.

17. Orville Freeman to President Kennedy, 5 February 1963, Orville Freeman Papers, Box 9, John F. Kennedy Presidential Library.

18. Orville Freeman to President Kennedy, 5 February 1963, Orville Freeman Papers, Box 9, John F. Kennedy Presidential Library.

19. North Dakota Farm Bureau pamphlet; Farm Bureau pamphlet, copies in Freeman Papers, Box 9, John F. Kennedy Presidential Library.

20. Orville Freeman diary, 11 April 1963, Freeman Papers, Box 14, Minnesota State Historical Society. Eleven days before the vote, Freeman informed Kennedy that while the contest had reached a "high pitch," prospects "for a successful referendum have increased substantially in the last month." Orville Freeman to John Kennedy, 10 May 1963, Freeman Papers, Box 9, John F. Kennedy Presidential Library.

21. Orville Freeman to President Kennedy, 31 May 1963, Freeman Papers, Box 9, John F. Kennedy Presidential Library. *U.S. News & World Report* blared that the "White House farm strategy has come unstuck." *U.S. News & World Report*, 16 September 1963.

22. *Fortune*, July 1963.

23. Orville Freeman to President Kennedy, 25 May 1963, Freeman Papers, Box 10, Minnesota State Historical Society. Privately, USDA officials were less equivocal, with one conceding that with the vote, "our Grand Strategy came to a screeching halt." Willard Cochrane to Orville Freeman, 5 November 1963, Freeman Papers, Box 10, Minnesota State Historical Society.

24. U.S. House of Representatives, Committee on Agriculture and Forestry, *Hearings, Wheat*, 88th Cong., 1st sess., p. 59 (23 July 1963). Freeman, on the other hand, informed Dole, "I don't want to suggest that anyone is extreme in his viewpoints, but I can't help that it is rather unrealistic to talk about removing all partnership between Government and farmers given the very peculiar complicated nature of agriculture." Orville Freeman to Bob Dole, 30 April 1963, Freeman Papers, Box 2, John F. Kennedy Presidential Library.

25. Kennedy quoted in Orville Freeman to John Schnittker, 25 May 1963, Freeman Papers, Box 9, John F. Kennedy Presidential Library.

26. Carl Albert and Hale Boggs, "Dear Colleague," 29 October 1963, Harold Cooley Papers, Box 82, Southern Historical Collection, University of North Carolina.

27. Henry Wilson to Larry O'Brien, n.d. [November 1963], Henry Wilson Papers, Box 2, LBJL.

28. *U.S. News & World Report*, 30 December 1963.

29. *Congressional Quarterly Weekly Report*, 20 December 1963.

30. Orville Freeman diary, 10 December 1963, Orville Freeman Papers, Box 14, Minnesota State Historical Society.

31. Daley quoted in "Notes on First Congressional Leadership Breakfast," Diary Backup, Box 2, LBJL; President Johnson, John McCormack, and Richard Daley, 10:00 A.M., 3 December 1963, Recordings of Telephone Conversations—White House Series, Recordings and Transcripts of Conversations and Meetings, LBJL.

32. Larry O'Brien, "Memorandum for the President," 2 December 1963, Wilson Papers, Box 2, LJBL.

33. Larry O'Brien, "Memorandum for the President," 2 December 1963, Wilson Papers, Box 2.

34. 109 *Congressional Record*, 88th Cong., 1st sess., p. 23303 (4 Dec. 1963).

35. Ibid., p. 23306.

36. Cooley to Albert House, 14 November 1963, Cooley Papers, Box 83; 109 *Congressional Record*, 88th Cong., 1st sess., p. 23282 (4 Dec. 1963); *Washington Star*, 5 December 1963.

37. Johnson quoted in the *New Republic*, 28 March 1964; President Johnson, John McCormack, and Richard Daley, 10:00 A.M., 3 December 1963, Recordings of Telephone Conversations—White House Series, Recordings and Transcripts of Conversations and Meetings, LBJL.

38. *New Republic*, 28 March 1964.

39. *Wall Street Journal*, 5 December 1963.

40. President Johnson, John McCormack, and Richard Daley, 10:00 A.M., 3 December 1963, Recordings of Telephone Conversations—White House Series, Recordings and Transcripts of Conversations and Meetings, LBJL.

41. Orville Freeman to President Johnson, 2 December 1963, WHCF-LE, Box 32, LBJL.

42. U.S. Senate, Committee on Agriculture and Forestry, *Hearings, Cotton Programs*, 88th Cong., 1st sess., p. 10 (20 May 1963); *Congressional Quarterly Weekly Report*, 21 June 1963.

43. Orville Freeman, "The Cooley and Talmadge Cotton Bills," 10 December 1963, WHCF-LE, Box 32, LBJL.

44. Harold Cooley to Charles Sayre, 12 December 1963, Cooley Papers, Box 82.

45. U.S. Senate, Committee on Agriculture and Forestry, *Hearings, Cotton Programs*, 88th Cong., 1st sess., p. 45 (20 May 1963).

46. President Johnson and Richard Russell, 29 January 1964, 10:30 AM, Recordings of Telephone Conversations—White House Series, Recordings and Transcripts of Conversations and Meetings, LBJL.

47. President Johnson, B. Everett Jordan, and Walter Jenkins, 5:34 PM, 6 December 1963, Recordings of Telephone Conversations—White House Series, Recordings and Transcripts of Conversations and Meetings, LBJL. Jordan followed up on this issue consistently over the next several months, bluntly informing the administration that it was "unwise" to consider any cotton measure other than the Cooley bill. B. Everett Jordan memorandum, enclosed in William Whitley to George Reedy, 5 February 1964, WHCF-LE, Box 32, LBJL.

48. John Williams memorandum, 15 January 1964, John Williams Papers, Box 30, University of Delaware Library.

49. U.S. Senate, Committee on Rules and Administration, *Hearings, Financial Interests of Senate Officers or Employees*, 88th Cong., 1st sess., pp. 452–461 (6 December 1963); Jeff Shesol, *Mutual Contempt: Lyndon Johnson, Robert Kennedy, and the Feud That Defined a Decade* (New York: Norton, 1997), 146–150.

50. *Wall Street Journal*, 23 March 1964, 24 March 1964.

51. Robert Dallek, *Flawed Giant: Lyndon Johnson and His Times, 1961–1973* (New York: Oxford University Press, 1998).

52. President Johnson, B. Everett Jordan, and Walter Jenkins, 5:34 PM, 6

December 1963, Recordings of Telephone Conversations—White House Series, Recordings and Transcripts of Conversations and Meetings, LBJL.

53. Orville Freeman, "Memorandum for the Files," 15 January 1964, Freeman Papers, Box 11, Minnesota State Historical Society.

54. Orville Freeman diary, 10 December 1963, Freeman Papers, Box 14, Minnesota State Historical Society.

55. Orville Freeman, "Memorandum for Files," 4 December 1963, Freeman Papers, Box 1, LBJL.

56. President Johnson and Orville Freeman, 6:35 P.M., Recordings of Telephone Conversations—White House Series, Recordings and Transcripts of Conversations and Meetings, LBJL.

57. In fact, the president would shortly commission a poll suggesting that Freeman was a political liability to the administration in the Midwest. President Johnson and Orville Freeman, 11:16 A.M., 18 March 1964, Recordings of Telephone Conversations—House Series, Recordings and Transcripts of Conversations and Meetings, LBJL.

58. Allen Ellender to Sam Smith, 30 October 1963, Senate Agriculture Committee Papers, Record Group 46, Records of the United States Senate, Tray 3, National Archives; Thomas Becnel, *Allen Ellender: A Biography* (Baton Rouge: Louisiana State University Press, 1995), 136–145. Freeman complained that Johnson was "talking to these people on the Committees and making no real organized effort to keep me informed at all." Orville Freeman diary, 10 December 1963, Freeman Papers, Box 14, Minnesota State Historical Society.

59. President Johnson and Allen Ellender, 9 December 1963, 12:45 p.m., Recordings of Telephone Conversations—White House Series, Recordings and Transcripts of Conversations and Meetings, LBJL. In fact, George McGovern, anxious to build support for his wheat subsidy plan, had offered this exact proposal to Ellender in late August 1963. Allen Ellender to George McGovern, Senate Agriculture Committee Papers, Reading File 1963–1964, Record Group 46, Tray 1, National Archives.

60. *U.S. News & World Report,* 30 December 1963.

61. Orville Freeman to President Johnson, 2 December 1963, WHCF-LE, Box 33, LBJL.

62. George Aiken to W. R. Church, 2 March 1964, Senate Agriculture Committee Papers, Reading File 1963–1964, Record Group 46, Tray 1, National Archives; *Congressional Quarterly Weekly Report,* 24 January 1964.

63. Henry Wilson to Larry O'Brien, n.d. [early November 1963], Wilson Papers, Box 3, LBJL; *U. S. News & World Report,* 16 September 1963.

64. Allen Ellender to George McGovern, 6 September 1963, Senate Agriculture Committee Papers, Reading File 1963–1964, Record Group 46, Tray 1, National Archives.

65. *Congressional Quarterly Weekly Report,* 24 January 1964. Purcell's hearings outlined the broad ideological framework through which the farm bill would be considered over the next few months. Representing the pro-administration viewpoint, Herchel Newsom of the National Grange and Freeman himself backed the McGovern bill, arguing that it would provide the benefits associated with the failed wheat plan of 1963 without the burden of coercion that the Farm Bureau had used effectively in the campaign. Robert Woodward of the U.S. Chamber of Commerce took a middle view, reasoning that a "transitional program" might be appropriate; Charles Shuman, unsur-

prisingly, denounced the perversion of the wheat referendum's principal lesson: that farmers "want to move from Restrictive Government programs." U.S. House of Representatives, Subcommittee on Wheat, Hearing, Wheat Programs, 88th Cong., 2d session, pp. 173–180 (17 February 1964).

66. Henry Wilson to Larry O'Brien, 23 March 1964, Wilson Papers, Box 4, LBJL.

67. Orville Freeman diary, 18 December 1963, Freeman Papers, Box 14, Minnesota State Historical Society.

68. U.S. Senate, Committee on Agriculture and Forestry, *Hearings, Wheat Programs*, 88th Cong., 2d sess., pp. 120–135 (10 February 1964).

69. U.S. Senate, Committee on Agriculture and Forestry, *Hearings, Cotton Programs*, 88th Cong., 2d sess., p. 593 (16 February 1964).

70. Taylor Branch, *Pillars of Fire: America in the King Years, 1963–1965* (New York: Simon and Schuster, 1998).

71. Robert Mann, *The Walls of Jericho: Lyndon Johnson, Hubert Humphrey, Richard Russell, and the Struggle for Civil Rights* (New York: Harcourt Brace, 1996), 334–385.

72. President Johnson and Allen Ellender, 15 February 1964, 5:04 P.M., Recordings of Telephone Conversations—White House Series, Recordings and Transcripts of Conversations and Meetings, LBJL.

73. 110 *Congressional Record*, 88th Cong., 2d sess., pp. 3850–3852 (27 February 1964). Keating's attack triggered a strong response from majority leader Mike Mansfield, who took to the floor to announce that while "it is very seldom that I let fury get the better of me—very, very seldom"—Keating's charge represented an exception. 110 *Congressional Record*, 88th Cong., 2d sess., pp. 3853 (27 February 1964). Ironically, several members of the administration had earlier considered Keating's strategy: Mike Mantaos, the deputy legislative liaison, urged delaying the bill, since it represented a "really fine inducement to counteract a filibuster." Mike Mantaos to Larry O'Brien, 15 February 1964, WHCF-LE, Box 32, LBJL.

74. President Johnson and Orville Freeman, 5:55 P.M., 19 February 1964, Recordings of Telephone Conversations—White House Series, Recordings and Transcripts of Conversations and Meetings, LBJL.

75. Orville Freeman diary, 18 February 1964, Freeman Papers, Box 14, Minnesota State Historical Society.

76. Richard Russell to R. F. Burch, 30 January 1964, Richard Russell Papers, series IX, Box 19, University of Georgia.

77. *New York Times*, 3 March 1964.

78. *Washington Star*, 5 March 1964.

79. *Christian Science Monitor*, 21 March 1964; *Newsweek*, 16 March 1964.

80. *New Republic*, 28 March 1964.

81. Henry Wilson to Larry O'Brien, 26 March 1964, Wilson Papers, Box 4, LBJL.

82. President Johnson and James Eastland, 7:11 P.M., 21 March 1964, Recordings of Telephone Conversations—White House Series, Recordings and Transcripts of Conversations and Meetings, LBJL. Pacifying Jordan, of course, remained important. The Baker hearings continued throughout January and February, when they implicated Walter Jenkins in an alleged kickback scheme involving Johnson's purchase of insurance in the 1950s. But as long as Johnson continued to support the textile subsidy, Jordan kept up his end of the bargain:

as the *Washington Star* observed, "whitewash" was the "unpleasant odor floating around the Senate side of the Capitol." The lethargic nature of the committee's inquiry, the paper predicted, would "leave in the public mind a deep and fully justified suspicion that the Senate Rules Committee is trying to cover up a major scandal of far-reaching dimensions." *Washington Star,* 12 March 1964.

83. In 1960, for instance, John Kennedy made a personal appearance with then-representative George McGovern, who was challenging incumbent Karl Mundt for his Senate seat in South Dakota. As the campaign party boarded its plane, Robert Kennedy remarked that he sensed the visit might very well cost McGovern the election—as, perhaps, it did. Arthur Schlesinger Jr., *Robert Kennedy and His Times* (Boston: Houghton Mifflin, 1978), p. 243.

84. President Johnson and John McCormack, 12:30 P.M., 7 March 1964, Recordings of Telephone Conversations—White House Series, Recordings and Transcripts of Conversations and Meetings, LBJL.

85. President Johnson and Larry O'Brien, 7:20 P.M., 6 March 1964, Recordings of Telephone Conversations—White House Series, Recordings and Transcripts of Conversations and Meetings, LBJL. As political commentator Richard Wilson observed in March, Johnson "appears to have reversed" his party's traditional weakness in the upper Midwest. *Washington Star,* 27 March 1964. In the end, Wilson was correct: Johnson swept the region in the fall campaign, carrying in with him nearly a score of Democratic freshmen in Iowa, Wisconsin, Illinois, Michigan, Minnesota, and Nebraska.

86. President Johnson and Larry O'Brien, 4:15 P.M., 7 March 1964, Recordings of Telephone Conversations—White House Series, Recordings and Transcripts of Conversations and Meetings, LBJL.

87. *Wall Street Journal,* 27 February 1964.

88. President Johnson and Larry O'Brien, 6:50 P.M., 21 March 1964, Recordings of Telephone Conversations—White House Series, Recordings and Transcripts of Conversations and Meetings, LBJL.

89. *Congressional Quarterly Weekly Report,* 7 February 1964; *Washington Star,* 7 February 1964; *New York Times,* 8 February 1964.

90. Orville Freeman to Eugenie Anderson, 10 March 1964, Orville Freeman Papers, Box 1, LBJL. Freeman himself long had believed that passing food stamp legislation "ought not to be too complicated." Orville Freeman to Bob Leonard, 4 June 1963, Freeman Papers, Box 9, John F. Kennedy Presidential Library.

91. *Congressional Quarterly Weekly Report,* 10 April 1964; *Washington Post,* 8 February 1964.

92. President Johnson and Larry O'Brien, 6 March 1964, 7:20 P.M., Recordings of Telephone Conversations—White House Series, Recordings and Transcripts of Conversations and Meetings, LBJL.

93. President Johnson and Carl Albert, 7 March 1964, 12:55 P.M., Recordings of Telephone Conversations—White House Series, Recordings and Transcripts of Conversations and Meetings, LBJL; President Johnson and Carl Albert, 25 March 1964, 6:55 P.M., Recordings of Telephone Conversations—White House Series, Recordings and Transcripts of Conversations and Meetings, LBJL.

94. President Johnson and Orville Freeman, 6 March 1964, 8:08 P.M.,

Recordings of Telephone Conversations—White House Series, Recordings and Transcripts of Conversations and Meetings, LBJL.

95. President Johnson and Carl Albert, 7 March 1964, 12:55 P.M., Recordings of Telephone Conversations—White House Series, Recordings and Transcripts of Conversations and Meetings, LBJL.

96. Henry Wilson to Larry O'Brien, 29 February 1964, Henry Wilson Papers, Box 4, LBJL.

97. President Johnson and George Grant, 9 March 1964, 5:50 P.M., Recordings of Telephone Conversations—White House Series, Recordings and Transcripts of Conversations and Meetings, LBJL; President Johnson and Tom Abernethy, 9 March 1964, 5:55 P.M., Recordings of Telephone Conversations—White House Series, Recordings and Transcripts of Conversations and Meetings, LBJL; *Wall Street Journal*, 5 March 1964. The committee's Republicans filed a minority report that denounced the program as "costly and inefficient" and as an invasion of state and local prerogatives. *Congressional Quarterly Weekly Report*, 13 March 1964.

98. President Johnson and Carl Albert, 10 March 1964, 6:55 P.M., Recordings of Telephone Conversations—White House Series, Recordings and Transcripts of Conversations and Meetings, LBJL.

99. President Johnson and Larry O'Brien, 7 March 1964, Recordings of Telephone Conversations—White House Series, Recordings and Transcripts of Conversations and Meetings, LBJL.

100. *Wall Street Journal*, 23 March 1964; Carl Brauer, "Kennedy, Johnson, and the War on Poverty," *Journal of American History* 69 (1982): 98–119; Lloyd Gardner, *Pay Any Price: Lyndon Johnson and the Wars for Vietnam* (Chicago: Ivan R. Dee, 1995), 99–100.

101. Among the few to recognize the significance of this development was Ken Birkhead, the chief congressional liaison in the Agriculture Department. He, for one, doubted that the House leadership fully realized the "'muscle' both in and out of Congress that may be behind this legislation": by March, labor, cotton interests, farm groups, textile manufacturers, prominent members of the House, and Democratic partisans all badly wanted the measure. Ken Birkhead to Larry O'Brien, 9 March 1964, Reports on Legislation, Box 5, LBJL.

102. President Johnson and Myer Feldman, 10 March 1964, 4:20 P.M., Recordings of Telephone Conversations—White House Series, Recordings and Transcripts of Conversations and Meetings, LBJL.

103. *Washington Star*, 11 February 1964. In a further testimony to his limited political skills, Freeman did not even know about the GOP's action until hours after it occurred, when—of all people—Johnson himself informed the secretary. President Johnson and Orville Freeman, 10 March 1964, 6:45 P.M., Recordings of Telephone Conversations—White House Series, Recordings and Transcripts of Conversations and Meetings, LBJL.

104. President Johnson and John McCormack, 7 March 1964, 12:30 P.M., Recordings of Telephone Conversations—White House Series, Recordings and Transcripts of Conversations and Meetings, LBJL; President Johnson and John McCormack, 10 March 1964, 7:35 P.M., Recordings of Telephone Conversations—White House Series, Recordings and Transcripts of Conversations and Meetings, LBJL.

105. President Johnson and Carl Albert, 12 March 1964, 6:45 P.M., Recordings of Telephone Conversations—White House Series, Recordings and Transcripts of Conversations and Meetings, LBJL.

106. Orville Freeman to President Johnson, 18 March 1964, Freeman Papers, Box 1, LBJL.

107. President Johnson and Carl Albert, 25 March 1964, 6:55 P.M., Recordings of Telephone Conversations—White House Series, Recordings and Transcripts of Conversations and Meetings, LBJL.

108. Orville Freeman to President Johnson, 26 March 1964, Freeman Papers, Box 1, LBJL.

109. Henry Wilson to Larry O'Brien, 23 March 1964, Wilson Papers, Box 4, LBJL.

110. *National Review*, 5 May 1964; *Wall Street Journal*, 10 April 1964.

111. *Christian Science Monitor*, 2 April 1964.

112. 110 *Congressional Record*, 88th Cong., 2d sess., p. 7125 (7 April 1964).

113. 110 *Congressional Record*, 88th Cong., 2d sess., p. 7311 (8 April 1964).

114. *Wall Street Journal*, 10 April 1964.

115. *New York Times*, 9 April 1964.

116. 110 *Congressional Record*, 88th Cong., 2d sess., p. 7127 (7 April 1964).

117. Orville Freeman to President Johnson, 18 March 1964, Freeman Papers, Box 10, Minnesota State Historical Society.

118. *National Review*, 5 May 1964.

119. *Wall Street Journal*, 10 April 1964; *Congressional Quarterly Weekly Report*, 7 February 1964; *Christian Science Monitor*, 2 April 1964; *Business Week*, 18 April 1964.

120. Johnson swept the region in 1964, while Democrats picked up congressional seats in North Dakota, Minnesota, Iowa, and Missouri, and rural areas of Illinois, Wisconsin, and Michigan.

8 | Lyndon Johnson and the Keynesian Revolution: The Struggle for Full Employment and Price Stability

David Shreve

TO LYNDON JOHNSON, as presidential assistant Jack Valenti once recalled, "the family pocketbook was the root-and-branch crucial connection to all his plans and hopes for the nation."[1] LBJ "considered a robust, non-inflationary economy so critical to his domestic program," Johnson domestic policy adviser Joe Califano added, "that he spent more time on economic matters than any other subject during my years at the White House."[2] Johnson's biographers, on the other hand, have likely focused less attention on his administration's economic policies than any other major subject, transmitting instead an all too simple story of "guns and butter," shortsighted manipulation, and incipient inflation. Examined closely, President Lyndon Johnson's political economy reveals a far more sagacious and complex, even revolutionary, design.

To LBJ, the American Century and his own plans for a Great Society rested upon the bedrock of full employment and increasing economic opportunity, shaped out of necessity by both active government management and enlightened private sector behavior.[3] Such a foundation, he believed, promised not only increased job opportunities and a dramatic decline in American poverty but also economic efficiency and innovation, improved productivity, and an environment conducive to private sector profitability and stable prices.

Only on the price front did it ever appear that LBJ had failed to deliver, yet it is the common assessment of this "failure" that may be the most misleading of all interpretations of this era or of Lyndon Johnson's presidency. Despite an unsurpassed record on jobs, profits, productivity, and the distribution of the nation's prosperity, and an approach to price stability at full employment that could best be described as painstaking and conscientious, Johnson is seldom credited with anything more than a reckless disregard for the price inflation implications of his economic policies. In a series of common variations, implicated along with the thirty-sixth president are the war in Vietnam, government activism, aid to the poor, designs for the Great Society, Keynesian economics, and even the New Deal. Tempted especially by their eagerness to blame Vietnam for a variety of the period's maladies, including the stagflation and economic policy confusion of the 1970s, prominent members of Johnson's Democratic Party have even been among those most willing to accept this deceptive interpretation. Meanwhile, LBJ's revolutionary approach to the emergence of price inflation at full employment—compromised and curtailed by organized opposition, divisions among erstwhile political allies, and thorough miseducation—continues to go unnoticed.

Essential to understanding this unfinished and largely forgotten revolution are two somewhat distinct narratives. The first of these is an intellectual and political history that demonstrates LBJ's economic philosophy. Perhaps the only U.S. president to have entered office as a full-fledged Keynesian, Johnson grasped the insights of John Maynard Keynes's *General Theory*—instinctively at first and then intellectually—and maintained an allegiance to this set of ideas throughout his administration. His appreciation of Keynes—the British economist whose revolutionary theories identified and explained the functional connection between consumer demand, investment, and employment—came gradually, through his early association with Texas Hill Country populists like his father, Sam Rayburn, and Wright Patman; from his intuitive grasp of and attraction to New Deal imperatives that underscored the importance of purchasing power and the capriciousness of private investment; and through his growing admiration for the young Keynesian economists who carried the New Deal torch into the Fair Deal and the New Frontier. For Lyndon Johnson, the most decisive merging of pragmatic politics and instinctive appreciation of cutting-edge economic theory came, perhaps, during his vice presidency, a mostly fallow and often depressing period during which he had become captivated, nevertheless, by the abilities and unprecedented importance of Kennedy's official and unofficial economic advisers. As Walter Heller, Council of Economic Advisers (CEA) chairman under Kennedy and Johnson, would declare in 1966, "The economist arrived on the New Frontier, and is firmly entrenched in the Great Society."[4]

While FDR, Truman, Eisenhower, and Kennedy all benefited from Keynes's insights and adopted policies that conformed to at least some of his most significant ideas, only President Johnson succeeded in crafting an economic policy consensus based squarely on an uncompromised and quite revolutionary Keynesian foundation. As it was with several of Lyndon Johnson's predecessors (and many of his successors), this implied the active use of fiscal policy—taxing and spending—to adjust national purchasing power and to close gaps between actual and potential output. In LBJ's case, however, this also implied adherence to other less well recognized but equally critical parts of the Keynesian formula.

Attention to relative inequality was one of these, for the federal government's ability to alter purchasing power and to influence investment and output stems most directly from its ability to channel income and wealth from those less inclined to spend additional dollars of income (the wealthy) to those much more inclined to do so (everyone else). LBJ grasped this fundamental tenet without hesitation, for it dovetailed with the experiences of his formative years in the 1920s and 1930s, his well-honed political affinities, and his long-standing desire to wage war against American poverty. "I want to say," Johnson told Bill Moyers in March 1964 as he prepared to launch his War on Poverty, "that this is not going to solve poverty. Thirty years ago Roosevelt talked about one-third. Today we're talking about one-fifth. But it is a beginning, and as President Kennedy said, 'Let us begin.'"5

Close attention to price stability was another of these guiding precepts, for it was inflation that most often jeopardized the full employment LBJ always prized. Indeed, as he had learned in the 1940s and 1950s, even the full employment of an incidental Keynesianism—promulgated largely by wartime (or cold war) spending requirements and periodic attention to the needs of the American worker—often came quickly undone as workers gained marketplace leverage and forced employers to share an increasing portion of the high demand–full employment profit premium. A classic predicament that Keynes had only begun to study at the time of his death in 1946, this inflation functioned, then, as a way for employers to cling to extraordinary profit margins they had suddenly come to regard as normal and worthy of staunch defense. That this behavior also produced instability that could be blamed readily on the marketplace wage pressure they hoped to deflate or vanquish only made it more difficult to resist. Accordingly, and quite contrary to most popular assessments of his presidency, Lyndon Johnson expended more energy than any other modern president in the struggle against incipient inflation and the mythology of the "overheated" economy.

The second of these narratives is the story of Johnson administration policy. On the macroeconomic fiscal policy front this included LBJ's budgets and his efforts to change the U.S. tax code, most significantly with the Revenue Acts of 1964 and 1968. Emerging here is Lyndon Johnson as the "prudent progressive," a largely forgotten but once well-known characterization that consistently marked the fiscal policy of the Johnson years.

On the microeconomic front, President Johnson's policy revolved around the Wage-Price Guideposts, an inflation-fighting tool designed to underscore productivity trends and real unit wage costs that was introduced early in the Kennedy administration. Efforts on behalf of international monetary reform, consumer protection, fair housing laws, health care reform, and education and training also carried significant microeconomic import, but these were largely subsumed under the effort to rein in what LBJ viewed as a mostly irrational inflationary psychology. Civil rights reforms carried similar weight—as a way to open new, long-overdue economic opportunities—but they, too, served in this realm as an adjunct to a more critical inflation-fighting strategy and to the fiscal and monetary policies made possible by such wage-price vigilance.[6]

Contrary to the conventional reading, then, LBJ did not neglect the gathering inflationary storm, nor did he embrace an economic strategy destined to produce price inflation. The inflation and stagflation of the 1970s and the concomitant U.S. economic decline—not to mention the economic theory and policy muddle that remained in its wake—appear to have stemmed instead from other forces. Most prominent among these was the maturation and veiled growth of U.S. managerial bureaucracies and perquisites, emerging in a precarious full employment setting that unleashed its more corrupting tendencies. Checked by few factors outside of Johnson administration initiatives that remained always under siege and only partly understood, this widespread development eventually combined with the more fleeting energy crises and early crop failures of the 1970s to create a much more insoluble inflation. Indeed, though the Wage-Price Guideposts and related initiatives served to subdue much of this confusion and instability, abrupt policy reversals in the Nixon administration only rendered the situation more difficult to comprehend or manage. "Guns and butter" loomed large all the while, but they functioned in general as positive, rather than debilitating, economic forces.[7]

Underscored here is LBJ's sense that the economy was most often mismanaged against the interests of the nation's working class and its poorest citizens, and against the ultimate interests, therefore, of all Americans. Also evident is his quiet but steady assault on the notion that the United States could neither afford full employment for very long nor tolerate its alleged impact on prices or profits. The revolutionary import of this approach remains hidden, perhaps, only because of the simplistic corporate liberalism to which Johnson's Democratic Party had often descended after the death of Franklin Roosevelt and the fastidious disdain with which the most doctrinaire liberals had often regarded the pragmatic Texas Hill Country politician.

Johnson Economic Policies: The "Prudent Progressive"

When Lyndon Johnson ascended to the presidency, amid the reverberating shock and horror of his predecessor's murder, he drew immediate attention to two public policy initiatives, announcing his intentions in direct fashion: "First, no memorial oration or eulogy could more eloquently honor President Kennedy's memory than the earliest possible passage of the civil rights bill for which he fought so long. . . . And second, no act of ours could more fittingly continue the work of President Kennedy than the early passage of the tax bill for which he fought all this long year."[8]

Adding that his administration and the U.S. government "will set an example of prudence and economy," President Johnson embarked on a crusade designed to convince skeptics that one could be frugal and yet still champion activist fiscal policy, Keynesian deficit spending, and, as he announced early the next year in his first State of the Union address, an "all-out war on human poverty and unemployment."[9] The accompanying drive for a strong civil rights bill only reinforced Johnson's demand, issued directly in his May 1964 "Great Society" speech, that American prosperity and greatness must entail "abundance and liberty for all."[10] Turning sharply from the economic policy orthodoxy that his predecessor had only begun to assail, away from the "trickle-down" economics that had never really lost its hold on American public policy, Johnson outlined his commitment to an economic strategy that was both revolutionary and the outgrowth of older, unfinished, or poorly tested economic policy experiments.[11] Journalists called it the New Economics, but it was at least as old as Keynes's *General Theory*, published in 1936. Though it would include critical microeconomic initiatives such as the Wage-Price Guideposts, it would begin with compensatory fiscal policy and the drive to pass the Kennedy-Johnson tax cut.

The economic strategy that began to unfold at this point, however, often was measured by those unable to see much beyond the deal making and the new, colorful brand of White House politics. Indeed, journalists tended to regard LBJ's first economic policy initiative—his attempt to submit a reduced federal budget for the upcoming fiscal year—as a symbolic exercise that lacked any significance for economic policy. "The campaign is regarded here," Tom Wicker noted in a special to the *New York Times*, "as more nearly a key to Mr. Johnson's political approach than to his basic economic ideas."[12] Following Wicker and other journalists, historians and biographers have typically characterized this initiative as a cynical exercise dominated by gimmicks or sleight of hand, or a parsimonious and unnecessary gambit that served to limit social progress.[13] When LBJ launched a campaign to conserve electricity at the White House, for example, Republican opponents ridiculed the effort, and some argued that he was bringing shame upon a great national monument (by turning off the floodlights at night). For a short while, "Light-Bulb Johnson" became a popular and intentionally pejorative sobriquet, and the symbolism of the campaign appeared empty and misguided. But the economy drive was at least partly designed to convince the conservative Senate Finance Committee chairman, Harry Byrd, to release the pending tax cut legislation to the Senate floor. "I told them," LBJ wrote in his presidential memoirs, "they might be able to sell me on the New Economics, but not Harry Byrd."[14] To Walter Heller, he declared, "I'd like an expanding economy, too, and I'd like a budget at $108 billion." But, he added later, "Unless the budget fell below $100 billion, you won't pee one drop."[15] The chief impediment, Heller learned soon enough, was Senator Byrd.

On the other hand, Johnson seldom feigned frugality. Although many of his biographers have noted the widespread ridicule he attracted while attempting to trim the White House electric bill and curtail the use of government limousines, less well known is his reaction to this ridicule and the ultimate fate of such initiatives.[16] As Johnson's friend and tax attorney Waddy Bullion recalled, "His feelings stung, LBJ stopped boasting about savings on the White House electric bill. He kept turning out the lights, though."[17] Spending cuts at the Pentagon were real and often quite substantial and were not washed out by increased spending in Vietnam until 1968. In 1965, President Johnson directed agencies to avoid excessive end-of-fiscal-year purchases. The General Services Administration realized substantial savings throughout the Johnson years by switching the sites of office buildings to government-owned land. Once established, the Office of Economic Opportunity relied on many unpaid volunteers, a practice continued throughout the Johnson presidency. The JOBS program, launched by LBJ in 1968 under the aegis of the National Alliance of Businessmen (NAB), operated in similar fashion. "It was a very, very cheap program," NAB director Leo Beebe recalled, "because everybody was volunteered. We did a little printing on the government presses, and used paper and typewriters and office space and that's about it."[18]

Admonished by LBJ, all government agencies realized additional savings through large-volume buying, new supply standards, and transfers of real and excess property, and even by switching to a new size envelope, the latter of which produced $300,000 in savings over the 1964–1968 period.[19] And though most Defense Department cuts came early in the administration (base closings, curtailed nuclear materials production), the search for additional savings continued throughout Johnson's tenure at the White House. When Vietnam first began to swallow some of these savings in the summer of 1965, the president scrawled a note to himself: "McNamara's got to find ways to drag his feet on defense expenditures."[20]

The Planning Programming Budgeting System (PPBS), introduced by Secretary of Defense McNamara and deployed in all departments afterward at LBJ's urging, opened up new opportunities for streamlined administration and frugal budgeting, even as it placed great demands on officials charged with the collection and analysis of relevant data. Faced with these demands and with far less concern for efficiency than his predecessor, Nixon scrapped PPBS in 1971. LBJ never ceased to push the concept, however, even after announcing his withdrawal from the 1968 presidential campaign. Two months after this surprising announcement, he admonished all cabinet officers to make a final, concerted push to streamline all programs.

Efficient delivery of services remained paramount—where possible in a complex, rapidly shifting arrangement of political power and new programs—and administration frugality, it appears, was at once symbolic gesture, genuine reform, and consummated performance. In many agencies and departments, this approach was discarded, and administrative costs ballooned for the first time not during the Johnson presidency but under Johnson's successor, Richard Nixon.[21]

The reorientation of budget priorities, also obscured later by mounting outlays for Vietnam, became an equally significant part of the early economy drive. Referring to himself in the third person, in a recorded telephone conversation with Walter Heller in December 1963, Johnson asked rhetorically, "Now, why is he cutting these expenses? He's cutting the waste and the things that he need not do in order that he has some money to do the things that he needs to do. . . . Faced between an installation or grandma, he's for grandma."[22] Following Johnson's lead, Heller assured George Meany that the administration did not intend to go beyond "squeezing out waste, duplication, and outmoded facilities" to free up funds for "pressing human needs."[23] To Walter Reuther, only days later, Johnson declared, "Now, don't you get alarmed about all this crap about economy. What I am doing is taking from the haves and giving to the have-nots."[24]

When it became clear that budget cuts—some real and some cosmetic—were a political necessity, that his advisers understood the validity of his approach, and that he could sell the crusade to liberal allies, LBJ immersed himself in the smallest details of the prospective budget. "I studied every line, nearly every page," he recalled, "until I was dreaming about the budget at night."[25]

The Revenue Act of 1964

In January 1964, when LBJ and budget director Kermit Gordon finished their work on the 1965 fiscal year federal budget, President Johnson called Virginia senator Harry Byrd. "I've got a surprise for you, Harry," he announced to Byrd. "I've got the damn thing down under $100 billion . . . way under. It's only $97.9 billion."[26] Because Byrd had agreed to release the administration's tax cut legislation from the Finance Committee if the budget came in under $100 billion, and because passage seemed very likely once the bill reached the Senate floor, this feat was the key to securing its enactment.

When it was signed into law by President Johnson on 26 February, the Revenue Act of 1964 reduced withholding rates immediately from 18 to 14 percent, introduced a new standard deduction, raised the maximum deduction for child care expenses from $600 to $900, and reduced personal and corporate income tax rates in two stages for calendar years 1964 and 1965. To aid small stockholders, the existing annual dividend exclusion was raised from $50 to $100, but the dividend credit—a boon for wealthier, large stockholders—was reduced from 4 percent to 2 percent in 1964 and then phased out completely in 1965. The total reduction for 1964 was approximately $7.7 billion, and for 1965, when all its provisions would become effective, $11.5 billion. In remarks broadcast on radio and television, LBJ called it "the single most important step that we have taken to strengthen our economy since World War II."[27]

Aimed decisively at Americans on the lower rungs of the income ladder and designed to widen a modest budget deficit in the interest of increased consumer demand, this tax cut was anything but the supply-side gambit for which it has often been mistaken.[28] As Nixon economic adviser Herb Stein noted in his brief analysis of the 1964 changes, output per person employed actually grew slower after the tax cut than before. "One would have expected the reverse," Stein wrote in 1984, "if the supply-side effects were dominant."[29]

Indeed, JFK, LBJ, and their economic advisers considered increased government spending as a suitable, even preferential, alternative to the tax cut. President Kennedy had been talked out of a tax increase proposal during the 1961 Berlin crisis spending bulge precisely for this reason. But as adviser James Tobin noted several months after the passage of the 1964 tax cut, "There is not a Keynesian majority in Congress, and conscious deficit financing is still not respectable."[30] Concern for the often irrational prejudices of bond markets (which would likely raise rates more readily in response to greater spending than decreased taxes) and the need for the rapid delivery of whatever product the administration proposed ultimately clinched the debate in favor of the tax cut. That the time was ripe for an overhaul of the existing tax code, the basic structure of which had been designed in the 1940s to dampen consumption during a period of global warfare and resource scarcity, only made it less problematic. Moreover, with feeling for the late president running very high, Johnson knew that he could exploit Kennedy's outspoken and often eloquent support for the measure to secure a speedy delivery. "No act of ours," LBJ informed a joint session of Congress in November 1963, "could more fittingly continue the work of President Kennedy than the early passage of the tax bill for which he fought all this long year. . . . This is no time for delay. It is a time for action."[31]

Confident in the eventual success of both the tax cut and the overall Keynesian strategy it helped introduce, President Johnson envisioned expanded opportunities for government spending initiatives and the diminished need for some ongoing "safety net" expenditures as prosperity and government revenue mounted. Redistribution and the elimination of waste and duplication would continue, in other words, but within a framework of larger budgets and greater public investment. Tipping his hand intentionally as he introduced his 1965 fiscal year budget to Congress, LBJ underscored this outlook, built largely on a vision of much larger but dramatically reoriented and streamlined future budgets. "But it is not a standstill budget," he declared on that occasion, "for America cannot afford to stand still. Our population is growing. Our economy is more complex. Our people's needs are expanding."[32] On timing and on political grounds, LBJ seized the unique opportunity that the tax cut proposal represented.

With substantial benefits for taxpayers at the bottom of the income scale most likely to spend the additional take-home pay, the tax cut would prime the pump quickly, help businesses exploit idle capacity, and encourage new investment outlays. But LBJ also regarded it as little more than a catalyst, knowing well that spending priorities, relative price stability, and policies for education and training, housing, and medical care also played critical roles. The federal government's potential for offsetting the regressive fiscal policies and tendencies of state and local government also came under intense scrutiny, resulting in proposals that were shunted aside at the end only after a series of damaging leaks and Vietnam-related political pressures. "I would hope," Walter Heller noted in 1966, "that the tax cut lesson of the past few years has been learned wisely, but not too well. The on-target success of the 1964 tax cut should not blind us to the special circumstances that made massive tax cuts the clear choice over more rapid expenditures at that time—circumstances that may not repeat themselves in the future."[33]

Guns and Butter Revisited: LBJ and Inflation

But the "prudent progressive," as *Time* magazine described President Johnson in early 1965, soon became known instead as the man who unleashed the Great Inflation.[34] Having risen $4.4 billion per quarter in the three quarters preceding the tax cut, consumption spending increased by approximately $8.4 billion per quarter in the three quarters after its implementation. One dollar of the tax cut produced just under an estimated two dollars of national income. And by the second quarter of 1965, the additions to national income produced added federal revenues of approximately $7 billion and added state and local revenues of approximately $1.5 billion.[35] Though LBJ never claimed that the tax cuts would pay for themselves, because they were tilted toward the lower income brackets and because they triggered substantial advances in national income as a result, they did produce enough new revenue to pay for at least a significant portion of the initial reductions.

LBJ's new spending priorities and additions to the budget—promised in his early 1964 budget message—also triggered substantial increases in national income, lessened inequality, and reduced unemployment to levels not seen since the Korean War. Shifts from defense spending to social spending and marked increases in the latter—not offset or stymied by Vietnam spending until late in the administration—led the way. When spending for Vietnam reached levels that offset and then surpassed the preceding defense spending reductions—by late 1967 or early 1968—the U.S. economy received another not insignificant stimulus. Business boomed, profits soared, unemployment fell below 4 percent by late 1965 (and remained at or under this level until the end of the Johnson administration), and poverty rates fell dramatically. When some price inflation appeared alongside these unmistakable advances, critics complained that President Johnson's willingness, even eagerness, to continue such progress had launched an inflation that could be controlled only by reversing course. "Call it walking inflation, call it creeping inflation," grumbled Everett Dirksen in 1966, "I don't care what you call it. Somewhere, somehow there has to be a halt in programs of the Great Society."[36]

But LBJ believed otherwise. "I have never held with the theory," he wrote, "that increasing unemployment is an appropriate cure for inflation. A progressive government and a responsible business and labor community can take care of inflation in more intelligent ways."[37] Yet, in most histories of his administration, this outlook is forgotten and the period's inflation is portrayed instead as a product of presidential disregard or myopia and an intractable problem of the greatest magnitude. Conflated also with the much more serious episodes of inflation (and stagflation) in the 1970s, it was LBJ's inflation, these narratives assert almost mechanically, that triggered the economic breakdown of the following decade.

In theoretical terms, Johnson's insistence on full employment and his unwillingness to tolerate even a mild recession ("The economy wouldn't have a recession while Lyndon Johnson was president; it wouldn't dare," recalled Walter Heller) apparently led the nation past what economists termed the "natural rate of unemployment."[38] Based loosely on the so-called Phillips curve concept introduced by New Zealand's A. W. H. Phillips in 1958, the natural rate thesis suggested that there exists a theoretical rate of unemployment under which all further declines result only in accelerating rates of inflation. In the 1960s, thanks in part to speculation on Phillips's thesis conducted by Kennedy economic advisers Paul Samuelson and Robert Solow at the dawn of the decade, 4 percent unemployment was the somewhat casually adopted figure. Yet, as Solow recalled, "we had remarked explicitly that any attempt to exploit the inflation-unemployment trade-off in policy terms, by buying low unemployment at the expense of permanently higher inflation, could easily have the effect of causing the Phillips curve to shift adversely, canceling the hoped-for gain."[39] Inflationary expectations could enter the picture quite readily, in other words, conveying unpredictable momentum.

But a "natural rate of unemployment" made even less sense to the Kennedy-Johnson economists than an unchanging Phillips curve tradeoff between jobs and price stability. "Of course at any given time," Solow declared, "you can imagine puffing up aggregate demand so much that inflation accelerates. . . . But what that critical level is depends on history, institutions, attitudes, and beliefs, including beliefs about the natural rate."[40] Mindful of the many positive effects of high demand and full employment, including enhanced productivity, improved forecasts, and smoother production cycles, LBJ sought to change the relevant attitudes, beliefs, and institutional behavior. Urging business leaders in particular to rethink their positions, he asked them to welcome the high demand of the period and to consider more closely what their markets were telling them about prices and price stability.

To President Johnson and the Keynesian economists on whom he depended, therefore, 4 percent unemployment served as little more than an interim target, and the Phillips curve only a reminder that institutions and beliefs—however misguided—played an increasingly significant role as the pressure of low unemployment and high demand mounted. The Phillips curve and the 4 percent target, in other words, served LBJ and his advisers mostly as symbols of the environment in which they labored, dominated still by economic orthodoxy and the mythology of excess demand inflation. But there was no single natural rate, only the presence of historical tendencies that could imperil sound policy or, alternately, be attenuated or vanquished. It is within this context that Lyndon Johnson sought to administer the most significant and demanding of all administration microeconomic initiatives: the Wage-Price Guideposts.

LBJ and the Wage-Price Guideposts

First popularized during the 1962 steel industry showdown during which President Kennedy forced the reversal of a steel price increase, the Wage-Price Guideposts became the principal means by which LBJ sought to curb price inflation. Based on the belief that prevailing prices in critical industries—such as steel—affected costs in many other industries and businesses, and that wage negotiations in these critical industries often ignored price implications or overwhelmed the careful consideration of actual costs, the guideposts sought a way to elucidate these potential consequences. The guidepost magnitude, never meant to be precise, was formulated upon a running average for annual productivity increases in the U.S. economy. Taking productivity trends into account, Johnson and his advisers reasoned, would teach company executives to acknowledge something approaching their actual costs, an acknowledgment seldom made with any precision or alacrity. Absent this calculation, corporations simply equated any wage increase with a general cost increase, building a flawed but compelling case for price relief in the process. Productivity changes—due to advances in worker training and education, the uptake of technological innovation, the replacement of obsolete or worn-out machinery, or increased capacity utilization—mattered little or not at all, yet savings from these factors could easily offset modest wage increases.

Although his advisers saw President Johnson as the ideal guidepost "enforcer," adherence was always designed to be voluntary, and the price objectives were neither arbitrary nor punitive but predicated upon real marketplace imperatives that were otherwise hidden or ignored. Indeed, recalling their experience administering wage and price controls during World War II and the Korean War, Gardner Ackley and others opposed more direct controls unequivocally. Ackley's successor as CEA chair, Art Okun, once sent what he referred to as a "screaming memo," written to dispel rumors in 1968 that LBJ was even considering such a change.[41]

Yet, because many companies ignored the ways in which full employment promoted stable or even declining prices and heeded only factors that suggested the opposite (typically the wage increases won by skilled labor in tight labor markets), voluntary compliance did not imply passive enforcement. The guideposts, as Ackley once described them, were a way to make price changes "a matter of private conscience" and to "create an informed public opinion" on the issue of corporate price policy.[42] To LBJ, they were a way to publicize and circumscribe a narrow corporate vision focused on short-term profits and incomplete or misleading accounting data, and built upon a blinding obsession with the power and costs of labor.

Indeed, recent investigations suggest that companies set prices without much regard for broad market factors and that publicity and education always play a significant role, particularly in the confusing realm of corporate costs.[43] Because easy-to-grasp information always carried more weight in decision making than more abstract or elusive information—regardless of accuracy—it was the principal role of the guideposts to provide a truer narrative, as easy to grasp as the more erroneous and incomplete but also more conventional reading.[44] With help from his closest economic advisers, LBJ preached an unequivocal message to the nation's business leaders: look at the details and the full dynamics of your own markets and begin to understand that high demand and increased wages need not imply rising costs or rising prices. To labor, the president's message bore a similar stamp: keep wage demands close to productivity advances, and employers can then be taught to alter market-defying behavior, share more of their income, and stabilize prices.

Fiscal and monetary policies, never insignificant and potentially more important, failed to take precedence at this point only because Johnson and his advisers viewed them, after the 1964 tax cut and the subsequent increase in federal spending, as less problematic and already close to their projected ideal.[45] With fiscal and monetary policies geared toward full employment, Johnson latched on to the guidepost concept, finding it indispensable in the struggle against inflation, and taking it even further than President Kennedy would have allowed. "He was such an activist on the wage-price front," Walter Heller recalled, "when he thought people were doing things against the national interest, he took it almost as a personal affront."[46] The guideposts, Heller added, were "tailor-made" for LBJ's "kind of approach to policy, his kind of personality. He embraced them. He gave them a real bear hug."[47]

Representing a response to entrenched corporate (and labor union) practices that had always goaded President Johnson into action, the guideposts dovetailed nicely with his populist/liberal economic philosophy. "I sure want to be prepared for them," Johnson warned Willard Wirtz in May 1964. "Looks like that these boys that are making the profits that they're making, and the fellas that are doing well with the wages, they'd share a little of it with the consumer."[48] Since the guidepost regime held the potential to sharpen the focus on all costs—including those associated with executive perquisites or hidden benefits like stock options—it also served LBJ's predilection for economy and his disdain for corporate greed. At unemployment levels at or under 4 percent and with profits soaring, this too was a critical function, for it was often in such circumstances that managerial costs increased dramatically, with little or no illumination from vague or misleading accounting systems.[49] Accordingly, the "prudent progressive" devoted an unusually large amount of time to guidepost popularization and enforcement, even when Vietnam commanded much of his attention.

The 1964 Economic Report of the President, issued only weeks into the Johnson presidency, enunciated LBJ's faith in the guideposts and reiterated the prevailing guidepost target figure (3.2 percent) adopted in the 1962 Economic Report.[50] Though all of Kennedy and

Johnson's advisers agreed that an exact figure would be impossible to select and that exceptions would ultimately have to be made, the 3.2 percent productivity figure was deemed a suitable, and relatively accurate, target.[51] Adopted after some debate, it also happened to represent the legal percentage of alcohol for beer produced in several states with large industrial economies. Anything that made the guideposts more memorable, it appeared, aided their enforcement.

Despite a general lack of enthusiasm at the outset, particularly with the memory of the 1962 steel price showdown still fresh in mind, an increasing number of managers and labor leaders began to welcome President Johnson's exhortation. Former Goldman-Sachs economist and assistant secretary of commerce (1968–1969) William Chartener recalled, for example, that in discussions with both corporate and union members of LBJ's Labor-Management Advisory Committee, he learned from many that the guideposts and the accompanying public pronouncements were "helpful" in obtaining moderate, noninflationary settlements.[52]

Very early in the administration, Harvard economist and CEA consultant (and later CEA member) Otto Eckstein, recommended that wage-price policy take into account "Johnson's persuasiveness on the telephone."[53] Though it is unlikely that LBJ required much prodding here, he soon began testing the telephone in this rapidly mounting rhetorical and pedagogical struggle. On the wings of just such an initiative in 1964, he succeeded in making a case for stable automobile prices. Many comparable successes followed, from aluminum, steel, copper, and automobiles again in 1965, to molybdenum, antibiotics, school textbook, and beef prices in 1967. "Sometimes I think he had more faith in what [the guideposts] could do, or more of a picture of individual misbehavior rather than general market conditions, than we did," recalled Arthur Okun.[54]

To business leaders who decried the apparent guidepost imperative—to transmit all productivity gains into wage increases—the Johnson administration reminded them of their faulty arithmetic and underscored the way in which full employment and higher wages redounded to their benefit. Productivity increases matched by equal percentage wage increases, they reminded detractors, also produced proportional increases in profits. Moreover, as Kennedy-Johnson adviser Kenneth Arrow pointed out, even in the event of wage increases only modestly above the guidepost target, a gradual increase of labor's share of the national income typically spurred the adoption of innovative technology and a modest accompanying increase in absolute profit. LBJ invoked the same explanation, noting repeatedly that prosperous workers in large numbers implied stable markets, much more forgiving of risky investments in new technology than those buffeted by recurring joblessness or stagnant wages.[55] Sustaining and creating markets for American products and services, making taxpayers out of "taxeaters," he asserted, was good business for all.

Despite the apparently commonsense character of such sermons, LBJ recognized his political and pedagogical limitations. Johnson and CEA chairman Gardner Ackley (November 1964–February 1968) expressed a continual reluctance, for example, to use certain high-pressure tactics—such as the threat of antitrust investigation—against corporations targeted for unnecessary price increases.[56] The president and the CEA also realized that guidepost effectiveness implied an ongoing educational effort that would likely bear little fruit in the short run. "It is very easy to exaggerate the extent of this transformation in attitudes," Ackley warned in 1965.[57] And, as he noted in 1967, despite the decline of the profits share of national income beginning in the second quarter of 1966, "Labor feels that the guideposts have done a better job of protecting corporate profits than real wages. Business leaders must ponder this fact of life."[58] Indeed, friends in the labor movement were among the most difficult to persuade. "I see you kicked my guideposts around the other day," LBJ once complained to AFL-CIO president and political ally George Meany. "Mr. President," Meany replied, "they're your guideposts and not mine."[59]

Consequently, when a well-publicized settlement between major airlines and the International Association of Machinists (IAM) was announced in August 1966—an agreement that included annual wage increases of approximately 4.9 percent—many read the settlement as the death knell for the guideposts. Coming on the heels of prominent guidepost-breaking labor settlements in the automobile industry and in the New York City transit workers strike, the consequences seemed dire. "We hoped that they could keep their increases as low as possible," declared President Johnson in the middle of the airlines negotiations, "but they could not be kept within 3.2."[60] On 27 July 1966, even before the agreement was announced, Gardner Ackley wrote to LBJ about the long-run implications:

> Every free industrialized country which tries to maintain full employment faces this problem: strong unions have the power to push up wages faster than productivity and thereby inflate costs and prices; and semi-monopolistic industries have the power to push up prices even if costs are stable. . . . This is not a problem for the next six months or two years but for the decade. The end

of the war won't solve it. A tax increase won't solve it (though it could help). It will have to be approached head on. Sometime, somewhere, we will have to find a way to convince the unions they cannot continually push wage costs up, and to convince business that profit margins cannot continually rise.[61]

But LBJ remained undeterred and considered the airlines settlement only a symbolic defeat. Profits in many industries, after all—including commercial airlines—appeared high enough to warrant both increased wages *and* lower prices.[62] And as Walter Heller had reminded Ackley and the president just before the end of IAM-airlines negotiations, industry return on capital was so great that the Civil Aeronautics Board was likely to mandate selective ticket price decreases even after the guidepost-breaking settlement.[63] Indeed, one reason many business leaders suddenly embraced the guideposts at this point was the early 1966 report that revised national trend productivity to 3.6 percent, significantly above the 3.2 percent benchmark.

When LBJ announced that the guidepost target would remain at 3.2 despite the new evidence, business groups cheered and the U.S. Chamber of Commerce hailed the move as an "act of economic statesmanship."[64] Hoping that labor would remain mostly in his corner, the president could do little but continue his more overt courtship and education of business leaders. As Eisenhower CEA member Henry Wallich noted, however, the dilemma was obvious. "The evidence is on the financial pages every day," Wallich wrote in his regular *Newsweek* column. "Profits have been rising rapidly, faster than the GNP, . . . and are now provoking excessive wage demands. Thus, though it is labor that is most ostentatiously turning its back on the guideposts, it is business that has done a large part of the damage."[65]

But the guidepost principle remained sound and the effects of its implementation significant. For fifteen consecutive quarters in which the Wage-Price Guideposts had been deployed (1962 IV–1966 I), wage rate gains actually fell below the predicted, hypothetical market rates for such a high-profit, tight labor market economy.[66] Their modest success also reflected fundamental market dynamics, for only in late 1966 or early 1967 did unit wage costs catch up to previous highs established late in the Eisenhower administration. With productivity advances proceeding apace, there was little to threaten high profits or stable prices.

In the end, securing a lasting and effective price-fighting strategy was more a pedagogical or political problem than an economic one. Accordingly, in late 1966, LBJ launched a drive to combine the Departments of Commerce and Labor, a reflection of his designs for a new consensus on which to base increasingly rational and cooperative private price-making behavior. When George Meany reported little support from the AFL-CIO, however, Johnson replied, "If you people feel deeply this way, that you think it's the wrong thing to do and you're going to fight it on the Hill, then that's the end of it. There are no recriminations, no bitterness. I just feel it's the right thing to do."[67] When the administration's Labor-Management Advisory Committee reported an equally negative reaction, Johnson capitulated. "Okay, it's shelved. Now, can you guys figure out how to get a handle on prices and wages?"[68]

There was, however, no mourning for the "death of the guideposts." Gardner Ackley had, early in 1966, called upon Saul Nelson to head up an administration price staff. Its efforts continued unabated. A veteran of the Korean War price controls, as was Ackley, Nelson chaired a three-man committee that met every Thursday and passed on its findings to the CEA. Ackley and Califano had also begun meeting every Friday to review this information and had begun issuing "Weekly Price Reports." When the Nelson committee stopped meeting in mid-1966, Califano recruited one of his Harvard Law classmates, John Robson, to head up a less formal but even more rigorous fact-finding group linked to the administration's inflation-fighting policies. "I need you more than I need a company of Marines," LBJ told Robson when he joined the administration in July 1966.[69]

The president continued to wire and telephone corporate executives, combining, as always, personal pleas with tangible government levers, and in many industries his success continued, unaffected by the rumored "death" of the guideposts in 1966. In February 1967, for example, he convinced Phillips Petroleum to roll back an attempted gasoline price increase. And in late 1968, he persuaded Humble Oil to rescind a modest fuel oil price rise.

In late 1967 and early 1968, when the automobile industry attempted increases based on new safety features (shoulder harnesses) and greater labor costs, the guideposts also wielded considerable influence. As was often the case, industry contracts with the federal government (more than $1 billion in this case, including military trucks and cannon shells) presented Johnson with a significant lever. While the early 1968 (January) "repricing" was a disturbing sign, increases were kept to a minimum (approximately $20 per vehicle) and mostly reflected improved product quality.[70]

LBJ's efforts on behalf of price stability were so substantial and unrelenting, even late in his term, that some of his advisers wondered if they were not somewhat misplaced. "When you think of all the problems that the world had at that time," economist Otto Eckstein recalled, "including . . . civil rights and the beginning of the Vietnam War . . . that all of this good talent and presidential leadership was being applied to chop two or three tenths off the [price] index may well have been a misallocation of resources."[71] Yet, when critics suggested that the whole guidepost operation entailed unseemly and unwarranted "ear twisting," Gardner Ackley replied: "Now, I have been trying to find out what people here mean by 'ear-twisting.' Is it, on the part of the President, being effective, persuasive, even passionate in private conversation? Do we want an inarticulate, unpersuasive, incoherent spokesman for what he believes in?"[72] Undoubtedly passionate about this endeavor, LBJ considered price stability an absolute prerequisite both for political success and for the longer-term acceptance of his as yet vulnerable economic strategy. Benign neglect was not an option.

If there was any lull at all in Johnson's struggle against price inflation, it came in 1967, when price advances did recede somewhat, and when more effort was directed toward securing the anti-inflationary tax surcharge he originally hoped to enact sometime late that year.[73] Urging Johnson to renew the struggle in mid-1968, Arthur Okun remarked, "Our record of activity here is considerably below any other period of the Kennedy-Johnson era."[74] But the low level of activity stemmed more from the surcharge debate and a number of key administrative changes than submission to an even moderate inflation. Once LBJ settled on a tax surcharge as a way to arrest inflationary psychology and to bridge old and new inflation-fighting strategies, asking bankers and corporate executives to endorse it rendered the guidepost gospel even more difficult to preach. And while the administration's personnel changes eventually constituted a move toward a more capable inflation-fighting effort, these also impeded guidepost enforcement in the short run.

The removal in January 1967 of the somewhat intransigent secretary of commerce, John Connor, represented one of the more notable changes. "Unless Jack [Connor] is willing to do some of the no-saying," Ackley reminded Johnson in 1966, "every case will wind up either in the White House or in the Council—or with a price rise. I have no objection to being the bastard; but in the long run, it may weaken the effectiveness of the Council to you."[75] Less than a year later, Connor was out, and Alexander "Sandy" Trowbridge was in.

Arthur Okun's ascension to the chairmanship of the CEA, on 16 February 1968, also represented a significant change. His predecessor, Gardner Ackley, had been an energetic and much admired chairman, but by late 1967 he had begun to tire. While Okun had been a member (the youngest ever at age thirty-five) and an integral part of the CEA since 1964 (replacing Walter Heller), he was especially well suited to the demands of the chairmanship and to the pedagogical requirements of the guidepost strategy. "He had a great gift for the presentation of ideas," Ackley noted, and, in the words of Kennedy CEA member James Tobin, "an unparalleled command of the facts of real world business fluctuations."[76] Okun was, as Ackley put it, "the best empirical economist I know, with surpassing skills as a forecaster."[77] If anyone could help guide Johnson out of the foreboding economic policy landscape that prevailed late in the administration, it was Okun. "That young Art Okun is a gem," LBJ remarked to Walter Heller in mid-1968; "he turns out more useful stuff for me than the Secretaries of [blank and blank] combined."[78]

When Ackley decided to retire from the CEA—accepting the Italian ambassadorship—he also introduced an important change that promised to strengthen guidepost enforcement. Proposing, in October 1967, a way to free the CEA from the handling of specific industry or company cases, Ackley convened discussions that led to the formation of the Cabinet Committee on Price Stability (CCPS). The CEA would become an active participant in the CCPS, but the new committee would take on much of the actual price fighting.

LBJ announced the formation of the CCPS in his 1968 Economic Report, and named Federal Trade Commission chief economist Willard Mueller as its executive director in April. Focusing initially on studies and proposals for new price-fighting initiatives such as improved controls on government procurement and cost containment measures for government expenditures on health care (Medicaid and Medicare), the CCPS reflected the "prudent progressive" who had engineered its creation, but it moved only slowly into actual price-fighting activities.[79] By midyear (1968) it had begun the practice of sending letters— termed "pre-sin sermonettes" by Okun—to companies and unions about to engage in important negotiations. According to Stanford Ross, who had replaced John Robson in early 1967, the CCPS was just becoming "workable and useful" when Johnson's term came to an end.[80]

Though Ackley once lamented that the "jawboning" process inherent to the application of the guideposts was like "telling children not to put beans up their noses," guidepost education and "enforcement" remained the key to long-term price stability at full employment. "Under such circumstances of generally excess demand," he admitted readily in 1966, "guideposts can play no significant part in avoiding inflation."[81] Neither Ackley nor LBJ, however, believed that the United States had reached such a point in the late 1960s, and the guidepost lesson remained decisive. Great advances in the nation's productive capacity had rendered excess demand an imprecise, even fundamentally inaccurate, characterization. Absent a deficient monetary policy, critical supply shocks, or a partial collapse of the normally robust and habitual channels for American investment, it might never occur.

Responding in May 1967 to charges that the guideposts were dead, Ackley replied: "I believe that voluntary restraint in the exercise of private discretion will continue because the natural leaders of labor, business and government know that it must. . . . And I believe that this continuing system of voluntary restraint must be based on the productivity principle because no other makes economic sense."[82] They remained somewhat crippled afterward not because they were ill-advised or ineffective but mostly because labor leaders remained unconvinced that their counterparts in management had truly learned and accepted the guidepost lesson. Indeed, when President Nixon jettisoned the guideposts abruptly within days of his first inauguration, corporate behavior changed dramatically, confirming these paralyzing suspicions. With inflation increasingly unchecked by public policy in the early 1970s, it also became easier for the American public to fall back on the mythology of the not-yet-vanquished orthodoxy, blaming LBJ for the inflation he had only begun to tame.

Accordingly, though fiscal and monetary policy remained the most significant economic policies in general, microeconomic tools reigned supreme in the battle against inflation. Unable to spell this out in clear enough terms for the American public, key politicians, and the leaders of U.S. business and labor, however, LBJ was compelled to battle on at least partly under the guise of the orthodoxy he hoped to vanquish. "I believe we can continue the Great Society while we fight in Vietnam," he declared in his 1966 State of the Union address. "But if there are some who do not believe this, then, in the name of justice, let them call for the contribution of those who live in the fullness of our blessings, rather than try to strip it from the hands of those that are most in need."[83] Connected debates on fiscal and international monetary policy made plain this predicament and necessity for compromise.

New Economics and Old Medicine

Despite President Johnson's efforts, his opponents continued to prophesy runaway inflation with full employment. "Educating the press and the public on fiscal policy," Gardner Ackley wrote to LBJ in August 1967, "is a long uphill fight."[84] On microeconomic anti-inflation policy, pedagogical success was even more elusive, and in the interest of buying time and changing expectations, LBJ found that he could scarcely avoid mixing the orthodox with the revolutionary. Much like Kennedy during his attempt to sell Keynesian economics (and his tax cut proposal) to skeptical business leaders and conservative congressmen, LBJ, too, was forced to chart a mostly traditional course, despite obvious misgivings. The assorted 1966 tax increases, the drive for an income tax surcharge in 1967 and 1968, and the administration's approach to the international balance of payments and gold "crises" all reflected in varying degrees this tendency and predicament.

Yet these actions also seemed to betray President Johnson as one who believed the assertions of his critics but who had offered in response only incomplete or insufficient measures. In 1968, his long-time supporter and unofficial economic adviser Eliot Janeway published *The Economics of Crisis: War, Politics, and the Dollar.*[85] Spurred by his aversion to the war in Vietnam, Janeway magnified the import of related economic policy decisions, exploited fears of runaway inflation, and urged Senator Vance Hartke to promote the message on Capitol Hill, mostly to make a forceful antiwar statement. His break with Johnson, a fellow New Dealer and friend, was sharp and laden with emotion. Shortly thereafter and in a similar vein—on the last page of the last chapter of *The Best and the Brightest*—David Halberstam set the tone for a generation of historians when he declared, "It was not the war which destroyed the American economy, but the essentially dishonest way in which it was handled."[86] Such dishonesty, Halberstam implied forcefully, led to greater public spending than the nation could handle, bigger deficits than anyone had predicted, and a virtually unstoppable and quite automatic inflationary momentum.

The measures judged incomplete or insufficient, however—particularly the tax surcharge introduced "belatedly" in mid-1968—were precisely what the prevailing political and economic environment demanded. Given undue deference to gain a political foothold for the New Economics, they were a dose of old medicine Johnson hated to prescribe but hoped to employ to inoculate the nation against larger, more harmful doses. Exploiting the "great psychological assets of sailing under the familiar colors," as Walter Heller described it, these actions also targeted problems that were quite real and difficult to surmount: the inflationary expectations and the genuine inflation or international monetary disturbances that such expectations always produced.[87] In the aftermath of the preemptive, ill-timed interest rate hike effected in late 1965 by Fed chairman William McChesney Martin, such deference could also stave off additional monetary shocks. On abundant display in 1966 in both housing and stock markets, the perils of tight money were just as significant as the perils of inflationary expectations.

In the case of the tax surcharge proposal, LBJ had also begun to realize that new programs simply needed new tax dollars; in 1967 and 1968, an increasingly conservative Congress would entertain no deficit spending alternative. The major problem with the 1968 fiscal year budget, budget director Charles Schultze informed the president, was that "we are not able to fund adequately the new Great Society programs."[88] In April 1968, speaking to the board of the newly formed Urban Institute, LBJ underscored the predicament: "Well, here's the number one problem for anyone that wants to help their country and the people in it. You've got to figure out how to raise the taxes to pay for these social programs our people need and to rebuild our cities and educate our children. . . . What we need is someone smart enough to tell us how to convince the American people that they should ante up."[89]

With unemployment rates under 4 percent and on their way to 3.3 percent at the time of Johnson's departure from office, there was also little need for additional deficit spending, however harmless and fleeting the current deficits remained. "In the near term," noted Johnson adviser Francis Bator—"once the economy was clearly in the neighborhood of potential output—pretty much everyone thought, including President Johnson, that the situation called for a large tax increase that would compress the consumption of the non-poor and thereby free up resources slated for the Vietnam War and for the increased consumption of Great Society transfer recipients."[90]

The drive for the tax surcharge in 1967 and 1968 was less a critical test, therefore, for the New Economics than a sound way to pay for expanded Great Society programs, a psychological tool wielded in the struggle against inflationary expectations, and a political tactic with which to blunt a rising conservative onslaught. "I am also struck," Arthur Okun wrote LBJ in April 1968, "by the illusion of some liberals that downward pressure on Federal programs will disappear if the tax bill fails. On the contrary, in that event, the atmosphere of financial emergency at home and abroad would give conservatives the upper hand in choking high-priority programs."[91] As had been true so often throughout the president's career, ostensible allies proved themselves once again far less capable of recognizing the persistent influence of orthodoxy and reaction.

Combined with efforts to scale back federal pay raises and slow down government construction projects, the surcharge also represented a way to encourage ongoing wage and price restraint. "How credible are you in asking for restraint by the private decision makers," Arthur Okun asked, reflecting on his tenure at the Johnson CEA, "if you don't show some kind of restraint in the decisions you make, even if they're relatively small decisions?"[92] An economy marked by little unemployment, burgeoning demand, and paralyzed production required a tax increase or a spending cut; this one required neither but could be aided, perhaps, by the new tax, especially if it targeted corporate and upper-bracket income.

Since the real targets of the surcharge were inflationary psychology and those capital and intermediate goods markets temporarily plagued by a mad scramble for increased capacity and profits, LBJ and his advisers pushed repeatedly for a progressive tax increase. "We should also resist a proposal," Okun reminded the president, "to raise all rates by the same number of percentage points in each bracket. In such a plan, upper income groups would be carrying much less of the added load than under the surcharge approach."[93] All surcharge proposals included a low-income exemption, and the surcharge vehicle itself—a tax on a tax—automatically imposed greater increases on those in higher brackets. Yet, as Gardner Ackley reminded LBJ in August 1967, "if we open up the whole question of the proper distribution of the tax burden, we will never be able to get temporary tax action in time to meet our needs." Until House Ways and Means chairman Wilbur Mills forced its hand in 1968, the administration also struggled to prevent the substitution of regressive spending cuts for progressive tax increases. If Mills's demands "are extreme," Ackley reported in December 1967, "that could mean a hopeless stalemate. With a reasonable budget we need a tax increase but can't get it; with a very tight budget we can get a tax increase but don't need it."[94]

Regarding the widely accepted Halberstam implication, that indecision here stemmed from deception on Vietnam spending, Ackley declared: "I would like to try very hard to disillusion anybody who believes that. In the first place we knew what numbers were being talked about . . . there was certainly no question about the absence of sufficient information to reach a policy judgment."[95] By December 1965, Ackley recalled, "the Council [of Economic Advisers] was actively discussing alternative tax increase programs with the Director of the Budget, the Secretary of the Treasury—and with LBJ."[96]

Paul Samuelson's advice, offered in *Newsweek* as the surcharge debate unfolded, typified the rather unsettled, equivocal nature of recommendations offered by economists, both inside and outside of the Johnson administration. "Like Oscar Wilde, who spent the morning putting in a comma and the afternoon taking it out," Samuelson noted in 1966, "I find myself oscillating."[97] Subsequent historical inquiries have only confirmed the president's candor and the primacy of political reckoning.[98] Delay in seeking the surcharge, as one study summarized it, "was a matter of calculation and timing rather than uncertainty and hesitation."[99]

Few, if any, however, have considered the surcharge debate in light of the New Economics and its new way of considering inflation at full employment. Even economists have focused almost exclusively on the largely irrelevant question of how effectively a temporary tax, such as the surcharge, can alter aggregate demand.[100] Since it was mostly a response to inflationary psychology and supply-side bottlenecks, and part of the struggle to maintain an evolving economic policy revolution, the answer to this question should matter only to the extent that it related to these problems.

In the realm of international monetary policy, LBJ faced similar limitations. Because the United States had decided at the 1944 Bretton Woods conference to underwrite much of the postwar economic recovery by agreeing to exchange gold for U.S. dollars held abroad (at the rate of thirty-five dollars per ounce), the mythology of gold would be counted on to support dollar integrity and international liquidity. As an overseas dollar shortage gave way to a more widespread accumulation by the end of the 1950s, however, any hint of unusually high or persistent U.S. inflation ran the risk of setting off a run on the American gold supply. Likewise, any appearance of U.S. current or capital account deficits—representing the difference between the imports and exports of goods, services, and loans, and precipitated in part by high levels of U.S. foreign lending and military aid—might also spark a decline of confidence in the dollar and a run on gold. Ignored whenever the specter of increasing gold shipments appeared—a vision often rendered quite vivid by political imprecations against "inflationary" domestic policy—were the international need for dollar-based liquidity and the vast returns earned by American capital exports. Such a situation compelled LBJ and his advisers—particularly

Francis Bator, Johnson's link to the Cabinet Committee on the Balance of Payments, George Ball at the State Department, and the CEA—to consider the prejudices of European central bankers, finance ministries, and economists along with those of domestic opponents. Barring the onset of irrational speculation or an uncontainable inflationary momentum, however, this was no fundamental roadblock to a high-demand, full-employment domestic economic policy.

This still forced Johnson, like Kennedy before him, to affirm steadfast support for a sound dollar and to cheer, ostentatiously, for those whose conservative views represented a bulwark against an irrational but powerful psychology. Prominent among these voices, Fed chairman Martin was said to be worth, alone, a billion dollars in gold. Martin, who once said that his principal role was to take away the punch just as the party began to swing, convinced European bankers solely by the force of his reputation, in other words, to hold on to their dollar balances and to abstain from cashing them in for U.S. gold. Both Kennedy and Johnson pleaded with him to stay on at the Fed throughout their presidencies.[101]

Yet, much as with similar prejudices on fiscal policy at home, international actors could quite readily promulgate inflationary expectations and dangerous self-fulfilling prophecies, despite their inaccurate forecasts or implausible theories. Some in their ranks, such as influential French economist Jacques Rueff, rang the excess demand alarm bells at the slightest hint of any broad currency accumulation. Though few expressed their sentiments as boldly as Rueff or cashed in their dollars for gold as readily as the French, these were actors the administration could not ignore.[102] The prevailing European prejudice for orthodox anti-inflation medicine and for hairtrigger invocations against dollar integrity had to be factored in to virtually all international monetary policy decisions.

As complex as the international currency and liquidity problems could be, they could still be reduced mostly to questions of domestic price stability and international confidence in the dollar. "The point of all the talk about fixing the deficit," Bator recalled, "the churning, the endless meetings and all that, was to position the U.S. politically in relation to the financial markets, the media, the Congress, foreign governments and central banks in such a way as to calm nervous dollar holders, strengthen the American position in the ongoing negotiations, and perhaps, just perhaps, give a gradual, collaborative process of reform a chance."[103] LBJ's clear preference was to go it slow, continue the use of "Bretton Woods band-aids," focus domestic policy on questions of price stability at full employment, and move cautiously toward international monetary reform that lessened dependence on gold and restraints upon domestic policy.[104] "There is a danger in too small and too weak a program," Gardner Ackley warned at the Cabinet Committee on Balance of Payments meeting of January 1965, "but there is also danger in too strong and restrictive a program."[105] The president's negotiation of "offsets" with West Germany—introduced to force the German financing of expanded U.S. military costs in that country—exemplified this approach. Where Eisenhower responded with alarm and Kennedy with puzzlement and concern, Johnson quickly came to understand that there was much more smoke than fire and that the United States had almost always been in a stronger position than it imagined. "I will not," he declared to a startled Fed chairman Martin on one occasion, "deflate the American economy, screw up my foreign policy by gutting aid or pulling troops out, or go protectionist just so we can continue to pay out gold to the French at $35 an ounce."[106]

In retrospect, LBJ's approach seems appropriate and judicious. Even before the United States formalized an official "standstill" agreement in March 1967, consisting of a German pledge to hold dollars and purchase special U.S. government securities, the West Germans had shown little inclination to draw on the American gold supply. Dramatic measures to remedy the dollar "overhang" would have inflicted much more harm than good.[107] "The president resisted the harsh proposals," one scholar of these negotiations noted, "and opted instead for measures which were, in essence, cosmetic."[108]

Yet because dollars remained the principal source of international liquidity and the U.S. government continued to back them with gold, LBJ would inevitably face rising doubts about dollar soundness and the threat of a still politically explosive gold drain.[109] Despite his desire to replace gold with a different kind of asset and to avoid the irrational psychology and limited breadth of gold-backed markets, he was forced to tread lightly, bowing ever so reluctantly to gold bugs in Congress and overseas. "Myths about gold die slowly," Johnson noted in his final Economic Report of the President.[110] When LBJ Federal Reserve appointee Sherman Maisel spoke of reducing the role of gold in the international monetary system, he met with an unquestionably cold reaction. "You know, young man," one international banker replied, "you may be right. But I consider it very unseemly for a Governor of the Federal Reserve to talk that way about gold."[111] As Francis Bator noted, "It seemed likely that there did not exist any gold price, and any configuration of U.S. payments, that would save the rules from causing trouble."[112]

To remedy this, LBJ pushed for reform, but all steps had to be taken tentatively. Building on the 1961 establishment of the London gold pool, a two-tiered gold market (1968), Special Drawing Rights (SDRs) at the International Monetary Fund (IMF) (1968–1969), and the removal of the 25 percent gold cover backing U.S. currency (1968) constituted the initial round of reform designed to loosen the "gold fetters" on international (and domestic) finance. The SDRs, in particular, held great promise as a new source of international liquidity. Other policies, such as the closing of the "gold window"—suspending the guarantee to exchange government gold for dollars held abroad at thirty-five dollars per ounce—had to be postponed. Ongoing negotiations in 1967 and 1968—for Kennedy Round tariff reductions, for the establishment of the IMF SDRs, and for military burden sharing in Europe among the Germans, British, and the United States—made rapid reform impossible. Flexible exchange rates, another potentially useful reform, had already been introduced in a somewhat disguised and limited configuration. Indeed, of the nine G-10 currencies that could be exchanged for dollars, five had adjusted their exchange rates relative to the dollar in the 1960s. "What we do have," William Fellner noted in 1970, "is a dollar-centered international monetary system into which the rest of the world can introduce as much flexibility as it desires."[113]

With even less opportunity to confront overseas the prejudices and orthodoxy with which he struggled at home, LBJ found himself facing these roadblocks with unenviable options. As Walter Heller once described it, it was a choice between bad macroeconomics (higher unemployment and higher interest rates to combat perceived domestic inflation) or bad microeconomics (restraining capital outflows and tying foreign aid to the purchase of U.S. goods and services).[114] When Johnson finally chose in early 1968, proposing to test mandatory controls on U.S. tourism and direct investment abroad, no department or agency really wanted to manage the Office of Foreign Direct Investment proposed to oversee it all. "Well," replied LBJ, "none of us are sitting around here in a clambake. This isn't fun for any of us."[115] According to Secretary of Commerce Trowbridge, "this was one of those miserable moments where you were really forced into a certain type of response." The immediate effect, however, as he also recalled, "was a very reassuring one to European doubters."[116] Yet, as Bator noted, "While in public—and sometimes, especially in larger meetings, even to each other—we pretended otherwise, I do not think that any of us thought, at least by mid-1966, that the actions we took would suffice to eliminate the deficit or even come close."[117]

Though more than a few Chancellors of the Exchequer liked to tell the story of how England suffered no balance of payments crisis for more than one hundred years simply because they lacked official balance of payments statistics, by the late 1960s there was no shortage of data or international payments alarm. Despite the soundness of the U.S. economy and the dollar, LBJ had little choice but to respond as he did, choosing "band-aids," negotiation and reform, and a renewed focus on domestic price stability. Much as he did with the tax surcharge, which targeted upper-bracket and corporate income obliquely and without fanfare, he chose the smallest possible dose of old medicine for the balance of payments affliction, mild in its effect and potentially useful for its impact on inflationary psychology. The British sterling devaluation of 18 November 1967 and the accelerated U.S. gold drain that it triggered proved, coincidentally, to be the principal factor by which LBJ convinced Congress to pass the long-debated surcharge, signed into law in June 1968. Directly imperiled at this point, however, was not his pursuit of full employment or the basic tenets of the Keynesian economics he had embraced but only international and domestic economic policy conducted without fear, irrational speculation, or self-defeating overreaction.

The Unfinished Revolution

In the end, LBJ bequeathed to the nation unsurpassed prosperity and an auspicious beginning to both a war on poverty and a struggle for price stability at full employment. "The accomplishments of this era," *Business Week* felt compelled to note in January 1969, "should not be underrated. Eight years ago, when John F. Kennedy took the oath of office, it was almost universally believed that recessions were an inevitable fact of life; there had been three in the previous decade. It is a proper tribute to the new economics that it is no longer considered noteworthy that the economy is in its 95th straight month of expansion."[118]

Yet it was as if many believed, right to the end, that there was no New Economics and no challenge to orthodoxy, only a dressed-up and more universally palatable version of the "old time religion." Blaming LBJ for Vietnam, many liberals found it difficult to see things any other way. Not yet sure how to explain the prevailing prosperity, business leaders and conservatives found it equally difficult to comprehend the emerging policy revolution. False cries of incipient inflation and imperiled profits from this quarter only increased the already destructive levels of myopia and confusion. And while Kennedy and Johnson had once exploited this ambiguity to sell the 1964 demand-side tax cut (disguising it partly as a supply-side maneuver to attract business support), by 1969 the capriciousness and confusion of the business community was no longer much of an asset.

Stymied politically on the price inflation front, President Johnson could not prove well enough what he always believed: that the nation did not have to buy full employment with unstable prices or stable prices with unemployment. When Nixon dumped the guideposts and flirted with monetary curbs in 1969, and when he asked John Ehrlichman to flush the Great Society in 1973, economic management had already reverted to an awkward combination of supply-side "riders," safety net reinforcements, and misplaced confidence in the Phillips curve path to price stability. Despite the obvious rewards, LBJ's frugality and judicious use of deficit spending and government-led redistribution seemed both dangerous and irrelevant. Public policy became all too circumscribed in general, and vacant antigovernment shibboleths suddenly appeared incisive or worthy of renewed attention. Married to a potent civil rights backlash, these transformations produced a new era of conservative politics and economic disappointment. Shrouded and derailed in the process was Lyndon Johnson's economic policy revolution, never completely adopted or understood, but perhaps, still, the best way to the Great Society he once envisioned.

Notes

1. Jack Valenti, *A Very Human President* (New York: Norton, 1975), 151.
2. Joseph A. Califano Jr., *The Triumph and Tragedy of Lyndon Johnson: The White House Years* (New York: Simon and Schuster, 1991), 75. The recently released Johnson presidential recordings make it clear that this preoccupation with economic affairs prevailed despite daily competition from a bewildering array of other issues and concerns.
3. For a persuasive account of this Johnsonian accent on opportunity, see Gareth Davies, *From Opportunity to Entitlement: The Transformation and Decline of Great Society Liberalism* (Lawrence: University Press of Kansas, 1996).
4. Walter W. Heller, *New Dimensions of Political Economy* (Cambridge, Mass.: Harvard University Press, 1966), 2.
5. Lyndon B. Johnson and Bill Moyers, 7 March 1964, Tape WH6403.04, PNO 12, Lyndon Baines Johnson Presidential Library, Austin, Texas (hereafter LBJL). In his second inaugural address (20 January 1937)—always a touchstone for LBJ—Franklin Roosevelt declared: "I see one-third of a nation ill-housed, ill-clad, ill-nourished. It is not in despair that I paint you that picture. I paint

it for you in hope—because the Nation, seeing and understanding the injustice in it, proposes to paint it out."

6. LBJ's outlook on affirmative action stands as a perfect example of this connection. Executive Order 11246, issued by Johnson in September 1965, introduced a new commitment to national affirmative action, but it did so with the implicit acknowledgment that without full employment such a program ran the risk of being both divisive and counterproductive.

7. Regarding Vietnam spending, for example, three of the most dynamic sectors of the U.S. economy in the late twentieth century—aerospace, telecommunications, and electronics—flourished on a foundation established by military contracts, many of which originated or reached critical mass during the Vietnam War. Widespread mergers and acquisitions and the rise of corporate conglomerates in the 1960s also assured that profits from purely military contracts would more readily underwrite productive capacity in civilian goods. As a result, manufacturing capacity utilization peaked in 1966 but declined gradually throughout the 1967–1969 period. By 1970, it was 79.4 percent, well below the conservative 83 percent threshold commonly employed by Federal Reserve inflation hawks.

8. "Address before a Joint Session of Congress, November 27, 1963," *Public Papers of the Presidents of the United States: Lyndon B. Johnson, Containing the Public Messages, Speeches, and Statements of the President*, 10 vols. (Washington, D.C.: Government Printing Office, 1965–1970), 1: 9.

9. "Annual Message to Congress on the State of the Union, January 8, 1964," ibid., 112.

10. "Remarks at the University of Michigan, May 22, 1964," ibid., 704.

11. For an example of this criticism, repeated many times by Johnson during his presidency, see "Remarks to Members of the Business Council, December 4, 1968," ibid., 2: 1168.

12. Tom Wicker, "Johnson's Frugality," *New York Times*, 13 December 1963, 25. T. Harry Williams, who died in 1980 just after having begun a political biography of Lyndon Johnson, mused in his early speculations on LBJ's career, "Johnson wanted to work within the system, manage and manipulate it. Could manage and believed in it, but had trouble explaining it. Reason? Probably did not have a philosophy of government or economics." See T. Harry Williams Papers, Location 34, Box 10, Folder 71, Louisiana State University.

13. See "Light Bulb Lyndon: A Phony Economizer," *Human Events*, 11 July 1964, 21.

14. Lyndon B. Johnson, *The Vantage Point* (New York: Holt, Rinehart, and Winston, 1971), 36.

15. Quoted in Walter W. Heller Oral History Interview II, 21 December 1971, by David McComb, p. 18, LBJL.

16. In this initiative, the White House electric bill was reduced from $5,000 per month to $3,000 per month.

17. Quoted in John Bullion, *In the Boat with LBJ* (Plano: Republic of Texas Press, 2001), 51.

18. Leo Beebe Oral History Interview, 4 February 1971, Tape 2, by Joe Frantz, p. 7, LBJL.

19. See "Administrative History of the General Services Administration," Volume I, Part II, Box 1, p. 531, LBJL.

20. Handwritten note, 20 August 1965, Papers of Lyndon B. Johnson, Presidential Papers, Handwriting File, Box 9, LBJL.

21. Such costs associated with Medicare and Medicaid were particularly notable examples.

22. Lyndon B. Johnson and Walter Heller, 14 December 1963, Tape K6312.08, PNOs 38 and 39, LBJL.

23. Walter Heller, "Further Report on My Meeting with George Meany," 17 December 1963, Papers of Walter Heller, Box 13, John Fitzgerald Kennedy Library, Boston, Mass.

24. Lyndon B. Johnson and Walter Reuther, 23 December 1963, Tape K6312.16, PNO 6, LBJL. In recorded calls to Kermit Gordon on 12 December 1963 and to Bernard Boutin on 19 December 1963, Johnson reiterated these budget management themes and priorities. Lyndon B. Johnson and Kermit Gordon, December 12, 1963, Tape K6312.07, PNO 27; Lyndon B. Johnson and Bernard Boutin, December 19, 1963, Tape K6312.10, PNO 14, LBJL.

25. Johnson, *Vantage Point*, 35–36. An example of cosmetic savings in the 1965 fiscal year budget was the "seignorage," or profit, the U.S. Treasury realized by switching from silver to alloy currency; real savings came mostly in the Pentagon budget, where LBJ and McNamara reduced civilian Department of Defense employment to under 1 million and also agreed to close twenty-six bases in fourteen states and seven overseas military bases. "I've never seen anyone," Treasury official Joseph Barr insisted, "who was better with the budget process, who understood it more thoroughly than President Johnson." Quoted in Joseph Barr Oral History Interview, 25 August 1969, interviewed by Joe Frantz, p. 29, LBJL.

26. Quoted in Richard Goodwin, *Remembering America: A Voice from the Sixties* (Boston: Little, Brown, 1988), 262.

27. *Public Papers of the Presidents, Lyndon B. Johnson*, 1: 311.

28. The mistaken belief that the 1964 tax cut was a supply-side prototype persists, due in part to the rhetorical flourishes employed by Presidents Kennedy and Johnson to sell the proposal to skeptical or defiant conservative politicians and business leaders.

29. Herbert Stein, *Presidential Economics: The Making of Economic Policy from Roosevelt to Reagan and Beyond* (New York: Simon and Schuster, 1984), 110.

30. James Tobin, "The Tax-Cut Harvest," in *The Battle against Unemployment*, ed. Arthur M. Okun (New York: Norton, 1965), 153.

31. *Public Papers of the Presidents, Lyndon B. Johnson*, 1: 9.

32. Ibid., 1: 113.

33. Heller, *New Dimensions*, 112.

34. "Man of the Year: Lyndon B. Johnson: The Prudent Progressive," *Time*, 1 January 1965, 14–27.

35. See Arthur M. Okun, "Measuring the Impact of the 1964 Tax Reductions," in *Perspectives on Economic Growth*, ed. Walter W. Heller (New York: Random House, 1968).

36. Quoted in "Senate Unit Bars Johnson Request for Rent Subsidy," *New York Times*, 26 April 1966, 1.

37. Lyndon B. Johnson, *The Choices We Face* (New York: Bantam Books, 1969), 98.

38. Walter W. Heller Oral History Interview I, 20 February 1970, by David McComb, p. 33, LBJL.

39. Robert M. Solow, "My Evolution as an Economist," in *Lives of the Laureates: Thirteen Nobel Economists*, ed. William Breit and Roger W. Spencer (Cambridge, Mass.: MIT Press, 1995), 199.

40. Ibid., 200–201.

41. Arthur Okun Oral History Interview I, p. 16, LBJL. "All through the Vietnam period we've been subjected to a flood of rumors on impending wage and price controls," Okun noted. "They really had no substance whatsoever—never close, and never really any work on it at all." Ibid., 15.

42. Memo, Ackley to Walter Heller, 11 December 1963, *CEA History*, vol. 2, Documentary Supplement, Part II, LBJL.

43. See Alan S. Blinder, Elie R. D. Canetti, David LeBow, and Jeremy B. Rudd, *Asking about Prices: A New Approach to Understanding about Price Stickiness* (New York: Russell Sage Foundation, 1998). This study revealed that many companies set prices based on explicit or implicit contracts, preferred nonprice competition, seldom responded to economy-wide inflation (preferring to focus only on business or industry-specific costs), and even appeared to believe that their marginal costs were either static or declining.

44. Daniel Kahneman earned a share of the 2002 Nobel Prize in Economics for clarifying this relationship between decision making and information.

45. This is so despite LBJ's effort to secure legislation enabling the president to adjust income tax rates, up or down by 5 percent per year, subject only to a legislative veto.

46. Heller Oral History Interview I, p. 33, LBJL.

47. Heller Oral History Interview II, 21 December 1971, by David McComb, p. 52, LBJL.

48. Lyndon B. Johnson and Willard Wirtz, 21 May 1964, Tape WH6405.08, PNO 24, LBJL.

49. Indeed, long forgotten is the widespread accounting chicanery and managerial chaos associated with this period. See John Brooks, *The Go-Go Years: The Drama and Crashing Finale of Wall Street's Bullish 60s* (New York: Weybright and Talley, 1973).

50. The 3.2 percent figure was not included in the text of the 1962 report but was interpolated from an accompanying table. See *Economic Report of the President, 1962, Transmitted to Congress, January 1963* (Washington, D.C.: Government Printing Office, 1963), 186.

51. In 1962, 3.2 percent represented the average annual increase in output per man-hour for the previous five years.

52. William H. Chartener Oral History Interview, 22 January 1969, by Paige Mulhollan, p. 21, LBJL.

53. Quoted in James L. Cochrane, "The Johnson Administration: Moral Suasion Goes to War," in *Exhortations and Controls: The Search for a Wage-Price Policy, 1945–1971*, ed. Crauford Goodwin (Washington, D.C.: Brookings Institution, 1975), 200n.

54. Arthur M. Okun Oral History Interview II, 15 April 1969, by David G. McComb, p. 30, LBJL.

55. Arrow cited in Cochrane, "Moral Suasion," 201–202n. Arrow noted

that since a 3 percent increase in nominal labor costs would typically induce a 2 percent increase in the capital-labor ratio, two developments beneficial to long-term profitability would result: the increased adoption of more efficient new technology; and a *slow* movement of the economy toward a position where wages constituted a larger share of the national income.

56. Gardner Ackley, Oral History Interview, in *The President and the Council of Economic Advisers: Interviews with CEA Chairmen*, ed. Erwin C. Hargrove and Samuel A. Morley (Boulder, Colo.: Westview Press, 1984), 261. Joe Califano was one of the few Johnson advisers who urged him to use this powerful lever.

57. Quoted in Gerald R. Rosen, "A Talk with Gardner Ackley," *Dun's Review and Modern Industry*, July 1965, 37.

58. Attachment to Report, Gardner Ackley to Members of Wage-Price Policy Task Force, 28 October 1967, Office Files of White House Aides, Joseph A. Califano, Box 57, "Wage-Price Guideposts," LBJL.

59. George Meany Oral History Interview, by Paige Mulhollan, 4 August 1969, p. 14, LBJL.

60. Quoted in Cochrane, "Moral Suasion," 261.

61. Memo, Ackley to LBJ, "A Longer Run View of the Airlines Case," 27 July 1966, Papers of LBJ, WHCF, Gen LA 6, Box 20, LBJL.

62. The recent conversion to jet engines provided the basis for much of this industry profit explosion.

63. Memo, Heller to Gardner Ackley, 19 July 1966, WHCF, Gen LA 6, Box 20, LBJL.

64. Cited in Cochrane, "Moral Suasion," 244.

65. Henry Wallich, "Desert Guideposts," *Newsweek*, 22 August 1966, 82.

66. George Perry, "Wages and the Guideposts," *American Economic Review* 57 (September 1967): 897–904. See also Perry's "Reply to Critics," *American Economic Review* 59 (June 1969): 365–370.

67. Quoted in James J. Reynolds Oral History Interview II, 1 October 1970, by Joe B. Frantz, p. 24, LBJL.

68. Quoted in Alexander Trowbridge Oral History Interview I, 19 February 1969, by Paige E. Mulhollan, p. 14, LBJL.

69. Quoted in Califano, *Triumph and Tragedy*, 139–140. Robson, an Illinois Republican, became an employee of the Bureau of the Budget, where he was hired ostensibly to use government procurement price policies to influence corporate price decisions.

70. This represented a break in the traditional auto industry practice of limiting sticker price changes to a once-a-year phenomenon.

71. Quoted in Crauford Goodwin, "A Report of the Conference," in Goodwin, *Exhortations and Controls*, 396.

72. Gardner Ackley, "The Contribution of Guidelines," in *Guidelines, Informal Controls, and the Marketplace: Policy Choices in a Full Employment Economy*, ed. George P. Shultz and Robert Z. Aliber (Chicago: University of Chicago Press, 1966), 74.

73. The CPI for all items signaled only a small change (from +2.5 percent in 1966 to +2.4 percent in 1967), but the wholesale price index went from +1.2 percent to +0.9 percent over the same period, and both food prices and wholesale prices actually dropped in the first two quarters of 1967. U.S. Bureau of

Labor Statistics, "Consumer Price Index" and "Wholesale Prices and Price Indexes."

74. Memo, Okun to Califano, 15 July 1968, Papers of LBJ, WHCF, LA 8, Box 33, LBJL.

75. Quoted in Cochrane, "Moral Suasion," 245.

76. Ackley, Oral History Interview, in Hargrove and Morley, *The President and the CEA*, 229; James Tobin, "Okun on Macroeconomic Policy: A Final Comment," in *Macroeconomics, Prices, and Quantities: Essays in Memory of Arthur Okun*, ed. James Tobin (Washington, D.C.: Brookings Institution, 1983), 299.

77. Quoted in Roland Turner, ed., "Arthur M. Okun," *The Annual Obituary, 1980* (New York: St. Martin's Press, 1981), 182.

78. Quoted in Walter W. Heller, Memorial Address for Arthur M. Okun, delivered at the Brookings Institution, 28 March 1980. "Out of respect for the living, I've deleted the executives," noted Heller.

79. Health care costs quickly became an area of great concern for Johnson. As early as April 1966, James Duesenberry (CEA) and John Douglas (HEW) conducted a joint CEA-HEW study of medical costs. Inflation figures for the following month (May 1966) illustrated the problem, for medical costs had risen by 0.5 percent (a 6.0 percent annual rate), while the overall CPI had risen by only 0.1 percent (a 1.2 percent annual rate). See Memo, Ackley to LBJ, 17 June 1966, LBJ Handwriting File, Box 11, LBJL.

80. Cited in Anderson and Hazleton, *Managing Macroeconomic Policy*, 173.

81. Ackley, "The Contribution of Guidelines," 68.

82. Ackley, to Society of Business Writers, May 1967, quoted in Hugh S. Norton, *The Employment Act and the Council of Economic Advisers, 1946–1976* (Columbia: University of South Carolina Press, 1977), 205.

83. "Annual Message to Congress on the State of the Union," 21 January 1966, *Public Papers of the Presidents, Lyndon B. Johnson*, 1: 4.

84. Memo, Gardner Ackley to LBJ, 27 August 1967, Administrative History of the CEA, Volume II, Part I, LBJL.

85. Eliot Janeway, *The Economics of Crisis: War, Politics, and the Dollar* (New York: Weybright and Talley, 1968).

86. David Halberstam, *The Best and the Brightest* (New York: Random House, 1972), 610.

87. Heller, *New Dimensions*, 39.

88. Memo, Charles Schultze to LBJ, 7 November 1966, WHCF, WE 9, Box 28, LBJL.

89. Quoted in Califano, *Triumph and Tragedy*, 284.

90. Francis M. Bator, "Concerning U.S. Balance of Payments and International Financial Policy, 1965–67" (paper presented at a Brookings Institution conference on the national economic policies of the 1960s), p. 3; published as "Comment by Francis Bator," in *Economic Events, Ideas, and Policies: The 1960s and After*, ed. George L. Perry and James Tobin (Washington, D.C.: Brookings Institution, 2000), 166–176.

91. Memo, Arthur Okun to LBJ, 27 April 1968, Administrative History of the CEA, Volume II, Part I, LBJL.

92. Arthur Okun Oral History Interview, in Hargrove and Morley, *The President and the CEA*, 300; emphasis in original.

93. Memo, Okun to LBJ, 23 April 1968, Administrative History of the CEA, Volume II, Part I, LBJL.

94. Memo, Ackley to LBJ, 12 December 1967, Administrative History of the CEA, Volume II, Part I, LBJL. To win Chairman Mills's support, in the end President Johnson agreed to a $6 billion reduction, virtually all of which was restored by subsequent congressional appropriation acts.

95. Ackley, Oral History Interview, in Hargrove and Morley, *The President and the CEA*, 247–248.

96. Correspondence, Ackley to the Editor, *Newsweek* magazine, 6 November 1978. A copy of this letter is included with the transcript of Ackley's Oral History Interview, conducted by Joe B. Frantz for the LBJ Library.

97. Paul Samuelson, *The Samuelson Sampler* (Glen Ridge, N.J.: Thomas Horton, 1973), 29.

98. See Donald F. Kettl, "The Economic Education of Lyndon Johnson: Guns, Butter, and Taxes," in *The Johnson Years*, vol. 2, *Vietnam, the Environment, and Science*, ed. Robert Divine (Lawrence: University Press of Kansas, 1987); Robert Dallek, *Flawed Giant: Lyndon Johnson and His Times, 1961–1973* (New York: Oxford University Press, 1998), 307–311, 391–399, 534–536; and James E. Anderson and Jared Hazleton, *Managing Macroeconomic Policy: The Johnson Administration* (Austin: University of Texas Press, 1986), 57–77.

99. Anderson and Hazleton, *Managing Macroeconomic Policy*, 237.

100. In the more protracted debate on the impact of the surcharge, Arthur Okun concluded that the surcharge had nearly full effect, William Springer suggested that it did not, and Alan Blinder found that temporary taxes in general carry a substantial impact *after* the first year of their implementation. See Arthur Okun, "The Personal Tax Surcharge and Consumer Demand, 1968–1970," in *Brookings Papers on Economic Activity: I, 1971*, ed. Arthur Okun and George Perry (Washington, D.C.: Brookings Institution, 1971), 167–204; William L. Springer, "Did the 1968 Surcharge Really Work?" *American Economic Review* 65, 4 (September 1975): 644–659; Okun, "Did the 1968 Surcharge Really Work? Comment," *American Economic Review* 67, 2 (March 1977): 167–169; and Blinder, *Economic Policy and the Great Stagflation*, 156–163.

101. Sherman Maisel, *Managing the Dollar* (New York: Norton, 1973), 148. Though Gardner Ackley suggested that LBJ "didn't like and really trust Bill Martin," and called Martin "absolutely zero as an economist," all evidence suggests that the White House and the Federal Reserve never were, and never have been, as close as they were during the Johnson administration. See Ackley Oral History Interview, in Hargrove and Morley, *The President and the CEA*, 236; and William McChesney Martin Oral History Interview, by Michael Gillette, 8 May 1987, pp. 17–18, LBJL.

102. Apparently, France even urged other nations over which it had some influence, such as Algeria, to buy U.S. gold whenever possible. See Larry Levinson to LBJ, 19 December 1967, Office Files of White House Aides, Joseph A. Califano, Box 8, LBJL.

103. Bator, "Concerning U.S. Balance of Payments," 7.

104. The "Bretton Woods band-aid" characterization is that of Diane B. Kunz. See Kunz, *Butter and Guns*, 103–104. Among these were tying U.S. foreign aid to the purchase of U.S. goods; forced purchase of U.S. goods by over-

seas military operations; General Arrangements to Borrow (a $6 billion backup fund at the IMF for currency stabilization); the establishment of the London gold pool; and currency "swap" arrangements (by which a nation fearing devaluation of its currency would borrow other currencies from other nations' central banks).

105. Quoted in Burton I. Kaufman, "Foreign Aid and the Balance of Payments Problem: Vietnam and Johnson's Foreign Economic Policy," in Divine, *Johnson Years*, 2: 86.

106. Quoted in Bator, "Concerning U.S. Balance of Payments," 9.

107. Only a heart attack suffered by Bundesbank president Blessing in 1963 created enough confusion to suggest otherwise. Until Blessing's return late that year, Secretary of the Treasury Douglas Dillon became convinced, incorrectly, that West Germany might begin cashing in dollars for gold.

108. Gregory F. Treverton, *The Dollar Drain and American Forces in Germany: Managing the Political Economics of Alliance* (Athens: Ohio University Press, 1978), 112.

109. See Robert Triffin, *Gold and the Dollar Crisis: The Future of Convertibility* (New Haven, Conn.: Yale University Press, 1960).

110. *Economic Report of the President, Transmitted to Congress, January 1969* (Washington, D.C.: Government Printing Office, 1969), 16.

111. Quoted in Maisel, *Managing the Dollar*, 197.

112. Bator, "Concerning U.S. Balance of Payments," 2.

113. William Fellner, "Comments and Discussion" on Lawrence B. Krause, "A Passive Balance of Payments Strategy," in *Brookings Papers on Economic Activity: 3, 1970*, ed. Arthur Okun and George Perry (Washington, D.C.: Brookings Institution, 1970), p. 364.

114. Heller, *New Dimensions*, 48.

115. Quoted in Alexander Trowbridge Oral History Interview II, 7 May 1969, by Paige Mulhollan, p. 15, LBJL.

116. Ibid., p. 19.

117. Bator, "Concerning U.S. Balance of Payments," 6–7.

118. "President Johnson's Economic Legacy," *Business Week*, 18 January 1969, 132. From this point, the expansion would continue an additional eleven months. At 106 months, this was more than twice as long as the previous record and was eventually surpassed only by the equally lengthy but somewhat less robust expansion of 1992–2001.

9 | President Lyndon Johnson and the Gendered World of National Politics

Julia Kirk Blackwelder

ON 10 FEBRUARY 1964, Congressman Jack Brooks telephoned President Johnson from Capitol Hill to report that the House had passed H.R. 7152, the 1964 civil rights bill, with "no crippling amendments at all, got a sex amendment on women."[1] Despite his opposition to the amendment, LBJ had no comment on this change that added women to the classes protected against employment discrimination under Title VII of the bill. On one level Johnson's silence on the inclusion of gender in Title VII bespoke his determination to see the civil rights bill through. On another level it bespoke his indifference to women's issues. Early in his presidency, LBJ gave some attention to the legal status of women, partly as impacted by Title VII, and the appointment of women to federal offices, but these interests were fleeting.[2] The ephemerality of women's issues in the Johnson White House reflected the president's biases on gender, the political culture in which he functioned, and the scarcity and powerlessness of American feminists in the early 1960s. Betty Friedan's *Feminine Mystique* had been excerpted in women's magazines in 1962, and it appeared as a monograph the following year, but the full impact of Friedan's ideas and nationwide consideration of the equal rights amendment did not come until after Johnson left the White House.[3]

The skirmish over Title VII in the House of Representatives, the limited roles and agendas of prominent women in the Democratic Party, and the public and private rhetoric of LBJ all demonstrated the hegemony of narrowly circumscribed views of women's rights during the Johnson years.[4] Johnson recognized the importance of Democratic women in grassroots organizing, but, in keeping with their minor places in the party, he did not seek their counsel in setting major policies.[5] In response to direct pressures from Democratic women, LBJ appointed an unprecedented number of female officeholders, but he did little to advance the status of women as a class. As former Johnson press aide George Reedy recalled, "During his presidency, he staged a show of high-ranking positions for women. But his heart was not truly in it and the posts were not really very high ranking."[6]

Women played significant roles in Washington politics in the 1960s, but the vast majority of female workers in government assisted and advised men in authority or held rank in agencies that dealt with women or children. Women held minimal influence in Congress, where the fate of the "sex" amendment rested and where Lyndon Johnson had mastered party politics. Of the eleven females in the House of Representatives Edith Green (D-Ore.) and Martha Griffiths (D-Mich.) spoke most strongly for passage of H.R. 7152. Green supported measures to improve women's wages and education, but she opposed the "sex" amendment by arguing, "Because of biological differences between men and women, there are different problems which arise in employment."[7] Martha Griffiths acerbically condemned the male debate on Title VII, then continued:

> And if you do not add sex to this bill, I really do not believe there is a reasonable person sitting here who does not by now understand perfectly that you are going to have white men in one bracket, you are going to try to take colored men and colored women and give them equal employment rights, and down at the bottom of the list is going to be white women with no rights at all.[8]

Equal rights amendment supporter Katharine St. George (R-N.Y.) condemned protective legislation for women in her defense of the "sex" amendment, while Frances Bolton (R-Ohio) also spoke for the amendment but insisted that "married women get along very well because they usually, after they have had their children and brought them to a certain age, go back into business to really protect the family against too little money."[9] Republican Margaret Chase Smith of Maine, who staunchly eschewed the label of feminist but supported equal rights for women, and Democrat Maureen Neuberger of Oregon, who had supported equal pay and benefits for women only as far as the reach of federal employment, were the only female senators. Smith spoke forcefully in support of the "sex" amendment at a Republican caucus on 7 April 1964, and both female senators supported H.R. 7152 after its final reading on the Senate floor on June 19.[10]

Although the nation stood on the brink of a revolution in women's roles when LBJ assumed the presidency, signs of the profound cultural change to come were barely visible in 1963, whereas the status of black Americans commanded nationwide attention. When Johnson addressed Congress only days after JFK's assassination, H.R. 7152 took center stage, and the new President continued to focus on African American rights through his first eight months in office. While eloquently advocating the rights of racial and religious minorities and artfully directing Congress and national opinion toward passage of the 1964 law, Johnson did not mention gender.[11] LBJ had initially opposed the inclusion of women in the civil rights bill because he feared it would spell defeat of the legislation.[12] Yet, the "sex" amendment had not doomed the rights bill in the House, and civil rights advocates had reason to be optimistic that a Senate campaign for civil rights could also be won. Title VII now warranted the president's full endorsement because any reservation on his part might open the door to Senate amendment and ultimate defeat of the bill. Accordingly, he changed his stance on women's employment rights because he cared passionately about the civil rights bill and because he (like most in Congress) did not fully appreciate the implications of the change to Title VII.

Johnson's indifference to women's rights mirrored the dominant paradigm in American politics during his years in public life, but it also reflected his own perspective on women in politics and in society. He admired many women individually, but he did not regard women as being the equals of men. He made patronizing, often disparaging, public and private remarks about women, statements that surface recurrently in the records of his administration, in memoirs and interviews of employees of the Johnson White House, and in the secretly recorded Oval Office telephone conversations.[13] Records of the Johnson years reveal that both women and men close to the president regularly reinforced the gendered order of Washington politics and seldom took issue with his intransigence.

Lyndon Johnson, Esther Peterson, and Women's Issues

Johnson's initial opposition to the "sex" amendment was consistent with the stance he had taken as vice president. Amid the 1961 to 1963 debates on minority rights, Representative Martha Griffiths, members of the National Woman's Party (NWP), and prominent individual feminists, including Marguerite Rawalt and Pauli Murray, had discussed amendments to the pending civil rights bill that would extend its coverage to women as a class. Although President Kennedy had sent a message to Congress early in 1963 that condemned gender discrimination along with racial, religious, and age discrimination, LBJ did not embrace the feminist position on civil rights.[14] JFK had also encouraged the linking of women's issues with race discrimination when he called together representatives of women's religious, social, and civic organizations to solicit their support for his civil rights bill. The delegates to this White House summit, including the White House's liaison Women's Bureau director Esther Peterson, began to discuss the status of women in the context of their support for African American rights.[15]

Peterson feared that women's rights advocates would undermine efforts to pass civil rights legislation by alienating men and women who supported racial change but opposed equality for women. She presented the president with a request for a federal study committee on women's issues with the hope of directing gender questions away from the debate on race. She also hoped that a separate study of women would remove any reservation that leading women might have about elevating race over gender in politics.

Peterson deeply believed that the cause of African American rights was the nation's first priority and that women ought to set aside gender issues to present a united front on race. She worried that enacting gender equity in employment, whether within the civil rights bill or in separate legislation, would invalidate existing state-level workplace protections for women. She presented JFK with a request for a commission on women partly to squash largely unnoticed feminist demands for full equality. Appropriating the cold war rhetoric that engulfed Washington, Peterson argued that a study commission would best serve the interests of women while undergirding America's war on international communism. She petitioned the president:

> I propose the appointment by the President of a Commission on Women in our American Democracy. Such a commission would substitute constructive recommendations for the present troublesome and futile agitation about the "equal rights" amendment. The commission would help the nation to set forth before the world the story of women's progress in a free, democratic society, and to move further towards full partnership, creative use of skills, and genuine equality of opportunity.[16]

Soon after receiving the request, Kennedy created the President's Commission on the Status of Women (PCSW). He named Eleanor Roosevelt to chair at Peterson's suggestion, and Peterson would serve as executive vice chairman. The president assigned responsibility for monitoring PCSW activities to LBJ, and the vice president and Mrs. Johnson held a welcoming reception for the commission at their

Washington home shortly after all members of the study group had been named. The decision that the vice president rather than the president should hold a function on behalf of the PCSW belied the secondary importance that the Kennedy administration ascribed to women's issues, but it placed Johnson in a position to claim later that he had taken an active interest in the status of women. Johnson kept in touch with PCSW member John R. Macy through the commission's life span, but he did not meet with the PCSW as a body after the opening reception at his home. Macy, who headed the Civil Service Commission under Kennedy and Johnson, worked to broaden women's access to civil service jobs and also advised Johnson on the appointment of women to executive posts.[17]

In October 1963, only weeks before the assassination, the PCSW concluded its work, presented its moderate findings to the White House, and disbanded. Kennedy and Johnson publicly endorsed the PCSW report *American Women* and its recommendation that the advancement of women's legal rights would appropriately be pursued at the state rather than the federal level, a finding that provided the basis for LBJ's position as president.[18] The PCSW also recommended the creation of two successor bodies to monitor the employment of women in federal government and to continue the study of women's legal status in America. President Johnson, at the urging of Esther Peterson, authorized the creation of the Interdepartmental Committee on the Status of Women (ICSW) and the Citizens' Advisory Council on the Status of Women (CACSW). He named Secretary of Labor Willard Wirtz and lawyer and *Ladies' Home Journal* editor Margaret Hickey as their respective chairs. Lyndon Johnson deprived Peterson of the central role she had played in setting the Kennedy White House women's agenda when he did not name her to chair or oversee the ICSW or the CACSW. Catharine East represented the executive branch on the CACSW and served as its executive secretary. Johnson attended the first meeting of CACSW and addressed the body on two subsequent occasions, but neither committee had notable influence on White House policy.[19]

Although Peterson's influence diminished in the Johnson years, LBJ depended on her to answer or deflect citizens' inquiries on women's issues. In responding to suggestions or questions about the status of women, the White House asked Peterson to draft letters or public statements reiterating the PCSW recommendations that equality for women might best be pursued at the state level through legislation or at the federal level by litigation under the Fifth and Fourteenth Amendments, the position presented by the PCSW.[20]

In March 1964 the president received a letter from Modell Scruggs, the president-elect of the Texas Federation of Business and Professional Women. Scruggs asked whether Johnson endorsed a Texas equal rights amendment sponsored by the federation and also asked him to clarify his stance on Title VII of the civil rights bill, since the administration had originally opposed the "sex" amendment. In penning LBJ's response to Scruggs, Peterson, who like Johnson had embraced the amendment after H.R. 7152 passed the House, wrote that "it is the firm conviction of the Administration that equal opportunity for women in hiring, training, and promotion should be the governing principle in private industry, and it is the hope of the Administration that the bill will be enacted in its present form." Peterson avoided speaking directly to the Texas rights amendment and echoed her PCSW position in declaring to Scruggs that the issue of gender equality in property and family law "must, of course, be determined at the State level and is not an appropriate matter for official Federal Government comment."[21]

Congressional Debate and the Dismissal of Women's Rights

Modell Scruggs's letter, along with others, had been prompted as much by the circus atmosphere in the House of Representatives during the debate on Title VII as by the content of the employment section of the bill. Observers of the floor debate on H.R. 7152 expressed surprise and cynical humor when Howard W. Smith of Virginia introduced the amendment to include women in the section of the bill that extended the life and the reach of the Fair Employment Practices Commission, a body that would become the Equal Employment Opportunity Commission under the civil rights bill. Yet Smith's action echoed his past behavior. He had supported a similar amendment to the Civil Rights Act of 1957 and, only days before his 1964 motion, he appeared on the Sunday evening television show *Meet the Press* and hinted that he might do something to help women's cause. According to some accounts, Smith presumed that the principle of gender equality would be offensive enough to the members of Congress to cause massive defections from the pro–civil rights coalition that he sought to defeat. Others have argued that Smith knew that the bill would pass despite conservative opposition and that he took the opportunity to reward NWP supporters who had long pressed him to act on behalf of women's rights.[22]

The gendered political culture that pervaded Washington and the nation in Lyndon Johnson's era framed the discussion of the "sex" amendment and placed women's rights in a ludicrous context. Smith's words rather than his past support of women's rights took center stage on 8 February as he entertained his colleagues. He introduced the amendment with the claim, "Now, I am very serious about this amendment. . . . I do not think it can do any harm to this legislation; maybe it can do some good." Continuing amid guffaws from the floor, Smith read from the letter of a constituent who suggested "that you might also favor an amendment or a bill to correct the present 'imbalance' between males and females in the United States" and asked for suggestions as to "what course our Government might pursue to protect our spinster friends in their 'right' to a nice husband and family."[23]

Smith had set the tone for what would follow. Supporters and detractors generally made their points at women's expense. Martha Griffiths, who had long supported the inclusion of women in civil rights legislation, observed that "if there had ever been any necessity to have pointed out that women were a second-class sex, the laughter would have proved it."[24] The Johnson White House made its opposition to the amendment clear in a letter from the Women's Bureau that had been drafted by Esther Peterson but signed by Secretary of Labor Arthur Goldberg as the cabinet official who oversaw the bureau. In reaction to the Peterson missive, "sex" amendment supporter John Dowdy of Texas asked if the letter had been signed by a man. When the question was answered in the affirmative, Dowdy concluded, "I had an idea that would be true—the letter from the Women's Bureau of the Department of Labor opposing this equal rights for women amendment was signed by a man. I think there is no need for me to say more." The letter, like others drafted by Peterson, asserted "that to attempt to amend H.R. 7152 would not be to the best advantage of women at this time."[25] At this point Peterson stood fast in her fear that an amended Title VII might defeat the bill. She also worried that the "sex" amendment would eradicate protective legislation for women, and both Goldberg and the president agreed with the potential she found in the House debate. The powerful chair of the House Judiciary Committee, New York's Emanuel "Manny" Celler, fought the "sex" amendment tooth and nail on grounds that mirrored Peterson's position but that denigrated women. Celler, an old-line labor Democrat, had steadfastly supported protective legislation out of his loyalty to AFL-CIO priorities and because he viewed women as being different from men in their mental and physical capacities.

After Smith had moved his amendment, Celler added his voice to the chorus of men poking fun at the notion of ascribing minority status to women. Celler informed his colleagues in the House that through his marriage of fifty years, his wife had had the upper hand, but that "I usually have the last two words, and those words are, 'Yes, dear.'"[26]

In the Senate, fierce debate on H.R. 7152 included numerous efforts to delete the "sex" amendment, but ultimately Title VII emerged from the upper house unaltered and by 1 July the Civil Rights Act of 1964 had reached the White House for Johnson's signature.[27] Once victory in the Congress had been achieved, the president presumed that the legislative agenda on gender had been concluded. Although he sought Esther Peterson's counsel in selecting female appointees, LBJ no longer needed her advice in responding to women's demands for gender-based legislation. Johnson began to establish distance between himself and the Women's Bureau head, giving the First Lady's press secretary Elizabeth (Liz) Carpenter a larger role than Peterson in recommending female appointees.[28] Lyndon Johnson and others did not fully trust Peterson to stick to the business of the Women's Bureau. Elected and appointed officials alike complained to Johnson, as did Senator Edward Long of Missouri, who said that she "causes everybody trouble."[29] By convincing her that the greatest needs of America's women lay outside the Women's Bureau and that relocation to the White House itself would augment her influence upon him, Johnson moved Esther Peterson from the headship of the Women's Bureau to the post of chairman of the President's Committee on Consumer Interests.[30] In reality, the president had acted to curtail her further meddling in legislative and cabinet-level matters. The new position deprived Peterson of influence, and the White House withheld funding sufficient to carry out the stated responsibilities of the office of consumer affairs. Peterson felt that she had been duped by LBJ, and his actions engendered frustration and deep resentment that led to her resignation in 1967. She returned to the position of assistant secretary in the Department of Labor but not as head of the Women's Bureau.[31]

Pursuant to Title VII

Although Johnson had finally endorsed the gender clause of Title VII, he took no steps to ensure compliance. The president's reticence left women to press their cases before a reluctant Equal Employment Opportunity Commission (EEOC), the agency that the 1964 legislation authorized to enforce the new regulations. Almost immediately after the Civil Rights Act took effect, EEOC head Herman Edelsburg announced that Congress had not intended to broaden women's employment and that the commission would undertake no efforts to ensure compliance with the "sex" amendment. Women pressed their cases despite the dismissive attitudes of the Congress at the time of its passage and notwithstanding the hostility of the EEOC to women's claims. Nine of the first forty-eight complaints filed under Title VII lodged charges of sex discrimination, but none of these cases gained a hearing at EEOC under Edelsburg's leadership.[32]

The orientation of the EEOC shifted almost imperceptibly when Franklin D. Roosevelt Jr. assumed the helm of the commission in 1965. Roosevelt announced that cases of employment discrimination pending before the EEOC involved women from shop-floor production workers to white-collar managers and that the EEOC was finding sex discrimination cases to be "terribly complicated."[33] Among the complications Roosevelt noted was a familiar employer concern voiced by Illinois Chamber of Commerce spokesman James B. O'Shaughnessy that firms would be compelled to "hire young, single girls for jobs that require extensive training [who would soon] marry and leave the job."[34] Subsequently the EEOC worked through these supposed complications only as female activists and the federal courts compelled change.

The hostility of the EEOC had helped mobilize women to petition for fair employment practices. Class interests, particularly on the issue of protective labor legislation, had long divided women seeking to better their economic status, but Title VII provided a common field on which working women campaigned to eradicate long-standing labor union and employer practices that barred them from many well-paying positions for which they were qualified. In 1966 Representative Martha Griffiths publicly excoriated the EEOC for "casting disrespect and ridicule on the law" through its "wholly negative" attitude toward enforcement of the ban on gender discrimination.[35] Griffiths's speech galvanized feminists and brought a broad spectrum of female advocates together on employment issues. Uniting around equal employment opportunities promised by Title VII, business and professional women established the National Organization for Women (NOW) only days after Griffiths's statement. Despite NOW's overwhelmingly middle-class membership, many clerical and industrial working women seeking better-paying jobs supported that organization's goals as they, too, sought redress from the EEOC.[36]

In the wake of the Civil Rights Act, the president had issued an executive order that stipulated the rules under which federal contractors could comply with the fair employment strictures of the legislation. Consistent with his perspective on gender, the mandate had not included women, but Johnson began to consider female employment somewhat more broadly as he widened his circle of consultants on gender beyond Esther Peterson and women employed in the White House. In 1967 the president received suggestions from a body of women in the executive branch who supported the objectives of NOW and of the National Business and Professional Women's Clubs. The women recommended that employment regulations for federal contractors be modified to include gender, and in 1967 the president signed Executive Order 11375, a measure that banned employment discrimination by sex among these contractors.[37] Shortly thereafter, Johnson affirmed his commitment to expand opportunities in federal employment when he signed into law a bill that removed some of the restrictions on the careers of women in the armed services. Still, these steps marked the virtual limits of his support of feminist goals. He did not press the EEOC to embrace the issues of women's work rights, and he had moved to protect those rights in the private sector only with respect to federal contractors. Similarly, LBJ did not embrace the 1966 efforts of female legislators of both parties to secure gender equality in jury service.[38]

Appointing Women to Federal Offices

Despite the limits of his commitment to fair employment for women, Johnson had acted energetically early on in his administration to reward the loyalty of female leaders in the Democratic Party.[39] In small groups and individually, party women beseeched him to improve female representation in executive posts in the federal government. In January 1964, in response to these pressures, LBJ embarked on a campaign to locate potential female officeholders and announced a campaign to name fifty women to appointive positions. The manner and procedures by which Johnson sought to locate potential nominees to public office revealed the hold of male networks on political structures. With the exception of Liz Carpenter, the Democratic women closest to the president largely held clerical or low-level administrative positions in the White House and had little authority to recommend appointments. In her affectionate but revealing portrait of her White House years, Carpenter remembered the president's efforts to promote women as an impetuous undertaking: "On one memorable day, President Johnson decided that women were being discriminated against in getting high level jobs."[40] The president had shortly before talked with longtime acquaintance Anna Rosenberg Hoffman, and Carpenter recounted LBJ's reaction to the conversation: "Anna Rosenberg Hoffman tells me that we need more women in government. . . . Call Esther Peterson and both of you be at the Cabinet meeting at ten o'clock in the morning, and we'll do something about it." Immediately after the January 1964 cabinet meeting attended by Peterson and Carpenter, Johnson launched his short-lived drive to name women to offices.[41]

Johnson took a shotgun approach to female appointments, entreating men across the Democratic Party to assist him. Johnson also turned to Carpenter and a few other women within the White House for advice on nominations. He issued an ultimatum that members of his cabinet report on progress made in appointing women, and he sought women for office without considering carefully what the job entailed or the pool of women available to fill the post. He thought first of the wives of his associates when trying to explain the types of women whom he sought to name, and he invited the wives of his political allies to fill some positions. Johnson attempted to identify potential nominees by pressuring men inside and outside the administration to find candidates for him. In February 1964 he jokingly threatened labor leader David Dubinsky, "I might have to steal that Evelyn [Dubinsky] from you and appoint her ambassador or something."[42]

Early in 1964 Johnson had told Secretary of Labor Luther Hodges, "Now if you want to do something real good for me next week, you find some vacancy you've got in top places and you get two or three women in them because I'm catching hell from them and Margaret Smith is running [for reelection]."[43] Days later Johnson talked with Secretary of Agriculture Orville Freeman about naming an assistant secretary of agriculture for international relations. In a virtual monologue addressed to Freeman, the president acted out the gendered views that both drove and bound his efforts to advance women:

> Why don't you find the greatest farm woman with an international background in this country and give [a job] to a woman and let these five million more women than men you've got think Freeman is a hero. . . . I'm thinking about Libby Smith or somebody that has the farm background, but that is outgoing. . . .
>
> Women, the truth is that they cast 5 million more votes than men. We've got a Cabinet made up wholly of men. We've got agencies that are made up wholly of men, the best thing we've got

is sometime we promote to a secretary. I mean a stenographer. . . . We just can't ever find one that's qualified. . . . If I could find some Eleanor Roosevelt with agricultural background as good looking and about forty years old and as outgoing and can talk why I'd do it and I'd be a hero.

I guarantee they'll support you. Why the only press I've got that's worth any god damn is these women writers and every one of them are writing all the time. Did you see Betty Beale take Charlie Bartlett's pants off last Sunday?

I'll appoint Jane [Freeman] to that job. . . . Doesn't she have a sister? A sister-in-law? I want someone like that.[44]

At the cabinet meeting of 18 February, the president asked that each member "report on the progress you are making in hiring women and members of minority groups."[45] A few days later Liz Carpenter sent out a blanket memorandum stating, "There is wide and increasing interest by the press in the upgrading and appointment of women and I would urge you to get going."[46] By March 1964 Carpenter reported that the goal of appointing 50 women had already been exceeded, and the administration moved on to a larger effort to name 150 women in total that concluded the following month.[47] The White House reached its goal of 150 female appointments by including on the list all women who had gained federal positions at Civil Service grades 12 through 18 and had been named between 1 January and 13 April 1964. The list included persons and posts as diverse as Jacqueline Kennedy, who had been selected for the Committee for the Preservation of the White House; Ann P. Donvost, a public health nurse assigned to the Agency for International Development; and Mary Keyserling, whom Johnson had named to succeed Esther Peterson as head of the Women's Bureau. In all, the list of 148, two shy of the announced accomplishment, included 55 women who had gained executive-level jobs through the Civil Service or through selections in which the president had played no role.

Although he occasionally named additional women to office through his years in the White House, LBJ's attention to female appointments dissipated rapidly after the efforts of 1964. Overall, his nominations fit into a twentieth-century trend of increasing numbers and rising prominence of women in the executive branch. In contrast with Johnson, Franklin Roosevelt and Dwight Eisenhower had both made cabinet-level female appointments, but LBJ chose more women for office than did his predecessors and fewer than those who succeeded him in the presidency.[48]

Johnson did continue to articulate the importance of women's contributions to the economy, although he took no steps to better women's status in the private sector. Following a Washington conference on women in medicine in 1968, he wrote Women's Bureau head Mary Keyserling, "I appreciate your sending me the report of the conference on the women's physician. . . . As you know, there is nothing more important to our welfare as a nation than the utilization of *all* our talent for the common good. That includes, above all, the fullest use of our womanpower in every segment of our national life."[49]

Despite hiring efforts and public statements praising women's accomplishments, an atmosphere of gender inequality permeated the White House. Following his female appointment campaign, the president asked Liz Carpenter and White House aide Bess Abell to arrange a reception for the 150 women whom he had named. In all seriousness the two women recommended a White House event graced by the marine band that would salute the new appointees by playing "There Is Nothing Like a Dame" and "Oh! You Beautiful Dame." Presidential assistant Jack Valenti seconded the recommendation, and the president endorsed the plan.[50] Johnson's remarks at the 13 April 1964 reception similarly bore the stamp of an administration that advanced women's employment at the same time that it manifested no sensitivity to feminist sensibilities. The president began by welcoming his female guests with the comment "I just attended a baseball game and returned to find my home filled with my favorite kind of people."[51] The president conceded, "I realize that some are still inclined to have second thoughts about the so-called emancipation of women, possibly including some of the husbands that are present in this room," but he affirmed the position that "there is no place for discrimination of any kind in American life."

Because she remained close to President and Mrs. Johnson throughout his years in the White House, Carpenter continued to recommend individual women for appointments long after the initial push to locate women had collapsed. In November 1966 she presented the president with her assessment of stockbroker Julia Montgomery Walsh for the post of U.S. treasurer:

She is a Democrat, an excellent speaker, lectures on stocks and bonds. She is fashionable looking. One good thing—she "mothers" about 12 children. She has four of her own (her husband died). She married a widower—Tom Walsh, a real estate man, and he had a bunch and now they have two together. This would be real good—politically, I think. All the people in the "money business" here respect her.[52]

Although women did gain hundreds of executive positions in the federal government while Johnson inhabited the White House, the president failed to support women for the highest posts in his administration, and he initiated no actions that improved the legal or economic status of women as a class. He appointed no women to the cabinet and nominated no woman for the Supreme Court. More telling of his perspective on gender issues, Johnson did not seek the naming of women to office until Democratic women lobbied him to do so, and when the pressure slackened, the president quickly lost interest in pursuing posts for women. Johnson publicly endorsed equal opportunity, but he did not encourage or participate in the sea change of culture that equality for women required. As summarized by Paul Conkin,

> Johnson verbally embraced the cause of women's equality, took pains to improve their opportunities in civil service appointments, and dutifully appointed a few women as ambassadors, as assistant cabinet secretaries, as head of consumer affairs, and as members of the Tariff and Atomic Energy commissions. But none of these became an intimate of Johnson or had any major role in shaping administration policy.[53]

Lady Bird Johnson and the "Complete Woman"

Through her husband's White House years, Lady Bird Johnson set the tone for his posture on gender issues. Lady Bird exemplified the accomplished and dutiful woman whom LBJ admired, a helpmate who excelled in affairs of the world as well as of the home but who did not outshine her husband. Competent and astute, but never strident or petulant, she epitomized the ideal political wife of the era. In the first year of the Johnson presidency, Lady Bird delivered a baccalaureate address at Radcliffe College in which she counseled the graduates that

> a quite remarkable young woman has been emerging in the United States. She is your sister, your roommate, and if you look closely enough, probably yourself. She might be called the natural woman, the complete woman. She has taken from the past what is vital and discarded what is irrelevant or misleading. She has taken over

the right to participate fully—whether in jobs, professions, or the political life of the community. She has rejected a number of overtones of the emancipation movement as clearly unworkable. She does not want to be the long-striding feminist in low heels, engaged in a conscious war with men. But she wants to be—while equally involved—preeminently a woman, a wife, a mother, a thinking citizen.[54]

Lady Bird Johnson epitomized the "complete woman" of whom she spoke. She played the helpmate in marriage, managed the Johnson radio station, raised two daughters, and never acknowledged Johnson's much rumored womanizing.[55] She coached Lyndon privately before his speeches and served as his spin doctor after his every public appearance. Lady Bird's skills particularly impressed Jacqueline Kennedy, who became better acquainted with her during the 1960 presidential campaign. In the 1970s Kennedy recalled Lady Bird's acute facility for bolstering Lyndon's command of persons and events. During an after-hours campaign gathering, Jackie was especially impressed that Lady Bird took careful notes of the conversations among Kennedy, Johnson, and top campaign staffers while simultaneously maintaining her own conversation with Jackie and the other women in the room. In the course of the discussion, Lyndon occasionally forgot the names of minor players in the campaign, and he called out to Lady Bird, who would remember the reference and remind him. Lady Bird advanced the president's political agenda through her campaigns on behalf of the environment and beautification, and she worked to build female volunteer efforts in the War on Poverty.[56]

Lady Bird facilitated Lyndon's career from Congress to the White House by advising him and by fulfilling an active role among the capital's women. In her public appearances and her political work behind the scenes, she strengthened the president and simultaneously reinforced the gendered culture of the era. In the 1964 campaign Lady Bird played her most demonstrative role as a political wife. Conceiving of the idea herself, she embarked on a whistle-stop train tour of the South amid presidential skepticism and fierce white resentment of Lyndon's civil rights campaign.[57] Despite the hostile climate, Lady Bird's southern manner and demeanor drew respectful hearings. *Washington Post* publisher Katharine Graham was at Washington's Union Station to greet the First Lady on her triumphal return. Of her public comments at the time, Graham later recalled, "Then Lady Bird talked in such a moving way about how the South had to turn away from hatred, how wounding the hatred was for everyone. She talked with such authority because she belonged there. It was very clear to me what a team they were. He couldn't have been Lyndon Johnson without Lady Bird."[58]

Lyndon Johnson and his colleagues expected wives to perform the difficult political tasks that Lady Bird had mastered, and they praised them for doing so. A thank-you note from then vice president Johnson to Missouri senator Stuart Symington and his wife underscored both Lady Bird's essential role in political campaigns and the expectation that the wives of other men in public life would contribute similarly. After a 1962 campaign stop in which Lady Bird and the Symingtons participated, Lyndon wrote, "Lady Bird tells me how much you contributed in St. Louis to the success of the meeting there. I'm not surprised, just proud of you both."[59]

Window Dressing

To Johnson, women were window dressing for political campaigns and for the White House, as well as being secretaries and organizers. He expected the women who worked around him to present an attractive and well-groomed appearance. While waiting for a phone connection one day, the president turned to White House secretary Vicki McCammon and chastised, "Vicki, I don't like your dress. It's too dull. You're prettier than that."[60] LBJ purchased clothing for White House employees, he repeatedly attempted to cajole Liz Carpenter into losing weight, and he sent his female staff members to have their hair restyled.[61] In a December 1963 phone conversation with Lady Bird, LBJ instructed, "When [the hairdresser] gets finished with Marie [Fehmer], tell him to do Yolanda [Boozer] because she's got to have about a bale cut off."[62] Boozer was scheduled to join the Johnsons at the Texas White House over the Christmas holidays, and LBJ did not want to see his assistant with the abundance of hair that presently adorned her.

Johnson believed that an attractive woman placed appropriately in the limelight might enhance his political fortunes. As planning for the Democratic National Convention of 1964 proceeded, the White House team discussed asking a southern woman to introduce a motion to nominate LBJ by acclamation. The president advised press secretary Bill Moyers to find a pretty, young woman to make a brief statement regarding the presidential nomination. He asked Moyers to "get some good woman or something. We don't want a boss image if you want a white woman to say something. She could get up and—say, some real

young pretty woman. . . . There's a pretty woman in the Georgia delega-
tion. They've acted pretty nice. I want to tie into the South a little bit.
Moyers responded, "Alright sir, let me find out who she is."[63]
After further conversation this line of discussion continued:

> LBJ: Christ almighty, there's bound to be some good looking
> woman in one of those delegations up there.
> Moyers: I will find one and get back to Jack with a suggestion.
> LBJ: And she's got to know what she's doin'. You got to tell her.
> She's got to sit with Carl Sanders if she's in Georgia. . . .
> Moyers: You don't think that's too much association with the
> South?
> LBJ: Probably is, but I thought a sweet woman. . . . And I damn
> sure want to carry Georgia if I can.

After Jack Valenti suggested that they call on Florida in the nomination protocol, Moyers added, "I've got a very attractive young
woman, about 35, who is on the platform committee. A little bit naive,
but she could be coached and she could do it. Her husband is going to
become president of the American Medical Association next year. Her
name is Damsey. . . . I don't know how that would appeal to you, but
she is attractive."
LBJ concluded the conversation: "All right I think Florida would
be better. I'd just go on and ask her. And get someone sitting right
there. Make sure there's someone sitting there—like Smathers."
Lyndon Johnson's supporters recognized and largely accepted the
president's efforts to surround himself with feminine pulchritude. In
private tape recordings made to aid in writing her White House diary,
Lady Bird included numerous mentions of the president's delight at
finding himself amid a bevy of beautiful women. Writing of Lyndon's
excitement over a new boat he had acquired, Lady Bird recorded that
the president "took all of the pretty girls he could gather . . . for a
ride." Preserving her thoughts only days later, Lady Bird again commented on the president's love of boats, noting that the presidential
yacht *Honey Fitz* was his favorite and that "Lyndon ensconces himself there and gets some pretty ladies clustered around him and spends
his evening."[64]
While LBJ sought the presence of attractive women, he could
not limit his company to women who appealed to his sense of beauty. Johnson had learned well that a politician did not get to dance
with only the beautiful people. Public life demanded courtesy to
women, but some social interactions constituted a private burden,

and he occasionally sought relief. Speaking to diplomat Thomas Mann before an evening gala, John pleaded with Mann to "dance with some of those short, fat women again. Old Mennen Williams was the only guy who delivered for me last night."[65] The political world in which he found himself, and not his admiration of feminine beauty, defined Johnson's public behavior as well as his policies on gender issues.

LBJ and Lady Bird understood political wives to be powerful symbols of American family values. Lady Bird epitomized this role, often traveling in the company of at least one of her daughters. With the exception of his sexual escapades, Lyndon rarely considered women apart from the men in their lives. Wives and daughters either enhanced or detracted from men on the political stage. After the JFK assassination, his appreciation of Jacqueline Kennedy's beauty, the tragic symbol of the young widow with two small children, and the former First Lady's popularity intertwined in his interactions with her. LBJ's shock in the first weeks after 22 November gave way to appreciation of Jackie's political currency. His exploratory efforts to offer Kennedy a diplomatic post, an exception to his initial lack of interest in appointing women, offered a singular opportunity to draw the nation's most revered woman into his circle.

Only a month after the assassination of the president, LBJ spoke to advisers and to Jackie herself about an ambassadorship for her, a position that he suggested would help the young widow rebuild her life. He presented the potential appointment to former Kennedy aides Pierre Salinger and Ken O'Donnell as a political coup for the Democrats, but neither received the idea warmly.[66] In telephoning Salinger to discuss the possibility of a nomination, Johnson disclosed the depth of his political ambition, his penchant for scatology, and his idealization of femininity. Upon reaching Salinger, Johnson sought confirmation that their conversation would not be overheard and then presented the question of whether it would "be just terrible" to offer Jackie the ambassadorship to Mexico, noting that "all she'd have to do would be to walk out on her balcony about once a week." Her appointment, the president insisted, would "electrify the Western Hemisphere. It'd be more than any Alliance for Progress. . . . She'd just walk out on that balcony and look down on them and they'd pee all over themselves every day." Responding to Salinger's skepticism Johnson replied, "You mean she wouldn't want to work this early? Do you think they'd think we were trying to use her or something?" Coming to the conclusion of the conversation, LBJ volunteered, "She's just the sweetest thing. She was always nicer to me than anyone in the

Kennedy family. . . . It would revolutionize Latin America . . . and it would give her something to do. . . . She and Tom Mann together would sew up this hemisphere. Her husband in heaven would look down and say my God he saw she had it just like I did."[67]

LBJ's consideration of Kennedy for an ambassadorship was not the sole instance of his efforts to exploit the nation's sympathy for the former first lady. His numerous interchanges with Kennedy exhibit a narrative style that seamlessly combined chivalrous concern with crass political manipulation. While Johnson wanted the world to know of his concern for her, he tried to guard against the appearance of using tragedy to advance his own political goals. On the evening of 23 December 1963, while in the presence of United Press International correspondent Frances Lewine, the president phoned Kennedy to wish her a merry Christmas. Later that night Johnson phoned Lewine for her assurance that she had not released any information about the content of his exchange with Kennedy because "I just don't want . . . my private conversations [aired] in public and have her think I'm using her or something."[68]

The Gendered Rhetoric of the White House

In numerous conversations with the former first lady, LBJ voiced his love and admiration for her, and she answered with thanks and expressions of concern for the president's well-being. Johnson addressed Kennedy as "Jackie," and she addressed him as "Mr. President," a pattern that acknowledged his status and reified a paternalistic relationship between them. Ten days after the assassination, LBJ assured the young widow of both his and the nation's love for her, urging her to "just come over and put your arm around me" and vowing that "you females got a lot of courage that we men don't have so we have to rely on you."[69] Johnson's invocation of female fortitude followed a series of exchanges in which Jackie's voice broke as she thanked him for a personal note that he had sent and told him that she had more hand-written correspondence from him than from JFK. LBJ then turned the conversation to a lighter note, telling Kennedy that not many women had been close to two presidents, after which she quipped, "She ran around with two presidents. That's what they'll say about me."[70]

On the day that he and Lady Bird moved into the White House, LBJ had also phoned Kennedy, opining that "I decided that I just wanted to flirt with you a little bit" and telling her that a photograph of her in the *New York Daily News* was "gorgeous," to which she responded "how sweet." LBJ asked about Caroline and John and requested that Jackie tell them that "I'd like to be their daddy." Kennedy revealed no hint that she found the remark presumptuous and assured the president that she would pass his words to the children.[71] Overall, Jacqueline Kennedy acted solicitously toward President Johnson, precisely the solace he looked for in women. She frequently expressed concern for his health and the burdens of his office. In one conversation she beseeched him to begin taking a daily nap, warning, "You just can't tear around."[72] LBJ tried repeatedly to get Kennedy to return to the White House, but she consistently demurred, and Johnson never seemed to understand the agony that a visit might cause her. After one of these appeals, she pleaded, "Oh, Mr. President . . . I just can't come down there. I wanted to tell you. I've barely gotten hold of myself. . . . I'm so scared I'll start to cry again. . . . I just can't. . . . Don't make me come down there again."[73]

LBJ's interactions with Kennedy epitomized the manipulation of women that his attitudes dictated. Judged by the opinions of those who knew him, equality of the sexes fell outside LBJ's worldview. As George Reedy summarized, "His view of the female role in society was not very flattering. They justified their existence as bed mates, cooks, housekeepers, mothers, and secretaries—with the last category at the top of the scale. The greatest destiny he could assign to a woman was that of a helpmate to a dominant male."[74]

The efforts of the Johnson administration to hire and promote women illustrate the president's ability to retain sex-role segregation while moving the best and brightest Democratic women into federal jobs. These actions confirmed underlying cultural assumptions about gender that LBJ acted out with Jacqueline Kennedy and others.[75] Intentionally or otherwise, he patronized women and thus kept them in their place. Condescending interchanges with or about women form a continuous strand through his private conversations during his White House years. When women's rights supporter Emma Guffey Miller wrote to the president concerning her leadership within the League of Women Voters, Johnson dismissed her views, writing back, "As per your suggestions, I read them with a big smile. You and I both know there are only two things more changeable than a woman's mind: a baby's diapers and the weather."[76] Through his years in the Senate, Johnson had developed an effective working relationship with Margaret Chase Smith, but gender framed their interactions, as it did all of Lyndon Johnson's written and oral expressions. As yet another honor came Smith's way, Johnson wrote, "I understand that you have just received your fiftieth honorary degree. I don't know whether this makes you the Hill's leading intellectual—but you are certainly the prettiest."[77] When Mary Keyserling submitted her resignation as director of the Women's Bureau in 1969, Johnson wrote her: "Under your guidance, equality of opportunity for women has advanced tremendously. You have accomplished, through charm, persuasion, and sensitivity, what an ordinary mortal would have been able to do only with greater statutory powers. As never before, women are able to participate in the progress of this nation toward the great goals we all share. Thank you, Mary, for being so very effective."[78]

With his family, his staff, and political figures from around the nation, Lyndon Johnson played out gendered scenarios that he and most men and women in public life had learned from childhood, and perfected in Washington. Lyndon Johnson commanded strict obedience from the men and women who served him in any capacity, and his concepts of loyalty and authority permitted him to speak to others in a condescending and often personal manner. Bawdy humor and off-color analogies peppered his verbal exchanges with men. Familiarity of expression and commentary on personal appearance charged his conversations with women. In his efforts to intimidate or to find rapport with men, Johnson occasionally questioned their manhood. Congruently, Johnson sought women's cooperation and admiration through flattery and terms of endearment. The gendered configuration of Johnson's behaviors had taken on a predictability of ritual over his years in public life. The secretly recorded tapes of phone conversations that Johnson made from the Oval Office draw the present-day listener into gendered verbal exchanges in which both sides to the conversation knew their roles and fit into a relationship of commander and deferential other. The White House tapes include dialogues not only with Johnson but also between others surrounding the president that further document the gendered political culture of the White House.

Casual flirtation had become a formalized pattern of interaction between men in politics and the wives of politicians or female staff, a pattern captured in the Johnson tapes. In February 1964 White House aide George Reedy, who had come to the White House with John Kennedy, reached staff member Marie Fehmer in the president's office when calling for Johnson's assistant Juanita Roberts. Reedy's exchange with Fehmer included friendly but gendered banter:

Reedy: Hi there . . . sweet feet. Is Juanita there?
Fehmer: She's on the phone, George. [Hold on] because she was trying to get you, to the phone, that is.

Reedy: Shucks, there you go dodging me again. How can I be a gay, dashing rogue when all of you women treat me this way? You can't drink champagne from a lady's slipper because they all have open backs.

Fehmer: Yes, we're all going to get them. . . .

Reedy: This has become a very lackluster world. It has all the excitement of a bar of American family laundry soap. The women all run. . . . This Irishman was born in the wrong time.[79]

Reedy later wrote, "In the Lyndon Johnson era, macho was the order of the day and the sexual analogue was impossible to avoid."[80]

By virtue of his office, the president stood atop a cultural pyramid in which his gendered language trumped the cleverness of other conversationalists. LBJ wrote and spoke of women in affectionate and sentimental terms, but he also displayed considerable warm-heartedness toward his male friends. He held out expressions of friendship as a reward for loyalty and service, and he withheld affection or countered affection with thinly veiled or outright insults as he sought compliance or support from male legislators or bureaucrats. Where he flattered or cajoled women, Johnson often challenged male pride. In a series of conversations with Sargent Shriver about his appointment as poverty czar, LBJ grew impatient and finally blundered into this spicy exchange:

LBJ: I'm going to announce your appointment at this press conference today. . . . Don't make me wait until next week. . . . I am going to make it clear that you are Mr. Poverty . . . and you can run the Peace Corps or not. . . .

Hell, it'll be a promotion. . . . I don't know why [the Peace Corps people] would object to that unless you've got some women who think you won't have enough time to spend with them. . . .

You've got the responsibility, you've got the authority, you've got the money, you may not have the glands.

Shriver: The glands?

LBJ: The glands.

Shriver: I've got plenty of glands.

LBJ: That's good because I haven't got the glands. I'd like to have your glands then. I need Dr. Brinkley myself and those goat glands.[81]

Conversations between Johnson and women from whom he sought commitments to public service document a gendered pattern of female responses that reinforced Johnson's paternalism. In January 1964, Johnson sought to persuade philanthropist Mary Lasker, a long-time friend, to accept an appointment as ambassador to Finland. Lasker's volunteer efforts on behalf of medical research and beautification as well as her campaigning for LBJ had advanced the agendas of both Lyndon and Lady Bird. In appealing for her to accept the ambassadorship, the president said he would let the Finnish president know that he had chosen "the most glamorous woman, the ablest person," and that the job required "somebody that's got some brains and some charm and besides I want a good female." Lasker demurred, claiming that she would not succeed in the post because she lacked "enough talent to speak" and "enough physical guts for it."[82]

Three weeks before he spoke with Lasker, Johnson phoned *New York Post* owner Dorothy Schiff to ask her to go to Africa to represent the United States at a celebration of one hundred years of Liberian-U.S. relations, but Schiff demurred, saying that she could not go because she feared flying.[83] While the fear of flying is not gendered, Schiff's spontaneous and rapid explanation for refusing the president's request exposes the ease with which highly visible professional women might admit to their weaknesses. After ending his conversation with Schiff, Johnson next tried to tap Helen Gahagan Douglas for the trip, telling her to "just get your little teddies ready" for travel. When Douglas responded, "Wait 'til I call [husband] Mel," Johnson cajoled, "I thought you ran your own house. Don't tell me you've got to clear it through Mel." Douglas answered, "Of course I have to clear things with Melvin," but then agreed to go. Before hanging up the phone, Douglas gave the president a parting feminine salvo: "One last thing, don't overdo."[84]

Conclusion

As Lyndon Johnson's conversational style and Lady Bird Johnson's White House assignments revealed, sharply defined gender roles characterized his private and his public life. Verbal crudities and an obsession with pretty women figured prominently in LBJ's private behaviors. His paternalism and his loyalty to male superiority reflected broadly shared American values of his time and consequently say as much about American culture of the 1960s and the role of gender in politics at the time as they reveal about the president himself. Lyndon Johnson stood with the Democratic Party with respect to gender and politics. Most prominent Democrats of the 1960s shared some behavioral expectations that precluded equality of the sexes. The ludicrous dismissal of women's rights in the Eighty-eighth Congress witnessed the powerlessness of feminists and validated LBJ's worldview. Men and women surrounding the president demurred in the face of his flirtatiousness and reinforced his paternalism.

Records of the Johnson presidency reveal the ways in which many Democratic women within or close to the administration worked to improve women's lives individually or collectively without capitulating to an equal rights agenda. Women with high visibility in Democratic circles confirmed Johnson's inclination to advance individual women in public office and to ameliorate the condition of working women without compromising the gendered order of Washington or of the nation.

The protectionism of Esther Peterson and the Women's Bureau rested on a concept of gender differences that defined men and women as different kinds of persons rather than persons whose abilities differed by circumstance. Peterson's views mirrored Johnson's own perspective within the strictly gendered world of Washington politics of the early 1960s. Lyndon Johnson could work to achieve the appointment of women to many government positions, but a society based on gender equity would be very different from everything he had known. For Johnson and the people with whom he associated, prescribed gender roles constituted the warp and woof of the fabric of politics. Mainstream Democratic women like Esther Peterson reinforced Johnson's paternalistic attitudes toward women at the same time that they advocated the broader hiring of women in the federal government.

LBJ's treatment of Peterson further informs our understanding of how the gendered world of the president guided his actions and policies. She was the senior spokesperson for Democratic women in federal employment and the acknowledged expert on women's working conditions. In his early months in the White House, LBJ saw these two issues as distractions and possible disruptions in his campaign to pass civil rights legislation. In the long run they mattered not at all to the president.

Women of the 1960s lacked the power to be major players in a presidential administration. In the 1960s, Democratic women constituted a major constituency but not a unified political force. Lyndon Johnson largely succeeded in balancing the requests and petitions of prominent Democratic women against the many responsibilities of the presidency, but women's agendas were too diverse and large for Johnson to succeed in satisfying all. Bound in a loose coalition of support for African American rights and for the advancement of women in public office, Democratic women did not represent a united pro-

Lyndon alliance. Over the course of the Johnson presidency, political developments drove some Democratic women from their earlier support for LBJ. As the Vietnam War increasingly occupied his and the public's attention, both women and African Americans within the Democratic Party increasingly criticized the president's leadership in domestic and foreign affairs.

The War on Poverty, the centerpiece of Johnson's domestic agenda, angered some minority women and some white feminists because it emphasized job development for male workers far more than for women and because of its implications for women's equality within the family.[85] Daniel Patrick Moynihan's report *The Negro Family*, a federal study completed during the Johnson years, condemned female-headed African American families, while welfare policies throughout the nation discouraged marriage among the poor by denying many welfare benefits to male-headed households. As Susan Hartmann has written and as the Moynihan report confirms, the designers of Johnson's antipoverty program consistently understood the poor to be mothers and children whose mates or fathers had failed to find their rightful places as breadwinners.[86] The War on Poverty mirrored the values of a Democratic Party whose leadership recognized social needs but did not acknowledge and perhaps did not understand the gendered implications of welfare policies. In other areas such as environmental protection, family planning, and public beautification, Johnson supported initiatives championed by women, but these actions did not enlarge women's civil rights. Lyndon Johnson took some steps to improve women's status, but gender was a fleeting political concern, and Vietnam ultimately overwhelmed the president's efforts to advance women as well as his agendas on class and race. Women's divisions over these several issues undermined their own abilities to put forth a coherent platform on women's issues.

President Johnson played a role in the transformation of gender roles in the United States not only through his appointments of women but also through his silence on or his repudiation of more aggressive steps that feminists desired. Johnson came to the presidency in the era before the feminism of Betty Friedan and other second-wave leaders had gained broad public hearing and while the reign of protectionists continued at the Women's Bureau and in the Department of Labor overall.[87] He left the White House without knowing how the Civil Rights Act would transform the horizons of working women, and his lack of foresight mirrored the nation's silence on gender issues in the early 1960s.

Notes

1. Lyndon Johnson and Jack Brooks, 10 February 1964, 8:22 P.M., White House Tapes, WH6402.13, PNO21, Lyndon Baines Johnson Presidential Library, Austin, Texas (hereafter cited as LBJL).

2. Susan M. Hartmann, "Women's Issues and the Johnson Administration," in *The Johnson Years*, vol. 3, *LBJ at Home and Abroad*, ed. Robert A. Divine (Lawrence: University Press of Kansas, 1994), 74.

3. Julia Kirk Blackwelder, *Now Hiring: The Feminization of Work in the United States, 1900–1995* (College Station: Texas A&M University Press, 1997), 180–181; Jo Freeman, *The Politics of Women's Liberation: A Case Study of an Emerging Social Movement and Its Relation to the Policy Process* (New York: David McKay, 1975), 1–54; Christine A. Lunardini, *Women's Rights*, Social Issues in American History Series (Phoenix: Oryx Press, 1996), 165; Janet M. Martin, *The Presidency and Women: Promise, Performance and Illusion* (College Station: Texas A&M University Press, 2003), 96.

4. Blackwelder, *Now Hiring*, 147–204; Alice Kessler-Harris, *In Pursuit of Equity: Women, Men, and the Quest for Economic Citizenship in Twentieth-Century America* (New York: Oxford University Press, 2001), 203–212.

5. Martin, *Presidency and Women*, 91.

6. George Reedy, *Lyndon B. Johnson: A Memoir* (New York: Andrews and McMeel, 1982), 39.

7. *Congressional Record: Proceedings and Debates of the 88th Congress, Second Session*, vol. 110, pt. 2, 8 February 1964 (Washington, D.C.: Government Printing Office, 1964), 2584.

8. Ibid., 2578–2580. Although her perspective differed, Griffiths echoed the rhetoric of white southern suffragists of the early twentieth century and of the National Woman's Party. Jo Freeman reported that Martha Griffiths intended to introduce Title VII herself, but that she demurred upon learning of Smith's intention because she believed that Smith could draw support for the amendment that she could not. Freeman, *Politics of Women's Liberation*, 53.

9. *Congressional Record*, 8 February 1964, 2578. Bolton's statement mirrored the perspective from the Women's Bureau in the 1950s; Blackwelder, *Now Hiring*, 159.

10. Charles Whalen and Barbara Whalen, *The Longest Debate: A Legislative History of the 1964 Civil Rights Act* (Cabin John, Md.: Seven Locks Press, 1985), 160; *Congressional Record*, vol. 110, pt. 11, 19 June 1964, p. 14511.

11. Johnson addressed a joint session of the Congress on 27 November 1963. He urged Congress to "enact a civil rights law so that we can move forward to eliminate from the nation every trace of discrimination that is based upon race or color." *Public Papers of the Presidents of the United States: Lyndon B. Johnson, Containing the Public Messages, Speeches, and Statements of the President*, 10 vols. (Washington, D.C.: Government Printing Office, 1965–1970), 1: 11.

12. Before H.R. 7152 passed the House, LBJ had good reason to fear that the inclusion of women could defeat the bill, partly because of the forces that had worked for the amendment to Title VII. As Modell Scrugg's query suggests, the debates over civil rights legislation that followed the Democratic presidential victory of 1960 breathed new life into American feminism.

During the Johnson years NOW emerged as a vocal advocate for women, but during the Kennedy administration the National Woman's Party (NWP) had spearheaded the drive for women's rights and played a critical role in keeping women's rights before the Congress. Although the NWP was a small and declining organization, its membership included militant feminists who had become well known in Washington circles through their relentless lobbying for passage of the equal rights amendment. The debate over the 1964 civil rights bill permitted the NWP to bring its equal rights agenda into national debate through the back door at a time when civil rights issues could not be postponed. Despite their traditional opposition to any measure short of a federal equal rights amendment, members of the NWP actively encouraged Virginia congressman Howard W. Smith to introduce the word "sex" into Title VII of the bill, the section of the proposed legislation that dealt with discrimination in employment.

Why would the NWP, which had steadfastly opposed anything short of the equal rights amendment, change its course? NWP members calculated that their cause would advance whether the bill won or lost. The equal rights amendment had been introduced repeatedly in Congress but had always died in committee. Failure to win the amendment in the face of women's contributions to World War II was a major blow to the NWP, and Title VII was a way to resurrect the faltering women's movement. Expectations that the bill would generate new enthusiasm for women's rights but that it would ultimately fail would advance NWP goals by laying the groundwork for the equal rights amendment and avoiding the compromise of partial legislative remedies. The NWP had not worked for the rights of racial minorities, and so its leaders did not voice concern over the prospect that the inclusion of gender would sink the 1964 bill. Virginia R. Allen to Alice Paul, 30 October 1963, Papers of the National Woman's Party, 1914–1974, Reel 108; Alice Paul to Lynn Franklin, 26 September 1963, ibid.; Alice Paul to Mary C. Kennedy, 23 October 1963, ibid.; Nina Horton Avery to J. Vaughan Gary, 8 January 1964, ibid.; "Resolution Adopted Unanimously by the National Council of the National Woman's Party," 16 December 1963, NWP Papers, reel 128; Hettie Milam Cook, "Equal Rights for Women," NWP Papers, reel 108; Jo Freeman, "How 'Sex' Got into Title VII: Persistent Opportunism as a Maker of Public Policy," *Journal of Law and Inequality* 9 (March 1991): 172–178.

13. On occasion, Johnson facetiously suggested that male politicians could win over women to their viewpoints by bedding them. Hartmann, "Women's Issues in the Johnson Administration," 56.

14. NWP Papers, Part I, Series 1, Section C, roll 108; Carl M. Brauer, "Women Activists, Southern Conservatives, and the Prohibition of Sex Discrimination in Title VII of the 1964 Civil Rights Act," *Journal of Southern History* 49 (February 1983): 37–56; Freeman, "How 'Sex' Got into Title VII," 163–184; Susan M. Hartmann, *From Margin to Mainstream: American Women and Politics since 1960* (New York: Knopf, 1989), 53–56; Martin, *Presidency and Women*, 85–86; Patricia Zelman, *Women, Work, and National Policy: The Kennedy-Johnson Years* (Ann Arbor, Mich.: UMI Research Press, 1982), 57–71.

15. Esther Peterson, who had built a network of congressional influence during her career as a labor lobbyist on Capitol Hill, took the helm of the Women's Bureau at the outset of the Kennedy administration. President

Kennedy had appointed Peterson to head the bureau at her request and in appreciation of her help in delivering her home state of Utah for the Democrats in the 1960 election. As director of the bureau, Esther Peterson ranked highest among women in the executive branch. From her vantage point in the bureau, Peterson exercised more influence on gender policy than any other White House appointee. From her bureau post, she both engineered the creation of the PCSW and guided the appointments of women and men to its numerous subcommittees. Esther Peterson's long history as an advocate for laboring Americans framed her views on civil rights. Through her years of unrelenting campaigns to better wages and working conditions for all blue-collar workers, Peterson had sympathized with the plight of African Americans, whom law or custom barred from fair competition with whites.

16. Interview with Esther Peterson by Emily Williams, 26 April 1979, Washington, D.C., Franklin D. Roosevelt Library; Esther Peterson to Arthur Goldberg, 2 June 1961, White House Central Files, box 206, John F. Kennedy Presidential Library.

17. Katherine Ellickson, "The President's Commission on the Status of Women," unpublished manuscript, January, 1976, p. 17, copy in the John Fitzgerald Kennedy Library, Boston, Mass.; Kessler-Harris, *In Pursuit of Equity*, 213–225; Martin, *Presidency and Women*, 65–69, 91–95. Roosevelt served as little more than a figurehead as she had largely retired from public life and was in fragile health, but her national stature brought notice and authority to the commission. By virtue of her office, her years in service to labor, and her acquaintance with public officials, Esther Peterson also commanded respect. Roosevelt and Peterson had consistently championed legislative measures and union contracts that protected working women from dangerous employment conditions, and both opposed an equal rights amendment because it would eliminate separate hours and conditions guidelines for the employment of women.

18. The report of the President's Commission on the Status of Women reached the public in the form of *American Women: Report of the President's Commission on the Status of Women, 1963* (Washington, D.C.: Government Printing Office, 1963). In this report the PCSW identified a plethora of legal disabilities that affected women, but it recommended that the states, rather than the Congress or the U.S. Supreme Court, should address issues of women's legal status.

19. Typed membership list of Citizens' Advisory Council on the Status of Women, Item 11, 6 February 1964, and invitation list for meeting of 12 February 1966, President's Appointment File—Diary Back-up, box 4, LBJL; Martin, *Presidency and Women*, 92.

20. Zelman, *Women, Work, and National Policy*, 1–54.

21. Modell Scruggs to President Lyndon B. Johnson, 12 March 1964, Lyndon B. Johnson to Mrs. Modell Scruggs, 23 April 1964, Memorandum to George B. Reedy from Esther Peterson, 16 April 1964, President's Papers, Human Rights, box 3, Equality for Women, LBJL.

22. Freeman, "How 'Sex' Got into Title VII," 172–178.

23. *Congressional Record, Proceedings and Debates of the 88th Congress, Second Session*, vol. 110, pt. 2, 8 February 1964, 2577.

24. Ibid., 2578.

25. Ibid., *Congressional Record, Proceedings and Debates of the 88th*

Congress, Second Session, vol. 110, pt. 2, 8 February 1964, 2577–2579; Brauer, "Women Activists, Southern Conservatives," 49.

26. *Congressional Record,* vol. 110, pt. 2, 2577–2578; Brauer, "Women Activists, Southern Conservatives," 48.

27. Senator Everett Dirksen did speak against the inclusion of women in the civil rights bill, but he did not succeed in changing Title VII, and he ultimately withdrew from a filibuster aimed at defeating the 1964 bill, Kessler-Harris, *In Pursuit of Equity,* 245.

28. Martin, *Presidency and Women,* 101–103, 107–108, 111–112.

29. Lyndon Johnson to Senator Edward Long, 29 July 1964, 10:32 A.M., WH6407.17, PN04, LBJL.

30. Copy of Executive Order 11136, 18 October 1965; White House Name File—Esther Peterson, LBJL.

31. Juanita Roberts to Esther Peterson, 5 December 1967, ibid. Under new leadership the Women's Bureau eventually endorsed the movement for the equal rights amendment, but this orientation did not emerge forcefully during the Johnson presidency. Peterson also reassessed her position on the ERA and ultimately embraced the amendment, but her subtle shift to the left in the 1960s did not shape White House policies or LBJ's perspective. Kessler-Harris, *In Pursuit of Equity,* 262–263; Winifred D. Wandersee, *On the Move: Women in the 1970s* (Boston: Twayne, 1988), 18, 38–40.

32. Caruthers Gholson Berger, "Equal Pay, Equal Employment Opportunity and Equal Enforcement of the Law for Women," *Valparaiso Law Review* 5 (1971): 326–338; Freeman, *Politics of Women's Liberation,* 54; Hartmann, *From Margin to Mainstream,* 57–59; Kessler-Harris, *In Pursuit of Equity,* 246–261; Rosalind Rosenberg, *Divided Lives: American Women in the Twentieth Century* (New York: Hill and Wang, 1992), 188; Zelman, *Women, Work, and National Policy,* 98–99. As Esther Peterson had understood, the Civil Rights Act of 1964 obviated industrial codes that set separate standards for men and women, although court interpretation of Title VII came after LBJ left office. What Peterson and other protectionists had not foreseen were the ways in which Title VII would change many blue-collar working women's perspectives. Worker advocates could continue to press for protective codes, but protective legislation now might aid men as well as women.

33. "Roosevelt Finds Sex Discrimination Is a Major Problem, Appoints Seven Key Aides," *New York Times,* 21 July 1965.

34. Ibid.

35. Freeman, *Politics of Women's Liberation,* 54.

36. Lunardini, *Women's Rights,* 168–169.

37. Hartmann, *From Margin to Mainstream,* 59.

38. Women in Congress pressed for the inclusion of gender equality in jury service in the 1966 civil rights bill. Although they failed at the time, Congress did ban gender discrimination on federal juries in 1968. Hartmann, "Women's Issues and the Johnson Administration," 63–65; Hartmann, *From Margin to Mainstream,* 60–61; Juanita Roberts to Esther Peterson, 5 December 1967, White House Name File—Esther Peterson, LBJL.

39. Hartmann, "Women's Issues and the Johnson Administration," 54–58.

40. Liz Carpenter, *Ruffles and Flourishes* (College Station: Texas A&M University Press, 1993), 34.

41. Ibid., 35. Anna Rosenberg Hoffman, a self-employed consultant in

labor negotiations and public relations in the 1960s, had held numerous government posts from the New Deal through the Truman administration.

42. Lyndon Johnson and David Dubinsky, 5 February 1964, 5:56 P.M., WH6402.06 PNO 8, LBJL.

43. Lyndon Johnson and Luther Hodges, 1 February 1964, 12:57 A.M., WH6402.01, PNO3, LBJL.

44. Lyndon Johnson and Orville Freeman, 19 February 1964, 11:25 A.M., WH6402.17, PNO 20, LBJL.

45. Agenda: Cabinet Meeting, 18 February 1964, President's Appointment File—Diary Back-up, box 4, LBJL.

46. Liz Carpenter to "Anyone interested in women," 24 February 1964, Human Rights—Hu 3, Equality for Women, box 58, LBJL.

47. Memorandum from Liz Carpenter to Pierre Salinger, 6 March 1964, Human Rights—Hu3, box 58, Equality for Women, LBJL.

48. Martin, *Presidency and Women*, 253–254.

49. Lyndon Johnson to Mary Keyserling, 26 November 1968. White House Name File, President's Papers, LBJL.

50. Memorandum from Liz Carpenter and Bess Abell to the President, 6 April 1964, Human Rights File, President's Papers, box 58, LBJL. While the administration had announced that 150 newly appointed women would be recognized at the reception, Johnson fell short of his goal.

51. "Remarks at a Reception for Recently Appointed Women in Government," 13 April 1964, *Public Papers of the Presidents of the United States, Lyndon B. Johnson*, 1: 257.

52. Memorandum, Liz Carpenter to Lyndon Johnson, 4 November 1966, White House Central Files—Liz Carpenter, LBJL.

53. Paul K. Conkin, *Big Daddy from the Pedernales: Lyndon Baines Johnson*, Twayne's Twentieth-Century Biography Series, No. 1 (Boston: G. K. Hall, 1986), 180–181.

54. Mrs. Lyndon Baines Johnson, "The Total Woman," Baccalaureate Address, Radcliffe College, 9 June, *Addresses by the First Lady, 1964*, pamphlet distributed by the Johnson Library, p. 3.

55. Lady Bird terminated all contact with her biographer Jan Jarboe Russell when Russell asked for the former first lady's comments on LBJ's relationship with other women. *Lady Bird, a Biography of Mrs. Johnson* (New York: Scribner, 1999), 12–13.

56. Interview with Jacqueline Kennedy by Joe B. Franz, 11 January 1974, *Oral Histories of the Johnson Administration, 1963–1969* (Frederick, Md.: University Publications, 1988), pt. 2, pp. 2–12; Lewis L. Gould, *Lady Bird Johnson: Our Environmental First Lady* (Lawrence: University Press of Kansas, 1999); Hartmann, "Women's Issues and the Johnson Administration," 70.

57. Carpenter, *Ruffles and Flourishes*, 142–168.

58. Russell, *Lady Bird*, 263. Michael Beschloss, ed., *Reaching for Glory: Lyndon Johnson's Secret White House Tapes, 1964–1965* (New York: Simon and Schuster, 2001), 47–49.

59. Lyndon B. Johnson to Senator and Mrs. Stuart Symington, 24 October 1962, Papers of the Vice President, 1961–1963, box 268, LBJL.

60. Lyndon Johnson and Clinton Anderson, 4 February 1964, 9:37 A.M., WH6402.04 PNO 13, LBJL.

61. Carpenter, *Ruffles and Flourishes*, 37; Doris Kearns, *Lyndon Johnson*

and the American Dream (New York: Harper and Row, 1976), 12; Reedy, *Lyndon B. Johnson*, 35–36.

62. Lyndon Johnson and Lady Bird Johnson, 23 December 1963, 7:35 P.M., K6312.16 PNO3, LBJL.

63. Lyndon Johnson and Bill Moyers, 26 August 1964, 12:50 P.M., WH6408.39, PNO10, LBJL.

64. Lady Bird Johnson, tape-recorded diary, 5 July 1965, 20 July 1965, quoted in Beschloss, *Reaching for Glory*, 385 and 401.

65. Lyndon Johnson and Thomas Mann, 19 February 1964, 11:32 A.M., WH6402.18, PNO2, LBJL.

66. Lyndon Johnson to Pierre Salinger, 23 December 1963, K6312.16, PNO 5; Lyndon Johnson to Ken O'Donnell, 27 December 1963, 3:00 P.M., K6312.19, PNO 6, LBJL.

67. Lyndon Johnson and Pierre Salinger, 23 December 1963, after 7 P.M., WH6312.16, PNO5, LBJL. Thomas Mann had also been mentioned as a potential nominee as ambassador to Mexico.

68. Lyndon Johnson and Frances Lewine, 23 December 1963, 9:54 P.M., WH6312.16, PNO12, LBJL.

69. Lyndon Johnson and Jacqueline Kennedy, 2 December 1963, 2:42 P.M., WH6312.1, PNO24, LBJL.

70. Ibid.

71. Lyndon Johnson and Jacqueline Kennedy, 7 December 1963, 5:20 P.M., WH6312.5, PNO 5, LBJL.

72. Lyndon Johnson and Jacqueline Kennedy, 9 January 1964, 11:30 A.M., K1295, LBJL.

73. Ibid.

74. Reedy, *Lyndon B. Johnson*, 32.

75. Johnson's reputation for womanizing fits comfortably with his patronizing behavior toward women, but the second condition did not depend on the first. Johnson always strove to be number one, and his ability to dismiss women's views made his success that much easier. Robert Dallek, *Lone Star Rising: Lyndon Johnson and His Times, 1908–1960* (New York: Oxford University Press, 1991), 188–191.

76. Lyndon B. Johnson to Emma Guffey Miller, 13 June 1964, Human Rights File, President's Papers, box 58, LBJL.

77. Lyndon Johnson to Margaret Chase Smith, 29 April 1967, White House Name File—Margaret Chase Smith, President's Papers, LBJL.

78. Lyndon Johnson to Mary Dubling Keyserling, 18 January 1969, White House Name File—Mary Dubling Keyserling, President's Papers, LBJL.

79. George Reedy and Marie Fehmer, 3 February 1964, WH6402.02 PNO 16, LBJL.

80. Reedy, *Lyndon B. Johnson*, 31.

81. Lyndon Johnson and Sargent Shriver, 1 February 1964, 5:47 P.M., WH6402.01, PNO16, LBJL.

82. Lyndon Johnson and Mary Lasker, 29 January 1964, 7:50 P.M., WH6401.17, PNO15; 29 January 1964, 8:45 P.M., WH6401.17, PNO17, LBJL.

83. Lyndon Johnson and Dorothy Schiff, 1 January 1964, WH6401.01, PNO1, LBJL.

84. Lyndon Johnson and Helen Gahagan Douglas, 1 January 1964, WH6401.01, PNO9, LBJL. Helen Gahagan Douglas served in the House of

Representatives as a member of the California delegation from 1945 through 1950. Richard Nixon defeated her in the 1950 Senate elections.

85. Julie Leininger Pycior, *LBJ and Mexican Americans: The Paradox of Power* (Austin: University of Texas Press, 1997), 158–159.

86. While welfare policies generally divided women, the administration succeeded in bringing together diverse female populations in its campaign to make birth control widely and cheaply available. By avoiding any mention of abortion, emphasizing voluntary participation, and billing family limitation as a method of shrinking poverty, bureaucrats succeeded in selling acceptance of federally funded contraceptive methods to the public. Hartmann, *From Margin to Mainstream*, 60–76.

87. For an account of changes in the perspective of the Women's Bureau after World War II, see Kathleen A. Laughlin, *Women's Work and Public Policy: A History of the Women's Bureau, U. S. Department of Labor, 1945–1970* (Boston: Northeastern University Press, 2000).

10 | The First Citizens of America: Lyndon Johnson and American Indians

Thomas Clarkin

MOST STUDIES OF LYNDON JOHNSON's presidency make no mention of his administration's efforts to assist American Indians. This scholarly neglect is not all that surprising. Throughout his years in office, Johnson expressed little interest in or knowledge of Indian policy. In 1963, when he first took office, most Native Americans lived in desperate poverty and as a group were politically marginalized. When he left office in 1969, little had changed—Indians remained the poorest Americans, and they had little political influence. Given the lack of presidential involvement and the absence of any notable improvement in reservation life, LBJ's Indian policy initially does not seem a productive area of scholarly inquiry.[1]

Yet the study of the Johnson administration's policies and programs is crucial for understanding modern American Indian history and contributes to a more accurate assessment of the achievements and failures of Johnson's Great Society. When LBJ entered the White House, federal Indian affairs were in disarray. Termination, the policy Congress enacted after World War II, had sought to bring Indians into the social and economic mainstream of American life by ending the government-to-government relationship between the various tribes and the United States. By the early 1960s, however, many observers had come to regard this attempt as an abysmal failure. American Indians desired a new policy of self-determination that would continue federal assistance to the reservations while allowing tribal members, rather than government bureaucrats, to design and direct programs. Lyndon Johnson presided over the continued erosion of termination and the beginnings of self-determination, which remains the guiding philosophy in federal Indian affairs today. His Great Society programs, especially the War on Poverty, played a crucial role in advancing this process.[2]

Assessing LBJ's influence on the nation's Indian policy is difficult because he offered little leadership on this issue. Stewart Udall, who served as interior secretary for both John Kennedy and Johnson, later noted that both presidents considered Indians "a low priority." In a 1998 interview, Udall could not recall either man "calling me with a new idea" regarding Indian programs or policies. Resources at the Johnson Library verify Udall's recollections—for example, the Oval Office tapes released to date make no mention of Native Americans, and there is no reason to believe that future releases will do so. The volumes of the *Public Papers of the Presidents* that cover the Johnson presidency include messages and statements devoted to Native Americans; however, records in the Johnson Library indicate that although the president signed these statements, he was almost never personally involved in drafting them. LBJ's postpresidential memoir, *The Vantage Point: Perspectives of the Presidency, 1963–1969*, reinforces his lack of involvement in this area; it does not mention Indians even once.[3]

Johnson's apparent neglect of Native American concerns stemmed from five sources—his background, a general perception of Indian affairs as a regional rather than a national issue, political realities, the historical relations between presidents and Indians that resulted from institutional structures within the federal government, and his relationship with Secretary Udall.

Johnson realized his greatest achievements in his efforts to secure civil rights for minority groups in the United States. He developed empathy for African Americans and Mexican Americans as a child and young man in Texas. He witnessed firsthand the sufferings of black Americans under the cruel hand of Jim Crow. As president, he pointed to his year as a teacher "in a small Mexican-American school" as a crucial experience in his life, one that taught him much about poverty and racism. Growing up in Texas, however, the future president knew few, if any, Indians. During the mid-nineteenth century, Anglo Texans drove most Indians who had survived the onslaught of white settlement out of the state. Thus, Johnson never developed a sense of the particular problems that Native Americans faced as a minority group.[4]

After the collapse of armed Indian resistance to Anglo expansion in the late nineteenth century, politicians in Washington, D.C., came to perceive Indian affairs as a regional concern, the province of westerners, rather than as an issue meriting national attention. In this regard, Texas, which had but one federally recognized tribe when Johnson entered Congress in 1937, was not a western state. As a representative and later a senator from Texas, Johnson had little reason to study Indian issues. Moreover, the regional nature of Indian affairs meant that members of Congress did not consider the Indian committees to be plum assignments—Clinton Anderson (D-N.M.) later recalled that Indian Affairs was regarded as one of the "rag-tag" or "lice and nits" committees. Service on such a committee was not a path to power, and Johnson had no reason to pursue such an assignment.[5]

LBJ was an avid political player who kept a close eye on the political implications of all his actions. His concern for minority Americans was in part a recognition of the votes that they brought to him and his party. Johnson recognized that African American votes were important to Democrats, and realized that civil rights legislation would secure black voters. Likewise, he wooed Hispanics throughout his career, working with congressmen such as Henry B. González (D-Tex.) to secure Mexican American support. In the case of American Indians, however, Johnson, and every other politician, accrued little political advantage. Impoverished, largely isolated from the cultural mainstream, and victimized by discriminatory laws—Indians could not vote in Arizona or New Mexico until 1948—Indians occupied the margins of American political life. Because they did not vote in significant numbers, most politicians and government officials ignored them. As Stewart Udall noted, "Everyone . . . tended to put the Indian off into a side pocket." Even Senator Henry Jackson (D-Wash.), who represented a state with a significant Indian population, complained, "Hell, they don't vote." Johnson and other politicians neglected Native Americans simply because they could—there was no penalty paid in ignoring Indians, and no gain in fighting for them.[6]

In his ignorance of Indian affairs, LBJ was no different from many of his predecessors (and successors) in the White House. Twentieth-century presidents paid little heed to Native Americans for the reasons just noted and because Congress, not the White House, is responsible for formulating Indian policy. Congressional control over appropriations and presidential appointments to the office of interior secretary and the commissioner of the Bureau of Indian Affairs (BIA) allowed that branch of government great influence over Native American concerns. As a result, during the 1960s the most powerful players in that policy area were senators from western states, men such as Clinton Anderson and Henry Jackson.

The final reason for Johnson's inattention to Indian affairs resulted from his attitudes toward the Department of the Interior, which housed the BIA. Johnson distanced himself from Interior because he did not want critics to charge that he favored Texas oil interests. LBJ told his interior secretary, "I want you to make all the oil decisions. . . . want oil out of the White House." As a consequence, Udall received little presidential guidance in running his department's operations, including the BIA. In a 1969 interview he noted that Johnson "substantially left it [Indian affairs] in my hands."[7]

The president's decision to retain Kennedy's advisers has drawn criticism from historians, especially in regard to events in Vietnam. Retaining Udall, however, earned Johnson the support of a dedicated conservationist whose vision coincided with his own and that of the First Lady, and Udall's legacy today rests on his role in shaping the nation's environmental policy. Because Udall was far more interested in resource management and the creation of national parks than running the BIA, Johnson's decision to leave Interior matters in his hands, while on the whole sound, meant that Indians received only intermittent attention from the administration.

What Indians needed, however, was a great deal of attention and assistance from the federal government. The 1960 census revealed that the nation's 546,228 American Indians were among the most impoverished, uneducated, and unhealthiest Americans. Median income for male Indians in 1959 was $1,792; for white males, $4,300. Only 1 percent of Indians had four or more years of postsecondary education. Infant mortality rates were twice the national average, and the average age at death was a mere forty-two years.[8]

Native Americans faced dire conditions and an uncertain future in part because of the vagaries of federal Indian policy, which constantly shifted during the nineteenth and twentieth centuries. As World War II drew to a close, many observers, both Democratic and Republican, argued that Indians would remain impoverished, second-class citizens as long as the special relationship between tribes and the federal government endured. They called for a new policy, later known as "termination," that would end federal recognition of Indian tribes as government entities with some sovereign powers. Instead it would make the states, rather than the BIA, responsible for providing most social services to them. Indian lands would lose their trust status, which included federal restrictions on the sale and use of those lands to prevent Indians from losing title. In some instances, jurisdiction in civil and criminal matters would be transferred from the federal and tribal governments to the states.[9]

In 1953 Congress stated its intent to advance termination in House Concurrent Resolution 108. The Alabama-Coushatta of Texas was listed as one of the tribes to be terminated immediately, but LBJ, then a senator from Texas, was absent from the hearing on this issue and neither supported nor opposed the Alabama-Coushatta termination. By the early 1960s many of the terminated tribes such as the Menominees of Wisconsin and the Klamaths of Oregon were in deep financial trouble. The distribution of tribal assets to individual members typically resulted in the loss of those assets and the further impoverishment of the community. Many Indians lost their lands in unwise or unfair dealings once federal trust restrictions were lifted. In addition, state governments objected to the extension of their criminal and civil jurisdiction without additional federal funding.[10]

Despite these problems, termination still had supporters in the U.S. Congress. The most influential terminationist in the early 1960s was Clinton Anderson, chair of the Senate Committee on Interior and Insular Affairs. Anderson and fellow committee members such as Henry Jackson, Frank Church (D-Idaho), and Gordon Allott (R-Colo.) kept the policy alive, which hampered the ability of Kennedy and Johnson administration officials to implement an effective Indian policy.[11]

As a result of a long history of failed policies, of which termination was only the most recent example, American Indians were leery of federal policy initiatives and suspicious of the motives of government personnel. However, they did not want the federal government to abandon them. Assistance was both needed and desired. What they wanted, and would soon demand, was self-determination, the right to manage their own communities with minimal interference from the BIA. The *Declaration of Indian Purpose,* a document produced by a pantribal meeting held in Chicago in 1961, offers a useful definition of Indian self-determination: "The basic principle involves the desire on the part of Indians to participate in developing their own programs with help and guidance as needed and requested."[12]

LBJ's first recorded encounter with the philosophy of Indian self-determination took place in August 1962. After meeting with President Kennedy at the White House, delegates from the Chicago conference met with Vice President Johnson and gave him a copy of the *Declaration.* This meeting lasted a short fifteen minutes, indicating that it was ceremonial rather than substantive. Nor did Johnson's appreciation of the move toward self-determination rise to new levels once he entered the White House. In more than five years as president, he met with Indian leaders only once, in a meeting that had been scheduled when Kennedy was still in office. On 20 January 1964, some two hundred officials from the National Congress of American Indians (NCAI), the leading pantribal organization, assembled in the East Room of the White House to meet with the president. To prepare Johnson for the meeting, Stewart Udall provided a "Fact Sheet on Indian Poverty." LBJ also received a statement on Indian housing from Marie McGuire, the commissioner of the Public Housing Administration.[13]

At the meeting Johnson offered an unimpressive performance that reflected the low priority his White House placed on Native American issues. He arrived late, and after acknowledging NCAI president Walter Wetzel, he launched into words of praise for members of Congress who were present. He then cited some statistics regarding poverty and housing (some of which he got wrong) gleaned from the briefing sheets. He made only one significant remark in his presentation, a pledge to "a continued effort to eradicate poverty and to provide new opportunity for the first citizens of America," a reference to his War on Poverty initiative, at that time in the planning stages. The remainder of the speech had almost nothing to do with Indian affairs. Johnson talked about the nation's gold supply, the voting record of Wright Patman (D-Tex.), and cutting waste from the government's budget. Although he concluded with the promise of future meetings "here again in the East Room," he never again met with any Indian leaders or representatives, never visited a reservation, and never made any unscripted remarks about American Indians for the remainder of his presidency.[14]

Despite the absence of the president in Indian affairs, the Johnson administration made some contributions to the advancement of Indian self-determination, improving upon the weak record of the Kennedy White House and setting the stage for several promising developments during the Nixon and Ford years. Interestingly, the BIA, the executive branch agency responsible for implementing Indian policy, did not create or operate the programs that best met the call for self-determination. Rather, it was Great Society programs, especially the War on Poverty, that brought new hope and energy to the reservations.

Numerous factors led to this surprising result, including the achievements and failures of the Kennedy administration in Indian policy, the actions of Congress, and the persistence of the termination policy during the early 1960s. Key to understanding these events is the role of Stewart Udall, Kennedy and Johnson's point man in Indian affairs.

As a member of the Arizona congressional delegation from 1955 to 1961, Udall boasted that he had "more Indian land and different Indian tribes than any other member of Congress." During the 1960 press conference at which Kennedy announced Udall as his choice for interior secretary, the nominee pointed to this experience and announced, "I have such a deep interest in Indian affairs that it might be said that I will be my own Indian commissioner." In truth, he would be overwhelmed by his responsibilities as interior secretary. He later recalled, "I had a big department, 16 agencies, 55,000 employees." He quickly earned a reputation as a poor administrator—as one interior official later complained, "he just played it by ear." The secretary focused his attention on a few significant issues—in his case the environment—and left other concerns, including Indian affairs, to subordinates. Without any pressure from the Johnson White House, Udall often let Indian issues languish, occasionally giving them intense consideration and then neglecting them for lengthy periods.[15]

At a congressional committee hearing in 1967, Udall described himself as a supporter of "gradual termination." He was committed to ending the federal-tribal relationships, but slowly, thereby allowing American Indian communities to prepare for their entrance into mainstream society. His stance would please neither those senators who called for immediate termination nor those American Indians who condemned the policy as a threat to their way of life.[16]

Udall's "gradual termination" influenced Indian affairs throughout the 1960s. While in office, Udall followed the recommendations of a 1961 task force that he authorized to study the nation's Indian policy. At meetings with tribal leaders, task force members received numerous complaints about the effects of the current policy. In their final report, they noted that termination made Indians suspicious of the intent of federal policymakers. Pointing to these concerns, task force members did not include termination as a major objective of federal Indian affairs. However, the refusal to cite termination as an objective did not constitute a wholesale rejection of that policy. The task force concluded only that federal services should be withdrawn from those Indians who evidenced sufficient economic and social skills.[17]

The task force's implicit acceptance of termination reflected Udall's gradualism, but there was also a critical political component. Task force members realized that any administration initiatives would require congressional approval. Philleo Nash, a task force member who later became Udall's first commissioner of Indian affairs, recalled, "You . . . could not fly in the face of congressional opinion." The opinion that Nash referred to was that of the terminationists who dominated the Senate Interior committee. Throughout the decade, Clinton Anderson and his colleagues inhibited the ability of administration officials to craft a policy that would garner support from American Indians.[18]

Although the task force called for increased Indian participation in policy formulation and program operations, it offered no organizational or administrative changes within the BIA to facilitate such participation. Once again the task force had followed Udall's lead. At a February 1961 meeting, the interior secretary had urged members to consult with Indian leaders. However, he made it clear that he would not let those leaders dictate policy. Udall, who regarded Indians as parochial, sought consultation and concurrence rather than their full participation in the policy process. Tribal officials perceived this position as opposition to self-determination, and it weakened the administration's efforts to build support within Indian communities. As a result, Johnson administration officials never received the unqualified backing of Indian leaders or their communities that desired self-determination.[19]

The initiatives that the task force recommended, and that Udall implemented, focused on the improvement of the physical and human resources on the reservations. Developing resources would spur economic growth, reducing Indian dependence on federal assistance. The BIA operated the Industrial Development Program, but it was too small to meet the task force's goals. However, Udall and Nash realized that requests for budget increases or the introduction of innovative legislation would only earn the wrath of congressional terminationists. Thus, they turned to other federal programs designed to assist impoverished Americans. During the Kennedy years, American Indians received funds and assistance from the Public Housing Administration, the Area Redevelopment Administration, and the Public Works Acceleration Act, among others.[20]

The results of these programs were less than encouraging. They brought much-needed funds to Indian communities and resulted in the establishment of some new businesses. Nevertheless, it became apparent that creating vibrant reservation economies represented an extraordinary challenge. Non-Indians made up a majority of the employees of the businesses established on the reservations, and most of these enterprises failed. Moreover, the BIA's education program, which the task force regarded as key to the development of human resources, was devoid of notable reform and remained ineffective. Thus, at the time of Kennedy's death, little had been achieved in the field of Indian affairs.

In November 1963 Lyndon Johnson inherited Kennedy's programs, and his decision to retain Udall as his interior secretary ensured continuity both in policy and in personnel. Yet Johnson's administration would fare better than his predecessor's with regard to Indian affairs. The initiative that most profoundly bettered the lives of American Indians during the late 1960s came directly from the White House itself. Although LBJ's War on Poverty eventually proved to be a political liability for the White House, American Indians came to regard it highly not simply because it provided economic aid but because it promoted self-determination.

Johnson announced his "unconditional war on poverty" in the 1964 State of the Union address, listing American Indians among the groups that would benefit from his program. However, the Economic Opportunity Act of 1964, which detailed the War on Poverty, contained scant reference to Native Americans. Indians were an afterthought in the development of the legislation and the poverty programs. Several cabinet officers attended initial planning sessions, but Udall, whose department represented Native Americans, was not among them. During a House subcommittee hearing on the poverty bill, Representative Peter H. B. Frelinghuysen (R-N.J.) questioned Udall on the apparent neglect of American Indians in the legislation. The interior secretary responded that the president "has said in very flat language that he wants Indians in the forefront of the program. If you think that the Director [of the Office of Economic Opportunity] will ignore the President, you may assume so. I do not." He declared, "You can expect us to be in there fighting and pounding the table" to ensure Indian inclusion in poverty programs.[21]

American Indians nonetheless feared that they might miss out on the benefits of the Great Society. To pressure lawmakers into making certain that Indians participated in the War on Poverty, the Council of Indian Affairs sponsored the American Indian Capital Conference on Poverty in Washington, D.C., in May 1964. Conference organizers invited luminaries such as Senator Hubert Humphrey (D-Minn.), Stewart Udall, and Philleo Nash. Humphrey, who delivered the keynote address, reassured the delegates, declaring that "no other group has been so totally victimized" by the ravages of poverty, and that Indians "must be one of the prime targets" of the president's new program. Jack T. Conway, a member of the President's Task Force on Poverty, outlined the administration's bill and claimed that almost all its features would be available to tribal organizations. Udall reminded delegates of the president's meeting with them the previous January and of LBJ's pledge to battle Indian poverty. In a follow-up interview with the New York Times, Udall noted that Johnson wanted Indians "in the very forefront" of the war on poverty."[22]

The American Indian Capital Conference on Poverty revealed the growing sophistication of Indian activists, who were turning to publicity and political pressure to achieve their goals. This development has received little attention from historians, who have focused on the Red Power activism of the early 1970s. In their efforts to battle termination, Native Americans used lobbying and press coverage to garner attention from lawmakers. That the interior secretary, a leading senator, and the commissioner of Indian affairs attended the conference, and promised to support the Indians in their efforts, highlights the changing nature of Indian political activism of the 1960s. In response to this activism, Johnson administration officials belatedly stressed the issue of Indian poverty, which to that point they had largely neglected.

One speech given at the conference revealed potential problems with the administration's approach to Native American affairs. Mel Thom, president of the National Indian Youth Council, declared, "The policy to push Indians into the mainstream of American life must be reevaluated. . . . That is not what Indians want." Rather, he maintained, "we want to remember that we are Indians. We want to remain Indian." Thom's assertions indicated a fundamental problem, almost a paradox, of federal Indian policy in the 1960s. On the one hand, Native Americans needed significant government assistance. Yet they also wanted greater control over their lives, freedom from the paternalism and economic dependence that had long been the hallmark of government policies. The programs initiated under the Kennedy administration, and the Great Society programs, offered many benefits to Indians, but they also pushed them into the "mainstream of American life," integrating them into the larger economy.[23]

The subtext of Thom's speech identifies another development in the arena of Native American life in the post–World War II era: the rise of new understandings of the positions Indians held in American society. The termination policy had sought to abolish a separate Indian identity. While it did not aim explicitly at the destruction of tribal cultures as earlier federal policies had, termination reduced tribes to little more than voluntary social organizations. American Indians, however, regarded themselves as a distinct group in the United States, not merely one among many ethnic minorities that had retained some traditional customs. They maintained that they had a special relationship with the federal government that accorded them a different status in American life, one that was evidenced by, and protected by, the rights enumerated in hundreds of treaties during the eighteenth and nineteenth centuries.[24]

Administration efforts to promote economic development and offer additional services on the reservations, while desirable, implicitly defined Indians as poor Americans like the people in Appalachia and urban ghettos. Thom and other leaders recognized the dangers in accepting this definition—in the long run, it might undermine the historical "special relationship" between tribes and the United States. Thus, many Indians feared that the Johnson administration policies would eventually constitute termination, albeit of the gradual kind that Udall countenanced. The secretary did little to soothe fears on this point when, at the Capital Conference, he announced that he saw the coming of "the last and triumphant phase in the relationship of the American Indian to American society," a statement that hinted at termination.[25]

Thom's speech raises another interesting issue regarding Johnson, Indians, and the civil rights movement. At the same time the delegates at the Capital Conference were articulating their goals, LBJ was pressing for passage of his civil rights bill. At first glance, it might appear that the civil rights movement dovetailed neatly with American Indian demands. Like African Americans, Indians had suffered impoverishment, racial discrimination, and political marginalization. Native Americans, however, expressed ambivalence toward the civil rights cause. In the early 1960s, most black Americans were calling for the guarantee of their constitutional rights, essentially demanding that society recognize them as individuals rather than as members of a stigmatized minority. American Indians, on the other hand, perceived themselves as members of a group, one whose relationship with the U.S. Constitution was unique. Thus, any alliance with the civil rights movement presented the same pitfall that the Johnson programs did—a redefinition of Indians that might erode their special status in American life.[26]

Udall and other administration officials never fully grasped the importance of these issues. At the Capital Conference the interior secretary discussed "Indian ideas from which all Americans can learn," including conservation. Praise for cultural values, however, did not translate into an appreciation of the social and political relationships that the tribes had negotiated with the dominant society over the centuries. That Udall missed this crucial point is evidenced by his defense of gradual termination. As a result of this failure, Johnson administration officials never earned the trust of Indians, and they crafted few policies that would resonate within Native American communities.[27]

The Office of Economic Opportunity (OEO) was the one significant exception to this general rule. The War on Poverty changed the lives of many American Indians, several of whom remembered it fondly in later years. Russell Means, a Yankton Sioux and a controversial Red Power activist of the 1970s, wrote, "OEO was the best thing ever to hit the Indian reservations." La Donna Harris, a Comanche married to

Senator Fred Harris (D-Okla.), declared in 1986, "I will stand up and defend OEO as long as I live." Means, Harris, and others held OEO in high regard because it provided them with the opportunity to design and manage programs in Indian communities. The Economic Opportunity Act called upon "urban and rural communities to . . . combat poverty through community action programs." The community action programs, typically called CAPs, allowed for the direct participation of community groups in the War on Poverty. Under OEO guidance, local groups including tribal councils formed Community Action Agencies (CAAs) responsible for developing poverty programs that met community needs. American Indians, usually under the auspices of tribal governments, created sixty-three CAAs operating on 129 reservations by mid-1968. Head Start, Neighborhood Youth Corps, legal services, and job-training programs were among the many services that Indians operated because of the efforts of the CAAs.[28]

Only recently have historians begun to investigate the ways in which these Johnson era programs worked on the reservations, and the study of Indian CAAs promises to be an exciting area of inquiry. One scholar has examined the ways in which the CAPs opened new opportunities for women in the Salt River Pima-Maricopa community. Women received employment in the reservation CAA primarily because they possessed clerical skills; over time they assumed more responsibility and became active in tribal governance. Another historian has researched Oklahomans for Indian Opportunity, a pantribal group that promoted economic independence, especially in rural areas. As more of these studies appear, scholars will gain greater insight into the operations and effectiveness of the War on Poverty in Indian communities.[29]

George Castile, an OEO grant reviewer who later became an anthropologist, has argued that "the content and economic impact of CAP programs was almost beside the point." Indeed, many CAPs had little economic effect, in part because sufficient funds were never available. The War on Poverty was chronically underfunded. In 1968 OEO spent some $35 million on programs targeted at Indian reservations, only 8 percent of total federal spending on Native Americans that year. Castile's remark points to the other consequences of Indian participation in the War on Poverty, specifically the promotion of self-determination. Many tribal leaders of the 1970s and 1980s, including Peter MacDonald and Peterson Zah of the Navajo Nation, had OEO backgrounds. Alfonso Ortiz of the San Juan Pueblo later noted that these new leaders "are not intimidated by bureaucratic procedures." Ortiz also indicated another benefit of OEO—it allowed Indians to circumvent existing institutional structures, especially the bureaucrats in the BIA, in their efforts to secure federal assistance. He remarked, "It was not necessary to worry about people who were defensive about keeping their jobs." In addition to providing a welcome alternative to the BIA, OEO also allowed Indians to receive funds without the approval of the Senate Interior committee, which remained committed to termination.[30]

Native American experiences with OEO were not always positive. There were instances of corruption and nepotism on some reservations. In addition, some activists worried that increased federal spending would only make their communities more dependent on federal moneys. If and when those moneys dried up, any benefits that Indians had experienced would soon disappear. Despite such problems, CAPs met the Indian desire for continued federal assistance in the context of increased Indian control over projects that affected their lives. Thus, Johnson's War on Poverty constituted a move toward self-determination. Ironically, federal officials who had planned the War on Poverty never considered the impact their ideas would have on American Indians, and so the shift toward greater self-rule was largely unintentional. Nonetheless, the promotion of Indian involvement in federal programs created a positive atmosphere and a sense of possibility long absent in federal-Indian relations.[31]

The War on Poverty programs were not the only Great Society initiatives available to American Indians. Created in 1965 to replace the Area Redevelopment Administration, the Economic Development Administration (EDA) offered technical assistance and grants to help communities with public works and other programs. The EDA experience revealed many of the problems that the Johnson administration faced as it brought the Great Society to Indian reservations. Officials hoped that developing infrastructure on or near reservations would attract businesses, which would in turn promote economic development in Indian communities. EDA covered up to 50 percent of the cost of some projects, and in distressed communities up to 80 percent. EDA officials quickly determined that they did not have sufficient funds to meet the demands of the many Indian communities expected to apply for assistance. To ensure that the limited funds were spent in areas where they would do the most good, EDA created the Selected Indian Reservation Program (SIRP) in 1967. This program relied on factors including location, manpower availability, and access to resources to determine which reservations would receive grants.[32]

By 1969 EDA had distributed some $53 million in grants and aid to various reservations. However, despite the SIRP, most EDA programs for Indians met with little success. An EDA study found that reservations "lack many of the fundamental necessities for economic development," including skilled workers and access to markets. As such, "it is little wonder that industry has serious misgivings about locating on reservations: it is a high risk venture." The report correctly concluded that "programs on reservations are likely to have a highly fair rate of unsuccessful projects."[33]

Officials in EDA were learning what BIA employees had long known—the problems that American Indians faced were almost overwhelming. However, EDA could not blame the seemingly intractable nature of Indian poverty for its failures. Although committed to efficient use of moneys, the agency funded projects that had no hope of succeeding. A study of seven EDA-funded industrial parks on or near reservations revealed that only one had attracted a business, and it was not faring well. Nor could EDA claim success as an engine of job creation—a 1972 study determined that the agency spent $30,000 for each job created, and most of those paid low wages.[34]

Despite such disappointing outcomes, Udall continued to support OEO and other programs because he realized that they brought needed services to Indian communities. He sought to convince BIA employees to embrace the president's initiatives. At a 1964 BIA conference, Udall spoke of LBJ's "historic commitment with regard to the elimination of poverty," declaring that "the purpose of this conference . . . is to raise our sights to the heights pointed to by the President." At a 1967 congressional hearing, Udall deemed OEO "instrumental" to the government's efforts to improve American Indians' lives.[35]

In addition to the tangible benefits that OEO brought to Indians, Udall hoped that the War on Poverty programs would inspire the BIA, an agency legendary for its bureaucratic inertia, to a higher level of performance. At a 1966 conference he told BIA workers, "I think maybe having OEO in our midst makes us rethink things." Many of the BIA's career bureaucrats, however, were not pleased. George Castile remembered one BIA official dismissing OEO with the comment, "It's been tried, it can't be done." OEO's involvement with Native Americans frustrated even Commissioner Philleo Nash, who believed that its offerings impinged on his bureau's responsibilities.[36]

Nash's unhappiness with the Great Society's expansion onto the reservations was not the only issue that separated him and Udall. The interior secretary had never been enthusiastic about Nash. He had hoped to appoint an American Indian as commissioner but had been unable to find one willing to take the position. Udall reluctantly turned to Nash, a member of the 1961 task force. A trained anthropologist who had worked in the Truman White House, Nash had some familiarity with Indian affairs.[37]

Udall was disappointed with his commissioner's failure to develop strong working relations with members of Congress, an essential component of the job. He later complained that Nash "was almost persona non grata to those people." He also blamed Nash for the BIA's failure to formulate any significant legislation to advance the administration's Indian policy. Tensions between the two men reached such a pitch that they hampered the performance of the BIA, and by 1964 Udall decided to seek a new commissioner. Nash, however, resisted, and it would be two years before he tendered his resignation.[38]

LBJ was well aware of the disagreements between the two officials. In September 1965, presidential aide Lee White and John Macy, the president's adviser on appointments, prepared a memo for him that detailed the conflict. Two months later, Udall asked Johnson to appoint Nash territorial governor of Samoa. Macy provided the president with a follow-up memo about the situation in December. However, LBJ loathed firing employees, so as long as Nash refused to resign, Udall did not have the president's support in forcing him from office.[39]

Johnson's unwillingness to back Udall on this point weakened the performance of the BIA. Nash complained in 1965 that the bureau "has been most unpleasant for the past ten months." He later acknowledged that his dispute with the interior secretary led his employees to "draw into their shells." At a time when the BIA needed to focus on Native American concerns, it was rendered ineffective by a bitter internal dispute and by LBJ's unwillingness to intervene directly. Perhaps the worst consequence of the Udall-Nash split involved educational funding. Interior Department officials were stunned when they discovered that BIA schools did not qualify for federal assistance under the provisions of the Elementary and Secondary Education Act (ESEA) of 1965. They had simply assumed the act applied to Indian education, an assumption that reveals the disarray that plagued the bureau at that time. Although a 1966 amendment allowed BIA schools to receive ESEA funds, the loss of funding for an entire year was inexcusable.[40]

In March 1966, Nash abandoned his long fight. He submitted his resignation to LBJ, who accepted it and sent it to John Macy with a note reading, "I've approved this—signed it, but I don't want to make any announcements myself. Let them make them over there." In a 1977 oral history interview Nash assessed Johnson's performance in Indian affairs. He noted, "As far as I was concerned Johnson was very remote and I did not have the opportunity to talk to him personally about Indian affairs." In regard to his conflict with Udall, Nash complained that LBJ "declined to intervene." Although Nash was some-what bitter about the treatment he had received, his assessment was generally correct. Johnson left Indian affairs in Udall's hands, and he refused to become involved directly in any way that might have undermined Udall's authority.[41]

A few days after accepting Nash's resignation, Johnson approved Udall's choice of Robert L. Bennett, a member of the Oneida tribe and a longtime BIA employee, to serve as his new commissioner. Bennett was more than capable of filling the position. Udall also realized that by appointing Bennett, who would become the first American Indian in nearly a century to hold the office, he had effectively muted any protests over Nash's departure.[42]

The terminationists on the Senate Interior committee used Bennett's nomination as an opportunity to register their disappointment with the administration's Indian policy. They took the unusual step of filing a written report on the Bennett nomination, declaring, "That Indians remain at the bottom of the economic ladder, have the highest rate of unemployment, live in the poorest housing, and suffer chronic poverty is a clear indictment of past programs and policies pursued by the Bureau." The "past policies" that the committee condemned were clearly intended to include the administration's conduct of Indian affairs. The terminationists asked Bennett to respond to their concerns in written form within ninety days. Their request revealed the persistence of termination within the most important congressional committee relating to Indian affairs. Although Congress had not passed any legislation terminating a tribe since 1962, the threat still hung over Indian communities, and Native Americans continued to regard federal officials with a high degree of suspicion.[43]

Before Bennett's response came due, the Senate approved his appointment. President Johnson led the swearing-in ceremony. As was the case with the 1964 East Room meeting with NCAI leaders, his remarks evidenced a lack of familiarity with Indian affairs. He opened with some general remarks about Bennett and then took the opportunity to "deviate just a moment" to discuss the budget and his efforts to control spending. In his conclusion, he suggested that if the new commissioner met any resistance in his job, he should "find some of those tomahawks that are still around the Smithsonian," the sort of stereotyping that made many Indians cringe.[44]

Some three months later, Bennett sent his response to the Senate committee. In it, he skillfully moved the blame for failures away from the BIA and onto the terminationists. He claimed that including the BIA in the process of terminating tribes meant that the bureau "ceases to be an advisor or partner and becomes an adversary" to Indian communities. This circumstance was "damaging to the kind of relationship in which the Bureau can be of maximum service." Bennett deflected the criticisms of the committee diplomatically, presenting his arguments in such a fashion as to not raise the ire of Anderson, Jackson, and other terminationists. The letter reflected Bennett's talents as he artfully defended his position while maintaining positive relations with the committee members and boded well for his future as commissioner.[45]

Despite his skills and a desire to work closely with tribal officials, Bennett was never able to take a full leadership role during his years in office. His ability to shape the conduct of the nation's Indian policy was limited because Secretary Udall took charge of Indian affairs in 1966. The secretary's dissatisfaction with Philleo Nash's performance had motivated him to take a more active role in Indian affairs. LBJ was aware of Udall's desire. In his September 1965 memo to LBJ, John Macy had noted, "Udall is anxious to establish himself as an important personality in Indian affairs."[46]

Udall's interest in Indian policy was tempered by the realization of the difficulties at hand. To that end, he promoted the eventual transfer of Indian welfare services to another cabinet department, Health, Education, and Welfare (HEW). However, he wanted Interior to retain control over Indian lands. In 1965 Udall proposed to Johnson that the BIA's education division be moved to HEW, and that Interior take charge of that department's water and air pollution programs. Ridding the Interior Department of Indian education programs would have been a relief, because the BIA's Education Branch was in a shambles. Hildegard Thompson, branch director since 1952, regarded education as preparation for assimilation into the mainstream society and paid little attention to Indians' calls for the inclusion of their cultural values in the curriculum. Udall later remembered her as "this nice old lady" who did not seek significant change. Because HEW officials were cool to the idea, the transfer did not take place, but administration officials would resurrect the proposal in coming years.[47]

The interior secretary sought to energize the BIA with a bold stroke. At the April 1966 BIA Area Directors' conference he announced a major new legislative effort, "the most important piece of Indian legislation ever written." While he offered few concrete proposals, Udall suggested that the legislation allow Indians to mortgage property in order to raise development capital. This casual remark ensured American Indian opposition to the effort. Any mortgage program, no matter how well intended, raised the possibility of Indians' losing land, a risk no community or leader would assume.[48]

The process of drafting a bill further alienated Native Americans. Following a promise made by Udall to consult with Indians, Bennett called for a series of regional meetings to discuss the proposed legislation. Indian leaders responded enthusiastically but soon were troubled by rumors that BIA officials already had begun drafting a bill. Bennett insisted that no such draft existed, but NCAI officials surreptitiously obtained a copy and distributed it at the first regional meeting. Bennett looked foolish, and Indian leaders became more determined in their opposition to legislation they already regarded as fundamentally flawed. As Vine Deloria Jr. of the NCAI later recalled, they decided to "beat it to death."[49]

American Indians voiced their opposition to the bill, now called the Indian Resources Development Act (IRDA), in a letter sent to President Johnson in February 1967. While praising LBJ for taking an interest in Indian affairs, they condemned the IRDA in its present form as a violation of long-standing treaty obligations. The focus of their anger was Udall's mortgage provision, which Indian leaders claimed would create economic pressures that would ultimately erode Indian economies and societies. Rather than completely dismiss the bill and risk angering Johnson, however, Indian leaders asked the president for time to study the positive aspects of the legislation and make a thorough response to its many provisions.[50]

While opposition to the IRDA mounted, Udall faced another crisis in Indian affairs. In August 1966, presidential aide Joseph Califano called for the creation of a White House task force to study Indian issues. Califano's reasons for convening this task force remain unclear. His timing was questionable, given that the interior secretary had just called for a major legislative effort. For his part, Udall exhibited understandable resistance to the proposal, as the task force constituted outside involvement in his department's activities. Notes from a planning session reveal that the interior secretary "initially opposed" the idea of the task force, although he later "seemed to agree that it would be a good idea."[51]

The 1966 President's Task Force on American Indians submitted its final report in December. Among its recommendations, the task force suggested transferring the BIA to the Department of Health, Education, and Welfare on the grounds that HEW could best provide the human services Indians required. Califano informed LBJ that Udall opposed the proposal, but he recommended that Johnson "tentatively" approve it should there be no congressional opposition. LBJ responded with a "See me" scrawled at the bottom of Califano's memorandum.[52]

The transfer proposal became public knowledge in late January 1967, when the *New York Times* ran a story about it. Many Indian leaders expressed outrage—once again, important policy issues were being discussed without their consultation. HEW Secretary John Gardner informed Johnson that he would defend the transfer recommendation at a meeting of Indian leaders to be held in February and asked the president to prepare a statement regarding it. After Califano convinced Gardner that a presidential message was unnecessary, the HEW secretary requested permission "to indicate that the proposed transfer is under discussion within the Administration." Johnson balked, noting to Califano, "See me about message—I have doubts about it." Johnson was right to dissociate himself from the transfer. Gardner's speech did not impress the Indians at the February meeting, who raised numerous objections. Members of Congress, including Wayne Aspinall (D-Colo.), chairman of the House Interior Committee, also stated their opposition, thus ensuring that the issue died.[53]

While the controversy over the transfer proposal continued, Udall pushed ahead with the IRDA. He believed that the legislation would receive considerable backing within Congress. Interior Department officials concurred, preparing a checklist that showed most members of the two Interior committees were favorably disposed to the bill. However, because of potential Indian opposition, Udall recommended that the Interior Department rather than the White House send the legislation to Congress. Johnson agreed, and the IRDA was sent to Congress on Udall's authorization.[54]

The interior secretary had assessed incorrectly congressional support for the IRDA. Not a single member of Congress agreed to sponsor the bill. The substantial cost—it called for a $500 million loan fund—elicited a cool response. In addition, many members of Congress objected to the numerous provisions that required secretarial approval before Indians could act. The lack of congressional support, combined with vocal Indian opposition, precluded any White House effort to secure the bill's passage. Although Udall declared that the legislation remained a priority, for all practical purposes the IRDA was dead.[55]

The failure of the IRDA may have prompted Joseph Califano's decision to create another task force on Indian affairs. He directed task force members, including Udall, to make specific recommendations for the administration's 1968 legislative program. He also reminded the study group to be mindful of budget constraints when drafting recommendations. As a result, the final report of the Interagency 1967 Task Force on Indians was not innovative, consisting of mundane calls for increased spending in already existing programs. To Udall's satisfaction, the task force rejected transferring the BIA to any other cabinet department on the rather obvious grounds that congressional opposition to such a move would be strident.[56]

The task force advanced one idea that administration officials seized upon—that of a special presidential message about American Indians. The proposal was by no means new. Udall had promoted the idea for years, and the 1966 task force had made a similar recommendation. In early 1967, Interior Department officials had worked on a message, which was to be delivered in conjunction with a Department of Labor pronouncement regarding migrant workers. However, it was not until the release of the 1967 task force report that administration efforts to draft a statement began in earnest.[57]

Drafting the message proved difficult because there was little new in the way of ideas or initiatives for the president to report. White House aide Ervin Duggan complained that, lacking any clear program or policy announcement, the resulting message was unimpressive. Nonetheless, by late February 1968 Lee White circulated a draft message among several agencies and departments, including the BIA, HEW, and OEO. Interior Department officials also ran it by key members of Congress, and by early March the message was complete.[58]

Udall and Bennett wanted the message issued on 5 or 6 March, to coincide with an NCAI meeting being held that week in Washington, D.C. The White House followed their suggestion, and it appeared on 6 March. However, administration officials had an additional motive for issuing the statement on that date. Joseph Califano had informed LBJ that Senator Robert Kennedy (D-N.Y.) was scheduled to make a speech on Indian education on 8 March. Releasing the presidential message earlier in the week would undercut the senator's speech and draw attention away from Kennedy, a man for whom Johnson's loathing remains legendary.[59]

The final product, entitled "Special Message to the Congress on the Problems of the American Indian: 'The Forgotten American,'" contained few surprises. It detailed the wrenching poverty that Indians faced and challenged Congress to increase funding for several programs. Its only new initiative was the creation of the National Council on Indian Opportunity. Johnson authorized this body, which would include several cabinet secretaries, the vice president, and numerous Indian leaders, to oversee federal Indian programs and to make policy recommendations.[60]

The message included a section entitled "Self-Help and Self-Determination," in which Johnson declared, "Indians must have a voice in making the plans and decisions in programs which are important to their daily life." He noted, "We have seen a new concept of community development—a concept based on self-help—work successfully among Indians." LBJ then argued that "this principle is the key to progress for Indians. . . . if we base our programs upon it, the day will come when the relationship between Indians and the Government will be one of full partnership—not dependency."[61]

This forthright defense of self-determination, and the call for a partnership between the tribes and the federal government, stands as the most significant portion of the message. However, Johnson's failure to repudiate termination as the goal of federal Indian policy undermined his call for self-determination. He came close to doing so, calling for a policy that "ends the old debate about 'termination' of Indian programs and stresses self-determination." American Indians, however, wanted the president to reject termination explicitly, thereby ensuring that members of Congress committed to that policy would face determined opposition from within the executive branch.[62]

Some administration officials supported an unequivocal denunciation of termination. The 1966 task force had called for such a statement, but a White House review of that report concluded that disavowing termination might spark congressional opposition that could harm other aspects of the administration's Indian programs. Although by the late 1960s termination had few congressional advocates, those who did remain committed to the policy, such as Henry Jackson and Clinton Anderson, exercised a great deal of authority over Indian affairs. They were powerful enough to make the White House unwilling to take the important step of reassuring American Indians that they would never again face the threat of termination.[63]

Despite this weakness, the message received praise from Indian leaders and members of Congress. Senator Sam Ervin (D-N.C.) offered a positive statement on the very day of its release. Ervin had good reason to draw attention to the president's message because Johnson had included remarks about an Indian civil rights bill then before Congress that Ervin had sponsored. Ervin saw the message as a means of gaining more support for his legislation, which he had submitted in various forms several times since 1964.[64]

The Ervin bill was not an administration initiative. While there was little doubt that American Indians were frequent victims of discrimination, Ervin focused on another issue. His legislation, which contained several provisions, extended the protections of the Bill of

Rights to Indians in their relations with tribal governments, which many Indians regarded as an attack on Indian sovereignty. However, because the bill also contained a provision requiring tribal consent before states could assume civil or criminal jurisdiction on their lands, some Indian leaders supported the Ervin bill.[65]

Johnson's approval put the administration behind the legislation, but Interior Department officials quickly realized that Ervin hoped to use the Indian civil rights legislation to scuttle an administration civil rights initiative. Fair housing legislation, which banned racial discrimination in the rental or sale of most housing, raised the ire of southerners such as Ervin. Seeing the opportunity to sink the measure, Ervin offered his legislation as an amendment to the fair housing bill then before the Senate. When the Senate approved the amendment, House Interior Committee chair Wayne Aspinall announced that he would hold hearings on the measure. Aspinall opposed the fair housing bill and was sure to tie the measure up in committee. As one Interior official noted, "Ervin hoped that tacking the Indian caboose onto the Civil Rights train would wreck the railroad." Ervin's ploy almost succeeded. Aspinall did hold hearings, but the bill was ultimately sent to the House Judiciary Committee, which supported it. President Johnson signed the bill, the Civil Rights Act of 1968, into law on 11 April 1968. The passage of this law marked the last significant act of Johnson's administration regarding Indian affairs.[66]

In the years after Johnson left office, federal Indian policy underwent profound changes. In July 1970, Richard Nixon released his own Indian message, one in which he called upon Congress to "expressly renounce, repudiate, and repeal the termination policy." Two years later, Congress approved the Indian Education Act, which expanded the Native American role in educational issues. In 1975, Gerald Ford signed into law the Indian Self-Determination and Education Assistance Act, which allowed tribes to provide many federal services to their members. During the 1970s, Congress also began the process of restoring the terminated tribes, reestablishing government-to-government relations that it had abolished in the 1950s and 1960s.[67]

The Nixon and Ford administrations were able to effect such dramatic shifts in Indian policy because of three changes involving Native American issues. First, by 1970 congressional support for termination had vanished. Clinton Anderson was in ill health, and Henry Jackson underwent a conversion, one brought on by his desire to sit in the Oval Office. To further his presidential ambitions, Jackson abandoned termination and became a champion of self-determination. Second, the rise of the Red Power movement brought considerable attention to Indian issues through dramatic protests such as the seizure of Alcatraz Island in 1969. Third, the public's perceptions of Native Americans became far more positive. Dee Brown's best-selling *Bury My Heart at Wounded Knee: An American Indian History of the American West*, published in 1970, portrayed Indians as victims of white expansionism rather than as the stereotypical savages that most non-Indians were familiar with from Hollywood movies and television westerns. The growth of the environmental movement, which often used Indians as symbols of harmony and balance with nature, further engendered public sympathy for Native Americans. As a result of these three factors, the Nixon administration had, in the words of one official, "an unobstructed policy shot."[68]

Lyndon Johnson, however, had not had Nixon's opportunities in the field of Indian affairs. The Johnson years are best understood as an era during which the commitment to termination collapsed and moved slowly toward a policy based on self-determination. The move toward self-determination during the 1960s was hesitant for two reasons. First, the paternalism that had long burdened federal Indian policy remained a reality. Udall and his Indian commissioners, Philleo Nash and Robert Bennett, recognized the growth of Indian activism and the need for Indian participation in the policy process. However, they were unable to devise effective mechanisms for bringing Indians into the policy process, in part because Udall was never convinced that Indians were capable of solving their own problems. Second, the persistence of support for the termination policy in Congress slowed the move to self-determination. For the most part, administration officials avoided ambitious legislative initiatives because congressional terminationists would thwart such efforts. As a result, the BIA offered few innovative or farsighted programs during this era. It was no accident that the only major legislation involving American Indians, the Civil Rights Act of 1968, came from outside the Interior department. Nor was it an accident that the most important federal programs involving Indians also came out of agencies and departments other than Interior.

The Office of Economic Opportunity and its War on Poverty efforts were the most important development in Indian affairs during the 1960s. Because they allowed Native Americans to create and operate programs to address their many needs, the Community Action Programs met the Indians' demand for self-determination. In addition to the direct benefits that CAPs brought to the reservations, they provided a new generation of Indian leaders with the knowledge and skills needed to improve the lives of the people in their communities.

As such, the War on Poverty set the stage for some of the successes that Native Americans realized in the years that followed, and the benefits the CAPS brought to the reservations long outlived OEO itself, which met its demise in the 1970s. The Great Society must be regarded as a significant turning point in the history of relations between American Indians and the federal government, one whose legacy still influences the lives of native peoples in the United States today.

President Johnson deserves credit for this achievement. Like his immediate predecessors in the White House, Johnson had little direct influence on the nation's Indian policy. Yet despite his lack of personal involvement, the thirty-sixth president left his mark on the nation's Indian affairs. He committed himself to a liberal agenda that created new opportunities for American Indians and inspired them in their struggle against the constraints and obstacles that had long burdened their lives. Lyndon Johnson brought the dream of Indian self-determination closer to reality.

Notes

1. Three studies that have examined the Johnson Indian policy are George Pierre Castile, *To Show Heart: Native American Self-Determination and Federal Indian Policy, 1961–1975* (Tucson: University of Arizona Press, 1998); Thomas Clarkin, *Federal Indian Policy in the Kennedy and Johnson Administrations, 1961–1969* (Albuquerque: University of New Mexico Press, 2001); and Christopher Riggs, "Indians, Liberalism, and Lyndon Johnson's Great Society, 1963–1969" (Ph.D. diss., University of Colorado, 1997).

2. The standard history of federal Indian policy is Francis Paul Prucha, *The Great Father: The United States Government and the American Indians* (Lincoln: University of Nebraska Press, 1984).

3. Udall quotations from Transcript, Stewart Udall Interview, 3 April 1998, by Thomas Clarkin, author's collection; Lyndon Baines Johnson, *The Vantage Point: Perspectives on the Presidency, 1963–1969* (New York: Holt, Rinehart and Winston, 1971).

4. *Public Papers of the Presidents of the United States: Lyndon B. Johnson, Containing the Public Messages, Speeches, and Statements of the President, 1965* (Washington, D.C.: Government Printing Office, 1966), 1: 286.

5. Clinton P. Anderson, with Milton Viorst, *Outsider in the Senate: Senator Clinton Anderson's Memoirs* (New York: World, 1970), 36.

6. Julie Leininger Pycior, *LBJ and Mexican Americans: The Paradox of Power* (Austin: University of Texas Press, 1997). For a discussion of Native American voting patterns, see Daniel McCool, "Indian Voting," in *American Indian Policy in the Twentieth Century*, ed. Vine Deloria Jr. (Norman: University of Oklahoma Press, 1985), 105–133; Udall quotation from Transcript, Stewart Udall Oral History, by Joe B. Frantz, 29 July 1969, interview no. 3, 5, Lyndon Baines Johnson Presidential Library (hereafter cited as LBJL); for

Jackson quotation, see Peter J. Ognibene, *Scoop: The Life and Politics of Henry M. Jackson* (New York: Stein and Day, 1975), 134.

7. First quotation from Transcript, Stewart Udall Oral History, by Joe B. Frantz, 18 April 1969, Interview no. 1, 20–21, 21–22, LBJL; second quotation from Transcript, Udall Oral History, Interview no. 3, 12, LBJL.

8. Statistical information from U.S. Bureau of the Census, *U.S. Census of Population: 1960: Subject Reports, Nonwhite Population by Race. Final Report PC(2)–1C* (Washington, D.C.: Government Printing Office, 1963), 2, 12, 104; U.S. Bureau of the Census, *U.S. Census of Population: 1960: General and Social Economic Characteristics, United States Summary. Final Report PC(1)–1C* (Washington, D.C.: Government Printing Office, 1963), xxxix–xl; William A. Brophy and Sophie D. Aberle, comps., *The Indian: America's Unfinished Business* (Norman: University of Oklahoma Press, 1966), 163.

9. For the termination policy, see Larry W. Burt, *Tribalism in Crisis: Federal Indian Policy, 1953–1961* (Albuquerque: University of New Mexico Press, 1982); and Donald Fixico, *Termination and Relocation: Federal Indian Policy, 1945–1960* (Albuquerque: University of New Mexico Press, 1986).

10. *United States Statutes at Large*, 67: B132; House, Subcommittee on Indian Affairs, *Termination of Federal Supervision of the Property of the Alabama and Coushatta Tribe of Indians of Texas*, 82d Cong., 2d sess., 16 July 1954, microfiche.

11. For insight into the position of Allott, Anderson, and Church, see Senate, Committee on Interior and Insular Affairs, *The Nomination of Philleo Nash to Be Commissioner of Indian Affairs: Hearings before the Committee on Interior and Insular Affairs*, 87th Cong., 1st sess., 14 and 17 August 1961.

12. American Indian Chicago Conference, *Declaration of Indian Purpose* (Chicago: American Indian Chicago Conference, 1961), 6.

13. *Public Papers of the Presidents of the United States: John F. Kennedy: Containing the Public Messages, Speeches, and Statements of the President*, 4 vols. (Washington, D.C.: Government Printing Office, 1962–1964), 1: 619–620; Daily Diary, 15 August 1962, "Aug., 1962," Box 2, Pre-Presidential Daily Diary, LBJL; Memorandum, Secretary of the Interior to the President, 20 January 1964, "11/22/63–2/29/64," EX IN, Box 1, White House Central Files (hereafter WCHF), Subject Files, LBJL; "Background of Indian Program: Statement of Marie C. McGuire, Commissioner of Public Housing Administration," "11/22/63–2/29/64," EX IN, Box 1, WHCF, Subject Files, LBJL.

14. *Public Papers of the Presidents of the United States: Lyndon B. Johnson, 1963–1964* (Washington, D.C.: Government Printing Office, 1965), 1: 149–152.

15. First and third quotations from Transcript, Stewart Udall Interview, author's collection; second quotation from *New York Times*, 8 December 1960, 3; fourth quotation from Transcript, John A. Carver Oral History, 20 September 1968, by John Stewart, Interview no. 2, 32, John Fitzgerald Kennedy Library, Boston, Mass. (hereafter JFKL).

16. Udall quotation from House, Committee on Interior and Insular Affairs, *Indian Resources Development Act of 1967: Hearings before the Subcommittee on Indian Affairs of the Committee on Interior and Insular Affairs*, 90th Cong., 1st sess., 13 and 14 July 1967, 48–49.

17. "Report to the Secretary of the Interior by the Task Force on Indian

Affairs," 10 July 1961, 5, 6. A copy can be found in "In/S Gen," IN, Box 4, White House Central Files, Subject Files, LBJL.

18. Transcript, Philleo Nash Oral History, by William W. Moss, 26 February 1971, Interview no. 3, JFKL.

19. "Task Force on Indian Affairs," 4, 8; "Official Report of the Proceedings before the Department of the Interior in the Matter of Secretary's Meeting on Report of Task Force on Indian Affairs," 9 February 1961, "Bureau of Indian Affairs (Task Force on Indian Affairs)," Box 89, Stewart Udall Papers, Special Collections, University of Arizona (hereafter cited as SUP).

20. "Task Force on Indian Affairs," 9; Castile, *To Show Heart*, 20–21; Clarkin, *Federal Indian Policy*, 67–77.

21. *Public Papers of the Presidents of the United States, Lyndon B. Johnson, 1963–1964*, 1: 114; Clarkin, *Federal Indian Policy*, 111; Congress, House, Committee on Education and Labor, *Economic Opportunity Act of 1964: Hearings before the Subcommittee on the War on Poverty Program of the Committee on Education and Labor*, pt. 1, 88th Cong., 1st sess., 17–20 March, 7–10, 13, and 14 April 1964, 4–18.

22. "Capitol [*sic*] Conference on Indian Poverty Sets Forth Needs and Aims," *Amerindian* 12 (March–April 1964): 3; George Eagle, "Poverty of American Indians Called Mirror of U.S. Problem," *Washington Post*, 10 May 1964, A12; Donald Janson, "U.S. Asked to Ease Poverty of Tribes," *New York Times*, 10 May 1964, 83; "Udall Sees Hope of Anti-poverty Aid for Indians," *Washington Post*, 11 May 1964, A7; Donald Janson, "Udall Asks for Help for Indian Poor," *New York Times*, 11 May 1964, 17.

23. Thom quotations from "A Statement Made for the Young People," printed in Congress, Senate, Committee on Labor and Public Welfare, *Economic Opportunity Act of 1964: Hearings before the Select Committee on Poverty of the Committee on Labor and Public Welfare*, 88th Cong., 2d sess., 340–341.

24. For shifting definitions of "Indianness" in the 1960s, see Daniel M. Cobb, "The Last Indian War: Indian Community Action in the Johnson Administration's War on Poverty" (M.A. thesis, University of Wyoming, 1998), 30–42.

25. "Udall Sees Hope," A7.

26. For a discussion of some of these issues, see Vine Deloria Jr., *Custer Died for Your Sins: An Indian Manifesto* (New York: Macmillan, 1969), 168–196.

27. "Udall Sees Hope," A7.

28. First quotation from Russell Means and Marvin J. Wolf, *Where White Men Fear to Tread: The Autobiography of Russell Means* (New York: St. Martin's Press, 1995), 137; Harris quoted in Kenneth R. Philp, ed., *Indian Self-Rule: First-Hand Accounts of Indian White Relations from Roosevelt to Reagan* (Salt Lake City: Howe Brothers, 1986), 223; House, Committee on Education and Labor, *Economic Opportunity Act of 1964*, 8–11; Alan L. Sorkin, *American Indians and Federal Aid* (Washington, D.C.: Brookings Institution Press, 1971), 165–166. For examples of specific CAPs that operated on reservations, see Riggs, "Indians, Liberalism," 183–217.

29. Paivi H. Hoikkala, "Mothers and Community Builders: Salt River Pima and Maricopa Women in Community Action," in *Negotiators of Change: Historical Perspectives on Native American Women*, ed. Nancy Shoemaker (New York: Routledge, 1995): 214–230; Daniel M. Cobb, "'Us Indians Under-

stand the Basics': Oklahoma Indians and the Politics of Community Action, 1964–1970," *Western Historical Quarterly* 33 (Spring 2002): 41–66.

30. Castile, *To Show Heart*, 33; Prucha, *Great Father*, 2: 1094–1095; Ortiz quoted in Philp, *Indian Self-Rule*, 221.

31. Robert Burnette, *The Tortured Americans* (Englewood Cliffs, N.J.: Prentice-Hall, 1971), 82; for dependence, see the testimony of Hank Adams in Congress, Senate, Committee on Labor and Public Welfare, *Examination of the War on Poverty: Hearings before the Subcommittee on Employment, Manpower, and Poverty of the Committee on Labor and Public Welfare*, pt. 14, Miscellaneous Appendix, 90th Cong., 1st sess., 4419.

32. Sorkin, *Federal Aid*, 93; Raymond H. Milkman, Christopher Bladen, Beverly Lyford, and Howard L. Walton, *Alleviating Economic Distress: Evaluating a Federal Effort* (Lexington, Mass.: Lexington Books, 1972), 293–294.

33. U.S. Department of Commerce, Economic Development Administration, "Summary of Case Studies: Evaluation of EDA Rural Activities in Fifteen Areas," quoted in Milkman, *Alleviating Economic Distress*, 304–306; for examples of EDA programs, see Boise Cascade Center for Community Development, *Indian Economic Development: An Evaluation of EDA's Selected Indian Reservation Program*, vol. 2, *Indian Reservation Reports* (Washington, D.C.: Department of Commerce, Economic Development Administration, 1972).

34. Milkman, *Alleviating Economic Distress*, 326.

35. Remarks by Secretary Udall at the Opening Session of Indian Affairs Conference of Superintendents, "June 13–16, 1964, Bureau of Indian Affairs, Conference of Superintendents (Santa Fe, New Mex.)," Box 115, SUP; Congress, House, Committee on Education and Labor, *Economic Opportunity Act Amendments of 1967: Hearings before the Committee on Education and Labor*, pt. 2, 90th Cong., 1st sess., 1550–1560.

36. Remarks of Secretary of the Interior Stewart L. Udall at his Bureau of Indian Affairs Conference, Santa Fe, New Mexico, 14 April 1966, "BIA Conferences with Stewart Udall, 1965–66," Box 7, James E. Officer Papers, Arizona Historical Society, Tucson, Arizona (hereafter cited as JOP); Castile, *To Show Heart*, 29.

37. Transcript, Stewart Udall Interview, author's collection; Margaret Connell Szasz, "Philleo Nash," in *The Commissioners of Indian Affairs, 1824–1977*, ed. Robert M. Kvasnicka and Herman J. Viola (Lincoln: University of Nebraska Press, 1979), 311–314; Transcript, Udall Oral History, interview no. 1, 1–3, LBJL.

38. Transcript, Udall Oral History, interview no. 3, 4, LBJL; Transcript, Stewart Udall Oral History, by W. W. Moss, 16 February 1970, 40–41, JFKL.

39. Memorandum, White and Macy to the President, 2 September 1965; Memorandum, Udall to the President, 15 November 1965, "FG 145—Dept. of the Interior," Box 145, WHCF, Confidential Files, LBJL; Memorandum, Macy to the President, 14 December 1965, "FG 145—Dept. of the Interior," Box 145, WHCF, Confidential Files, LBJL; Richard L. Schott and Dagmar S. Hamilton, *People, Positions, and Power: The Political Appointments of Lyndon Johnson* (Chicago: University of Chicago Press, 1983), 168–170.

40. First quotation from Letter, Nash to Burke, 10 December 1965, "Misc. 1965 Indians," Box 181, Philleo Nash Papers, Harry S. Truman Library

(hereafter cited as PNP); second quotation from Transcript, Philleo Nash Oral History, interviewer unidentified, 7 April 1977, 37, "Writings of Philleo Nash—Oral History Interview—Lyndon B. Johnson Library," Box 208, PNP; Congress, House, Committee on Education and Labor, *Elementary and Secondary Education Amendments of 1966: Hearings before the General Subcommittee of the Committee on Education and Labor*, pt. 2, 89th Cong., 2d sess., 990.

41. Johnson quoted in Schott and Hamilton, *People, Positions, and Power*, 169–170; Szasz, "Philleo Nash," 320; Transcript, Nash Oral History, 21, PNP.

42. Richard N. Ellis, "Robert L. Bennett," in *The Commissioners of Indian Affairs*, 325; Transcript, Udall Interview, 3 April 1998, author's collection.

43. Ellis, "Robert L. Bennett," 325; Congress, Senate, Committee on Interior and Insular Affairs, "Executive Report No. 1, To accompany the nomination of Robert LaFollette Bennett, 8 April 1966," 89th Cong., 2d sess.

44. *Public Papers of the Presidents of the United States, Lyndon B. Johnson, Containing the Public Messages, Speeches, and Statements of the President, 1966* (Washington, D.C.: Government Printing Office, 1967), 1: 457–459.

45. Letter, Robert L. Bennett to Henry M. Jackson, 11 July 1966. Copy available in Folder 10, Box 69, Association of American Indian Affairs Archives, Seely G. Mudd Library, Princeton University.

46. Memorandum, White and Macy to the President, 2 September 1965.

47. Castile, *To Show Heart*, 46–47; Margaret Connell Szasz, *Education and the American Indian: The Road to Self-Determination since 1928* (Albuquerque: University of New Mexico Press, 1999), 123–140, 141–142; Transcript, Udall Oral History, Interview no. 2, 41, JFKL.

48. Udall quotation from Transcript, Informal Remarks by Secretary of the Interior Stewart L. Udall at the Bureau of Indian Affairs Conference, Santa Fe, New Mexico, 15 April 1966, at Morning Session on "The World of Work," 15 April 1966, "Vol. II Documentary Supplement (2 of 2)," Box 2, Administrative History: Dept. of the Interior, LBJL. On the IRDA, see Castile, *To Show Heart*, 50–52, 57; Clarkin, *Federal Indian Policy*, 202–209, 217–225; and Christopher K. Riggs, "American Indians, Economic Development, and Self-Determination in the 1960s," *Pacific Historical Review* 69 (August 2000): 431–463.

49. Transcript, Informal Remarks, 15 April 1966; Vine Deloria Jr., *Behind the Trail of Broken Treaties: An Indian Declaration of Independence* (Austin: University of Texas Press, 1974), 32; Riggs, "American Indians," 450; quotation from Transcript, Vine Deloria Jr., Oral History Interview, by Christopher Riggs, 17 July 1999. I thank Dr. Riggs for providing me with a copy of this interview.

50. Letter, Indian Conference on Policy and Legislation to President Johnson, 2 February 1967, attached to letter, T. W. Taylor to Joseph Califano Jr., 15 February 1967, "In 12-21-66–," GEN IN, Box 2, WHCF, LBJL. There is no evidence indicating that President Johnson ever saw this letter.

51. Notes, Meetings on Indians, 25 August 1966, "American Indians," Box 329, Office Files of James C. Gaither, LBJL.

52. "A Free Choice Program for American Indians: Report of the President's Task Force on American Indians," 92, December 1966, Box 3, Task

Force Reports, LBJL; Castile, *To Show Heart*, 52–56; Memorandum, Joseph Califano to President, 5 January 1967, "10/5/64–2/29/68," EX IN, Box 1, WHCF, LBJL.

53. William W. Blair, "Panel Asks Shift of Indian Bureau," *New York Times*, 28 January 1967, 14. Blair learned of the proposal during congressional hearings on Indian affairs held that week; Memorandum, John Gardner to the President, 11 February 1967, attached to Memorandum, Joseph Califano to the President, 13 February 1967, "10/5/64–2/29/68," EX IN, Box 1, WHCF, LBJL.

54. Committee Check List: Omnibus Bill, attached to Memorandum, Udall to Califano, 12 May 1967, "LE/IN Ex," EX LE, Box 74, WHCF, LBJL; Memorandum, Califano to the President, 13 May 1967, "LE/IN Ex," EX LE, Box 74, WHCF, LBJL.

55. Riggs, "American Indians," 454–457.

56. Transcript, James Officer Interview, by George Castile, 18 April 1990, 11–12, "Correspondence and Interview w/Officer—George P. Castile," Box 15, Folder 170, JOP; Memorandum, Joseph Califano to Lee C. White, 19 August 1967, reprinted in "Interagency 1967 Task Force on Indians," Box 20, Task Force, LBJL; Memorandum, Lee C. White to Joseph Califano, 23 October 1967, reprinted in "Interagency 1967 Task Force on Indians."

57. Transcript, Udall Oral History, no. 3, 13, LBJL; "A Free Choice Program for American Indians," 102; Letter, Charles F. Luce to Joseph Califano, 26 January 1967, "Indians/Mig. Workers," Box 67, Office Files of Joseph Califano, LBJL.

58. Memorandum, Ervin Duggan to Matthew Nimitz, "EX Sp 2–3/1968/ In Indian Message Backup Material V," EX SP, Box 122, WHCF, LBJL; Memorandum, Lee C. White to Joseph Califano, 26 February 1968, "EX Sp 2–3/1968/ In Indian Message Backup Material IV," EX SP, Box 122, WHCF, LBJL; Memorandum, Joseph Califano to the President, 2 March 1968, "EX Sp 2–3/ 1968/In Indian Message Backup Material II," EX SP, Box 122, WHCF, LBJL; Memorandum, Stewart Udall to Joseph Califano, 2 March 1968, "EX Sp 2–3/ 1968/In Indian Message," EX SP, Box 122, WHCF, LBJL.

59. Memorandum, Joseph Califano to the President, 5 March 1968, "EX Sp 2–3/1968/In Indian Message," EX SP, Box 122, WHCF, LBJL.

60. *Public Papers of the Presidents of the United States: Lyndon B. Johnson, Containing the Public Messages, Speeches, and Statements of the President, 1968–1969* (Washington, D.C.: Government Printing Office, 1970), 1: 335–344.

61. Ibid., 337.

62. Ibid., 336.

63. "A Free Choice Program for American Indians," 3–4; Draft Memorandum, to Joseph Califano, n.d., "Pricing Files: Indians 1 of 2," Box 10, Office Files of John E. Ross and Stanford G. Robson, LBJL; Memorandum, White to Califano, 23 October 1967.

64. Press Release, "Ervin Praises Presidential Call for Indian Rights Bill," EX Sp 2–3/1968/In Indian Message," EX SP, Box 122, WHCF, LBJL.

65. Castile, *To Show Heart*, 65–66. On the issue of American Indians and constitutional rights, see John R. Wunder, *"Retained By the People": A History of American Indians and the Bill of Rights* (New York: Oxford University Press, 1994).

66. Vine Deloria Jr. and Clifford M. Lytle, *The Nations Within: The Past and Future of American Indian Sovereignty* (New York: Pantheon Books, 1994), 210. This account contains some factual errors but is correct in its conclusions. Memorandum, JEO to SLU, 27 March 1968, "S.L.U. and Staff (James Officer)," Box 138, SUP; Clarkin, *Federal Indian Policy*, 267–268; *Public Papers of the Presidents of the United States, Lyndon B. Johnson, 1968*, 1: 509–510.

67. *Public Papers of the Presidents of the United States: Richard M. Nixon, 1970* (Washington, D.C.: Government Printing Office, 1971), 1: 564–576. For Nixon's Indian policy, see Castile, *To Show Heart*, 73–160; and Dean J. Kotlowski, *Nixon's Civil Rights: Politics, Principle, and Policy* (Cambridge, Mass.: Harvard University Press, 2001), 188–221.

68. Clarkin, *Federal Indian Policy*, 271; Castile, *To Show Heart*, 105; Kotlowski, *Nixon's Civil Rights*, 188–189; quotation from Leonard Garment, *Crazy Rhythm: My Journey from Brooklyn, Jazz, and Wall Street to Nixon's White House, Watergate, and Beyond . . .* (New York: Times Books, 1997), 225.

About the Contributors

David L. Anderson is dean of the College of Undergraduate Programs at California State University, Monterey Bay, and the 2004 president of the Society for Historians of American Foreign Relations. His books include *Imperialism and Idealism* (Indiana University Press, 1985), *Trapped by Success* (Columbia University Press, 1991), *Shadow on the White House* (University Press of Kansas, 1993), *The Human Tradition in the Vietnam Era* (Scholarly Resources, 2000), and *The Columbia Guide to the Vietnam War* (Columbia University Press, 2002). *Trapped by Success* received the Robert H. Ferrell Book Prize from SHAFR, and *The Columbia Guide to the Vietnam War* was recognized as one of the "Best of the Best from University Presses" by the American Library Association and the Association of American University Presses. He has also written approximately seventy-five articles and reviews and made some fifty conference presentations.

Julia Kirk Blackwelder is associate dean of the College of Liberal Arts and a professor of history at Texas A&M University. Dr. Blackwelder is a social and urban historian of the United States in the twentieth century whose research focuses on gender, race, and the labor force. Among her publications are *Styling Jim Crow: African American Beauty Training during Segregation* (Texas A&M University Press, 2003), *Women of the Depression: Caste and Culture in San Antonio, 1929–1939* (Texas A&M University Press, 1984), and *Now Hiring: The Feminization of Work in the United States, 1900–1995* (Texas A&M University Press, 1997). She has also published essays on fundamentalism and the civil rights movement, on women in the South, and on urban crime and is currently completing research on gender issues during the Lyndon Johnson presidency.

Thomas Clarkin is an independent scholar specializing in American Indian policy. He is the author of *Federal Indian Policy in the Kennedy and Johnson Administrations, 1961–1969* (University of New Mexico Press, 2001). He has also written numerous essays, articles, and book reviews for academic journals and textbooks and is currently at work on a study of American Indians in Texas.

Michael Flamm is an associate professor of history at Ohio Wesleyan University, specializing in post–World War II political history. He is the author of *Law and Order: Street Crime, Civil Unrest, and the Crisis of Liberalism in the 1960s* (Columbia University Press, 2005). Dr. Flamm has also written numerous essays and articles for such journals as the *Journal of Policy History*, *The Historian*, and *Agricultural History* and is the coauthor of *The Chicago Handbook of Teaching* (University of Chicago Press, 1999).

Peter L. Hahn is a professor of history at Ohio State University, specializing in U.S. diplomatic history in the Middle East. His publications include *Caught in the Middle East* (University of North Carolina Press, 2004), *The United States, Great Britain, and Egypt, 1945–1956* (University of North Carolina Press, 1991), and *Empire and Revolution* (co-edited with Mary Ann Heiss, Ohio State University Press, 2001). Dr. Hahn is also the executive director of the Society for Historians of American Foreign Relations and winner of the 1998 Stuart L. Bernath Lecture Prize from that organization. He has won research grants from the J. William Fulbright Foreign Scholarship Board, the National Endowment for the Humanities, the Truman Library Institute, the John F. Kennedy Library, the Lyndon Johnson Foundation, the Eisenhower World Affairs Institute, and the Office of United States Air Force History.

Robert David Johnson is a professor of history at Brooklyn College and the CUNY Graduate Center. His books include *Ernest Gruening and the American Dissenting Tradition* (Harvard University Press, 1998), *The Peace Progressives and American Foreign Relations* (Harvard University Press, 1995), and *Running from Ahead* (W. W. Norton, 2004). He has also written extensively on modern American politics and diplomacy in such journals as *Diplomatic History*, *Political Science Quarterly*, and *International History Review*. He is currently at work on a study of Congress and the Cold War, to be published by Cambridge University Press.

Mark Atwood Lawrence is an assistant professor of history at the University of Texas. A specialist in the history of U.S. foreign relations, Dr. Lawrence is the author of *Constructing Vietnam: The Making of the Cold War in Southeast Asia* (University of California Press, 2004), which explores the process by which the three western powers arrived at a common policy in Vietnam and marginalized dissent at home and abroad. Recently he has turned his attention to the Johnson years, beginning projects on the administration's relationships with India and Panama, and is coediting a collection on the First Indochina War.

Mitchell B. Lerner is an associate professor in the Department of History at Ohio State University in Newark, Ohio, specializing in modern American diplomatic and political history. He is editor of *Passport: The Newsletter of the Society for Historians of American Foreign Relations* and author of *The Pueblo Incident* (University Press of Kansas, 2002), which won the 2002 John Lyman Book Award. He has published articles on the Johnson administration in numerous anthologies and journals, including *Diplomatic History, Presidential Studies Quarterly,* and the *Journal of Cold War Studies.* He is currently working on an all-encompassing study of the policies of the Johnson administration.

David Shreve is an assistant professor of history at the University of Virginia and deputy director of the Presidential Recordings Project at the Miller Center of Public Affairs at that university. A former budget analyst for the Louisiana House of Representatives, Dr. Shreve is currently at work on a history of presidential economic policymaking during the Kennedy, Johnson, and Nixon administrations. His book *A Precarious and Uncertain Liberalism: Lyndon Johnson and the New Economics* is expected to be published shortly.

Jeremi Suri is an assistant professor of history at the University of Wisconsin. He is the author of *Power and Protest* (Harvard University Press, 2003), which won the 2003 National History Honor Society's Best First Book Award. Dr. Suri has published articles about American diplomacy in such journals as *Diplomatic History, Reviews in American History, International Security,* and the *Journal of Cold War Studies* and was a 2003–2004 National Fellow of the Hoover Institution, where he is working on his next book, *Henry Kissinger and the Transformation of International Society.*

Index